ALSO BY BOB WOODWARD

The War Within: A Secret White House History, 2006–2008

State of Denial

The Secret Man
(*with a Reporter's Assessment by Carl Bernstein*)

Plan of Attack

Bush at War

Maestro: Greenspan's Fed and the American Boom

Shadow: Five Presidents and the Legacy of Watergate

The Choice

The Agenda: Inside the Clinton White House

The Commanders

Veil: The Secret Wars of the CIA, 1981–1987

Wired: The Short Life and Fast Times of John Belushi

The Brethren
(*with Scott Armstrong*)

The Final Days
(*with Carl Bernstein*)

All the President's Men
(*with Carl Bernstein*)

OBAMA'S

WARS

Bob Woodward

SIMON &
SCHUSTER

London · New York · Sydney · Toronto

A CBS COMPANY

First published in Great Britain in 2010 by Simon & Schuster UK Ltd
This paperback edition published in 2011 by Simon & Schuster UK Ltd
A CBS COMPANY

Copyright © 2010 by Bob Woodward

The right of Bob Woodward to be identified as the author of this
work has been asserted by him in accordance with sections 77 and 78
of the Copyright, Designs and Patents Act, 1988.

1 3 5 7 9 10 8 6 4 2

Simon & Schuster UK Ltd
1st Floor
222 Gray's Inn Road
London
WC1X 8HB

www.simonandschuster.co.uk

Simon & Schuster Australia
Sydney

A CIP catalogue copy for this book is available
from the British Library.

ISBN: 978-1-84983-220-5

Designed by Paul Dippolito
Printed in the UK by CPI Cox & Wyman, Reading, Berkshire RG1 8EX

To those who serve

CONTENTS

AUTHOR'S PERSONAL NOTE

I had two of the most exceptional people assist me full-time on the reporting, writing, editing and thinking about this book:

Josh Boak, a 2001 cum laude graduate of Princeton and later of the
Columbia University master's program in journalism, came to work
after reporting at *The Blade* in Toledo, Ohio, and the *Chicago Tribune*. He
may be the most energetic, resourceful, fair-minded and good-natured
young man I have had the good fortune to work with. On his résumé
he described himself as "skilled in shoe-leather reporting and phone-
jockeying." True, but he is much more. Josh immersed himself in all
the details and nuances of the Afghanistan War, the Obama administration and Washington politics. He became a part of my brain—the
better part. At times, I came to think he knows everything. What is
not in his head, he can and does find almost instantly. He is a skilled
writer and a superb investigator. I leaned on Josh, pushed him as he
pushed me. We never had even a half-serious disagreement. The result
has been permanent trust and permanent friendship. There would be
no book without him—not even close.

Evelyn M. Duffy, who worked with me on *The War Within: A Secret White House History, 2006–2008*, continued on this project. Thank
God. At age 25 now, she is a wizard at everything—thinking, prod-
ding and again transcribing hundreds of hours of recorded interviews

with people ranging from President Obama to generals and intelligence officials. A 2007 English and creative writing graduate of George Washington University, she is a truly gifted writer. She has written and produced a one-act play, *Nighthawks*, based on Edward Hopper's famous late-night diner painting. In her spare time, Evelyn has written a stunning young adult novel, which I'm sure will be published soon once I give her time to meet with agents and editors. She is both intellectual and practical—a rare combination. I stand in awe of her maturity, drive and independent spirit. A friend for life, Evelyn left her stamp of integrity on every idea, scene and page in this book.

NOTE TO READERS

A word of explanation about how the information in this book was obtained, evaluated and used. This book is designed to present, as best my reporting could determine, what really happened.

The core of this book comes from the written record—National Security Council meeting notes, personal notes, memos, chronologies, letters, PowerPoint slides, e-mails, reports, government cables, calendars, transcripts, diaries and maps.

Information in the book was supplied by more than 100 people involved in the Afghanistan War and national security during the first 18 months of President Barack Obama's administration. Interviews were conducted on "background," meaning the information could be used but the sources would not be identified by name. Many sources were interviewed five or more times. Most allowed me to record the interviews, which were then transcribed. For several sources, the combined interview transcripts run more than 300 pages. I have attempted to preserve the language of the main characters and sources as much as possible, using their words even when they are not directly quoted, reflecting the flavor of their speech and attitudes.

Many key White House aides were interviewed in-depth. They shared meeting notes, important documents, recollections of what happened before, during and after meetings, and assisted extensively with their interpretations.

Senior and well-placed military, intelligence and diplomatic officials also provided detailed recollections, read from notes or assisted with documents.

Since the reporting was done over 18 months, many interviews were conducted within days or even hours after critical discussions. This often provided a fresher and less-calculated account.

Dialogue comes mostly from the written record, but also from participants, usually more than one. Any attribution of thoughts, conclusions or feelings to a person was obtained directly from that person, from notes or from a colleague whom the person told.

Occasionally, a source said mid-conversation that something was "off-the-record," meaning it could not be used unless the information was obtained elsewhere. In many cases, I was able to get the information elsewhere so that it could be included in this book. Some people think they can lock up and prevent publication of information by declaring it "off-the-record" or that they don't want to see it in the book. But inside any White House, nearly everyone's business and attitudes become known to others. And in the course of multiple, extensive interviews with firsthand sources about key decision points in the war, the role of the players became clear.

Given the diversity of sources, stakes and the lives involved, there is no way I could write a sterilized or laundered version of this story.

I interviewed President Obama on-the-record in the Oval Office for one hour and 15 minutes on Saturday, July 10, 2010.

Bob Woodward
July 25, 2010
Washington, D.C.

CAST OF CHARACTERS

THE PRESIDENT OF THE UNITED STATES
Barack H. Obama

VICE PRESIDENT OF THE UNITED STATES
Joseph R. Biden

THE WHITE HOUSE
White House Chief of Staff
Rahm I. Emanuel

Senior Adviser to the President
David M. Axelrod

White House Press Secretary
Robert L. Gibbs

NATIONAL SECURITY COUNCIL
National Security Adviser
General James L. Jones, U.S. Marine Corps, retired

Deputy National Security Adviser
Thomas E. Donilon

Senior Adviser and Coordinator for Afghanistan-Pakistan
Lieutenant General Douglas E. Lute, U.S. Army, retired

National Security Council Chief of Staff
Mark W. Lippert   January 20, 2009–October 2, 2009
Denis McDonough   October 2, 2009–

Assistant to the President for Counterterrorism and Homeland Security
John O. Brennan

National Security Adviser to the Vice President
Antony J. Blinken

Deputy National Security Adviser for Strategic Communications
Benjamin Rhodes

Chairman, Interagency Policy Review of Afghanistan-Pakistan
Bruce O. Riedel   February 10–March 27, 2009

DEPARTMENT OF STATE

Secretary of State
Hillary Rodham Clinton

Special Representative for Afghanistan and Pakistan
Richard C. Holbrooke

United States Ambassador to Afghanistan
Lieutenant General Karl W. Eikenberry, U.S. Army, retired

United States Ambassador to Pakistan
Anne W. Patterson

DEPARTMENT OF DEFENSE

Secretary of Defense
Robert M. Gates

Undersecretary for Policy
Michèle A. Flournoy

Pentagon Press Secretary
Geoffrey S. Morrell

THE INTELLIGENCE COMMUNITY

Director of National Intelligence

Vice Admiral Michael McConnell,   February 13, 2007–January 29, 2009
    U.S. Navy, retired

Admiral Dennis C. Blair,   January 29, 2009–May 28, 2010
    U.S. Navy, retired

Director of the Central Intelligence Agency

General Michael V. Hayden,   May 30, 2006–February 19, 2009
    U.S. Air Force, retired

Leon Panetta   February 19, 2009–

Deputy Director of the Central Intelligence Agency

Stephen R. Kappes   July 25, 2006–April 14, 2010

Michael J. Morell   May 6, 2010–
    (previously CIA Director for Intelligence, 2006–2010)

UNITED STATES MILITARY

Commander, United States Central Command

General David H. Petraeus,   October 31, 2008–June 30, 2010
    U.S. Army

Commander, U.S. and NATO forces, Afghanistan

General David D. McKiernan,   June 3, 2008–June 15, 2009
    U.S. Army

General Stanley A. McChrystal,   June 15, 2009–June 23, 2010
    U.S. Army

General David H. Petraeus,   July 4, 2010–
    U.S. Army

Chairman of the Joint Chiefs of Staff
Admiral Michael G. Mullen, U.S. Navy

Vice Chairman of the Joint Chiefs of Staff
General James E. "Hoss" Cartwright, U.S. Marine Corps

Director of the Afghanistan-Pakistan Center of Excellence, Central Command
Colonel Derek Harvey, U.S. Army, retired

Spokesman for General Petraeus
Colonel Erik Gunhus, U.S. Army

AFGHANISTAN

President of Afghanistan
Hamid Karzai

Leader, Provincial Council of Kandahar; President Karzai's half-brother
Ahmed Wali Karzai

PAKISTAN

President of Pakistan
Asif Ali Zardari

Chief of Staff of the Army of Pakistan
General Ashfaq Kayani

Pakistani Ambassador to the United States
Husain Haqqani

1

On Thursday, November 6, 2008, two days after he was elected president of the United States, Senator Barack Obama arranged to meet in Chicago with Mike McConnell, the director of national intelligence (DNI).

McConnell, 65, a retired Navy vice admiral with stooped shoulders, wisps of light brown hair and an impish smile, had come to present details of the most highly classified intelligence operations and capabilities of the vast American espionage establishment he oversaw as DNI. In just 75 days, the formidable powers of the state would reside with the 47-year-old Obama. He would soon be, as the intelligence world often called the president, "The First Customer."

McConnell arrived early at the Kluczynski Federal Building, an austere Chicago skyscraper, with Michael J. Morell, who had been President George W. Bush's presidential briefer on 9/11 and now headed the Central Intelligence Agency's analysis division.

Two members of Senator Obama's transition team from the last Democratic administration greeted them: John Podesta, Bill Clinton's chief of staff for the final two years of his presidency, and James Steinberg, a former deputy national security adviser in the Clinton White House.

"We're going to go in with the president-elect and hear what you guys have got to say," Podesta said.

McConnell paused awkwardly. He had received instructions from President Bush. "As president," Bush had told McConnell, "this is my decision. I forbid any information about our success and how this works" except to the president-elect. McConnell knew Bush had never been comfortable using the terminology "sources and methods." But what the president meant was that nothing should be disclosed that might identify human spies and new techniques developed to infiltrate and attack al Qaeda, fight the wars in Iraq and Afghanistan, and defend the nation.

"John, sorry," McConnell said. "I'd love to be able to accommodate, but I didn't make these rules." He related Bush's instructions—only the president-elect and anyone designated to take a top national security cabinet post could attend. "Neither of you are designated. So I can't. I'm not going to violate the president's direction."

"Okay, I got it," Podesta said, barely concealing his irritation. Podesta had had all-source intelligence access before, as had Steinberg. He thought this was not helpful to Obama, who was largely unfamiliar with intelligence briefings.

Obama arrived still in full campaign mode with ready smiles and firm handshakes all around. He was buoyant in the afterglow of victory.

Two months earlier, after receiving a routine top secret briefing from McConnell on terrorism threats, Obama had half joked, "You know, I've been worried about losing this election. After talking to you guys, I'm worried about winning this election."

"Mr. President-elect, we need to see you for a second," Podesta said, steering him off to a private room. When Obama returned, his demeanor was different. He was more reserved, even aggravated. The transition from campaigning to governing—with all its frustrations—was delivering another surprise. His people, the inner circle from the campaign and the brain trust of Democrats he had carefully assembled to guide his transition, were being excluded. The first customer–elect was going to have to go it alone.

McConnell and Morell sat down with Obama in a private, secure room called a Sensitive Compartmented Information Facility, or SCIF. It was an unusually small room in the center of the building where a bathroom might normally be located. Designed to prevent eavesdropping, the SCIF was windowless and confining, even claustrophobic.

At first, this would be something of a continuation and amplification of the earlier briefing McConnell had given candidate Obama. There were 161,000 American troops at war in Iraq and 38,000 in Afghanistan. Intelligence was making significant contributions to the war efforts. But the immediate threat to the United States came not from these war zones, but from Pakistan, an unstable country with a population of about 170 million, a 1,500-mile border with southern Afghanistan, and an arsenal of some 100 nuclear weapons.

Priority one for the DNI, and now Obama, had to be the ungoverned tribal regions along the Pakistan-Afghanistan border where Osama bin Laden, his al Qaeda network, and branches of the extremist insurgent Taliban had nested in 150 training camps and other facilities.

Combined, the seven regions forming Pakistan's Federally Administered Tribal Areas (FATA) were about the size of New Jersey. The extremist groups and tribal chiefs ruled much of the FATA and had footholds in Pakistan's Northwest Frontier province.

In September 2006, Pakistan had signed a treaty ceding full control of the FATA's North Waziristan region to Taliban-linked tribal chiefs, creating a kind of Wild West for al Qaeda and the Taliban insurgents attacking the U.S. forces in Afghanistan.

In the earlier briefing, McConnell had laid out the problem in dealing with Pakistan. It was a dishonest partner of the U.S. in the Afghanistan War. "They're living a lie," McConnell had said. In exchange for reimbursements of about $2 billion a year from the U.S., Pakistan's powerful military and its spy agency, Inter-Services Intelligence (ISI), helped the U.S. while giving clandestine aid, weapons and money to the Afghan Taliban. They had an "office of hedging your bets," McConnell said.

Dealing with the ISI would break your heart if you did it long enough, McConnell had explained. It was as if there were six or seven different personalities within the ISI. The CIA exploited and bought some, but at least one section—known as Directorate S—financed and nurtured the Taliban and other terrorist groups. CIA payments might put parts of the ISI in America's pocket, McConnell had said, but the Pakistani spy agency could not or would not control its own people.

The Pakistani leadership believed the U.S. would eventually withdraw from the region, as it had toward the end of the Cold War once the occupying Soviet forces retreated from Afghanistan in 1989. Their paranoid mind-set was, in part, understandable. If America moved out again, India and Iran would fill the power vacuum inside Afghanistan. And most of all, Pakistan feared India, an avowed enemy for more than 60 years. As a growing economic and military powerhouse, India had numerous intelligence programs inside Afghanistan to spread its influence there. Pakistan worried more about being encircled by India than being undermined by extremists inside its borders.

The best way out of this would be for Obama to broker some kind of peace between India and Pakistan, the DNI had said. If Pakistan felt significantly more secure in its relations with India, it might stop playing its deadly game with the Taliban.

In his September overview, McConnell also discussed strikes by small unmanned aerial vehicles such as Predators that had sophisticated surveillance cameras and Hellfire missiles. The covert action program authorized by President Bush targeted al Qaeda leadership and other groups inside Pakistan. Although classified, the program had been widely reported in the Pakistani and American media.

Only four strikes had been launched in the first half of 2008, Obama had been told. The U.S. had uncovered evidence that the Pakistanis would delay planned strikes in order to warn al Qaeda and the Afghan Taliban, whose fighters would then disperse. In June 2008, McConnell had taken human and technical intelligence to President Bush showing multiple conversations between an ISI colonel and Siraj Haqqani, a guerrilla commander whose network was allied with the Afghan Taliban.

"Okay," Bush had said, "we're going to stop playing the game.

These sons of bitches are killing Americans. I've had enough." He ordered stepped-up Predator drone strikes on al Qaeda leaders and specific camps, so-called infrastructure targets. It was like attacking an anthill—the survivors would run away in the aftermath. These "squirters" were then tracked to the next hideout, helping to build the intelligence data on terrorist refuges.

Bush had directed that Pakistan receive "concurrent notification" of drone attacks, meaning they learned of a strike as it was underway or, just to be sure, a few minutes *after*. American drones now owned the skies above Pakistan.

In addition, McConnell had given President Bush intelligence showing that the Pakistani ISI had helped the Haqqani network attack the Indian embassy in Kabul, Afghanistan, on July 7, four months earlier. The U.S. had warned India, which had put its embassy in a defensive posture. But it was not enough. Fifty-eight people were killed and more than 100 injured in a suicide bombing.

McConnell had then moved during the September briefing to one of the most pressing worries. Al Qaeda was recruiting people from the 35 countries who didn't need visas to enter the United States. It was paying them good money, bringing them into the ungoverned regions by the dozens, training them in all aspects of warfare—explosives and chemical—and trying to have them acquire biological weapons.

"We're a big open sieve," McConnell said. "They're trying to get people with passports that don't require a visa to get into the United States." Al Qaeda had not succeeded yet, but that was the big worry. "We can't find any cell in the United States, but we suspect there may be some."

That got Obama's full attention. Some of the 9/11 hijackers had operated for nearly 18 months in the United States before their attacks. As he had said at the end of that meeting, there were reasons to worry about winning the election.

The November 6 briefing to Obama picked up exactly where that earlier presentation had left off. McConnell could now provide him with a fuller description of how the intelligence community culled and collected information.

"Mr. President-elect, we can share anything with you," McConnell said in the soothing accent of his native South Carolina.

For example, the top secret code words for the Predator drone operations were SYLVAN-MAGNOLIA. The code words set up Sensitive Compartmented Information (SCI) to which only people with the highest-level security clearances and a need to know were granted access. The president-elect was now, of course, one of those people.

The U.S. had scored an extraordinary intelligence coup in the ungoverned regions of Pakistan as the result of blending two intelligence cultures—human sources and technical intelligence such as communications intercepts and satellite and drone imagery.

But, he said, the real breakthrough had been with human sources. This is what President Bush wanted to protect at all costs. The drones were basically flying high-resolution video cameras armed with missiles. The only meaningful way to point drones toward a target was to have spies on the ground telling the CIA where to look, hunt and kill. Without spies, the video feed from the Predator might as well be a blank television screen.

McConnell provided extensive details about these human sources, who had been developed in an expensive, high-risk program over five years. The spies were the real secrets that Obama would carry with him from that moment forward. They were the key, in some respects, to protecting the country.

President Bush had absolute views on protecting them. "His instructions to us are no one except you or one of your designated cabinet officials can be provided the information," McConnell said. President Bush did not want any "tourists," as he called them, and no "professors" who might be part of the Obama transition team but later reveal the spies in a speech, a book or a careless comment.

Obama indicated he understood.

The CIA is so guarded with human sources that each one has a randomly selected code name such as MOONRISE. If the source is productive and undertaking great risks, word might get around the agency. He's doing great, but when too many people know about him he is killed off. There is a burial ceremony, everybody's sad. MOONRISE paid the ultimate price, his CIA case officer would say. Except MOON-RISE is not actually dead. His code name has changed. And now the CIA has another source called SHOOTING STAR. Same guy, new name. MOONRISE is SHOOTING STAR. It's an elaborate and manipulative ruse in order to grant MOONRISE the ultimate protection—death.

On the technical side, McConnell explained, the National Security Agency (NSA), which he had headed from 1992 to 1996, had developed a breakthrough eavesdropping capability. It had begun years before with a project code-named SHARKFINN that was designed to speed the acquisition, storage, dissemination and availability of intercepted communications, including cell phone calls and e-mails. The project advanced and was soon referred to as RT10, which increased the speed in real time to factors of up to 10 to the 10th power, or 10 billion times faster. It was now called RTRG—Real Time, Regional Gateway. RTRG meant there was a way to capture all the data, store it, and make it instantly available to intelligence analysts and operators, allowing the U.S. to react quickly in response to the enemy.

In Afghanistan, the program code name was JESTER. Specialized units called JACKAL teams operated countrywide to monitor the insurgency.

"They talk, we listen. They move, we observe. Given the opportunity, we react operationally," McConnell said.

The human and technical intelligence pointed with confidence, McConnell said, to the Quetta Shura Taliban as the central insurgent group in the Afghanistan War. This "shura," an Arabic word meaning council, was headed by Mullah Muhammad Omar, the Taliban leader who had fled Afghanistan after the U.S. attack into his country after 9/11. There had been a $25 million reward on his head ever since.

Mullah Omar was in the Pakistani city of Quetta, just about 60 miles from the Afghan border in the province of Baluchistan. Unlike the vast desert of the FATA, Quetta had a population of almost 900,000, which made drone strikes virtually impossible.

"Here's the center of gravity," McConnell said.

"Well," Obama asked, "what are we doing about that?"

Not that much, McConnell indicated.

The problem was sending American forces across the border into Pakistani cities where drones could not strike. Just two months earlier, on September 3, a day after McConnell had given candidate Obama his first briefing, President Bush authorized a cross-border operation into Pakistan. It was supposed to be a quiet, in-out Special Forces ground raid by about two dozen Navy SEALs on a house believed to be used by al Qaeda in the town of Angor Adda in the FATA. The plan was for the SEALs to seize al Qaeda's documents and computers, their "stuff," as McConnell called it.

But in that part of the world, people often ran toward automatic weapons fire and explosions—instead of away from the danger—to see what was happening, McConnell explained. Civilians were killed in the raid, causing all hell to break loose in the Pakistani press.

The raid had been poorly planned and coordinated, McConnell acknowledged. The Pakistani government angrily claimed it was a violation of their sovereignty. Bush was extremely upset about the civilian casualties, and said America would not do that again. In the Bush administration, there would be no more ground operations into Pakistan, period.

One important secret that had never been reported in the media or elsewhere was the existence of the CIA's 3,000-man covert army in Afghanistan. Called CTPT, for Counterterrorism Pursuit Teams, the army consisted mostly of Afghans, the cream of the crop in the CIA's opinion. These pursuit teams were a paid, trained and functioning tool of the CIA that was authorized by President Bush. The teams conducted operations designed to kill or capture Taliban insurgents, but also often went into tribal areas to pacify and win support.

McConnell said a second immediate threat was al Qaeda in Yemen, which was commonly referred to as al Qaeda in the Arabian Peninsula, or AQAP. The group had attacked tourists and in September 2008 detonated two vehicle bombs outside the U.S. embassy in Yemen, killing 19 people, including six of the terrorists.

McConnell and Morell turned to the Iranian nuclear program. It was well known that Iran was trying to get nuclear weapons. Despite the suspension of some of the Iranian nuclear programs, others continued or could be restarted. And there were hidden facilities. McConnell said he was convinced that Iran was going to get a gun-type nuclear weapon—probably primitive—but one that could be detonated in the desert with great dramatic effect. This would be done, in his view, between 2010—less than two years off—and 2015. It would create an incredibly unstable situation in the Middle East. Saudi Arabia would call in their chips with Pakistan, which had been receiving Saudi oil, and try to get help developing a Saudi nuclear weapon. Egypt and other countries in the region could go all out to develop their own weapons.

Another main threat, McConnell said, was North Korea, which had enough nuclear material for six bombs and an effort underway to increase that. The North Korean leaders were loony. Attempts to negotiate with the regime would likely repeat the Bush administration's experience. It would be "negotiate, prevaricate, escalate and renegotiate," he said. The North Koreans would talk, they would lie, they would escalate and threaten to walk away, and then they would try to renegotiate. "That's how it's going to work," McConnell insisted.

Iran and North Korea were particularly difficult intelligence targets because of their closed societies. The absence of U.S. embassies in the countries made spying more of a problem. The nuclear programs in both had, in part, been penetrated by U.S. intelligence, McConnell said. But, Iran and North Korea represented serious short- and long-term threats.

"What else?" Obama asked.

"We haven't talked at all yet about cyber," McConnell said. "What the Chinese did to you."

The Chinese had hacked into the Obama campaign computers in the summer of 2008 and moved files and documents out at an astonishing rate.

"Yeah," Obama said, "they got McCain too."

Yes, McConnell confirmed. "The point is what they did to you and did to McCain, they took your data. And they're clumsy, so they got caught." U.S. intelligence had detected it, and the FBI had warned both campaigns, which had taken some defensive steps. "But the real issue would have been, what if they had destroyed your data?"

That would have been a problem, Obama said.

"All right," McConnell said, "roll that over to the nation."

"This is important," Obama said.

McConnell explained how the Real Time, Regional Gateway gave the NSA an incredible exploitation capability—reading other people's mail, listening to their conversations, and sorting their data. That was NSA's traditional speciality. But there was also an attack capability that Bush had approved in 2007 against computers and communications in Iraq. The NSA had argued that it was one of the most powerful capabilities in the world, so it had been used with the utmost care and restraint in order to avoid starting a cyber war.

The NSA's offensive capability, called Computer Network Attack (CNA), was the most sophisticated stealthy computer hacking. Cyber teams could break into computer systems in foreign countries. Their digital work somewhat resembled the targeted quick strikes by the Delta Force or a Navy SEAL team. The highly secret operations were run through the Army Network Warfare Battalion of the 704th Military Intelligence Brigade at NSA's Fort Meade headquarters outside Washington, D.C.

There was another tier—Computer Network Defense (CND).

McConnell noted that the United States was vulnerable to cyber attacks. If the 19 terrorists from 9/11 had been cyber-smart and attacked a single bank, it would've had an order of magnitude greater impact on the American and global economies than dropping the two World Trade Center towers, he said. The Bank of New York and Citibank each handle about $3 trillion a day in financial transfers. To put that in perspective, the size of the entire American economy, its annual Gross Domestic Product, is $14 trillion. If the bank data was destroyed, there would be financial chaos. People wouldn't be able to get their money, know whether they had it, or if they had made payments. Imagine if you disrupted that process? Wealth was most often just an entry on a computer. Modern banking was built on assurance and confidence in those digital entries rather than gold and currency. A few people could ruin the U.S. and the global economy and destroy faith in the U.S. dollar, McConnell said. There were no real protections and the system was totally open to attack, he said. Power grids, telecommunication lines, air traffic control—all computer-dependent enterprises—were likewise vulnerable to cyber attacks.

"I want you to brief my entire cabinet," Obama said. "I want you to give me a roadmap about what the nation should do about this."

He thanked McConnell and Morell.

Obama later told one of his closest advisers, "I'm inheriting a world that could blow up any minute in half a dozen ways, and I will have some powerful but limited and perhaps even dubious tools to keep it from happening."

In an Oval Office interview on July 10, 2010, President Obama told me he did not want to confirm or deny specific quotes for this book. "What I'll try to give you is a general overview of how I was thinking at any particular point in time."

He said McConnell's assessment of the situation in Afghanistan, Pakistan and along the countries' border region was "sobering" but not "surprising."

The president explained, "It did corroborate some of my deepest concerns about the fact that the Taliban had strengthened, were controlling more parts of the territory, and that we did not have a strategy in Pakistan for the FATA and the Northwest region."

He said the briefings "confirmed that fact that you had the Taliban, the Quetta Shura, the Haqqani network, a whole range of these al Qaeda affiliates, essentially, who were operating very aggressively. And we were not putting a lot of pressure on them."

"And did you say, okay," I asked, "this is one of the things I'm going to try to fix?"

"Yes," he said.

He also generally confirmed the ideas in his comment to an aide about what he was inheriting. "Events are messy out there," Obama told me. "At any given moment of the day, there are explosive, tragic, heinous, hazardous things taking place. All of which, objectively, you would say, somebody should do something about this."

Obama acknowledged that after the election the world's problems were seen as his responsibility. "People are saying, you're the most powerful person in the world. Why aren't you doing something about it?"

2

John Podesta had been quietly heading Obama's transition team. He had one central message for the president-elect: Pick the White House staff before the cabinet. Podesta, 59, a wiry long-distance runner who started out as a junior aide in the Clinton years, said that one of Clinton's earliest mistakes was focusing on cabinet selections and almost as an afterthought picking as his first White House chief of staff Thomas "Mack" McLarty, an amiable natural gas executive who had been Clinton's friend since kindergarten in Arkansas.

Podesta believed he had imposed some order and discipline during his time as chief of staff. Government policy should be decided, organized and monitored through a centralized White House system.

Two basic models for White House chief of staff existed, Podesta advised Obama. One is a senior statesman, an old Washington hand who could be a chairman of the board type. The other is a fighter, someone who could naturally play the heavy.

Obama said he had one person in mind: Representative Rahm Emanuel, 48, a three-term congressman from Chicago and also a former aide in the Clinton White House. One of the most combustible operatives in Washington, known for his profanity-laced diatribes, the 5-foot-8, 147-pound Emanuel delivered a giant political punch, having risen to the No. 3 House leadership position.

Obama first raised the chief of staff job with Emanuel weeks before the election. Emanuel had two major reservations. First, he was on track to become House speaker someday, a personal ambition. Second, he and his wife, Amy Rule, had agreed to raise their three children—ages 9, 10 and 11—in Chicago, where they had an established life. A White House chief of staff had no life, in Chicago or Washington.

On the Saturday before the election, Obama told him, "Rahm, you have to do this." This was no longer a matter of choice. "I'm going to make you do it. I'm going to be president of the United States. And I tell you that you have to do it." Emanuel understood it was a historic moment, the country was in trouble, and as White House chief of staff he could be a kind of deputy president in the right circumstances. Though he and Obama were from Chicago, they did not know each other well. On one hand, Emanuel was surprised he was being offered such a critical assignment. On the other, Emanuel, who was known for his bluster, confided to associates that the driving force in his life was a fear of failure. It was as if he knew his entire career was a dangerous high-wire act and he was being forced to take the wire to new heights, requiring that he move faster and not look down. Despite his misgivings, he finally said yes, and his appointment was announced Thursday, November 6, after McConnell briefed Obama.

During the week of the presidential election, General David H. Petraeus was 7,000 miles from Washington in Afghanistan and Pakistan. The distance was perhaps symbolic. Petraeus, 56, did not exactly share the ecstatic sense of renewal among Democrats and Obama supporters, many of whom had criticized the Iraq War, not least among them the president-elect.

Only months earlier, candidate Obama had visited Petraeus in Iraq. According to Obama, he told the general, "My job, if I have the honor of being commander in chief, is going to be to look at the whole picture. I expect you, as the commander of our forces in Iraq, to ask for everything you need and more to ensure your success. That's what you owe the troops who are under your command. My job, then, which in some ways is more difficult, is I've got to choose. Because I don't have infinite resources."

If President Bush told Petraeus yes, Obama was prepared to say no.

Now Petraeus had a bigger job. Shortly before the election, he had taken over the Central Command, putting him in charge of both the Afghanistan and Iraq wars.

Over the two previous years as the Iraq commander, Petraeus had led the efforts that turned the war around, stabilizing the country and dramatically reducing violence. This was a result of the "surge" of 30,000 more troops and new top secret operations to locate, target and kill insurgents.

Petraeus had almost redefined the notion of warfare, authoring the new *Counterinsurgency Field Manual* and implementing it in Iraq. His primary insight was that the U.S. could not kill its way out of the war. It had to protect and win over the population, living among them, providing security so that a stable and competent government could thrive. A new kind of soldier in the Petraeus mold had to be a social worker, urban planner, anthropologist and psychologist.

Perhaps no general in America had been held in such near-universal esteem since General Dwight David Eisenhower after victory in World War II. Young-looking with his neatly parted brown hair, Petraeus could pass for a 35-year-old. He had few hobbies—no fishing, no hunting, no golf. When he jogged, it was "physical training." He could run five miles in about 30 minutes. A solid pace put him in a good mood and helped with sleep. "I prefer running to Ambien," he had said. When he read a book, it was often about a renowned general. He had a Ph.D. from Princeton, finishing the course work in double time, just two years. When his 92-year-old father died in the summer of 2008, Petraeus did not attend the funeral but stayed in Iraq to oversee the war.

He put other workaholics to shame, monitoring military business and his personal e-mail day and night. His new office on the second floor of the Central Command headquarters in Tampa, Florida, made the bridge of Starship *Enterprise* seem modest. It was filled with regular and special secure phones, computers and numerous screens arranged around a clean desk marked by its compulsive orderliness.

When Petraeus had turned over his Iraq command six weeks earlier, Secretary of Defense Robert Gates had flown to Baghdad to de-
clare that Petraeus had overseen a near-miracle.

The evening before the formal change of command, Petraeus was
treated to a testimonial dinner. It was more like an Academy Awards
ceremony, ending with a film of his 19-month tour called *Surge of Hope*.

"The darkness has receded," Gates said in a speech. "General
Petraeus leaves this country transformed."

Six weeks later, on October 31, the 5-foot-9, 155-pound four-star
had just been sworn in as the central commander, the combatant
commander in charge of both the Iraq and Afghanistan wars. His appointment was in part an insurance policy taken out by the Bush administration in hopes of avoiding a precipitous withdrawal from Iraq.

Gates again showed up to hail Petraeus as "the preeminent soldier-
scholar-statesman of his generation."

The Iraqis called him "King David." Some on his staff called him
"The Legend of Iraq." Colleagues believed that Petraeus was so competitive that he preferred fighting a war when the odds were against
him, even with both hands tied behind his back, so that his eventual
victory would be all the greater. Petraeus was the recipient of countless
awards, and the celebrity selected to do the coin toss at the upcoming
Super Bowl.

But Obamaland was potentially hostile. When candidate Obama
had visited Iraq over the summer, the conversation between the two
had not gone well. Here were two of the most ambitious, driven men
of their era. Obama, an outspoken, acerbic opponent of the Iraq War,
said he still wanted to withdraw and would have to consider Iraq in the
context of all the other pressing national security concerns, including
Afghanistan.

The Obama presidency was going to dramatically alter Petraeus's
status. He had direct access to President Bush, and his mentor, retired
General Jack Keane, the former vice chief of staff of the Army, had an
extraordinary pipeline to both Bush and Vice President Dick Cheney.

But Petraeus had gone to Afghanistan and Pakistan in early November to emphasize the forgotten war. "I was trying to send a signal," he said later. "You show by where you go and by the use of your time what's most important."

He was no expert on Afghanistan, but he had gone there four years earlier to assess for then Secretary of Defense Donald H. Rumsfeld the training of the Afghan army and police. Petraeus had immersed himself in the details. He studied the police training schedule for an eight-week course. He kept looking at it. Something was missing. He soon realized there was no time on the shooting range. None. He asked about it.

The response: "Oh, General, we don't have time to go to the range."

He looked at the schedule. "You have time to march for an hour each morning and an hour each afternoon?"

Yes.

It was almost day care, Petraeus concluded, not serious training.

On this November trip, he saw firsthand the lack of troops, the training problems, the absence of structure. There was no cell working to bring the insurgents over to the U.S. and Afghan side—a key tenet of counterinsurgency. His bottom line was that without more troops, money and attention, "We're not going to achieve our objectives."

Petraeus told his closest aides that Afghanistan would be different from Iraq, where he had become the poster boy of the war. "I do not want to be the face of policy," he told one aide. "They can't dump it on me." Petraeus later denied this was his intent. He just wanted to be "a good soldier," as he put it, and keep a very low public profile.

Obama's campaign aides saw his prominence through a political lens. A popular war hero like Petraeus, a registered Republican, was always a potential presidential candidate. It had happened before. Petraeus denied he had political ambitions.

On Monday, November 10, Obama met with Bush alone in the Oval Office. The focus was the financial crisis, but Bush said the intelligence problem was hard to get right. He had made his share of mistakes.

The different agencies did not always play nicely with each other. It is not as easy as it might look, he said. It's finally running well under McConnell as DNI and Air Force General Michael Hayden as the CIA director. Both have said they would stay on for a year or so. Keep these guys for a while, Bush urged. Don't throw them overboard, give yourself some continuity. This is working. Leave this alone. They are professionals.

But the professionals—despite the successes they could claim with the drone attacks, the human penetrations and real time signals intelligence—had yet to capture the prize. McConnell and Hayden had a special cell devoted to getting Osama bin Laden and his al Qaeda deputy, Ayman Zawahiri. President Bush had set the last year of his administration as the deadline for accomplishing this task. On one level, it was a running joke. And on another, it was deadly serious. "I want him," Bush had said.

At a regular Thursday morning briefing on terrorism, the president would ask at least every other week, "How are you coming on getting number one and number two?"

Their best answer that was they were working the problem, night and day.

"You only got three more months," Bush was now saying.

Later on November 10, Ed Henry appeared on CNN reporting on the president-elect's day in Washington: "As soon as he left the White House this afternoon, he headed over to Reagan National Airport. And, while his jet was waiting, he went to the firehouse at National Airport for a long meeting with either a mystery person or persons— a lot of speculation tonight. Maybe it had something to do with first responders, since it was in the firehouse. Maybe it was a meeting with a potential secretary of homeland security. But I have been e-mailing Obama advisers tonight. They're all in lockdown, saying they can't talk about it."

The mystery person was Secretary of Defense Robert Gates, whom President Bush had brought into the Pentagon two years earlier to salvage the Iraq War. Gates, 65, knew Washington, the White House, the world of espionage, war—and survival. No one else had ever held so many key positions in the CIA and the White House. A career CIA man, he had never been a covert operator but was an analyst with a doctorate in Russian history. Methodical and driven, he had served on the NSC staff from 1974 to 1979 and after Ronald Reagan's election became the chief CIA Soviet analyst, executive assistant to CIA Director William J. Casey and later Casey's chief deputy.

In 1987, Reagan nominated Gates to be CIA director but Gates withdrew because of too many questions about the Iran-contra scandal and his relationship with Casey. In his 1996 memoir, *From the Shadows*, he made it clear he had learned about public humiliation, writing that he was "embarrassed" and felt "like a leper for whom people have sympathy but still don't want to get too close." When George H. W. Bush became president in 1989, Gates served as deputy national security adviser before Bush nominated him to be CIA director. He was confirmed that time, serving in the top post from 1991 to 1993.

Probably no one had better mastered the art of holding back in meetings, press conferences or congressional testimony than Gates. It was a disarming quiet that appealed to Obama, who saw Gates as someone who kept his ego in check, seemingly humble yet forceful. Obama had asked Podesta to set up a secret, one-on-one meeting.

Retaining Gates at the Pentagon might make sense, the president-elect said. Continuity during the wars could be essential. And it might be helpful as U.S. troops pulled out of Iraq to have at the Pentagon someone who had overseen the stabilization and reduction of violence there.

Podesta, who had other names in mind, was not sure Defense should be given to a Bush-appointed Republican. And, to his knowledge, no one else in the transition was arguing to keep Gates.

Set it up, please, Obama said. He didn't want a public event that could raise the expectations and the stakes, in case Gates preferred not to stay or it might not work out.

Podesta realized that Obama seemed to have already made up his mind.

Obama told aides that he thought Gates was a breath of fresh air after the overbearing, fear-and-loathing approach of Donald Rumsfeld, the previous secretary of defense. Gates was liked in the Congress, and he seemed to be dismantling the Rumsfeld autocracy. All the signs were that this was a straight shooter.

Gates was aware of the speculation that Obama might ask him to stay. His public position was that he had promised his wife, Becky, that they would be getting back to Washington state, where they had a home.

But he was carrying around a personal secret, and it was a major reason he might agree to continue as secretary, according to what he had told one of his closest aides and advisers. It was not a secret about the strategies for the wars, nor was it privileged information about military operations or capabilities, or a piece of intelligence that could change the world.

It had been extensively reported in the media that Gates had launched aggressive, personal campaigns to help the troops in the field with armored vehicles, more sophisticated intelligence gathering equipment, and almost anything else to protect them. When he had talked about the problem publicly he blamed it on the "institutional base," and the "bureaucratic structure" of the Pentagon.

What had not been reported was that he realized it was not just the structure, but the people. Inside the Pentagon, the uniformed military, the generals, admirals, colonels and thousands of other officers and civilians, were largely focused on planning and equipping the force for future wars rather than effectively fighting the wars they were in—Iraq and Afghanistan. There were too few officers on the Joint Staff or the various services working every day to help the war fighters come home alive, Gates believed.

Many of the Pentagon's endless meetings, schedules and intense debates seemed to be about some distant, theoretical war. Those officers were busy designing and buying the new ships, jets, tanks, radars, missiles and the latest high-technology equipment in their modernization programs. They were gearing up to fight the wars of 2015 or 2020, while ignoring the wars of 2008.

At first, Gates couldn't believe it. "He was shocked," said one of his closest advisers inside the Pentagon. "We've complained the government's not on a war footing when we're not on a war footing ourselves." It was as if nearly all of them were playing some role in an ugly parody of the military brass behaving badly. This aide went so far as to say, "It's the only reason he stayed in the job."

When Gates had taken over from Rumsfeld in December 2006, one of the biggest problems was the improvised explosive devices (IEDs) or roadside bombs that were killing dozens of U.S. personnel a month in Iraq.

Gates read one of several articles in *USA Today* about the Mine Resistant Ambush Protected (MRAP) vehicle. These MRAPs had a passenger compartment high off the ground, V-shaped hulls and heavy armor to deflect a blast away from the troops inside. It was an existing technology. The South Africans had used them, and the Marines were experimenting with them.

"Why aren't we buying these things?" he asked the senior military leaders.

The MRAPs were expensive, nearly $1 million each. A large purchase would cost billions, the military explained.

They feared that any funding for MRAPs would come out of their programs, out of the hide of the Navy, Army, Marines or Air Force: the stealth F-22 fighter or the Navy's latest ship or the Army's exotic unmanned vehicles in the Future Combat Systems. They talked as if the two wars were some kind of passing distraction, and their pet projects took precedence.

The brass also argued that the MRAP had only limited use. They were transport vehicles to take troops from one place to another. The military needed fighting vehicles. MRAPs wouldn't be part of a long-term arsenal. A big buy would eventually wind up in surplus.

"If anybody thinks IEDs are going away, you're crazy," Gates told them. "I think this is the new threat we face, and will probably be for this generation." As for the worry about a big surplus, the U.S. military always had a surplus after a big, long war. It was the price of winning, he said.

The uniformed military in the Pentagon didn't get it. No one picked up the ball and ran with it. Frustrated at the lack of response, Gates took ownership of the issue himself. As one of his first actions, he officially asserted it was a national priority to buy the ballistic steel used in making the MRAPs. That legally forced private industry to sell the steel to the military before all other customers. Gates ordered the Pentagon to begin buying the ballistic steel even before it was decided which company would build the MRAPs.

Instead of taking the money out of the budgets of the services, Gates asked Congress for more than $20 billion for about 16,000 MRAPs. Congress readily agreed. Such was the power of the secretary of defense when it came to getting money to protect the troops. Gates ordered crash production to begin in May 2007.

Gates had served in government long enough to not be surprised by government failure. It didn't take a former CIA director to realize the power of aerial surveillance, which was known as Intelligence, Surveillance and Reconnaissance, or ISR. Commanders and troops on the ground in Afghanistan and Iraq told Gates that the Predators were a game changer, key to seeing where the lethal IEDs were being planted and to tracking IED networks. These were so-called Find, Fix and Finish operations—the finding of targets, fixing their locations, and then attacking them from the air or ground. Yet only about 25 percent of the military's aerial surveillance aircraft were in the war zones. There were only 36 Predator drones allocated to the Central Command for both wars. Most of them were in Iraq.

Gates formed a task force and found that getting the services to go along with adding more Predators to Afghanistan was grinding. He had to push for additional air surveillance with two-engine propeller Beechcraft. Military pilots, who preferred the fast jets, didn't want to be assigned to fly at slow speed, circling for 12 hours over Afghanistan.

So Gates ordered changes, and soon three round-the-clock facilities were opened to retrofit the planes with sensor packages.

For four years before becoming secretary, Gates had been the president of Texas A&M University. He loved "Aggieland" and quickly formed a deep emotional bond with the school that, other than the service academies, produces more military officers than any other college. As secretary, Gates realized there had been cases over time in which he signed the diploma for an A&M graduate, the deployment order sending him into combat, and the condolence letter to his family.

The afternoon of November 10, firemen pulled their trucks out of the firehouse at Reagan National Airport so Obama's and Gates's cars could enter.

Gates was 18 years older than the president-elect. He was low-key and calm. Nothing about him seemed to be in a hurry, but this masked a big ego and a supreme confidence in his own judgment. Gates also had a streak of self-righteousness.

Obama told me that from his time in the Senate, he found Gates "possessed a hardheaded, clear-eyed view of America's national interests, was not interested in grandstanding, was willing to take on the Pentagon bureaucracy but also would defend it when it needed defending."

The two Mr. Cools connected quickly and easily. Obama came to the point. There was no way he wanted to string along a man who did not seek the post. For several months, Obama had been working quietly with Senator Jack Reed, a Rhode Island Democrat, as a go-between with Gates to explore the possibility. Gates had already worked for seven presidents. So in the name of continuity and bipartisanship Obama asked him to continue as secretary in his new administration.

Later, Obama recalled for me the conversation with Gates. "What I said to him was that we were in the middle of two wars. That I thought he had done an outstanding job as secretary of defense." He said he found Gates's efforts "sound" for reducing the U.S. combat mission in Iraq. "And that it did not make sense, from my perspective, for us to change secretaries of defense. I thought he was going to be an important part of my team, and I wanted him to stay."

According to Obama, Gates responded, "I take very seriously your desire to make sure that we are building on the progress we've made in Iraq. I share with you your concerns about the direction in Afghanistan. And I'm willing to stay and work with you, but I'll have to talk to my wife."

Obama later said he was glad to hear that Gates had to check with his wife, because if he hadn't he would know "it's not a real yes."

Gates also said he agreed with Obama that at least another two combat brigades needed to be added to Afghanistan.

Afghanistan would be the new priority, Obama said, as he had promised in his campaign.

Gates said that, given that the uniformed military was often serving three, four or more tours in the war zones, he did not see how he could decline. It was his duty.

Obama replied that he was not surprised Gates saw it that way.

There needed to be a back end, Gates said, a time in the unspecified future when he would leave.

They shook hands.

At a later press conference, Gates remarked on how unprecedented all of this was. He said with pride, "Since the creation of the position of secretary of defense some 60 years ago, no secretary has been asked to continue in office under a newly elected president, even when the president has come from the same party."

3

On Wednesday, November 12, CIA Director Mike Hayden went to New York City to discuss Predator drone strikes inside Pakistan with its president, Asif Ali Zardari.

Hayden, 63, was a four-star Air Force general who had also been the NSA director from 1999 to 2005. He wore rimless eyeglasses that accentuated his arched eyebrows and bald head. As CIA director, he had some reservations about the drone attacks. There had been 20 against terrorist camps in Pakistan since July, when President Bush stepped up the program.

Killing senior al Qaeda leaders with drones had a debilitating impact on al Qaeda's ability to plan, prepare and train. That counted as a big counterterrorism win.

But each strike was tactical and would not change the big picture. As an Air Force officer, Hayden knew that to get a strategic victory— to defeat al Qaeda—America had to change the facts on the ground. Otherwise, the U.S. would be doing piecemeal drone strikes forever. The great lesson of World War II and Vietnam was that attacks from the air, even massive bombings, can't win a war.

Hayden and the CIA deputy director, Steve Kappes, were ushered into the presidential suite of the InterContinental Barclay hotel, where

Zardari and the Pakistani ambassador to the U.S., Husain Haqqani, awaited them.

The Pakistani news media had been clobbering the U.S. for civilian casualties from drone strikes. But the accidental death of Pakistani citizens was only half of the story.

Many Westerners, including some U.S. passport holders, had been killed five days earlier on the Kam Sham training camp in the tribal area of North Waziristan, Hayden told the Pakistani president. But the CIA would not reveal the particulars due to the implications under American law.

A top secret CIA map detailing the attacks had been given to the Pakistanis. Missing from it was the alarming fact about the American deaths. Was al Qaeda developing a fifth column of U.S. citizens who did not need visas to pass through immigration and customs?

The CIA was not going to elaborate.

How are you choosing targets? the Pakistani ambassador asked Hayden.

The CIA is exercising the utmost care, Hayden said. Seven of the top 20 al Qaeda leaders had been killed this year alone. Al Qaeda was struggling to replace those leaders.

After an hour of conversation, the Pakistani president met one-on-one with Hayden. Zardari wanted to clear the air about the controversy over civilian deaths from drones. He had only been president since September and could afford a drop in his approval ratings. Innocent deaths were the cost of doing business against senior al Qaeda leaders.

"Kill the seniors," Zardari said. "Collateral damage worries you Americans. It does not worry me."

Zardari had just given the CIA an important green light. Hayden appreciated the support, but he also knew it would not achieve the goal of destroying al Qaeda.

In one of their long conversations, Obama raised the Hillary question with David Axelrod, his senior political aide and closest adviser.

Axelrod, 53, was a former *Chicago Tribune* reporter turned campaign consultant who had embraced Obama with a convert's zeal. When Axelrod listened to himself gush about Obama, he felt silly because he sounded like such a homer—a simpleminded hick. But "Axe" was also as hard-boiled as any strategist in the Democratic Party. A 1987 *Chicago* magazine profile summed up his aggressive approach with its title—"Hatchet Man."

Axelrod braced himself. Hillary Clinton had been their nemesis during the long Democratic presidential primary, a rivalry that had grown into visceral suspicion.

"Hillary and I were friends before this started," Obama said. "We had this very vituperative campaign, but, you know, she is smart and we ought to be able to do something with her." She did her homework, showed up, fought hard. She was relentless. She'd make a great Supreme Court justice.

"How could you trust Hillary?" Axelrod asked. Maybe Obama was not a vengeful person and could put past grievances aside. But there had been some raw, ugly moments on the trail, with Clinton accusing Obama of not telling the truth. After a February rally in Ohio that year, she had scolded him with a line that continued to sting: "Shame on you, Barack Obama."

"I have a really strong feeling," Obama said. "I think I know her pretty well. If she's going to be on the team, she's going to be loyal."

After all, Hillary Clinton had stood by her husband during the Monica Lewinsky scandal more than a decade earlier, and Obama was impressed by her resilience.

As he went over the list of candidates for secretary of state, Obama realized he needed someone with enough stature to be seen as a major player on the world stage. What about Hillary Clinton? What would it mean? Would she accept? What was she thinking?

Well, Axelrod said, she certainly wasn't confiding in him.

Obama decided to find out. John Podesta passed word to Clinton's staff that Obama wanted to discuss the possibility of her becoming secretary of state. "Think about it," Podesta said to Clinton's staff. "Talk to her. This is serious."

Clinton assumed Obama had no choice but to sit down with her. She had garnered 18 million votes in the primaries, and those voters might be upset if he didn't at least consider her for something. Just as he had faked consideration of her for vice president, he would fake consideration for State. As far as she was concerned, it was part of a bullshit political Kabuki dance.

She flew to Chicago on November 13. "Personal business," a spokesman claimed when the media spotted her black Secret Service–driven SUV going in and out of the parking garage at Obama's transition headquarters.

Obama made it clear he was serious. He wanted her to be his secretary of state.

Clinton returned to Washington and spoke with Podesta. Wow, he's serious about this, she said. She was stunned, yet not convinced the position would be right for her.

Podesta was encouraging. No one else could do the job as well as you, he said. And look at the alternatives, he said. Hanging around the Senate? Seniority ruled on the Hill, and there were no leadership opportunities for her there. "Bush fucked up the world," Podesta said, "and fucked up America's place in the world, and digging out of that would be very tough." No one else came close to having her clout and visibility. There was a big agenda, Podesta said, and she would be a big deal.

Clinton didn't argue with that, but it would mean giving up her independence in the Senate. What would the relationship be like working for Obama? She knew how the White House worked. If a president wanted to control, he controlled or used his staff—or even his wife—to do it. There wasn't exactly a reservoir of trust between her camp and his. She might find it difficult, if not impossible, to operate. "Will I really be able to do the job?" she asked.

Podesta said he could probably get a guarantee from Obama that she could pick her own deputies and staff.

Then came the various "Bill" problems. Her husband, the former president, maneuvered visibly on the world stage. What about the big-bucks donors to his presidential library, his foundation and his

Clinton Global Initiative? Obama's transition lawyers had said these enterprises could not accept foreign money if Hillary became secretary of state.

The Bill issues were a major stumbling block, she said, noting with a smile and a laugh that she wasn't about to send Bill to live in a cave for four or even eight years.

"I'm not going to tell him to shut down operations in 26 countries that are saving people's lives," Clinton said. Just because someone thinks it might look bad? People would die if his charities collapsed. "It's not worth it," she said. Her husband had told her he would do what was necessary. "I'm not going to tell him to do it. So we'll work it out in a way that permits that work to go forward, or I'm going to say no."

Podesta spoke with former President Clinton. "I only have one argument," Podesta told him. "Nobody can do this job better. It's really important to the country that she does it."

Oh, come on, the former president said. His own relationship with Obama from the campaign remained tense, to say the least. It had offended him that critics interpreted his comments about Obama as racist. Some political feuds, particularly those arising from the hothouse of a presidential campaign, never get settled.

"We'll work this stuff out," Podesta said. "It'll cause some inconvenience, but it's worth it." Podesta was pleased to learn that Chelsea, the Clintons' 28-year-old daughter, wanted her mother to accept.

"Let's work it out," Bill Clinton said. The former president went public on Wednesday, November 19, saying, "I'll do whatever they want." He agreed to release the names of 200,000 donors to his library and foundation. Previous donors were grandfathered in, meaning no money would have to be returned.

Vice President–elect Joseph R. Biden joined in the outreach to Bill Clinton, and Biden and Rahm Emanuel both spoke with Hillary.

By midweek, she decided no.

"This is never going to work," she told Podesta. She was a Clinton. She was not an Obama acolyte. It was a matter of retaining her identity. She had submerged herself all those years as the governor's wife in Arkansas, then for eight years as first lady, and the roles had sub-sumed her. Not again. "It's too complicated, forget it."

A formal statement was prepared that thanked Obama but an-nounced her decision to decline. A phone call was scheduled so she could tell Obama directly, but Podesta arranged it so the two didn't connect that night. "Let her sleep on it," he said. Podesta knew the most intense conversations were taking place within the family—Hillary, Bill and Chelsea.

Podesta talked with her again early the next morning.

"Are you really sure I should do this?" she asked.

Absolutely, he said. No doubt. And everyone else was too, most im-portantly the president-elect. She would be able to pick her own people and have direct access to the president—instead of going through his national security adviser.

Podesta could see that her hard "no" had turned into a "maybe," if not a soft "yes."

Not quite a yes, Podesta reported to Obama.

During the course of this courtship, Clinton had exchanged e-mails and spoken by telephone with Mark Penn, the pollster and chief strat-egist for her failed presidential campaign. The rumpled polling guru, who as an outside consultant had controlled virtually every important policy pronouncement out of Bill Clinton's White House during his second term, thought she should say yes.

Penn listed half a dozen reasons. It would show she was a good sport who didn't carry a grudge—a trait often attributed to the Clin-tons. Being secretary of state would give her absolute bona fides in foreign policy and national security, a weakness that had become evi-dent in the campaign. Accepting Obama's offer would put her under the umbrella of the Democratic Party, where she and Bill had often been suspected of playing Clinton-first politics. In addition, the Senate was not as welcoming as it once had been and its leaders had turned on her during the presidential contest. No matter what her future, the top cabinet post would give her an unmatched record of public service. Also, Penn believed the people in the country, especially Democrats, wanted to see her and Obama together, on the same team. And it might be possible that Obama's favorable press could spill over to her. As secretary she would be in the public eye all the time, and the post would once and for all establish her independence from her husband.

Penn defined diplomacy as getting someone to do something they did not want to do without shooting them—a skill she had.

With the prolonged emotional strain of the campaign over, she needed to apply her considerable energies to something, he said.

Penn always had his eye on the prize—the White House. If she did the job for four years, Obama might be in trouble and have to dump Biden and pick her to run with him as vice president. She had nearly beaten Obama and had won substantial margins in the primaries among four important constituencies—women, Latinos, the working class and seniors—voting blocs Obama would need in 2012. Her addition to the ticket might be a necessity.

In terms of 2016, Penn noted, if she served eight years at State, she could not be better positioned to run for president again. She would only be 69—the age Reagan had been when he took office. And statistically, women lived longer and generally stayed in better health during their later years.

Plus, it fit with the Clinton style, since the family motto was "We're going to keep on going." Say yes, Penn urged. You're still in the game, he basically told her. It's a "no brainer, a five-minute decision."

Clinton later said these political considerations played no role in her decision.

When Obama called Clinton personally, he turned on all the spigots.

He said he wanted her to accept. This is a particularly momentous period in our history, he said, and you would have the authority to conduct diplomacy and to act as a major player. It was a better, more meaningful opportunity than going back to the Senate, said the former junior senator from Illinois. He needed her to do this.

It was the voice of a president asking a lot. She had heard it many times before. She said yes.

•   •   •

Admiral Michael Mullen received an important phone call several days after the election, a confirmation perhaps of the clout he hoped to have in the next administration. The president-elect wanted to speak alone in Chicago with Mullen, the chairman of the Joint Chiefs of Staff.

Though putatively the highest-ranking military man, in reality the chairman is a kind of sixth finger in the military hierarchy. By law he is the principal military adviser to the president, the secretary of defense and the National Security Council, but he is not in the all-important chain of command. The power to give orders and control wars ran from the president, as commander in chief, to the secretary of defense to combatant commanders such as CentCom's General David Petraeus. Mullen had no actual command authority over combatant forces.

His predecessors as JCS chairman, Air Force General Richard B. Myers and Marine General Peter Pace, had been mostly irrelevant, because Secretary of Defense Rumsfeld so thoroughly dominated the Pentagon.

Mullen, 62, was something of an accidental chairman. He had been chief of naval operations in 2007, when Gates hastily decided Pace did not have the Senate votes for reappointment.

Obama's invitation was a chance for Mullen, who was in the middle of his two-year term, to get back in the game, restore the status of the chairmanship, and establish a personal relationship with the new president. The model was Colin Powell, the Army general who held the position from 1989 to 1993 during the first Gulf War. Powell had been front and center in that war, publicly promising to "kill" Saddam Hussein's army. He formulated the Powell Doctrine, the use of overwhelming and decisive force to minimize casualties and ensure victory.

Mullen is tall with a hearty, almost booming voice. As he speaks, his hands tend to fly around him. He had been carefully neutral in the 2008 presidential campaign. A 1968 graduate of the Naval Academy at Annapolis—ten years after Senator John McCain, the Republican presidential nominee—and the son of a Hollywood publicist, he was deferential to anyone with political power.

Right after he attended President Bush's State of the Union address in January 2008, there was one of those moments in life, an accidental encounter, that might change everything. Mullen passed Obama on a stairwell. He thought Obama, stuck on the presidential campaign treadmill, looked like he hadn't slept for a month.

"God," Mullen said, taking Obama's hand, "get some sleep!"

"My staff won't let me," Obama replied.

The chance meeting was a bit of good luck for Mullen. Had he encountered a sleep-deprived McCain, he would likely have said the same thing. But to politicians in the heat of a national campaign, the country is binary—either for you or against you. Mullen, in his dress blues with a breastful of ribbons and the gold braid of a full admiral—one thick and three thin around each forearm above the wrist—felt he had successfully reached out to the Illinois senator.

Obama, who had never served in the military and possibly knew as little about it as any major presidential candidate in years, called Mullen two or three times during the campaign, just to check in, say hello, not talk about anything really. Mullen believed the calls were designed to build a personal connection. The admiral could not have been more responsive, eager, gentlemanly or deferential.

In one of the presidential debates, Obama even used Mullen to back up his position, noting that the chairman himself had "acknowledged that we don't have enough troops to deal with Afghanistan."

The invitation to Chicago was almost as welcome as another promotion, and it could practically amount to that. On a hunch, Mullen concluded that Obama wanted to have more of a conversation and less of a briefing. Accompanied by a single aide, he arrived about 20 minutes before his noon appointment on Friday, November 21.

"I'm here to see President-elect Obama," Mullen told a young female staffer at the Obama headquarters.

"Well, who are you?" she asked.

"Mike Mullen, Admiral Mullen."

"Who are you?"

"Chairman of the Joint Chiefs."

"Well, he just left for lunch," the woman explained. She quickly got up to check.

Mullen gazed out the window as he waited. When he turned around, there was Obama three inches from his face, inviting him into his office, which was strewn with campaign memorabilia—a football, a basketball and posters.

Mark Lippert, a key Obama foreign policy aide and a lieutenant in the Navy Reserve, came in to take notes.

"I've been running for this bus," Obama said, "and now I caught it." Almost as an afterthought, he added, "And it's a big bus."

There is an economic crisis, Obama continued, and it would have to get most of his attention.

I got that, Mullen said, adding, as the former budget guy for the Navy, he had no expectations Defense would ever be exempt from trimming expenditures.

"I'll give you some time here at the end," Obama said. "I want to ask questions."

On Afghanistan, and by extension Pakistan, he asked, what is the degree of difficulty?

The Afghanistan War has been under-resourced for years, Mullen said. In truth, there was no strategy, he added, knowing that Bush's national security adviser, Stephen Hadley, would kill him for saying that. It was an indictment of Bush, Hadley, Gates and, in a way, himself. Mullen had testified the previous year that, "In Afghanistan, we do what we can. In Iraq, we do what we must."

Obama made it clear that would change.

With the proper resources, Mullen said, they could succeed in Afghanistan. But there are almost no resources on the civilian side, and the U.S. embassy has a very bad relationship with just about everybody, even the military.

I want to get Afghanistan and Pakistan right, Obama said, but I don't want to build a Jeffersonian democracy.

He said he still intended to withdraw U.S. forces from Iraq but would do so responsibly. On Iran, Obama said he would open a dialogue with the Iranians. But he also made it clear that he had no intention of pulling the military options off the table.

•   •   •

But Obama soon found out there were problems with the options. The existing contingency plan for Iran seemed to have dated from Jimmy Carter's presidency. It started with 90 days of bombing before a Normandy-style invasion from World War II that involved more troops than the U.S. had in its inventory. No serious process had been in place for updating the many contingency plans a president needs.

Nor did adequate plans exist for Somalia or Yemen, two countries with a growing al Qaeda presence. And most tellingly, nothing on the shelf specifically addressed securing Pakistan's nuclear weapons. Obama's team would have to develop a graduated plan dealing with a range of circumstances from Pakistan losing a single nuclear weapon all the way up to the Pakistani government falling to Islamic extremists, who would then have a nuclear arsenal. Compounding the problem was a lack of knowledge about the location of all of Pakistan's nukes. The sites were scattered across the country, with the weapons frequently moved in a classic shell game.

One of the closest held secrets of President Bush's inner circle was that the president had lost his appetite for military contingency planning. The tough-talking, saber-rattling Bush administration had not prepared for some of the worst-case scenarios the country might face.

Obama later said he would neither confirm nor deny any specifics about contingency plans, but he acknowledged that he had inherited unfinished business from Bush. "Wars absorb so much energy on the part of any administration," Obama told me, "that even if people are doing an outstanding job, if they're in the middle of a war—particularly one that's going badly, as it was, obviously, for a three-year stretch there in Iraq—that's taking up a huge amount of energy on the part of everybody. And that means that there are some things that get left undone."

4

Two weeks before his election, Obama had asked retired General James L. Jones to Richmond, Virginia, for a private meeting. Jones, 64, was a figure out of a Marine Corps brochure, 6-foot-5, with a brush haircut, a long handsome face, bright blue eyes, a boyish smile and a genial manner. He was called "Gentleman Jim" because he treated everyone from presidents to corporals with respect. His national security credentials appeared gold-plated, having served in the Marines for 40 years and rising to the top position, commandant, then four years as NATO commander, the top U.S. and allied commander in Europe, before retiring in 2007.

Jones had expressed distaste for Secretary of Defense Rumsfeld's leadership, publicly confirming a report that the secretary had "systematically emasculated" the Joint Chiefs and warning a fellow Marine general, then Chairman Pete Pace, "You should not be the parrot on the secretary's shoulder." Secretary of State Condoleezza Rice had asked him to be her deputy, a post he declined. Jones instead served as Rice's part-time envoy for security in the Middle East, but he made no secret of the fact that he found the Bush administration woefully disorganized and embarrassingly unserious about Middle East peace.

In the Richmond hotel, Obama told Jones, "It looks like I might win this." He wanted to talk to him about being secretary of state or national security adviser.

Jones said he would be a better fit as secretary of state than as a presidential aide. "What I can do is set up an organization to get the best people to help you as president" at State, he explained. Noting that he had served as chief aide to the Marine commandant and later as senior military aide to Secretary of Defense William S. Cohen, Jones acknowledged, "I wasn't very good" at being an aide.

Obama drew him out on how he thought the National Security Council should work.

Jones said he had seen the Bush NSC up close. It was understaffed, under-resourced and deeply dysfunctional. The national security adviser had little clout and failed to think strategically by plotting out the detailed steps and plans of a policy for a year or two. This was the biggest missing piece in the Bush operation. The national security adviser had to develop measurements to ensure reasonable progress was being made toward the goals. If not, the plans had to be revised—radically if necessary. Too much policy was on automatic pilot. Second, Jones said, the national security adviser had to find a way to get results without "micromanaging" what the departments and agencies should do.

How should that be done? Obama asked.

Convince your subordinates that your vision is their vision, Jones said. That meant giving them a stake, creating "buy-in" so they also have personal ownership of the policy. If a president tried to do all the work by himself, he added, his subordinates would let him. An example of this was President Bush's secure videoconferences every two weeks or so with the leaders of Afghanistan and Iraq. That meant no one else in the U.S. government had any real leverage or could speak with authority. Afghanistan President Hamid Karzai and Iraqi Prime Minister Nouri al-Maliki always insisted on taking up any dispute directly with Bush, who effectively had both the Afghanistan and Iraq accounts, living deeply in the tactical weeds—precisely where a president didn't belong.

•   •   •

From that meeting on, Obama made it clear to Podesta and his foreign policy campaign aides that he wanted Jones as national security adviser. It would, he said, give him someone outside the Pentagon with the credibility to deal with the secretary of defense and the generals on a more or less equal footing. It looked like Jones could manage big personalities, and he had a theory on how to energize the National Security Council.

After hearing Obama out, Podesta had the strong impression that Obama wanted a national security adviser who wasn't perceived as his guy, a mere extension of the president. He seemed to have reached the baffling conclusion that the lack of a personal relationship could be an asset. Jones would not only be speaking on behalf of Obama, but as a retired Marine general, a former commandant and NATO commander. It could give Obama more leverage with the Pentagon. Jones's record of outspokenness and independence might make him a counterweight to the military establishment.

But most of all, Jones knew the military as well as anyone, and that was the terrain Obama knew the least. In the White House, Jones could help him navigate what could be a difficult relationship, particularly given Obama's fervent opposition to the Iraq War. Jones could be an inoculation, guide and shield.

Podesta and several of the others were coming to realize that once the president-elect got an idea for who should fill a critical post, he stuck with it, unless something disqualifying was found. Podesta examined Jones's record and talked to several people in the national security community. He did not find Jones to be very strategic, certainly not in the mold of what he called "the Kissingerian, master-, überstrategist."

Maybe that would be less crucial under Obama, Podesta thought, because Obama's approach was so intellectual. He compared Obama to Spock from *Star Trek*. The president-elect wanted to put his own ideas to work. He was unsentimental and capable of being ruthless. Podesta was not sure that Obama felt anything, especially in his gut. He intellectualized and then charted the path forward, essentially picking up the emotions of others and translating them into ideas. He had thus created a different kind of politics, seizing the moment of 2008 and driving it to a political victory.

But, Podesta thought, sometimes a person's great strength, in this case Obama's capacity to intellectualize, was also an Achilles' heel.

Obama had several more phone conversations with Jones. Since Clinton was going to get State, the top foreign policy job, he offered national security adviser to Jones. If it was a consolation prize, it certainly had its own appeal. It required no Senate confirmation and the corner West Wing office carried its own highly visible cachet.

Jones was astounded that the president-elect would give such a position of responsibility and trust to someone he hardly knew. His basic philosophy was that everything hinged on personal relations, and he didn't have one with Obama.

Jones told Obama that he would have to consult his family.

In retirement, he was heading the energy program for the U.S. Chamber of Commerce, serving on several boards, consulting and speaking, earning over $2 million a year. Accepting would mean an 80 percent pay cut. But the family agreed it was worth the chance to cap his career with one of the most important posts in government. What sealed the deal for Jones was a promise Obama made. If he accepted, Obama said that on national security issues, "I will always ask your opinion or judgment before I do anything." It was a personal pledge. To the former commandant of the Marines, whose motto is "Semper Fidelis" ("Always Faithful"), it meant everything. Jones said yes.

One of the first orders of business for Jones was picking a deputy—a key post that had been occupied by half a dozen men who had then gone on to be promoted to national security adviser. Obama had told him that he could pick whomever he wanted. His deputy would occupy a small, closet-size office critically located in the West Wing suite of the national security adviser. All other senior NSC staffers were down one floor in the basement or in the Eisenhower Executive Office Building. Most importantly, the deputy would run the deputies committee meetings to tee up issues and decisions for the principals and full NSC.

Emanuel had suggested Jones consider Tom Donilon, a 53-year-old lawyer and former chief of staff to Secretary of State Warren Christopher in the Clinton administration. A political junkie and workaholic who attended foreign policy seminars as recreation, Donilon was a detail man and extremely close to Vice President–elect Biden. Donilon's wife, Cathy Russell, would become Jill Biden's chief of staff. He was a member of nearly every council, advisory board, group or institute that dealt with foreign affairs, and had served as co-head of the transition team for the State Department. His friendship with Emanuel went back several decades.

Donilon had been preparing all his life for a top national security post. He had helped Democratic presidential candidates going back to Jimmy Carter. He had advised Obama in the presidential debates and wanted to be deputy secretary of state. But Donilon had served seven years as in-house counsel to Fannie Mae, the federally chartered mortgage giant that had nearly gone bust in the financial crisis, costing taxpayers billions of dollars. The Fannie Mae connection was toxic, and Donilon might have serious problems in a Senate confirmation.

Emanuel lowered the hammer. First he had suggested and now he was almost insisting. He wanted Donilon in the White House.

Jones did not know Donilon but agreed to interview him. They hit it off. Clearly a Democratic Party insider with what appeared to be sterling national security credentials could be a help, since Jones didn't know the political insiders. He quickly decided to pick Donilon, and could almost hear the collective sigh of relief from Obama's political and transition teams.

On Wednesday, November 26, President Bush convened one of his last National Security Council meetings. It was to consider a highly classified report on the Afghanistan War. The report was the work of Army Lieutenant General Douglas Lute, the "war czar" Bush had appointed the year before as the top NSC deputy for the wars in Iraq and Afghanistan.

Lute, 56, lived under the public radar as much as General David Petraeus lived in it. The West Point class of 1975 graduate—a year after Petraeus—had also earned a Harvard master's degree in public administration. It might be easy to assume he was another "Bush general," but Lute had a streak of daring independence. His favorite military book was Thucydides' history of the fifth-century B.C. Peloponnesian War between Sparta and Athens. The book taught him about the relationship between the military and civil society, two cultures he now bridged at the NSC. He remained a three-star general, yet by serving in the White House he was no longer among the Army brotherhood.

Lute personally briefed Bush about both wars each morning at 7 A.M. Because Bush was sometimes early, Lute made sure to be outside the Oval Office at 6:45. That summer, Bush had ordered Lute to do an Afghanistan strategy review. Go deep, go wide, Bush had said, get to the bottom of where we are after seven years. Lute wasn't entirely sure whether he was on a fact-finding or a rescue mission. Perhaps both. He wanted to see the entire horizon and the ground truth in a way that he couldn't from a Washington office. Lute traveled with a high-powered team from the departments of State and Defense and the CIA.

In his 33-year Army career, Lute had punched some of the key command and operational tickets overseas and on the Joint Staff. But nothing was quite like being at the center of the turmoil in the White House, where he acted as unofficial information link with cabinet officers, generals, admirals, diplomats and intelligence officers in two wars. He kept in touch with an exhaustive list of officials through secure telephone calls and one-to-one conferences on a Tandberg video phone.

Lute had arrived in Afghanistan from Iraq, where the United States had 150,000 troops, a 1,000-person embassy that coordinated with the military, and a foreign assistance program of several billion dollars a year. In Iraq, Prime Minister Maliki had shown surprising leadership skills, while the Iraqi security force was becoming stronger and better. The United States had stared failure in the eye in Iraq, and, for the moment, failure had blinked. Overall, the strategy that accompanied the 2007 troop surge seemed to be working as planned.

The contrast with Afghanistan was stark. Afghanistan had about 38,000 U.S. troops, plus 29,000 from NATO and other allies. They were thinly dispersed across the country, so it was impossible for the troops to have a big impact. The U.S. embassy was not working well with the military. Economic development for most Afghans was minimal. Afghan President Hamid Karzai proved a growing disappointment, while the Afghan security force remained woefully inadequate. Put simply, all the hopeful signs in Iraq were missing in Afghanistan.

Lute also found that while Taliban insurgents had a clear presence in the southern Afghan provinces along the Pakistani border, the U.S. hadn't dedicated the resources to stop them. Over the summer, attacks and security incidents had doubled to about 200 a month in the south alone. The insurgents' capability was deemed "strong, effective" or "demonstrated" in nearly half the country, predominantly in southern Afghanistan, according to intelligence reports.

As Lute examined the situation there, he found about 10 distinct but overlapping wars in progress. First, there was the conventional war run by a Canadian general in charge of the region for NATO. Second, the CIA was conducting its own covert paramilitary war. The Green Berets and the Joint Special Operations Command each had their own wars, tracking down high-value targets. The training and equipment command ran its own operations. The Afghan National Army, the Afghan National Police and the Afghan National Directorate for Security, the country's CIA-sponsored intelligence agency, were also fighting separate wars.

Lute and his team visited the southern province of Kandahar, which had 2 million people in its namesake city and the surrounding area and was the cradle for the Taliban movement, which had governed the country from 1996 to 2001. The province and the city appeared to be slipping back into Taliban control.

By placing different icons on a map of the regional command that included Kandahar, he could see how the ten different wars were sprinkled around. They looked like the scribbles of a child. Nobody was in charge. There was no unity of effort or command.

Afghanistan was the poor man's war, Lute concluded. But as the czar of both wars knew, the only way to get more resources and capabilities would be to remove them from Iraq. This was a zero-sum game. There were no more troops, the military was stretched to the brink.

Upon returning to Washington, Lute set up a series of 19 in-depth meetings over six weeks with all the interagency representatives—State, Defense, CIA—in Room 445 of the Eisenhower Executive Office Building next to the White House. In all, these meetings took some 45 hours, grinding down to the finest detail. They grilled Afghan ministers, the military commanders and the CIA people about what was really going on.

Lute and his team summarized their findings in a report of about 25 pages, keeping it short so it would be easy to read.

"I know this is kind of bad timing, but here it is," Lute said when he delivered the review to President Bush earlier in November. He was tossing a rock into a quiet pond. There would be ripples.

"I'd rather not be reading this," Bush said, "but I appreciate your candor. You're doing what I asked you to do." Bush took the review with him for the weekend.

"We're not losing, but we're not winning, and that's not good enough," was one of the opening lines in the review. The effort was barely enough to keep from losing, but that was all.

The report identified Pakistan as a much more strategically troubling problem than Afghanistan, because the sanctuaries there for al Qaeda and other affiliate groups were more of a threat to the United States.

The review concluded that the U.S. couldn't prevail in Afghanistan unless it resolved three large problems. First, governance had to be improved and corruption curtailed. Bribes and embezzlement were rampant. There were, for example, about 42 steps to get an Afghan driver's license, nearly all an opportunity for someone to pocket a bribe. Second, the opium trade was out of control. It fueled corruption and partially financed the Taliban insurgency. And third, the Pakistani safe havens had to be reduced and eventually eliminated. If the United States didn't accomplish these three things, it could never claim to be done in Afghanistan.

With Pakistan, the review said the U.S. should expand the scope of its aid beyond that country's military and try to stabilize its economy. If Pakistan's $168 billion economy collapsed, the chaos in the tribal areas would then spread to the country's more cosmopolitan cities.

Bush's secretary of state, Condoleezza Rice, was unhappy with the review. After four years as national security adviser and then three and a half as secretary of state, she treated this as a legacy issue, kind of a last semester report card. She pushed back on the notion that Pakistan was more important than Afghanistan. She thought they were doing better than the disorder and weakness suggested in the review, arguing that they were doing more than just hanging on.

On Wednesday, November 26, Bush convened a National Security Council meeting to consider what should be done with the highly classified and critical document.

"We're not going to release this publicly," Bush said. "Look, I'm in my last couple of months. A public release will just make people scratch their heads." Release could also prejudice the incoming administration from at least taking the review under consideration, he said. What was left unsaid was that the review could also be embarrassing because it exposed the extent to which the Afghanistan War had been neglected.

"I don't want any public rollout," Bush said. "There won't be any rollout plan. The rollout plan will be up to the new administration coming in, because this is going to be their bailiwick now."

Just as Bush was deciding not to release the damning Afghanistan War report, 10 gunmen were roaming the Indian city of Mumbai, effectively holding its 15 million people captive. The gunmen created a spectacle of chaos and violence on live television for about 60 hours. Terrorist theater had not been anything like this since the 9/11 attacks.

When the gunfire ended, the body count totaled 175, including six American citizens. The siege had been organized by a group called Lashkar-e-Taiba, which means the Army of the Pure and is commonly referred to by the acronym LeT. One of LeT's primary goals is to overthrow India's control of Kashmir, a Muslim-majority province that borders Pakistan. Its broader mission involves founding an Islamic nation across South Asia. Intelligence showed that ties between LeT and al Qaeda were increasing.

The open secret is that LeT was created and continues to be funded and protected by the Pakistani ISI. The intelligence branch of the Pakistani military uses LeT to inflict pain and hardship on India, according to U.S. intelligence. These gunmen had, quite possibly, committed an act of war.

President Bush called his national security team into the Oval Office as Mumbai sorted through the blood and rubble.

You guys get planning and do what you have to do to prevent a war between Pakistan and India, Bush told his aides. The last thing we need right now is a war between two nuclear-power states.

But what worried the president was not just tensions between India and Pakistan. Americans had been killed in an act of terrorism. In his nationally televised address on the evening of 9/11, Bush had declared what became known as the Bush Doctrine: "We will make no distinction between those who planned these acts and those who harbor them." The doctrine was the basis for launching the war in Afghanistan to overthrow the Taliban, which had harbored and given sanctuary to al Qaeda.

Bush was extremely proud of the hard-line doctrine and told me in an interview the doctrine meant, "We're going to root out terror." A foundation of his presidency was this zero tolerance for terrorists and their enablers.

The Mumbai attacks presented him with something of the same problem—hard-core LeT terrorists and their enablers, the Pakistani intelligence service. An upset Bush asked his aides about contingency plans for dealing with Pakistan.

This is like 9/11, he said.

The United States military did not have "war" plans for an invasion of Pakistan. Instead, it had and continues to have one of the most sensitive and secret of all military contingencies, what military officials call a "retribution" plan in the event of another 9/11-like attack on the U.S. by terrorists based in Pakistan. Under this plan, the U.S. would bomb or attack every known al Qaeda compound or training camp in the U.S. intelligence database. Some locations might be outdated, but there would be no concern, under the plan, for who might be living there now. The retribution plan called for a brutal, punishing attack on at least 150 or more associated camps.

Within 48 hours of the Mumbai attack, CIA Director Hayden contacted Pakistan's ambassador to the U.S., Husain Haqqani. CIA intelligence showed no direct ISI link, Hayden told him. These are former people who are no longer employees of the Pakistani government.*

Bush informed the Indians himself. He called Indian Prime Minister Manmohan Singh, with whom he had a strong personal relationship. My intelligence shows that the new Pakistani government is not involved, Bush said.

It looked like a war had been averted for the moment.

In a call to Lieutenant General Ahmed Shuja Pasha, the head of the Pakistani ISI, Hayden said, "We've got to get to the bottom of this. This is a big deal." He urged Pasha to come clean and disclose all. On the day after Christmas, Pasha flew to the United States, where he briefed Hayden at CIA headquarters.

Pasha admitted that the planners of the Mumbai attacks—at least two retired Pakistani army officers—had ISI links, but this had not been an authorized ISI operation. It was rogue.

"There may have been people associated with my organization who

---

*The CIA later received reliable intelligence that the ISI was directly involved in the training for Mumbai.

were associated with this," Pasha said. "That's different from authority, direction and control."

He provided details that fit with the picture developed by U.S. intelligence. Hayden told Bush he was convinced it was not an official
Pakistani-sponsored attack, but it highlighted the problem of the sanctuaries in Pakistan. The ease of the planning and execution, the low
cost, and the alarming sophistication of the communications system
that LeT had used were all troubling. The attackers relied on an easily
obtainable global positioning system device, Google Earth maps, and
commercially available encryption devices and remote control triggers.

They spoke with handlers back in Pakistan with satellite phones
that went through a Voice over Internet Protocol (VoIP) phone service
in New Jersey, making the calls difficult, if not impossible, to trace and
routed them in a way that also concealed the locations of those talking.

The FBI was horrified by the low-cost, high-tech operation that
had paralyzed Mumbai. American cities were just as vulnerable. A senior FBI official responsible for thwarting similar attacks in the United
States said, "Mumbai changed everything."

5

Up in his seventh-floor office at CIA headquarters in Langley, Virginia, Director Michael Hayden had been stewing for months, waiting in frustration to be contacted by Obama. But Hayden had been cut out of the loop with the next first customer.

During the summer, candidate Obama had asked to see him. On June 18, Hayden was being driven to Capitol Hill for their meeting when his phone rang. Obama apologized, explaining he had to cancel. The memorial service for NBC newscaster Tim Russert, who had died of a heart attack the week before, had unexpectedly run late.

"General, I really want to talk with you," Obama said. "I feel really bad." They would get together. We'll do lunch, he in effect promised.

Obama never rescheduled. Hayden tried to pretend he didn't take the slight personally, concluding it showed that Obama didn't understand the importance of the CIA. But being stiff-armed for months bruised his ego. He figured he was being blocked from Obama, refused a chance to advertise his achievements as director.

Hayden had built his career around selling his intelligence wares person to person. Able to think and talk about 20 percent faster than most people, Hayden seemed to have an edge in any debate.

When he became CIA director in 2006, Hayden had inherited an agency suffering from what he called "battered child syndrome." There was the botched intelligence that mistakenly concluded Iraq had weapons of mass destruction, the main premise of the Iraq War, and the accusations that the CIA's enhanced interrogation techniques, such as waterboarding or simulated drowning, amounted to torture. Hayden felt he was restoring morale, putting the CIA on the road to recovery. During the controversy about the interrogation methods—techniques Obama had promised to abolish—Hayden had persuaded President Bush to drop the harshest practices. He was eager to brief Obama, convinced he could sell the next president on the need for an independent CIA interrogation program that played by more flexible rules than the U.S. military.

Hayden also hoped to stay on as CIA director, at least for six more months. He thought he deserved to be asked, even though his wife, Jeanine, reminded him that this was unrealistic. Hayden believed he could provide continuity during the first year of the new presidency—a time of maximum vulnerability. The first bombing of the World Trade Center had been in 1993, at the start of the Clinton administration. And 9/11 occurred during Bush's rookie year. With a large foreign policy agenda and two wars, Obama would need the CIA. "No contact," Hayden complained. "I'm in absolute limbo. No one's talking."

Obama's closest national security advisers from the campaign, Denis McDonough and Mark Lippert—whom Obama affectionately referred to with the Dr. Seuss book nicknames of Thing One and Thing Two—had told Hayden they would reach out to him during the transition. But weeks of silence had passed.

"We do covert action at the CIA," Hayden reminded them, convinced they underestimated the importance of these missions—the stuff of spy thrillers—that were specifically designed to disguise America's hand. By law, the president authorized covert actions in a "finding," a document stating that the action was necessary for national security.

"It is authorized by the office of the president, not the person," Hayden explained. "So everything we do will be popping at 4 P.M., January 20"—just hours after Obama would take the oath of office. "If there are changes the president-elect wants to make, I need to brief him on the active covert action programs."

One of Hayden's top CIA deputies went to McDonough and Lippert to ask again, what about Hayden?

Tell the general not to worry, we will reach out to him, they said. That meeting was finally arranged in Chicago for December 9.

Hayden did not alert or invite DNI McConnell, who found out about the meeting on his own.

McConnell worried that the temptation of covert action might entrance Obama. Any president, especially a new, relatively inexperienced one, could be vulnerable. Imagine the allure of solving a foreign policy problem by secretly funding a regime change—literally buying a country's government. As Richard Helms, the CIA director from 1966 to 1973 during Vietnam and Watergate, once said, "Covert action is like a damn good drug. It works, but if you take too much of it, it will kill you."

The CIA did some spectacular work, McConnell knew. It essentially recruited people to betray their countries through espionage. Recruitment was a delicate art, fraught with opportunity and peril. The one target the CIA loved to recruit was the American president, to unfurl the secrets and wonders of spying for the first customer. The CIA wanted no one between it and the White House.

McConnell phoned the CIA chief when he heard about the December 9, 2008, Obama briefing.

Did Hayden plan to discuss RDI, meaning Rendition, Detention and Interrogation, the controversial CIA counterterrorist programs? McConnell asked.

Hayden said he would because they were covert actions. The CIA director was certain the president-elect would be impressed that the modified interrogation techniques made sense and were legal.

"I will be there," McConnell said, giving an RSVP to the invite he should have received.

"Well, that'd be nice," Hayden replied.

On the morning of Tuesday, December 9, Hayden and McConnell were in Chicago, ready to have the president-elect focus for two hours on the CIA's covert actions. A somewhat astonished and distracted Obama greeted them.

"They just arrested the governor for trying to sell my seat," he said. The FBI had taken Illinois Governor Rod Blagojevich into custody that morning after wiretaps showed he was asking various politicians for money in exchange for being appointed to the Senate seat Obama had resigned.

The entourage of intelligence and administration officials crammed into the Sensitive Compartmented Information Facility, or SCIF.

Hayden sat directly across from Obama at a table so narrow that they were uncomfortably close to each other. His bald head was about 30 inches from the president-elect's face. Vice President–elect Joe Biden, Jim Jones, Greg Craig, the designated White House counsel, and several others sat on Obama's side.

"Mr. President-elect," said McConnell, who was next to Hayden, "we're going to give you the background on the findings and covert actions, where we are and how it's working. We talked to you about this in summary terms when we briefed you in September. We gave you a little more detail in November. But now we're going to get down to more sources and methods."

Hayden jumped at this opening, practically brushing McConnell aside, several from the Obama camp noticed. This was his opportunity and he wanted to create what he called an "oh, shit moment" to prove how grave the threats were and to show how seriously the CIA was taking them. He had brought a chart the size of two dinner place mats. It listed 14 highly classified covert actions, the nature of those actions, and the written findings from Bush and other presidents. Referring to the chart he spread in front of Obama, Hayden said the current covert actions were authorized to:

- Conduct clandestine, lethal counterterrorism operations and other programs to stop terrorists worldwide. Operations were active in more than 60 countries. Bush senior signed the initial finding, which his son, the current president, later modified. If al Qaeda planned to detonate a nuclear weapon in an American city or launch an influenza pandemic by using a biological agent, these covert actions are all you've really got to try to stop them, Hayden explained. The finding included unmanned aerial Predator drone strikes on terrorists and terrorist camps worldwide.

"How much are you doing in Pakistan?" Obama asked.

Hayden said about 80 percent of America's worldwide attacks were there. We own the sky. The drones take off and land at secret bases in Pakistan. Al Qaeda is training people in the tribal areas who, if you saw them in the visa line at Dulles, you would not recognize as potential threats.

• Stop or impede Iran from developing nuclear weapons.

The CIA director described a range of secret operations and techniques—some of which had been effective, some of which had yet to work. After stopping attacks from terrorists, the covert efforts against Iran were President Bush's top priority.

• Deter North Korea from building more nuclear weapons. The regime headed by Kim Jong Il, among the world's most erratic and irrational leaders, probably had enough weapons-grade plutonium for another six bombs. This finding was supported by an array of clandestine intelligence gathering operations aimed at that closed and oppressive society.

• Conduct anti-proliferation operations in other countries to prevent them from acquiring weapons of mass destruction.

• Carry out lethal and other operations independently or in support of the U.S. military in Afghanistan. This included the unmanned aerial drone attacks and the CIA's 3,000-man army of Counterterrorism Pursuit Teams (CTPT).

• Run an array of lethal operations and other programs in Iraq. The CIA had a continuing and deep involvement with the Iraqi government and the Iraqi security forces. Hayden claimed they "owned" certain entities and people.

Greg Craig, for one, was shocked by the term. He thought Hayden might be overstating it. The director was showboating, he concluded, and could have conveyed the same degree of influence without resorting to "We own them."

In addition, Hayden said the CIA pumped tens of millions of dollars into a number of foreign intelligence services, such as the Jordanian General Intelligence Department, which he said the CIA also "owned."

- Support clandestine efforts to stop genocide in the Darfur region of Sudan. President George W. Bush, who signed the finding, had said, "I want to fix Sudan and stop the slaughter."

- Provide Turkey with intelligence and other support to stop the Kurdistan Workers' Party (PKK) in northern Iraq from setting up a separatist enclave inside Turkey.

The Turks had deployed about 100,000 troops along the Iraqi border in late 2007 and threatened to clean out the PKK camps. That could have opened another front in the Iraq War. Vast portions of the U.S. air cargo and fuel flowed through Turkey.

"Do something," President Bush had ordered. The small-scale covert operation appeared to be the lowest cost option to help Turkey conduct limited air strikes and force the PKK back into Iraq.

Hayden also described several covert actions, including counternarcotics and propaganda operations. Disclosure of these could hamper U.S. foreign relations and possibly jeopardize the lives of operatives and others, so they are not revealed here.

The last on the list of covert actions was Rendition, Detention and Interrogation (RDI). This was what Hayden was itching to explain.

Rendition—picking up suspected terrorists abroad and transporting them to another country or the United States for interrogation or prosecution under American law—had first been used in the Clinton administration and remained in effect. The suspects might be transported to various countries in the Middle East.

Biden interrupted Hayden right there, almost as if the CIA director was testifying before the Senate Committee on Foreign Relations.

"General," Biden said, "suppose we send somebody to Egypt or so forth, and they torture him. You know if you send them to that country they're going to be tortured."

"No, no, no," Hayden said, insisting the CIA received assurances there would be no torture. The legal standard was that they had to have the highest confidence there would be no torture.

Biden and several others stared skeptically at him.

Hayden then noted that the secret overseas CIA detention facilities had been closed and all the prisoners transferred to Guantánamo Bay, Cuba—a facility that President Bush said he wanted to shut down. During the presidential campaign Obama had repeatedly said he would close the prison.

On enhanced interrogation techniques, Hayden said only six remained. A participant at the meeting later said that because sleep deprivation appeared to be the lone technique that worked on hard-core terrorists, these six methods were to prevent a detainee from falling asleep. President Bush had approved them in 2006, supplanting the earlier finding that authorized additional harsher techniques. That finding included sleep deprivation for up to 96 hours, which could be extended under exceptional circumstances.

"I want to talk about that," Obama said. "What are they?"

Hayden said: Isolation of the detainee; noise or loud music; and lights in the cells 24 hours a day. There was limited use of shackles when moving a prisoner or when the prisoner was a danger. In addition, blindfolds were used when moving prisoners or when the prisoners might gain information that could compromise the security of the facility.

"David, stand up please," Hayden said to David Shedd, the DNI's deputy director for policy. Shedd rose. Hayden gently slapped his face, then shook the deputy DNI.

It was as rough as what might happen in "Little League football," Hayden said. The key to a successful interrogation was to make it intimate, not violent. By subjecting suspected terrorists to these methods, he said, it took less than a week to break them. This entailed getting them to a point where they feel that Allah can release them, that they've endured enough and can now tell their story. Hayden said that the revised interrogation program was essential to fighting terrorism.

McConnell thought Hayden's presentation conveyed the impression that this was all the CIA had ever done.

"Okay," Obama said, "what used to be on the list?"

There had been 13, Hayden said, including waterboarding one terrorist 183 times (see chapter notes for full details).

Several of the techniques described were new to Obama. He seemed transfixed. McConnell detected a trace of disbelief in the president-elect's stoic face.

Hayden, too, looked hard at Obama. He was accustomed to Bush, who in a briefing would spontaneously let you know how you were doing and react, often emotionally. Obama offered no clear reaction other than an acknowledgment that the transmission had been received.

"I'm going to have Greg come talk to you about this," Obama said, referring to designated White House counsel Greg Craig.

Obama then thanked McConnell, Hayden and the others for coming to Chicago. Now, he noted, he had to go back to the pressing issues of the transition, which suddenly included the arrest of the Illinois governor.

As best Hayden could tell, he had made the sale on the whole package of covert actions. He believed that the reduced interrogation program would win broad support inside the new White House. And he believed that the very existence of the interrogation program was more important than its content. Terrorists would know they faced a more severe interrogation if picked up by the CIA than by the military, which used the *Army Field Manual*.

On the way out, the CIA director told McConnell that he thought he had surprised Obama and his team by showing that the interrogation tactics were strictly limited. The bad stuff was gone. He had aced the exam.

Not so fast, McConnell thought. Hayden had gotten cocky, a little flippant. He had misread the audience.

Hayden spoke confidently about making a sale.

"We'll see. I hope so, Mike," McConnell said.

Later as president, Obama abolished the CIA's enhanced interrogation program—even in its reduced form. The agency would have to follow what was in the *Army Field Manual.*

When I asked the president about this covert action briefing, he said, "I'm not going to comment on my reaction to our deep secrets."

In discussions with Jones, McDonough and Lippert, DNI McConnell urged that the Obama administration come up with some intelligence professionals for the top jobs. "If you're not going with Hayden and me, at least pick a professional—an apolitical professional, someone who grew up in that world," he said. Hayden and he had 74 years of combined experience, and experience mattered. It was too easy to get misled or sidetracked if you didn't know about the hardware, personnel, special language, rituals, protocols and the traditions—good and bad—of the secretive and turf-conscious intelligence agencies.

Put people in charge who have lived in that world. It's different than anything else. You can't learn it overnight. It would make no sense and might have a tragic outcome to use the top intelligence posts for political appointees.

The Obama team responded politely, but indicated that the president-elect had a different agenda. They had to get people confirmed, and a large part of the Obama win had turned on the country's attitude toward President Bush. In their eyes, they made it clear, Bush had tarnished the image of the nation, especially with the enhanced interrogation techniques and expansive electronic eavesdropping.

At minimum, McConnell said the law on intelligence had to be rewritten so someone was clearly in charge. The 2004 reform law didn't make the DNI the boss of the CIA director, who still had authority on covert actions and reported to the president on them. They needed a

Department of Intelligence just as they had a Department of Defense and the Department of State. He and Hayden had worked it out. But it was an uneasy alliance among old hands, and with the wrong people it could spin out of control.

If you don't fix it, he warned, you will pay an enormous price.

But neither McConnell nor Hayden was given the opportunity to talk to Obama about the basic dysfunction of the intelligence organization. As the transition of government proceeded, neither requested a chance to explain to the president-elect how intelligence was not working.

Obama had told Podesta the kind of person he wanted in his administration. "I don't want just the same old crowd in Washington who do the same old things the same old way," he said. Change would be the dominant factor.

The selection of Clinton, Gates and to some extent Jones contradicted this approach. No one better represented the same old crowd than Republican Gates and Clinton, the wife of the former two-term president. Filling the two top intelligence posts would give Obama a chance to repot the plant, find people of broad experience and proven capability, and thrust them squarely in the middle of the espionage game. This was an opportunity to emphasize the "change" theme as the president-elect rounded out his national security team.

Rahm Emanuel had an idea for CIA director. In his view, one of the strongest men in the Democratic Party was Leon Panetta, a former California congressman and Clinton White House chief of staff. Their friendship went back to the mid-1980s, when Panetta was in the House and Emanuel was political director of the Democratic Congressional Campaign Committee.

Podesta had previously thought Panetta could be Gates's deputy at the Pentagon. Because Gates was a Republican, the White House would need someone with Democratic credentials. "A guy on our team," as Podesta put it. But after Obama had selected Bill Lynn, an executive at defense contractor Raytheon, as deputy secretary of defense, Emanuel felt there was still room for the 70-year-old Panetta. If he could do Pentagon deputy, why couldn't he do CIA?

Podesta called Panetta. "Your name's come up for CIA director."

"You're kidding me," Panetta replied. The idea floored him. Panetta had said he was ready to serve in the new administration if something came up, not that he expected it would. But the CIA? Was this a genuine offer?

It's serious, Podesta said. Will you come back out to talk? The reasoning: Panetta knew the intelligence programs from his time as chief of staff and had considerable exposure to national security issues, having served on the Iraq Study Group, which examined the war in 2006. Panetta was not a political or bureaucratic naïf. And Obama needed someone with unquestioned integrity who could pick up, reorient, reenergize and redefine the CIA.

Obama phoned Panetta, who was in Minneapolis visiting his son.

"Leon," he said, "I really want you to take the job of CIA director."

"I'm honored that you would ask me," Panetta replied. "You should know that my record in office is to be very truthful and to not pull any punches."

"That's exactly why I want you in that job."

By that time, the Obama team had publicly floated a replacement for McConnell as DNI, though it had yet to be made official. Dennis Blair—a Rhodes Scholar and retired four-star admiral—had an impressive résumé and none of the associations with the Bush administration that McConnell had.

Blair was astonished to be under consideration. "Before the election of last November, I had a grand total of one conversation with then Senator Obama," he said in a later speech to the U.S. Chamber of Commerce. It was an hour-and-a-half meeting when Blair had been head of the U.S. Pacific Command. "But I was, at any rate, quite surprised to receive a phone call the day of the election asking me to join his team."

Podesta had known Blair from work both had done for the CIA

during 1995, when Podesta consulted for the CIA director and Blair was the agency's associate director for military support.

On Monday, January 5, 2009, Hayden read an online *Washington Post* story confirming the rumors he had heard the day before about Panetta succeeding him as CIA director. "Rahm Emanuel's goombah," he said in disgust. Being replaced by a politico was a personal humiliation, as was learning about it from a newspaper.

Steve Kappes, Hayden's deputy at the CIA, called the transition office to say, "Is anybody ever going to talk to Mike Hayden?"

That next evening, Obama phoned Hayden. "General, this will make it easier for us to focus on the way ahead . . . to look forward, not backward," he said. "I will have pressure on me, and this will make it easier for me."

After the Panetta nomination was announced, Hayden and Panetta met at transition headquarters. Panetta can exude congeniality and breaks easily into giddy laughter. Among the political class, his ability to build personal relations might be equaled, though it probably was not exceeded. But Hayden was there to brief his successor, not to make a new friend. The CIA director pulled out a 3x5-inch card.

"Number one, Leon—don't know if you expect this—but you are the nation's combatant commander in the global war on terrorism," Hayden said. "You're going to be making some interesting decisions." The word "interesting" was a sufficiently vague substitute for "lethal." The CIA director had Predator drones to attack terrorists and a 3,000-man army inside Afghanistan. Panetta would have to help settle the rules for how the agency captured, transported and interrogated terrorists, the outcome of which might stop a terrorist attack.

Yeah, yeah, Panetta agreed.

"Number two," Hayden said. "You have the best staff in the federal government. If you give them half a chance, they—like they did for me—will not let you fail."

Panetta indicated that he revered the CIA.

"Number three, I've read some of your writings while you've been out of government," Hayden said. "Don't ever use the words 'CIA' and 'torture' in the same paragraph again."

Panetta said nothing.

"Torture is a felony, Leon," Hayden said. "Say you don't like it. Say it offends you. I don't care. But just don't say it's torture. It's a felony." The Justice Department had approved what the CIA did in long, detailed memos, so—legally—the CIA had not tortured anyone.

Again, Panetta did not respond.

McConnell had drafted an order that he knew could exacerbate tensions between the CIA and DNI. The order declared that the DNI, not the CIA director, would decide the senior intelligence representative in each foreign country. This power had traditionally belonged to the CIA station chief. While McConnell knew the station chief would remain the intelligence representative about 99 percent of the time, the intelligence issues in some countries were mostly military. For example, with 28,500 troops stationed in South Korea, it would be logical for the top U.S. intelligence person to be the J-2, the military intelligence chief, of the Korean command. That was where the critical intelligence issues resided.

McConnell had told Hayden, "I won't break CIA. I won't push it to the point where they lose face or stature." He thought he was getting close to persuading Hayden. So in transition meetings between Bush National Security Adviser Steve Hadley and Jones, he announced he was close to issuing the directive.

"This will be a knife fight," said Steve Kappes, who was likely to stay on as Panetta's deputy.

McConnell talked to Blair, who was going to replace him as DNI, and explained his plan. "This is a fight. CIA believes they're losing manhood. . . . I am prepared to sign it and walk out the door . . . blame it on me."

"You leave it for me," Blair said. "I'll work it out with Leon. We can solve this." They were friends.

"Okay, it's your call. I'll take the heat or leave it for you."

"Leave it for me," Blair said confidently.

McConnell was blunt, "You have to understand the battle you're going to have with the CIA, because they see you as the enemy, as taking their birthright. And any way they can, they'll cut you off at the knees."

6

Obama asked Vice President–elect Joe Biden to go to Afghanistan and Pakistan before the inauguration. Biden, a six-term senator from Delaware, was 19 years older than Obama and as chairman of the Senate Foreign Relations Committee had traveled the world. This should be a bipartisan effort, Obama said. Biden ought to bring a Republican along.

"Lindsey Graham has the best instincts in the Senate," Biden said. Obama agreed. Senator Lindsey Graham of South Carolina was 54, but his toothy grin and good ole boy charm made him look a decade younger. He was a lawyer and colonel in the Air Force Reserve. Graham could tap-dance between the red-meat right and moderates, and had acted as a kind of shadow and best friend during the presidential campaign for the volatile Senator John McCain. He also had a back-channel relationship with Obama's camp through Emanuel.

On Friday, January 9, 11 days before the inauguration, Biden and Graham landed in Islamabad. President Zardari rolled out the red carpet. Pakistanis often referred to Zardari as "Mr. 10 Percent," a nickname he earned for allegedly taking kickbacks during the premiership of his late wife, Benazir Bhutto. Zardari had a playboy reputation, yet his office contained loving photographs of Bhutto, who was assassinated by terrorists during the 2007 national parliamentary campaign. The widower had inherited a political dynasty from her family. In August 2008, Pervez Musharraf—an army general who had seized control of the government in a 1999 bloodless coup—stepped down as president. Zardari was elected as his successor.

The Pakistani leader conferred the Hilal-e-Pakistan award on Biden. The ceremony had an absurd pomp to it. The Pakistanis joked that the one requirement was that Biden wear the medallion on inaugural day and every January 20 after that. The office then cleared out so that Biden and Graham could talk with Zardari behind closed doors.

Biden told the Pakistani president about Obama's thinking, "Afghanistan is going to be his war." Obama might soon send more troops, but this would be meaningless if Pakistan and the U.S. were not working together. "We can't fix Afghanistan without Pakistan's help." American success would depend on Pakistan, and U.S. taxpayers would not support assistance to Pakistan if the Taliban and al Qaeda continued to operate from Pakistani sanctuaries to kill U.S. soldiers and plot attacks.

The ISI ties with the Taliban cast doubt in American minds, Biden said. Pakistan has got to stop providing safe haven. Your military and intelligence service have to get their act together.

Zardari talked about his wife.

"I may not be as experienced and knowledgeable, but my mission is not different from hers because it is about my children. You need to help me gain sufficient ground at home. You know this country is awash with anti-Americanism, and they're going to hate me for being an American stooge. You have to give me economic resources so that I can win over the people, that there's something in it for them."

The extremists have the money to fight and the Pakistani government lacked the funds to match them, Zardari said. Pakistan needs a stimulus package of its own. His claim about the anemic economy was accurate. An emergency loan from the International Monetary Fund in November had saved Pakistan from defaulting on its foreign debt, rescuing the nation from possible bankruptcy.

"I get that," Biden said. "I'm a politician."

"I am going to help clean up the ISI," Zardari said. "We have to get out of these games."

Biden said that the Obama administration would like a fresh start with Pakistan, one where their interests were better aligned. "If you do not show spine," he said, "then all bets are off." Biden mentioned that his own son, Beau, was in the U.S. Army serving in Iraq.

Graham thought Biden had ably walked a fine line between reassuring and pressuring. When his turn came, he said the American public was "war weary," tired of the conflict that had dragged on for more than seven years.

"Mr. President," Graham said, "the indecision that plagues your country has got to come to an end. You've got to figure out who your enemies are, who your allies are, and act accordingly. We're your allies. We're not your enemies. But there's limitations to what we can do to help because of public opinion and resources back home. For every school we try to build in Pakistan, there's somebody in South Carolina saying, 'Why aren't you building a school here? We need it just as much.' Joe and I understand the strategic importance of your country or we wouldn't be here. It was the first place we came. It wasn't an accident.

"I was Senator McCain's chief ally. The election is over. We lost the election. I am part of the loyal opposition, but I'm here with my friend, the vice president [elect], to let you know that Senator McCain and myself . . . the people who were on our side, are going to follow this president in terms of giving you the help you need."

"You've got to pick," Biden said. "You can't keep playing one side against the other. We got briefed by the CIA. The CIA thought that a lot of our intelligence was compromised" by the ISI alerting the terrorist camps we were targeting for drone strikes.

Zardari responded with emotion about how he had been fighting terrorism all his life, and reminded them that his wife had been killed by terrorists.

"I appreciate the loss of your wife," Graham said.

Zardari raised the eternal problem of India, and the endless hostility between the two countries.

"You know," Biden said, "we're looking for change."

•   •   •

To Graham, Zardari did not inspire confidence. He would have liked to tell him exactly what was on his mind, "The whole fucking place is burning down here, pal, you know? You may not see it, but I do."

Biden was struck by the CIA analysis. Segments of the Afghan Taliban insurgency such as the Haqqani network had virtual immunity in Pakistan, and al Qaeda was free to set up and run training camps. Who was in charge?

Next on the agenda, Biden and Graham were flying to Kabul to meet with Afghan President Hamid Karzai.

A small, gentle-looking man with a salt-and-pepper beard, Karzai had been selected to lead Afghanistan after the Taliban regime fell in late 2001. A minor Pashtun tribal leader, Karzai spoke pristine English, causing American officials to often think their conversations with him could be more candid. But he had been diagnosed as a manic-depressive, according to intelligence. Karzai was on medication and had severe mood swings.

After 9/11, CIA and U.S. Special Forces teams brought him back from exile into Afghanistan under the cover of night. He rallied villages to fight the Taliban. In the middle of the battle to retake the city of Kandahar, the U.S. accidentally dropped a bomb near Karzai. A CIA officer known as Greg V. threw himself atop Karzai and saved his life. Both men survived and Karzai frequently spoke with great emotion about his rescue.

But after an Afghan constitution was in place and Karzai was elected president in 2004, his relationship with the U.S. became more volatile. He began to routinely berate the Americans for civilian casualties.

The evidence of corruption in Karzai's government and family only exacerbated the tensions with the United States.

His half-brother, Ahmed Wali Karzai, ran Kandahar like an Afghan version of New York City's infamous Boss Tweed. Ahmed Wali had been on the U.S. and CIA payroll for years, beginning before 9/11.

He had belonged to the CIA's small network of paid agents and informants inside Afghanistan. In addition, the U.S. government paid him
money through his half-brother, the president.

More importantly, he was the landlord of some CIA and military
facilities in Kandahar. A measure of his influence—and corruption—
was that he was getting hefty rents from U.S. taxpayers on properties
in Kandahar that he arguably did not own or control. His government-
sponsored tenants included the Kandahar Strike Force, a paramilitary
group of Afghans the CIA used to attack suspected insurgents. There
was also evidence that Ahmed Wali profited from the opium trade.

Among senior U.S. policymakers there was a constant debate:
Should we be in bed with this guy? The CIA argument was standard—
he gets results, provides intelligence and support for important counterterrorist operations. It was necessary to employ some thugs if the
United States was going to have a role in a land of thugs. Cutting him
off might break Ahmed Wali's control of the city, and Kandahar might
be lost entirely. Lose Kandahar and we possibly lose the war.

But the CIA had few illusions about him. He was not in any sense a
controlled agent who always responded to U.S. and CIA requests and
pressure. He was his own man, playing all sides against the others—
the United States, the drug dealers, the Taliban and even his brother
if necessary.

On the flight to Afghanistan, Graham said, "I dread this meeting."

"Me too," said Biden. CIA reports showed a staggering level of corruption, inaction and snarled intelligence relationships that went back
decades. Biden wanted to break the dependency relationship that had
developed between Karzai and the Oval Office. President Bush had a
videoconference with Karzai almost every two weeks. At times, Karzai
sat his infant son in his lap during the head of state tête-à-têtes. When
anyone in the U.S. military or the U.S. embassy in Kabul confronted
Karzai, he invoked his special relationship with the president of the
United States.

Biden and Graham agreed to push Karzai. The planned state dinner would not be the traditional feel-good session.

For about 30 minutes before the dinner, Biden and Karzai spoke alone.

"We have no interest in making life tougher for you," Biden told Karzai. "But you have a real stake in our success. And you have no interest in making life tougher for us.

"We need to understand whether you're able to do the hard things that need to be done to move this forward, just as we're going to have to look whether we're able to do the hard things necessary to move this forward."

That's exactly right, Karzai said.

Graham and the American entourage as well as Karzai's cabinet milled outside the door, waiting as if this was a papal conclave to see what color smoke emerged from the chimney. Karzai and Biden came out seemingly pleased by their conversation. They sat down opposite each other at a massive dinner table, with about 15 people on each side.

Karzai had staged the evening. He called out to each of his cabinet members. "Defense Minister, tell us what you're doing." Afghan Defense Minister Abdul Rahim Wardak stood up and delivered a report. "Interior Minister, tell us what you're doing." Afghan Interior Minister Mohammad Hanif Atmar did the same. Once the performance ended, Biden turned to Karzai.

"I wanted Senator Graham to come to let you know that the election is over at home," he said. "We're here to make a commitment to your country, but, Mr. President, things have got to change. President-elect Obama wants to be helpful, but this idea of picking up the phone, calling President Obama like you did President Bush, is not going to happen."

I understand, Karzai said. He seemed eager to accommodate, gushing with lines like "Wonderful" and "No problem" as Biden talked.

"Mr. President," Graham said, "the economy in America is on its knees. If we don't see some progress on corruption, on better government, Republicans are not going to continue to vote for more troops, more money for Afghanistan if we don't see some real change."

Biden criticized Karzai's failure to govern with all of Afghanistan in mind, his unwillingness to travel the country and build a political consensus among the many tribes and ethnicities. He mentioned the ornate homes of Afghan officials near the presidential palace, no doubt paid for by the U.S.

"You're the mayor of Kabul," Biden said, meaning Karzai was isolated in the capital. "Replacing governors willy-nilly has got to stop." Karzai routinely doled out provincial governorships as favors to his political supporters.

Graham broached the subject of Ahmed Wali Karzai. "Mr. President," he said, "now you can't come to Afghanistan without hearing about your brother."

"Well, show me the file, Senator," Karzai replied.

"We will, one day," Graham said.

The mood began to sour. Karzai seemed offended.

"There's only one issue that troubles us," Karzai said, "and that's civilian casualties. We need to work together on this. People here don't want you to leave. Your interest is to defeat terrorism. We will help."

"We're doing everything we can to minimize civilian casualties," Biden answered. "In a war, they can't all be avoided. You know that." It would help, he added, if Karzai didn't hold news conferences denouncing the U.S. every time there were allegations of civilian casualties. "You need to come to us. We will find the facts each time, but what we have to avoid is immediate public statements that don't reflect the facts."

Graham, the Air Force Reserve lawyer, jumped in. "Our rules of engagement are very sensitive to civilian casualties," he said. "And nobody hates it more than the people involved, but, Mr. President, we cannot be accused of every bad act the moment it happens based on what a Taliban press release says. You're feeding the enemy. You're empowering them to get more involved in the civilian population." The requirement to get a warrant before a raid was absurd, he said. "We're in the middle of a war." Graham realized he was getting hotter. "We're not going to ask our troops to become cops. We want to be partners. Nobody would like the first person to go through the door [in a raid] to be an Afghan more than Lindsey Graham, but the first person through the door is an American. And the hope is that one day the first person through the door will be an Afghan." But, he told Karzai, he had to cease playing to his domestic audience.

"You have to be in on this with us," Biden added. "If this is not a war for you, then we won't be sending our warriors." The death of innocent Afghans sets back American interests, Biden said. "When we break their hearts, we'll lose their minds."

Karzai seemed to realize he had hit a sensitive nerve. "It's not a criticism," the Afghan president said. "It's letting you know there's a problem."

But let's deal with that problem in private instead of press conferences, Biden said.

Karzai's tone sharpened. Civilian casualties were a public matter. The Americans seemed to believe the death of, say, 30 Afghan villagers was insignificant. And Biden should not have belittled him in front of his own cabinet.

"This has gone on for too long," Karzai said. "The Afghan people will not support it."

"We may have reached that point ourselves, and we'll have to cut our losses," Biden said.

"The Afghan people must be partners, not victims," Karzai said.

"I believe we can and will do a better job on this," Biden said. "But if you don't want us, we're happy to leave. Just tell us. Instead of sending 30,000, maybe it'll be 10,000. Or maybe it'll be nothing. Or we could just send you economic assistance. If you don't want us, just tell us."

At that, the U.S. ambassador to Afghanistan, William Wood, interrupted them as a desperate marriage counselor might.

"I think this has been a useful conversation," he said. "It shows frustrations on both sides."

"We're just poor Afghans," Karzai said. "I know no one cares about—"

Biden threw down his napkin. "This is beneath you, Mr. President."

It appeared to be a struggle for both men to contain their tempers. Graham had been to so many of these freaking dinners he could barely count them. But this was "a dinner to remember," he later said. It ended shortly after that exchange. By the time they returned to the embassy, the ambassador was flooded with calls from distressed Karzai cabinet members asking, is this okay? What's going on?

Biden's visit was shrouded in secrecy. There were no public statements or press briefings. Biden and Graham later met with the commander in Afghanistan, U.S. Army General David McKiernan, who didn't share as pessimistic a view. Biden indicated to McKiernan that he would be getting more troops and asked: Can you pull this off?

McKiernan said, "We're not losing, but to get off the fence to where we're actually winning we need these additional troops." He had a pending request for 30,000 that the Bush administration had not acted on.

There were positive signs in Regional Command East, which contained the Hindu Kush mountains. American troops had performed admirably, securing the valleys and towns. "We're getting to the point where the gains are irreversible," McKiernan said.

But in sharp contrast, Regional Command South was rapidly deteriorating. RC South included Kandahar and Helmand provinces. It was the nexus of the Taliban insurgency, the drug trade and Karzai's nepotistic corruption. What was being done in the east that was not being done in the south? Biden asked.

McKiernan struggled to answer. More emphasis had been put on the east and there was better cooperation with the Afghans there, he said.

Biden was not persuaded. If the U.S. was really winning in the east, then the best move would be to reverse-engineer that success and replicate it in the south.

What about al Qaeda? Biden asked. The terrorist group was the reason the Americans were in this country. What was their presence like in Afghanistan now?

"We haven't really seen an Arab here in a couple of years," McKiernan said. For all practical purposes, there was no al Qaeda there. That confirmed what Biden suspected. Al Qaeda—the impetus of this war—was a Pakistani problem.

"I'm looking forward to working with you," Biden said, shaking McKiernan's hand.

The vice president–elect believed that off-the-cuff conversations often yielded more insights than formal presentations. As he made his rounds with the troops, after asking the basic "How's it going?" he then slipped in a "What are we trying to do here?" Everyone—colonels, lieutenants, sergeants—gave a different answer.

"Basically, we're trying to rebuild this country," said one, "so that it can stand on its own two feet."

Another said, "We're trying to get al Qaeda."

Biden replied, "But I was just told they're not here."

A more common answer from the front-line troops was, "I don't know."

Tony Blinken, 46, Biden's top foreign policy adviser for the last seven years and now his national security adviser, was on the trip. A lawyer who had served as a staffer on the Clinton National Security Council, Blinken joined his boss and Graham for a session about what they had seen. "I don't know if they can ever pull this off," he said.

This idea of building up the Afghan government, Biden said, and the army and the police in a functioning way, is maybe a bridge too far. Was it doable?

"I don't know if it's doable or not," Graham said. "I had the same doubts about Iraq," but this seemed to be the best chance they would get. "How does it end? Does Karzai ever govern better? I don't know," Graham said. "He's been given too much room to maneuver without accountability." He was certain, however, that this visit had been a good start for engaging anew with Karzai.

Blinken was in the doubters' camp. "How do you leave?" he asked.

• • •

Back in Washington, Biden hauled Graham into the transition head-quarters to meet with Obama on Wednesday, January 14.

He told Obama the major headline from the trip. "If you ask ten of our people what we're trying to accomplish here, you get ten different answers," he said. "This has been on autopilot."

We can't be on autopilot, Obama responded. We need to get a grip on this and that's going to be the first order of business.

The CIA briefing on the region and the conversation in Pakistan was disheartening, Biden said. We have our work cut out for us, but I support sending more troops in.

Floated in the media that day was the appointment of Richard Holbrooke as the State Department's special representative for Afghanistan and Pakistan. Hillary Clinton would likely select her friend Holbrooke, a 67-year-old veteran diplomat best known for resolving the Bosnian War in 1995, to handle Karzai and Zardari.

"He's the most egotistical bastard I've ever met," Biden told Obama, "but he's maybe the right guy for the job." Though absorbed with being a hero, Holbrooke was so committed to succeeding that he would focus his extraordinary talent, energy and ego on the assignment and might just pull it off.

"We know your view about Holbrooke," Obama said, cutting Biden off and turning to Graham.

"I talked to Senator McCain," Graham said. "I just think Afghanistan's going to take a lot more resources. And Pakistan is double dealing." He thought Biden's tough approach with Karzai was necessary. "I would urge you, Mr. President," he said, though Obama was six days away from inauguration, "to deal with Karzai from a distance. And pick your engagements with him wisely and let the pressure build to push for better governance. And at the end of the day, you can count on me and Senator McCain . . . and others to stand by you as we try to turn around Afghanistan."

Obama smiled but didn't betray his thoughts.

Graham said that it was essential that Obama show progress in the next year—better governance in Afghanistan, prosecutions for corruption, send people to jail, or an Afghan army that could go through the door first in a raid. Without those game changers, he said, "You're going to lose the public." Traction for the 2010 midterm congressional campaigns would take hold and Republicans would be running against Obama, just as the Democrats did against Bush. "Your responsibility for Afghanistan will be solidified in a year. And if this thing is bumping along, I can tell you now that the Republican Party will not walk off a cliff for another unpopular war. And I may be the only guy standing on the cliff with you."

"Thanks," the president-elect said.

"Mr. President, we're losing this battle," Graham said. "Your assessment of the importance of Afghanistan is dead-on. And your assessment of we've taken our eye off the ball is right." As senators, they had disagreed about sending more troops into Iraq, since Graham believed winning in Afghanistan would be impossible if we lost in Iraq. But now Graham was encouraging Obama to reset things in Afghanistan.

As Obama, Biden and Graham headed for a news conference, Obama pulled Graham aside to thank him.

"Mr. President," Graham said, "this is not your war. This is our war."

7

On Tuesday, January 20, inauguration day, David Axelrod encountered President Bush on the platform at the Capitol. As Obama's chief campaign strategist and now his senior adviser, Axelrod had repeatedly criticized Bush.

"Mr. President, I was on television this morning," said Axelrod.

"I don't watch television," Bush snapped back.

"Well, I'm going to tell you what I said," Axelrod continued calmly. "I said you conducted this transition like a true patriot and we really appreciate it."

"Oh, that's great," the president said, warming. "Listen, you're in for the ride of your life and you just sort of hang on and really enjoy it."

The day before, Rahm Emanuel—Axelrod's friend for more than 25 years—had told him there were contingency plans to cancel the inaugural. Credible intelligence showed that a group of Somali extremists planned to attack Obama by setting off explosives.

"We might have to shut this thing down," Emanuel had said. "We would have to be prepared for that."

An inaugural attack never occurred. The attention instead was squarely on the speech. What would Obama say? One of the people wondering was General Jones, who as Obama's national security adviser ought to know. But he had not seen a draft. "I had asked," he said, almost trembling. Emanuel and the political operatives would not show it to him. It was not a happy beginning given Obama's promise to ask Jones his "opinion or judgment before I do anything." But Jones knew the Obama team was still in campaign mode, which hopefully would end when they all settled into the White House. Still, being kept in the dark about the speech was insulting.

In his address, Obama devoted one sentence to the wars: "We will begin to responsibly leave Iraq to its people and forge a hard-earned peace in Afghanistan."

As Obama spoke, General Petraeus was again in Afghanistan. He had spent the past week visiting its neighboring countries, trying to line up safe supply routes into the war zone. Getting supplies into Afghanistan was hard. Most traveled through Pakistan, but a gauntlet of Taliban insurgents lurked along the Khyber Pass, the mountainous road linking the countries. Petraeus had explored alternative routes that bypassed Pakistan by entering Afghanistan from the former Soviet republics in the north.

On the evening of January 20, his C-17 lifted off the tarmac in Kabul, bound first for refueling in Germany and then Washington.

When the plane landed in Germany, Petraeus took one of his brutal five-mile runs, hoping to avoid sleep medication for the transatlantic flight. He was racing the sun to be at the new president's first meeting on Iraq.

Obama called his national security team to the Situation Room at 4:15 P.M. on January 21. Located in the basement of the West Wing, the Situation Room is a high-tech bunker.

Many of the senior officials and White House staffers had been up late partying at the inaugural balls the night before, and they showed it. Not the president.

Opposing the Iraq War had been central to Obama's rise, causing some members of the Bush administration, including Gates, to fear what the new president might do. During the campaign, Obama had promised to remove all combat troops from Iraq within 16 months of becoming president, by the middle of 2010. But several Bush administration decisions made such a quick withdrawal unlikely. These decisions would prevent what Bush officials considered to be a precipitous withdrawal.

The key decision was installing Petraeus at CentCom. Second was appointing Army General Raymond Odierno, who had been Petraeus's deputy and had received much of the credit for helping stabilize Iraq, as the overall commander in Iraq. The third was the Status of Forces Agreement signed by Bush little more than a month before Obama's inauguration. It said U.S. combat forces would not be out until the end of 2011.

At the January 21 meeting, Obama directed that he wanted three options.

He commissioned a 60-day review, saying, "I want to do a thorough review in Iraq and I want to figure out how we're going to get to where we want to be." There had been no forewarning about this assessment to the continuing NSC staff who would be conducting it. Among the options they were to consider at the president's request was the 16-month withdrawal.

After the meeting, Petraeus was about to board his plane and return to Central Command headquarters in Tampa. Sorry, he was told, on Friday the president and the National Security Council would talk about the war that wasn't faring well—Afghanistan—and he had better stay in Washington.

With an extra day in Washington, Petraeus spent the afternoon of Thursday, January 22, on the red-brick campus of the National Defense University, going over an internal review of the entire Central Command region. He liked to joke about the Pentagon's abuse of PowerPoint, the software program that often tortures audiences with its tedious, jargon-laden slides. But after about four months of work, the CentCom regional review had reached an epic length of 1,000 PowerPoint slides.

A team of 80 was drilling down on the Afghanistan component of the review, including Derek Harvey from the Defense Intelligence Agency (DIA). The 54-year-old retired Army colonel had been among Petraeus's most trusted intelligence advisers in Iraq, a country Harvey first explored during the 1980s by taxicab.

Harvey approached intelligence with the step-by-step methodology of a homicide detective. Intelligence analysts tend to rely on secret reports—human agents, intercepted electronic communications, and pictures from satellites and drones. Harvey "widened the aperture," studying prisoner interrogations, battlefield reports, and reams of enemy documents—financial records, propaganda and Taliban communiqués. By sifting through the enemy's paper trail, he pieced together clues that others might miss.

What have you dug up? Petraeus asked him.

"It is the blind leading the blind," Harvey said. The U.S. remained dangerously ignorant about the Afghan insurgency. Basic questions had gone unasked over the course of the war: Who is the enemy? Where are they? How do they see the fight? What are their motivations?

"We know too little about the enemy to craft a winning strategy," Harvey said, implying that the current strategy put America on the path to defeat and—unless the intelligence gaps were filled—a new strategy would be futile.

Harvey said the Afghanistan commander, General David McKiernan, believed the reconciliation successes—making peace with elements of the insurgency—from Iraq could not be duplicated in Afghanistan, so he had not directed intelligence collection toward economic, social and political issues of the Afghan tribes and villages. But having reconciliation efforts was likely the only way out of the war. McKiernan had also complained to Harvey that he barely had the military resources to fight the insurgency, saying, "I don't have enough to do my own job."

Harvey was willing to concede that Afghanistan was a Band-Aid effort. More than seven years into the war, the Director of National Intelligence—the agency established to coordinate intelligence across the government—had yet to hire a mission manager for Afghanistan and Pakistan. Petraeus wrote the new DNI, Blair, asking him to remedy the situation. He then followed up personally until the matter was resolved. A former CIA officer was appointed as an associate DNI. But that wasn't nearly enough.

What Harvey had told him was a forehead-smacking moment for Petraeus. The problem was obvious. He needed to fix the intelligence shortcomings immediately. Shuffling things among the DNI, CIA, NSA, DIA and other agencies would only prolong the problem.

Petraeus decided to create his own intelligence agency inside CentCom. Regional commands in Europe and the Pacific had intelligence divisions. CentCom should too.

Can you draft plans for an agency modeled on your approach? Petraeus asked Harvey.

Soon, Harvey was appointed director of the new Afghanistan-Pakistan Center of Excellence based at CentCom headquarters in Tampa, Florida. Petraeus rearranged funds within CentCom to cover the projected $108 million in annual expenses, leaving Congress unaware of the center's existence for several months.

Harvey was trying to revolutionize intelligence collection. Most intelligence agencies rotated their staff through two-year postings. The center would commit its analysts to five-year assignments, with the goal of having them gain fluency in Dari and Pashto, the primary languages spoken in Afghanistan.

Harvey threw his life into the job. He started each morning at 4 A.M., worked 15-hour days, and rarely slept through the night. The obsession came at a personal cost. Harvey's wife filed for divorce. One of his three sons was having trouble. As a result, friends worried about Harvey's health.

Harvey preferred sources that gave him a feel for the ground. Valuable insights came from unclassified material, such as the weekly summaries of engineers in Afghanistan who oversaw bridge and road projects. He also regularly logged on to Harmony, a government site that posted translated copies of enemy documents.

A counterinsurgency strategy relied on rock-solid intelligence. It meant breaking down a province village by village; and knowing a village house by house. Tracking the relationships among tribal elders, mullahs, farmers and opium merchants mattered as much as spotting the enemy. When the objective was to protect the population, soldiers had to distinguish between whom to defend and whom to shoot. Insurgents had the advantage, since they looked like civilians.

American intelligence analysts tracked 90 distinct categories of information from Afghanistan. Harvey wanted to expand that to 500. The insurgency's resources, leadership, financing, freedom of movement, popular support and group cohesion all had to be measured. No such metrics had existed before, and huge disparities existed among the reports from the international coalition in Afghanistan. Out of more than 40 U.S. allies, only the Romanian soldiers stationed in Zabul province consistently recorded what Harvey wanted to know. So Harvey fashioned uniform questionnaires.

He then color-coded Afghanistan based on the data. Information about the international coalition was blue. The insurgents were red. The Afghan army and police were green. And the Afghan people were white. Harvey could chart the relationship between the Taliban and Afghan people by checking where red overlapped with white. He plotted the information on maps, searching for patterns amid the mountains, valleys, villages. As he parsed the data, Harvey concluded that the war could be won, but the U.S. government would have to make monumental long-term commitments for years that might be unpalatable with voters.

"I think Afghanistan is doable, it's not sellable," Harvey concluded.

On Friday, January 23, at 11:20 A.M., the president took his seat in a large black leather chair at the head of the Situation Room conference table for his first National Security Council meeting on Afghanistan.

"I have campaigned on providing Afghanistan with more troops, but I haven't made the decision yet," Obama said. "When we send them, we need to announce it in the context of a broader strategy." He planned to reorient U.S. foreign policy and the approach to terrorism, he said. The military will, of course, be a piece of our national security but not the overwhelming driver of how we achieve our goals.

General Lute, Admiral Mullen and General Petraeus each had either finished or were completing strategic reviews of Afghanistan and Pakistan. All the reviews should be gathered together, Obama said. As he saw it, there was no coherent strategy. The ultimate strategy must explain the logic for adding more troops and show how the fight would be carried out going forward.

"I've got to lay this out to the American public," the president said.

The Afghanistan War would be a priority, Obama said, but the economic crisis needed most of his attention as president. "I want you to feel free to speak your mind."

Petraeus had carefully scripted what he wanted to say. He had been a little offended during the presidential campaign, when it seemed to him as if a bidding war had developed over who could get out of Iraq the fastest and who could do the most for Afghanistan. So he warned, "This is going to be very difficult. It is going to get harder, much harder before it gets easier."

Petraeus continued, "We cannot achieve our objectives without more troops." By his understanding, the objective was to prevent Afghanistan from again becoming a sanctuary for transnational extremists such as al Qaeda. You can't just do counterterrorism with drone strikes and infantry raids, you have to do counterinsurgency to stabilize the country and that is a whole host of tasks, he said. American soldiers had to protect Afghans. The local government must deliver services to the people. And the Afghan National Army and National Police need to expand in size.

The U.S. should fulfill McKiernan's pending request for 30,000 more troops, Petraeus concluded.

Mullen said he supported fulfilling the McKiernan request.

Obama asked for clarification. "Do you have to have all of this now?"

No one answered before Vice President Biden nearly erupted.

"We have not thought through our strategic goals!" he complained. Everyone should agree to a strategy before the president ordered up more troops. "We've got to put together the decisions that he has to make," he said.

Obama, Biden and chief of staff Rahm Emanuel raised more questions about the proposed troop increase. Where does this lead? Where are we going with this? Is this the beginning of a larger ramp-up? This needs to be done in connection with a strategy and not in isolation.

Petraeus thought these questions indicated that Obama's political advisers realized that the Afghanistan War would continue into the 2012 election. The war would not be settled in one or two years. The president already seemed to understand this, Petraeus thought, but it seemed to have just dawned on the other folks who had run his presidential campaign.

The president had to leave for another engagement and excused himself.

Biden and Emanuel stayed on. Petraeus said that they would need to build additional infrastructure and push more supplies into Afghanistan, a very complicated, time-consuming process. He was going to move forward on the 30,000 new troops, he said.

"Hold on," Emanuel said. "The president hasn't made any decisions and I want that to be absolutely clear. General, I appreciate you're doing your job, but I didn't hear the president of the United States give that order."

8

A few days after the inaugural, retired Army General Jack Keane phoned the new secretary of state. Keane had built a friendship with Hillary Clinton after she was elected to the Senate from New York and joined the Armed Services Committee. With both West Point and Fort Drum located in New York, Clinton had a vested interest in the Army. She had charmed Keane, who was impressed with her willingness to do the homework to understand the military.

At 65, Keane resembled an aging linebacker and still spoke with a blue-collar accent tinged by the outer boroughs of New York City. He had risen from a Vietnam War paratrooper to Army vice chief of staff. Keane had had friends in the Bush administration as well. Known as the father of the Iraq surge, he had played effectively behind the scenes, not only for the 30,000-man surge but for the promotions of General David Petraeus, first to Iraq commander and then Central Command. Petraeus still called him "sir." The two were as close as any in the Army brotherhood.

Keane now saw the same problems in Afghanistan that had compelled him to push on Iraq. He told Clinton, "The strategy in Afghanistan is wrong. And I had conversations with you about this in Iraq, so I'm telling you again. And not only that, but the leadership is wrong."

"How bad?" Clinton asked.

McKiernan, the Afghanistan commander, was the wrong man for the job, Keane said. Too old-school. And McKiernan would not accept coaching from Petraeus. McKiernan was too cautious, conservative to a fault. He preferred more conventional operations, a counterterrorist approach designed to kill Taliban fighters. Counterterrorism would not be decisive, Keane said. It hadn't been quite enough in Iraq.

High body counts alone cannot end an insurgency. The deaths often had the opposite effect, swelling an insurgency's ranks as recruits joined to avenge what they deemed to be a family member's murder. Insurgents do not fight on American terms. To cope with their disadvantages—no helicopters, no tanks, dented ammo and poor vision because they don't have eyeglasses—they play by their own rules. They plant improvised explosive devices, spreading fear with the suddenness and randomness of each blast.

The only way out of Afghanistan, Keane indicated, was an intensive counterinsurgency geared toward protecting Afghans. When American troops take the risk of living among the Afghans they're protecting, the population becomes personally invested in the cause. To beat an insurgency, there had to be safety and security. That meant adding troops to cover more of Afghanistan's cities, villages and mountainous terrain.

The Taliban insurgency is an alternative to the existing Afghan government, a competitor for legitimacy and loyalty. This meant that the U.S. must help establish an Afghan government that the people endorse, a government capable of maintaining peace. Keane had heard that McKiernan was not interacting with provincial governors, which limited American influence on the Afghan political regime. Failure to perform a textbook counterinsurgency would doom the U.S. mission. Petraeus thought McKiernan would come around. Keane did not.

"I think he should be fired," Keane told Clinton. "He's got to come out of there. He's not going to solve the problem. We've got to get new leadership in."

"I've got to have you talk to Dick," Clinton said. "Do you know him?"

"Dick" was Richard Holbrooke, the new special representative for Afghanistan and Pakistan. He had been the foreign policy consigliere in her presidential campaign. His new job entailed coordinating the entire government effort in the AfPak region. Holbrooke's first assignment, 46 years ago, as a junior Foreign Service officer, had been in Vietnam. Now at 67, he was looking for one more big play. Though he insisted this was his last government job, if he somehow succeeded—and Secretary Clinton decided to move on—secretary of state might be his.

"No, I met him a couple of times, but I don't know him," Keane said.

The next day, Keane found Holbrooke at the State Department working out of a cubbyhole office, temporary quarters until there was space for his team. He looked distracted as Keane repeated what he had told Clinton the night before. Phones kept ringing, interrupting Keane mid-sentence.

Holbrooke, his blue eyes burning with intensity, was human evidence of Newton's first law of physics—an object in motion tends to stay in motion. But after one last phone call, Holbrooke wound to a stop.

"By the way, Hillary wants to see you," he told Keane. "I was surprised that she wanted to see you."

"It doesn't surprise me."

Clinton greeted Keane with a bear hug, astonishing Holbrooke because—and he should know—Hillary rarely bear-hugged anyone.

Keane outlined his argument. "We're relying on counterterrorism too much, and we have a very uneven counterinsurgency strategy. And we don't have nearly enough forces to use a counterinsurgency strategy, either." He had little faith in the current training efforts for the Afghan army. Keane was aware of Petraeus's skepticism going back years and had recently been briefed about the subject as a member of the Defense Policy Board, an advisory committee for the secretary of defense composed of old government hands—including Henry Kissinger and three former defense secretaries, William Perry, James Schlesinger and Harold Brown. Because of Afghanistan's shallow pool of officer candidates and high illiteracy rate, the Defense Policy Board was told it would take years to grow the Afghan army and police to a sufficient size.

"Hillary, this is rubbish," Keane said. "We're fighting Afghans, and the Afghans that we're training and organizing just have to be a little bit better than the Afghans that they're fighting. We're not trying to build some military in the image of ourselves or in the image of the West or in the image of Europe.

"Don't let people tell you we can't do this," Keane said.

Who should be McKiernan's replacement? Clinton asked.

The officer Keane had in mind was Army Lieutenant General Lloyd Austin III, second in command in Iraq, but he needed a rest.

"Well, who else?" Clinton asked.

"There's another guy named McChrystal," Keane said.

"I've heard that name," she said.

Army Lieutenant General Stanley A. McChrystal had led the secretive Joint Special Operations Command from September 2003 to August 2008. The gaunt runner who ate only one meal a day had essentially lived cocooned in a plywood box at Balad Airbase in Iraq for five years. During that time, he lived a vampirelike existence, rarely seeing the light of day. The stealth JSOC missions were usually at night. When JSOC had killed the Iraqi al Qaeda leader Abu al-Zarqawi in 2006, McChrystal accompanied his men to verify the burned remains. For the past five months, McChrystal had served as director of the Joint Staff of the Joint Chiefs, a high-profile job in which he interacted daily with Chairman Mullen and, often, Secretary Gates.

"He's, without a doubt, the best candidate," Keane said.

During an early 2007 visit to Iraq after the surge was announced, Keane had been impressed by McChrystal's understanding that aggressive counterterrorism might not be enough to win. McChrystal set up an 11 P.M. videoconference for Keane about the latest missions by the classified forces in Iraq and elsewhere. It was extraordinary how McChrystal kept the enemy off guard, Keane thought. JSOC planned, prepared and executed missions without pause, using signals intelligence and even the "pocket litter" found after one attack to immediately launch the next assault. But Keane spotted the flaw in these successes.

"Stan, let me come at it differently for you," he had told McChrystal. "What you've done here, purely in terms of taking out high-value targets, is significant. And your ratios of killed and captured to your own casualties is remarkable. And the efficiency and the effectiveness of these kinds of operations, you've reached a new level in the state of the art.

"That's powerful, what it's done, but what difference does it make strategically? We are losing. The Iraqi security forces are losing. We are losing. The government is fractured."

McChrystal had organized a jaw-dropping counterterrorism campaign inside Iraq, but the tactical successes did not translate into a strategic victory. This was why counterinsurgency—blanketing the population in safety and winning them over—was necessary.

Keane respected the fact that McChrystal did not instantly become defensive.

"That's a hell of a point," McChrystal had said.

Shortly after being appointed special representative for Afghanistan and Pakistan, Holbrooke phoned Husain Haqqani, a casual acquaintance and the Pakistani ambassador to the U.S. since 2008. He invited him to lunch and was prepared to negotiate on the restaurant.

"I believe you are very media-savvy," Holbrooke said. "You and I should have lunch, but we should have lunch somewhere public so it gets reported in the newspaper, if you don't mind."

"I don't mind," Haqqani said.

What about the Hay-Adams Hotel, across from the White House? They agreed on Friday, January 30.

The 52-year-old Haqqani, a former journalist, academic and adviser to the late Pakistan Prime Minister Benazir Bhutto, talked regularly with U.S. cabinet officers and top White House aides. His chipper English flowed into Urdu at the chime of his BlackBerry.

While teaching at Boston University in 2005, Haqqani published a

397-page book, *Pakistan: Between Mosque and Military,* which exposed the Pakistani army and ISI's entanglement with Islamic extremism.

Haqqani laughingly referred to himself as "Pakistan's Mr. America." Rivals and critics back home harbored a creeping paranoia that their ambassador was somehow conspiring with Washington. Haqqani dreaded the fallout of what would happen if the next terrorist attack against the U.S. was postmarked from Pakistan.

The northern view from the Hay-Adams Hotel second-floor dining room looks across Lafayette Square to the White House gates. In a touch of discretion, the elegant tables are spaced so that eavesdropping is nearly impossible. The Hay-Adams, as advertised, is a place to be seen, not heard.

Haqqani asked about the scope of Holbrooke's new assignment.

Without missing a beat, Holbrooke confidently laid out his ambition. He hoped for nothing less than a successful end to the war in Afghanistan and a stable Pakistan and Afghanistan.

When it came to India—a country outside of Holbrooke's portfolio but central to Pakistan's concerns—Holbrooke said in his theatric baritone, "I will deal with India by pretending not to deal with India."

Was Karzai the best man to lead Afghanistan under the current circumstances or were alternatives available? Holbrooke asked provocatively.

Haqqani maintained a diplomatic silence. Mutual friends had told him that Holbrooke possessed an incredible memory and that an economy of words was best.

Holbrooke said he understood Pakistan's need to protest the drone strikes, since the government could not afford to be seen as complicit. But the protests should not fuel uncontrollable anti-Americanism.

The lunch ended after two hours. Holbrooke's strength, Haqqani realized, was his fierce and desperate desire to succeed. It wasn't clear to Haqqani who his primary contact would be on U.S. foreign policy toward Pakistan.

Yet Holbrooke had failed in one of his first missions—to get his tête-à-tête with Haqqani into the media. No journalists, bloggers or gossips reported on their lunch. Apparently, no one had noticed.

While Holbrooke and Haqqani lunched, about ten miles across the Potomac River a tall, academic 56-year-old sat reading in his Alexandria, Virginia, town house. Sprawled in his lap was his King Charles spaniel, Nelson, named after the celebrated British admiral. It was about 1:30 P.M. when the phone rang.

"Please hold for the president," the operator said.

"Hey, Bruce, it's Barack," a familiar voice said.

Just ten days into the Obama presidency, Bruce Riedel felt certain he had dodged a recruiting call. He had done his time—29 years in the CIA, the Pentagon and the Clinton National Security Council staff—and he didn't want another government job. Riedel had worked undercover for the CIA for 10 years, and had briefed three presidents. He had retired to the comparatively tranquil Brookings Institution, a Washington think tank where he was a senior fellow.

In 2007 Riedel had agreed to be the South Asia team leader for what was then Senator Obama's long-shot presidential campaign. As "leader," Riedel was at first the entire team. He was an expert in Islamic extremism, al Qaeda, its leader Osama bin Laden, Afghanistan and Pakistan. His main stipulation before joining the campaign was that he not be asked to return to government service.

"I know you don't want to work full-time in government," Obama said, "but here's a proposition. Will you come into government for 60 days, work in the NSC, do a strategic review of Afghanistan and Pakistan?

"All my people are telling me you're the person that I should ask to do this," the president said. "You'll work with General Jones. You'll report directly to me, and it really will be 60 days."

"I'll call General Jones, sir. Can I think about it overnight?"

Sure, the president said. With Riedel, he would be guaranteed that his own man, someone trusted and experienced from the campaign team, would set the course in the neglected war.

Riedel knew he would accept. Four months earlier, he had published a book, *The Search for al Qaeda*, a 181-page treatise about the true national security threat: Pakistan, which he called "the most dangerous country in the world today, where every nightmare of the twenty-first century" converges—terrorism, government instability, corruption and nuclear weapons. The book described how the Pakistani military and its notorious spy agency, the ISI, had a direct hand in creating, supporting and bankrolling Islamic extremists. Even after 9/11, the ISI continued clandestine partnerships and lethal dabbling with al Qaeda, the Taliban and LeT, while simultaneously assisting the U.S.

He concluded that there was a "battle for the soul of Pakistan." Riedel could answer the questions Obama and his national security team might have about al Qaeda, the Taliban, Afghanistan and Pakistan with three simple words: "Read my book."

Obama was giving him the rarest of gifts, a once-in-a-lifetime chance to apply the insights of his career and convert them to an action plan. Others might or might not read his book, but he was now going to implement it.

The next Monday, February 2, Riedel went to the White House to see Jones and accept the job. He matched the description coined by the late CIA Director William Colby of a "gray man," someone "so inconspicuous that he can never catch the waiter's eye in a restaurant."

Sixty days for the review was not much time as Riedel saw it, because of the time-consuming interagency bureaucratic process that required it to be vetted at all levels, including by cabinet officers. He would then have to consult with the Afghans, the Pakistanis, Congress, NATO allies and outside experts. He figured he actually had about 21 days to get a thorough draft together to help the president make what might be the most important decision of his presidency.

Shortly after, Doug Lute, the holdover war czar who was still the NSC's top Afghanistan deputy, approached him at the NSC offices.

"Welcome," said Lute, handing Riedel a cup of coffee. "Look, I know you're only going to be here for a short period of time. All my guys have their feet on the ground. We'll give you all the admin support. Don't worry about computers, rooms, secretarial support. We'll set up your meetings. You just tel! us, you direct this, and we'll make it happen. We'll make this easy for you."

Riedel made it clear that he wouldn't need much help.

That next Wednesday was the first organizational meeting of the "Riedel review" committee, up in Room 445 of the Eisenhower Executive Office Building. Lute had an allergic reaction to the room. It was where he had put in so much time on his own Afghanistan review, the one that now two administrations—Bush and Obama—had accepted politely and then ignored.

Seated around the table were Holbrooke and undersecretary of defense for policy Michèle Flournoy, the committee co-chairs. Riedel outlined what he knew about the project. Many of them wondered how the review could be delivered in just 60 days.

"By Friday, we'll have the first draft of the report out to everybody for a first look," Riedel said. That was two days away.

Lute was astounded. He had spent months digging, traveling, weighing, evaluating. Inside that very room, he had devoted more than 40 hours—a standard workweek—fleshing out his own review. Now some former CIA man from the campaign was parachuting in to present a draft in two days. It was clear to him that the president would get a cut-and-paste from Riedel's book.

9

Leon Panetta appeared for his CIA director confirmation hearings before the Senate Intelligence Committee on February 5, 2009, two weeks after the inaugural.

Outgoing Director Hayden was watching on C-SPAN from his office at the CIA headquarters when Panetta testified that the agency would no longer send suspected terrorists to another country "for the purposes of torture" because it was forbidden by the president's new executive orders. Under questioning, he said he suspected the CIA sent people for interrogation to other countries using techniques that "violate our own standards."

An angry Hayden wondered if Panetta had simply ignored their conversations last month about the word "torture." He hit the button on the internal intercom system to the chief of the counterterrorism center, a senior officer still undercover.

"You watching TV?"

"Yeah."

"How's it going?"

"Not well."

"Okay, no bullshit, have you ever—?"

"No."

"You have always sought assurances?" Under CIA rules, they were supposed to ask the foreign government, intelligence service or police to make sure there would be no abuse or torture.

"Absolutely."

"And beyond the assurances, you used all the tools available to an espionage agency to ensure they're living up—"

"All the time." The claim indicated that the CIA was using spies and communications intercepts from phones, computers and room microphones to ensure foreign intelligence services were not torturing the suspected terrorists dispatched to them by the agency.

"I'm not talking about your watch," Hayden said. "I'm talking about forever."

"Forever," the CT chief said. Forever went back more than 60 years, and there was probably no way anyone—even with extensive research—could have made such a categorical claim. But it was another "slam dunk," a statement in absolute terms. This is the way some CIA people, including past directors, talked, suggesting they were all-knowing in a world of doubt and uncertainty.

Hayden thought they had caught a break because the hearing was cut short by Senate votes, so Panetta would have to return the next morning. He contacted Jeff Smith, a former CIA general counsel who was helping with the transition for Panetta.

"He walks that sentence back tomorrow in his public testimony," Hayden threatened, "or we will have the spectacle of the current director of the Central Intelligence Agency saying the prospective director of the Central Intelligence Agency doesn't know what he's talking about." He said he would say this publicly. "That's not in anybody's interest."

The next day, Friday, February 6, Senator Kit Bond of Missouri, the senior Republican on the Intelligence Committee, pressed Panetta.

"Thank you for the question, Senator, because I think there is some clarification required. . . . We may very well direct individuals to third countries," Panetta said. "I will seek the same kind of assurances that they will not be treated inhumanely."

Would he retract his statement from the previous day about torture? Bond asked.

"Yes, I would retract that statement."

Bond rubbed it in. So "liberal blogs" and "rumors or news stories" were insufficient sources for someone nominated to be CIA director. "I would ask you to assure this committee that you will not make rash judgments based on hearsay."

"Senator, you have my assurance that I intend to do that."

Hayden met Panetta for a last heart-to-heart. He wanted to clear the air, correct the record as he understood it.

"Leon," Hayden said, "I've been reading some of your writings while out of government. You claim the [Bush] administration cherry-picked the intelligence for Iraqi WMD." Panetta had blamed a special unit set up by Rumsfeld at the Pentagon. "That's not true. We got it wrong. Okay? It was a clear swing and a miss. It's our fault."

Panetta said he got it. There had been a catastrophic intelligence failure at the agency he was taking over.

During Hayden's last week as CIA director, he gave the president one final Situation Room report about the latest Predator strikes in Pakistan. There had been two attacks on January 23 in the Federally Administered Tribal Areas (FATA). Neither strike killed the intended "HVT," or high value target, but at least five al Qaeda militants died.

The president said good. He had fully endorsed the covert action program and made it clear he wanted more.

Afterward, Hayden spoke to Emanuel. It was good stuff, Emanuel said, praising the CIA program.

"Rahm," Hayden said, hoping his last piece of advice didn't fall on deaf ears, "you have to understand what we just talked about was a counterterrorism success." It was intoxicating, but only tactical and short-term. "Unless you're prepared to do this forever, you have to change the facts on the ground. That requires successful counterinsurgency." And the counterinsurgency must be on both the Afghan and

Pakistani sides of the border to be effective. "You've got to change the facts on the ground."

Petraeus wasn't sure that his protect-the-population strategy was looked on with favor in the Obama White House. So in early February 2009, he had the national security adviser, Jim Jones, approve every word in advance of a speech he was scheduled to give in Germany. Jones went along with the whole draft, in which Petraeus made it clear he was seeking a rerun of the Iraq strategy. The approval made him confident that his approach was getting traction. But the pending 30,000-troop request had hit a bump in the road.

At an NSC deputies committee meeting—the seconds in command at the major departments and agencies—Tom Donilon, Jones's deputy, said he wanted to understand the basis for the 30,000. Troops constantly flowed in and out of Afghanistan. The amount of traffic made it hard to get a perfect snapshot.

"Wait a minute," he said, "let's build it in a way that's completely, totally transparent, and that we've identified the pieces here." He wanted a firm answer to Obama's question about how many troops were absolutely necessary. Why should the president send more troops before finishing a strategy review?

"Time out," said Marine General James "Hoss" Cartwright, vice chairman of the Joint Chiefs of Staff. "We need to go back and let's get the numbers exactly right and then we'll reconvene this."

The stated reason for deploying more troops before the strategy review was to provide security for Afghanistan's August presidential election, to keep the polls open for what could be a major turning point for the country.

The Pentagon had sent a troop breakdown to General Lute. The immediate need was for only two brigades, around 13,000 troops. Another 10,000 wouldn't be ready until later in the year. The initial 30,000 had already been scaled back, making Donilon even more distrustful of numbers from the Pentagon. Lute had put together these kinds of figures from his previous job as director of operations for the Joint Staff. The 13,000 actually looked low, so Lute went to Donilon.

"These numbers are really soft," he said. "For example, there's no helicopters in here. How do you get around Afghanistan with no helicopters? And where are the counter-IED teams? Where's the intel that goes with this? Where's the UAV [unmanned aerial vehicle] support?" There was nothing for medical evacuations. "We should make them go back," the general said.

Donilon told the Pentagon, "Unacceptable. Do over. You know what? We're starting all over again. You guys want this decision today, but you can't get the numbers straight. So you've got thousands of people over there. Do it again and send it back, and we'll get you the decision in a timely way, which is our commitment to you."

Donilon's tone didn't help. His condescension offended some Pentagon staffers.

JCS Chairman Mullen suggested that the White House butt out of Pentagon business. "We're in charge of the numbers," he said. "We've got the numbers. We've done our homework."

Well, okay, was the NSC response. The request was about to go for a presidential signature as is when Gates intercepted it.

"We don't have the numbers right," the secretary of defense said, somewhat chagrined. "The complaints that you raise, I went back and looked into. And I've got to tell you, I now don't have confidence in those numbers. So please pull the package from the president, and I'll get you the right numbers."

After a couple of days, the Pentagon provided a revised number—17,000. They acknowledged they needed an additional 4,000 enablers for intelligence and medical evacuation that Lute had identified. The scaled-down request and incomplete math added to the suspicion Donilon and others had of the military. It shook their confidence in the charts and numbers the Pentagon churned out. It almost appeared as if someone was trying to pull a fast one on a new president. The 30,000 had gone down to 13,000, then up to 17,000. Gates seemed to understand the White House's concern, but Mullen did not.

Donilon was thankful to have Lute at the NSC. "This is exactly why we kept these guys, because they know what the hell's going on," Donilon said. "And we never would've caught this. We would've had the president and press releases approve one number, only days later to have to come back and increase the number, make us look foolish."

On Friday, February 13, the president met with the National Security Council, and Jones, the national security adviser, presented four options on Afghanistan troop deployments.

Option one: Decide only after Riedel completes the strategy review. The argument for: It was logical to define the strategy and then make the troop decisions. Jones believed that if everything was equal, this is what the president would do. The arguments against: Security was deteriorating in Afghanistan and a delayed decision meant the troops would arrive after the August election. Plus, a deployment decision, according to the options paper, "would send a strong statement to the allies, the Pakistanis and the world." It was a belief in the declaratory impact of such a decision; just ordering troops would help.

Option two: Send all 17,000 at once.

Option three: Send the 17,000, but do so in two parts. This would be something of a compromise between the first two options. The argument against was that this decision would send a message of hesitancy and uncertainty to the allies, Afghans and Pakistanis.

Option four: Send 27,000, which, given the troop flows, would fill General McKiernan's entire request. This included about 10,000 troops that would not be needed until later in the year.

Given those options, the president had the appearance of a choice, when for practical and political purposes there really was none. Clinton, Gates, Mullen and Petraeus backed the full 17,000 deployment, which in the end was Jones's recommendation as well.

The core argument was that it could be disastrous if the president declined to send the 17,000, or split it into two parts, and the election was a bloodbath with the Taliban overrunning the Afghan government defenses.

Richard Holbrooke, on the secure video from Kabul, noted that 44 years ago President Lyndon Johnson and his advisers were debating the same issues for Vietnam.

"History should not be forgotten," he said. Vietnam had taught him that guerrillas win in a stalemate, and he strongly supported the 17,000 option.

A confused silence greeted the Vietnam reference.

"Ghosts," Obama whispered.

Biden opposed any deployments before the Riedel review was wrapped up.

What is your view? Obama asked Riedel. Should we do it?

"Yes, to some extent," Riedel said. "In a perfect world, we'd like to put every Afghan decision in the refrigerator for two months. But it's not a perfect world, and making this decision now will actually give you more options, come August. Because with more troops on the ground in August, your capacity to have a real election will increase. If you don't do it, you may find yourself in August unable to hold an election."

The 17,000 was an insurance policy, so that the president would have the flexibility to make choices in the future.

A poker-faced Obama said he would wait to let them know his final decision.

When Lute returned from the NSC meeting, staffers asked him, What did the president decide?

"I don't know," he said.

When do you think we're going to have a decision?

"I don't know. Stand by."

Over the weekend, Obama considered his options.

Obama later said that the worries about the Afghan election largely drove his decision. "There were strong warnings, both from the military as well as our intelligence agencies," the president told me, "that if we did not bolster security in Afghanistan rapidly, that the election might not come off, and in fact you could see a country that splintered.

"This is always the toughest decision that I make as president," he told me. "I just think that the first time that you sign off on an order to send young men and women into a battle theater, you feel the weight of that decision. And it is . . ."

"Do you pause?" I asked.

"Yes."

"How many times?"

"You pause."

The president added, "Look, I think that you make sure that you have thought through all the alternatives, and that you feel confident enough that this is the best decision, that it justifies potentially some of those kids not coming back. And the challenge is that you never have 100 percent certainty."

He said he decided the 17,000 was the best option he could see. The president told me he made this decision "knowing that some of those kids may not come back, or if they come back they're going to be grievously injured, it is still in the country's interests to do it."

On Monday, Obama notified the Pentagon that he had decided on 17,000.

The next day the White House press secretary issued a four-paragraph release saying the president had decided to deploy more forces. "There is no more solemn duty by a president than the decision to deploy our armed forces into harm's way," the release said. It was left to the Pentagon to provide the details on the 17,000 troops going to Afghanistan. There was no presidential press conference, no presidential speech announcing what was one of Obama's most important decisions in his first 30 days in office.

Of the 17,000, the first 8,000—a Marine Expeditionary Brigade—would deploy to an area in the rural Helmand province that had less than one percent of Afghanistan's population. They would provide security in a place with few voters.

10

On Wednesday, March 11, Jones invited Gates and Mullen to his West Wing office to give the Pentagon leadership a sneak preview of the Riedel strategy. Gates and Mullen had to be on board if they were going to get anywhere.

Riedel presented his diagnosis and cure. The focus must shift to Pakistan and away from Afghanistan. Pakistan had to end its complex, schizophrenic relationship with terrorists in which they are "the patron and the victim and the safe haven all at the same time," Riedel said. In a major shift, the U.S. would confront Afghanistan and Pakistan as two countries but one challenge: AfPak. Extremists based in Pakistan were undermining the Afghan government. And in a self-destructive cycle, Afghanistan's insecurity fed Pakistan's instability.

Riedel had an answer to the president's question of what the goal should be. "The goal is to disrupt, dismantle and eventually defeat al Qaeda and its extremist allies, their support structures and their safe havens in Pakistan and to prevent their return to Pakistan or Afghanistan."

Saying there were no quick fixes in AfPak, the review listed several recommendations. First, the U.S. should execute and resource an integrated civilian-military counterinsurgency strategy in Afghanistan, and the Afghan army should be increased to 134,000 troops over the two years. Other recommendations centered on Pakistan, including increased financial assistance to Pakistan's military, economy and civilian government.

"Have you looked for a silver bullet to solve the Pakistan problem?" Gates asked.

Yes, Riedel said. His team had examined several carrot-and-stick options. In the carrot category, for example, suppose Pakistan was offered a civil/nuclear power deal similar to the one that President Bush gave India? Pakistan would probably just pocket it, claim they were entitled to equal treatment, and not change their behavior.

On the stick side, Riedel said, they had looked at the extreme option of invading Pakistan, and, of course, immediately dismissed it. Invading a country that possessed dozens of nuclear weapons would be something beyond madness.

Everyone agreed.

The best thing we've come up with, Riedel said, is to give the Pakistani military what it needs to fight a counterinsurgency war against the terrorist groups: helicopters. During the Bush administration, the Pakistanis received 12 helicopters. It was practically nothing. But even this would not be a silver bullet, he said. There weren't enough helicopters in the world to change Pakistani behavior.

As for his recommendation to work on issues between India and Pakistan, everyone in the room said it had to be done without fanfare or public attention. Otherwise, India would go berserk. India thought the United States was filled with closet Pakistani lovers.

Mullen found that idea laughable. Riedel was obviously the opposite. He was hard-over against Pakistan. Mullen might have the closest relationship with the Pakistani military. He had the account dealing with General Ashfaq Kayani, the Pakistani army chief who had been the ISI chief from 2004 to 2007, when the al Qaeda stronghold was built and the Afghan Taliban revived. In many ways, the Pakistani military had vastly more authority over the direction and fate of the country than its historically weak civilian leadership.

Jones and Gates—and Mullen to a lesser extent—asked whether it was possible to trust the Pakistanis.

"I've known every head of ISI since the mid-1980s," Riedel said. Kayani either is not in control of his organization or he is not telling the truth. The U.S. should see the obvious and connect the dots.

The Pakistanis are lying, he said. Addressing Mullen, he said, you've met Kayani some dozen times, you know him better than anyone else here. My impression is that he falls into the second category—liar.

Mullen didn't disagree. But he valued the personal bond he had forged with Kayani. He knew there were things that Kayani didn't tell him. But Mullen thought Riedel, like many CIA analysts, had a jaded, cynical view of Pakistan and had lost his objectivity. And as a practical matter, they had to work with Kayani out of necessity. He had the most power in that country.

Later Mullen asked Dennis Blair, the DNI, for a favor—four-star admiral to retired four-star admiral. "Denny, help me here," he said, "I need an objective view of Pakistan." He was not getting it from the intelligence world. Distrust consumed most analysts, but some in the CIA suffered from a severe bout of client-itis with the ISI, having worked with them for so many decades.

Blair told Mullen that Riedel had it about right.

Jones met with the NSC principals the next day, March 12, to go over the Riedel review.

"I want Bruce to talk for 30 minutes and explain what's in this paper," Jones began. Let's have no interruptions. Riedel reprised his presentation from the day before and Jones opened up the meeting for comments.

"Just let me take two minutes here," Biden said. "I only have a couple of things to say, and this'll only take me a minute or two." Historically, he said, it's been very difficult—impossible—for foreign interventions to prevail in Afghanistan. With tens of thousands of troops on the ground already, if we can't do it with this number and we don't have a reliable partner in the Afghanistan government, then it seems irresponsible to inject additional troops on top of that. We're just prolonging failure at that point, he said.

The war was not politically sustainable, he said. It has been nearly eight years. If we put in more troops, statistically, we're going to see our casualties go up, adding fuel to public and congressional disillusionment.

Biden proposed what he called counterterrorism plus. Focus on al Qaeda in Pakistan. The U.S. and NATO troop presence in Afghanistan would soon reach about 100,000—enough to ensure that al Qaeda would not move back there, and enough to hold the Taliban insurgency at bay.

The vice president's lecture lasted almost as long as Riedel's talk. An NSC staff director sitting on the back bench clocked Biden as speaking for 21 minutes.

Jones turned to Secretary Clinton, the ranking principal after Biden.

"Well, Joe, tell us what you really think!" she said.

Those in the room burst into laughter. Clinton argued for sustained counterinsurgency—protecting the Afghan people, winning them over, getting popular "will" on our side, improving the legitimacy and competency of the Karzai government. Do you understand what the alternative would be if we don't stick with this? she asked. The gains for women would evaporate and the United Nations would be driven out. She fully supported Riedel's strategic review and the recommendations.

Lock, stock and barrel, Riedel thought. It was a ringing endorsement that he appreciated.

Gates took the floor briefly and said that he too agreed with Riedel's review—but without the warmth of Clinton's blanket endorsement.

Jones said there appeared to be three force options since the president had approved 17,000 more troops the previous month.

The first was counterterrorism "lite" as they called it: no more troops, maybe even bring some out, basically the vice president's position.

Second was 4,000 more trainers for the Afghan army, which General McKiernan, General Petraeus and Secretary Gates had recommended.

Third would be ramping up to full counterinsurgency, meaning one member of the U.S., NATO military, Afghan army or police for every 40 to 50 people in Afghanistan. This was the standard ratio in the theoretical model for counterinsurgency, or as the military called it, COIN. To do that would require another 100,000 U.S. troops—a position that no one had even come close to advocating, including Petraeus.

At one point, Riedel spoke with Rahm Emanuel, who was astounded that the intelligence on bin Laden was not better. "What do you mean you don't know where he is?" the chief of staff asked. Some $50 billion a year spent on intelligence "and you don't have a clue where the most wanted man in the history of the world is?"

We let the trail go cold back after 9/11 when the Bush administration turned to Iraq, Riedel answered. The solution by the Bush White House and the Congress had been to add more people, throw more bodies into the CIA, the DNI and the National Security Agency. They were highly motivated but inexperienced. About two thirds of those in the CIA's Near East and South Asia office of analysis, for example, had less than five years' experience, roughly an inversion of how it had been when Riedel joined the CIA almost three decades ago.

In a later discussion with Jones, Riedel said, "The intelligence community is always better off when it's given direction rather than too much love." They're big boys and can handle the discipline.

The NSC principals met again five days later, March 17, for final approval of the Riedel strategy and to choose among the military options.

"Bruce has done the classic Henry Kissinger model," Gates said, referring to the military options. "You have three options, two of which are ridiculous, so you accept the one in the middle."

"Yes, that's right," Riedel said. "Guilty as charged." It was a vintage White House trick, one that offered the illusion of choice. But even though everyone recognized this for the stunt it was, the Kissinger model remained popular.

Gates and the others voiced objections to the third option of 100,000. Though it was the theoretical model, it was not serious, so they took it off the table, and all, with the exception of Biden, backed the Riedel strategy with the military option of 4,000 trainers.

Biden, whose opinion Gates had called ridiculous, said he wanted his dissent noted.

Emanuel interjected that they now had to get the review paper to the president. "The president's got to get his head into this, in depth," Emanuel said. "He's got to read it carefully, and he's got to have some-body walk him through it."

Jones agreed.

"So guess what, Bruce?" Emanuel said, turning to Riedel. "You're going to California tomorrow." Obama was taking Air Force One to appear on *The Tonight Show* with Jay Leno and conduct several town hall meetings. The flight would give him five hours of unscheduled time—an ideal opportunity for him to digest the 44-page report. Rie-del could ride along, walk him through it, and answer his questions.

The next day, March 18, Riedel boarded Air Force One. Over the years, he had flown numerous times on the presidential plane and had a fa-vorite seat, a window seat, well behind the private cabins used by the president and isolated from the chairs clustered around tables. Riedel didn't feel like chitchatting. He sat down and looked over his notes to make sure he had it right.

Emanuel's plan was to stage the presentation away from the White House so none of the national security team—Clinton, Gates, Jones, Mullen, Blair, Panetta, Holbrooke or Petraeus—would feel they had been excluded from an important presidential meeting. Obama would be able to give Riedel his undivided attention.

About two hours into the flight, Axelrod came over to Riedel. Both the president and he had finished reading the report.

Showtime, Riedel thought as he stepped into the president's office in the front.

Obama was behind his desk, in a shirt and tie, with his suit jacket nearby for their arrival in California.

Riedel told Obama that the written report was by necessity a bureaucratic document, a reflection of the interagency process. The 20 recommendations were serious and focused, he hoped, and the 180 sub-recommendations fixed around actions that should be taken. It was dense—not Shakespeare—and there were parts that required some decoding. Mr. President, what I can do is read between the lines for you, he said.

You might remember, Riedel said, that during the campaign I told you that al Qaeda was as dangerous now as they were on the 10th of September, 2001. After a review of the intelligence, he said, it turns out that I was underestimating the danger.

Though my first recommendation is an integrated civilian-military counterinsurgency for Afghanistan, you, Mr. President, have to be focused on the real, central threat—Pakistan.

Some al Qaeda watchers would argue that bin Laden, hiding in Pakistan, is irrelevant, Riedel said. He's stuck in a cave somewhere, and yes, he puts out these audiotapes once in a while, but he's more of a symbol than the commander of a global jihad.

What I learned is that's just not true, Riedel said. He communicates with his underlings and is in touch with his foot soldiers. His troops believe they are getting his orders, and we know from good intelligence that they are. But we don't know the exact mechanism by which this happens. And that we don't know is one of the more troubling facts. We know that, say, four people get his messages. What we don't know is if 40 other people are getting his messages. Or even 400? If you are seeing a slice of the picture, how big is what you're not seeing? It could be huge.

You could ask, Riedel said, what was the last thing al Qaeda or its affiliates did on the world stage. And the answer, as Obama knew, was the brutal Mumbai attack organized by Lashkar-e-Taiba that previous Thanksgiving. That was a big deal, and LeT is growing.

Al Qaeda is clearly plotting against targets in Western Europe and, less clearly, in North America. For Europe, al Qaeda is using Pakistanis who have relocated to the United Kingdom, Norway and Denmark and can pass through our screening and defenses. They are not young Saudis or Somalis, but the children of immigrants, with British, French, Belgian passports. So this is a triple problem—recruiting, plotting and traveling with relative freedom.

"These guys are serious," Riedel said. "They are clever, and they are relentless. Until we kill them, they're going to keep trying to kill us."

You have to see the threat as a syndicate, Riedel continued. Al Qaeda is part of a larger militancy in Pakistan. It incubates the Afghan or Pakistani Taliban or LeT. The groups all interact. Bin Laden can't be found because he is swimming in a sea of like-minded people.

The singular feature of the syndicate is that despite the Bush administration's efforts—the extreme rendition, detention and interrogation techniques—no one has turned in bin Laden, his deputy, Ayman Zawahiri, or the Taliban leader, Mullah Omar. Lost in the entire torture controversy is the fact that none of those interrogated ever gave up the major intelligence priority—the location of bin Laden. Whether the Bush-Cheney approach was right or wrong, it did not get us what we most want to know.

That fact suggests a greater discipline than is normally attributed to al Qaeda now, Riedel warned.

You could make the case, he continued, that we were surprised once on 9/11 for all kinds of reasons. It's going to be pretty hard to explain what happened to the American people if we're surprised again. We can't be complacent. It's great that drones are killing bad guys, but we don't know where the top leaders are, where "the essence is." Drone strikes are similar to going after a beehive one bee at a time. They would not destroy the hive.

Predator drone strikes only work because CIA paramilitary teams have an ultra-secret presence on the ground in Pakistan. Without the local informants these teams develop, there would not be good signals intelligence so that the drones know where to target. This was a risky enterprise that might collapse overnight. So don't rely on drones, Riedel said. They look like a cheap way out, but they're not.

Turning to Afghanistan, Obama asked if sending in 17,000 and then 4,000 more troops would make a difference.

Yes, Riedel said, or at least you will know the answer in a reasonable time frame. Given what President Bush and you have ordered—nearly 33,000 more troops this year—that will double the number there now. The additional forces will be there by summer or early fall. We're going to go into parts of southern Afghanistan where nobody's been in a long time. If that doesn't have a measurable impact on the Taliban, then you've got a fundamental problem. In his 44-page report, Riedel wrote that the Taliban's momentum "must" be reversed that year.

When an 18-year-old Pashtun warrior has 5,000 Marines in his neighborhood he may say, "You know, I think I'll sit out the next campaign season. I'll just go home." I wouldn't call that reconciliation between a Taliban insurgent and the Afghan government, but I would call that victory, Riedel said.

"But you should have a measurement over the course of six to 12 months whether you're succeeding," Riedel said.

If you don't see progress, there are lovely words in the bureaucratic process. You can "on-ramp" more forces or you can "off-ramp" them, meaning that because of the months of delay between your approval and actual deployment, you can decide to not deploy them. Basically, you're not locked in.

How much does this cost? Obama asked.

We don't know, Riedel answered. This is a review, not a budget. But to put an American soldier in Afghanistan, to pay everything including his veteran's bill, his health insurance, take care of his family, feed him and arm him, is roughly $250,000 a year. Having an Afghan solider on the ground is roughly $12,000. And a committed, well-trained Afghan army unit knows the language, terrain and neighborhood. But remember, the United States would still have to pay for the Afghan forces because their government does not have anything near the revenue.

"The principals are in consensus on this," Riedel said. "The vice president, however, has a different point of view," a modified counterterrorism strategy. But that is what the Bush administration did, and it's how we ended up where we are today. Biden's basic argument is that the war is not politically sustainable, Riedel said. That's politics, and not in my purview. "Mr. President, that's better left for you to decide."

"Yes, that's right," Obama replied. "That shouldn't be part of your writ."

The president also had to think about how to respond to what might happen, Riedel said. For example, we're attacked again and the address is Pakistan, what do you do about it? Obama knew about the retribution plan against Pakistan, to bomb more than 150 sites linked to al Qaeda and other groups. But, Riedel said, problem two, Pakistan's internal situation continues to deteriorate and you get a jihadist government there. What do you do?

Third bad thing. Pakistan attacks India again, either directly or indirectly, Mumbai redux. What are we going to say to the Indians this time? We admire your Gandhi-like self-restraint? I think we've probably reached the threshold in India, Riedel said. The next attack will get a military response. And that means you're talking about the potential for nuclear war.

Another problem would be responsibility for the next attack, which Riedel said he wanted to underscore again. We simply don't know enough about al Qaeda. There are dimensions, capabilities or quirks we don't understand. Al Qaeda may be more formidable than we think.

And when it came to Pakistan, Riedel said bluntly, the president and his team should not rely on Admiral Mullen's latest conversation with General Kayani. At best, it would be half the story.

To summarize, Riedel said that they would have to change the strategic direction of Pakistan. Making the necessary kind of strategic change in any country would be difficult, but particularly with Pakistan.

"That is not something you do in two years," Riedel said. "It may take two decades. It may not be possible." This was an extraordinary—and chilling—prospect.

When Air Force One landed at the Costa Mesa County Fairground, Obama and Riedel were still talking. Obama put on his jacket to greet the crowd of 1,300.

Taping *The Tonight Show* that afternoon, Obama told Jay Leno that he had picked the University of North Carolina to win the NCAA basketball tournament known as March Madness.

"Isn't that a swing state?" Leno teased.

"Complete coincidence," Obama said. "Absolutely."

There was no hint in Obama's demeanor that he had just received a devastating analysis of the threats against the U.S., a warning that al Qaeda was as dangerous as it had been on September 10, 2001.

At one point during their time in Southern California, Axelrod explained to Riedel why Obama went with UNC in his bracket. North Carolina, which Obama had carried in the presidential election, was normally a swing state, so he wanted a team from that state to win. Supporting Duke University would have been too blue, an appeal to the Democratic base. UNC, however, could be seen as more red, a way to reach Republicans.

The former CIA agent could not tell if Axelrod was joking. Politics was not Riedel's writ. On the way back from California, Obama, Axelrod and Riedel watched nearly five hours of the college basketball tournament.

Later, the president confirmed that Pakistan would have to be the centerpiece of any new strategy. "Bruce felt very strongly, as I did," he told me, "that we had to have a serious heart-to-heart with Pakistani civilian, military and intelligence leaders."

"And it continues to this day, does it not?" I asked on July 10, 2010, more than a year after Riedel briefed the president.

"It continues to this day," Obama said.

•   •   •

The National Security Council met with the president on March 20 to review the Riedel strategy. Everyone was now familiar with it, and they discussed Biden's argument that the war was politically unsustainable.

"I think I have two years with the public on this," Obama said. "They'll stand by us for two years. That's my window."

Gates said that the Afghan National Army and National Police would be the key—increasing their numbers, their training, professionalism and commitment. "That's our ticket out."

"I think the die is cast," Biden said. With his dissent noted, he would support the president's decision. "We've pretty much reached agreement with how to go forward. I have some concerns about it, but the die is cast."

"I think this is right," Obama said. "I'm in general accord with it." But he indicated it was not a done deal. "I'm going to think about it a little bit more and I will get back to you." Nonetheless, the die was cast. And unlike the deployment announced in February, this would have to be explained to the American public.

11

In the overcast night, General Petraeus hurried along the sidewalks of Washington's Georgetown neighborhood. His spartan frame looked smaller in real life than in photographs.

The general's fame evolved from a strategy in which soldiers lived as the locals did, no matter the squalor, danger or—in the case of Washington—luxury. He had a dinner reservation and a draft of Obama's planned speech on the Afghanistan-Pakistan strategy.

There was some dissonance between the speech and the Riedel strategy review it was based on. The review's first recommendation on page 19 was to put a "fully resourced" counterinsurgency into Afghanistan. The president's draft gave scant attention to that and, ominously, the word "counterinsurgency" was not mentioned.

This concerned Petraeus. Some thought the general was transfixed by his protect-the-people counterinsurgency success in Iraq. But Petraeus was aware of his infatuation. He worried about becoming the victim of his previous triumph. It was possible a counterinsurgency could be the wrong track for Afghanistan.

"I've looked very hard at that," he had told some of his staff. "That is something that can have you spring awake in an early hour of the morning, that you turn over a thousand different ways when you're running." Petraeus had assigned a "red team"—groups of intelligence and operations experts who developed the contrarian view—to study the issue.

More to the point, it seemed that the president was not buying his counterinsurgency argument.

Petraeus met Holbrooke—his civilian counterpart and "wingman"— on M Street at La Chaumière. It was a Georgetown institution and Holbrooke lived a few blocks away. With its wood-beamed ceiling and central stone fireplace decorated with wine bottles, the restaurant re- sembled a French country inn. By 9 P.M. on Thursday, March 26, the crowd was thinning out.

Petraeus and Holbrooke huddled intently, reviewing each line of Obama's speech. Holbrooke had what he said were important edits about the Afghan police. As the restaurant cleared out, Petraeus sud- denly jumped to his feet to greet the elderly woman passing by their table.

"Helen Thomas," he said, in a courtly display of military manners and charm. "It's David Petraeus. It's so good to see you."

There was the 88-year-old columnist for Hearst newspapers, the scourge of ten presidents and their press secretaries.

"What the hell are you doing in Afghanistan?" she asked. Not even a hello. Why escalate the war? she prodded. "This is Vietnam all over again."

No, Petraeus said, trying to respond.

But Thomas barged into his answers with more questions, some of which she recalled later in an interview. "Come on, don't give me that stuff." "What's your exit strategy?" "How are you going to solve this?" "What are you talking about?" "And anyway, what are you screwing around in Iraq for? You know it's going to hell when we leave." "What are we going to do? Are we going after al Qaeda?"

About her conversation with Petraeus and Holbrooke, she later re- flected, "They had very soothing words. Everything is going to be fine. They were very confident. But I am passionate about Vietnam. I feel it is a repeat of Vietnam—impossible terrain, [the Afghans] are fight- ers. The Russians spent 10 years and they pulled out and no one called them cowards.

"Petraeus was not bragging," explained Thomas. "All I know, I didn't feel reassured."

As Obama's foreign policy speechwriter, Ben Rhodes, 31, read the president's final edits to the text. Rhodes, who had moved from the campaign to the NSC, thought Obama did not fully own the strategy in the speech. The young would-be novelist, who had set aside his literary ambitions to craft political rhetoric, was a diligent note taker. Obama had been frustrated that he had to commit 17,000 troops to Afghanistan before the Riedel review was completed. And as part of the speech, Obama announced that another 4,000 would be sent to train the Afghan security forces.

At 9:40 the next morning, Obama calmly took the stage in the Eisenhower Executive Office Building next to the White House. Sporting a crimson tie and flanked by his cabinet, advisers and a row of American flags, the president said the mission was to "disrupt, dismantle and defeat al Qaeda.

"Multiple intelligence estimates have warned that al Qaeda is actively planning attacks on the United States homeland from its safe haven in Pakistan," Obama said. "And if the Afghan government falls to the Taliban or allows al Qaeda to go unchallenged, that country will again be a base for terrorists who want to kill as many of our people as they possibly can."

The president continued, "For the Afghan people, the return to Taliban rule would condemn their country to brutal governance, international isolation, a paralyzed economy and the denial of basic human rights to the Afghan people, especially women and girls."

A *Washington Post* editorial praised the plan with the headline: "The Price of Realism." A *New York Times* editorial entitled "The Remembered War" commended Obama for taking a "good first step toward fixing the dangerous situation that former President George W. Bush created when he abandoned the necessary war in Afghanistan for the ill-conceived war of choice in Iraq."

The speech surprised Army Colonel John Wood, who since 2007

had been a senior director for Afghanistan on the National Security staff and reported to Lute. Wood popped into Denis McDonough's office.

McDonough, a foreign policy adviser for the Obama presidential campaign, managed strategic communications for the NSC. Wood said he was impressed by how strong the speech was with a counterinsurgency push to protect common Afghans. That had not been in the Rhodes draft.

"I thought that was much better than the version I saw yesterday," Wood said.

Those changes had been made personally by the president, McDonough said.

But Obama had not committed to the full troop request made by the military. McKiernan's request for more troops at the end of the year was still pending.

"No," Obama had told Rhodes. "We'll revisit this after the election" in Afghanistan. That was five months away in August. He wanted to wait to see where they were after the presidential election, and how the 21,000 he ordered to Afghanistan were doing. "We're not making any more troop decisions right now."

Secretary of Defense Gates seemed comfortable with the decision, telling Fox News two days later, "My view is there's no need to ask for more troops, ask the president to approve more troops, until we see how the troops we—he already has approved are in there, how they are doing."

The troop issue troubled Lute. It was a leap of faith by the Riedel review to believe that a fully resourced counterinsurgency could somehow equate to what McKiernan had requested. As they knew, the math disproved that. And Lute knew that McKiernan had requested troops based on when they became available from Iraq, instead of based on mission requirements. The U.S. desperately needed more trainers in

Afghanistan, for example, but McKiernan had asked for them to arrive when they became available in five months.

"Look, sir," Lute said to the Afghanistan commander, "just tell us what you need when you need them, not when Mother Army is telling you they're available."

McKiernan didn't really respond.

There was a fundamental trade-off on resources between Iraq and Afghanistan that Lute felt should be addressed. This had been masked by how the requests were made. But the trade-off had never been presented to Bush, and was not being presented clearly to Obama.

On Thursday, May 7, Pakistani President Zardari and his 20-year-old son, Bilawal, an Oxford University student, stepped into the Oval Office for a meeting with Obama. This was a chance for the two presidents to forge a personal connection. The U.S. was hosting a trilateral summit with Afghanistan and Pakistan.

Obama greeted them warmly, calling himself an enormous admirer of Benazir Bhutto, the former prime minister who was Bilawal's mother and Zardari's late wife. He recalled visiting Pakistan with college friends and learning to cook keema and dal, a lentil chili.

"We do not begrudge you being concerned about India," Obama said. "I know that many Pakistanis are. But we do not want to be part of arming you against India, so let me be very clear about that."

"We are trying to change our worldview," Zardari said, "but it's not going to happen overnight."

Obama turned to the Swat Valley, a former tourist region in the northwestern part of Pakistan. About three months earlier, the Pakistani government signed a cease-fire that ceded control of the region to an Islamic extremist group that was forcing people to obey religious Sharia law. But these extremists—who were allied with the Pakistani branch of the Taliban—broke the cease-fire and continued to gain control of more territory. When they came within 60 miles of the Pakistani capital of Islamabad and close to the nuclear weapons stored in Tarbela, the Pakistani army finally snapped to action and counterattacked.

"You've made progress in Swat," Obama said, "but there was a time we were all concerned you guys would do deals." The cease-fire had let the extremist groups subvert the Pakistani government's legitimacy. "It also gives the wrong impression that nobody is in charge," Obama said.

"If I had sent the military in without mobilizing public opinion, it would not have succeeded," Zardari tried to explain. "Once I showed that these guys are not well-meaning people, that even after they had an agreement to enforce Islamic law, that they really want power and not Islam, I was able to turn public opinion around."

Obama recognized that the Pakistani government was showing more resolve than it had before. Progress was evident by the move into Swat, and by the CIA having averaged a drone strike every three days for the past month.

The president then escorted Zardari and his son around the Rose Garden. As they walked, Obama draped his arm around the son's shoulders.

Later Obama told me that the operation in Swat was an important step by the Pakistanis, one that "you would not have seen two or three years ago." The Pakistanis had sent 15,000 troops in one of the largest operations against the Taliban.

One evening during the trilateral summit, Zardari had dinner with Zalmay Khalilzad, the 58-year-old former U.S. ambassador to Afghanistan, Iraq and the U.N. during the Bush presidency.

Zardari dropped his diplomatic guard. He suggested that one of two countries was arranging the attacks by the Pakistani Taliban inside his country: India or the U.S. Zardari didn't think India could be that clever, but the U.S. could. Karzai had told him the U.S. was behind the attacks, confirming the claims made by the Pakistani ISI.

"Mr. President," Khalilzad said, "what would we gain from doing this? You explain the logic to me."

This was a plot to destabilize Pakistan, Zardari hypothesized, so that the U.S. could invade and seize its nuclear weapons. He could not explain the rapid expansion in violence otherwise. And the CIA had not pursued the leaders of the Pakistani Taliban, a group known as Tehrik-e-Taliban or TTP that had attacked the government. TTP was also blamed for the assassination of Zardari's wife, Benazir Bhutto.

"We give you targets of Taliban people you don't go after," Zardari said. "You go after other areas. We're puzzled."

But the drones were primarily meant to hunt down members of al Qaeda and Afghan insurgents, not the Pakistani Taliban, Khalilzad responded.

But the Taliban movement is tied to al Qaeda, Zardari said, so by not attacking the targets recommended by Pakistan the U.S. had revealed its support of the TTP. The CIA at one time had even worked with the group's leader, Baitullah Mehsud, Zardari asserted.

Khalilzad listened calmly, even though the claims struck him as madness. The U.S. was using the Taliban to topple the Pakistani government? Ridiculous. But Khalilzad knew Afghanistan's President Karzai also believed in this conspiracy theory, more evidence that this region of the world and its leaders were dysfunctional.

Despite Zardari's claims, Pakistani government officials had received top secret CIA briefings about drone strikes against Baitullah Mehsud's TTP. A March 12, 2009, attack against a Mehsud compound killed more than two dozen militants, who quickly retrieved the remains of their fallen comrades. And on April 1, another five militants linked to Mehsud, including an al Qaeda trainer, died in a drone strike, according to a CIA briefing given to Pakistan in April. Around 30 were killed in those two CIA attacks to help protect the Pakistani political and military establishment.

Almost everything about Afghanistan was troubling Mullen. As Obama was giving intense focus to the war, Mullen was feeling more personal responsibility. Afghanistan had been marked by "incredible neglect," he told some of his officers. "It's almost like you're on a hunger strike and you're on the 50th day, and all of a sudden you're going to try to feed this person. Well, they're not going to eat very quickly. I mean, every organ in the body is collapsing. The under-resourcing of Afghanistan was much deeper and wider than even I thought. It wasn't just about troops. It was intellectually, it was strategically, it was physically, culturally."

Perhaps the biggest missing resource was leadership, in Mullen's view. Obviously, Afghanistan needed absolutely the best commander. And for all his skills and experience, the general who currently held that post, David McKiernan, was not the best.

"I cannot live when I know I have a better answer," Mullen said, "when kids are dying every single day."

The chairman of the Joint Chiefs realized that the solution to Afghanistan was right before his eyes, walking through the ringed hallways of the Pentagon. Army Lieutenant General Stanley McChrystal had been director of the Joint Staff for more than seven months. The Joint Staff director was essentially the chairman's deputy. It was the premier assignment for a three-star, an almost certain path to four-star rank. Among McChrystal's predecessors in the post were DNI Dennis Blair, former CentCom commander John Abizaid and the current Army chief General George Casey.

McChrystal was already a legend within the Joint Staff. He worked harder than anyone, fixing problems rather than complaining about them. He was open-minded and carried out all requests and orders seamlessly. He skipped lunch, staying at his desk and munching instead from a plastic container of large, salt-encrusted Bavarian pretzels. McChrystal started the Pakistan Afghanistan Coordination Cell, which brought officers with multiple deployments in Afghanistan into the Pentagon so their experiences could inform Washington.

Gates, who often worked with McChrystal, agreed he was the man for the job. He and Mullen told the president they wanted to replace McKiernan. Obama said he would approve whoever the secretary and Mullen recommended.

Gates told others in the White House, This is my test for the president, whether I'm going to succeed here. I've got to have the best team on the field.

In late April, Admiral Mullen arrived in Afghanistan and told McKiernan in a private meeting that it was time for him to retire.

You'll have to fire me, McKiernan responded.

McKiernan had given his word to Afghan officials that he would be there for two full years. He would not break it. Perhaps he had not thumped his chest enough, bragged to the Pentagon leaders, or charmed the visiting congressional delegations. Some of his advisers wondered if maybe McKiernan should have been more of a public presence. Other commanders seemed to benefit from media exposure.

At a Monday, May 11, Pentagon press conference, Gates's voice quivered slightly as he announced that McChrystal would be the new Afghanistan commander.

"Our mission there requires new thinking and new approaches from our military leaders," he said. "Today we have a new policy set by our president. We have a new strategy, a new mission. . . . I believe that new military leadership also is needed."

Gates listed the questions he expected McChrystal to answer as the new commander: "How do we do better? What new ideas do you have? What fresh thinking do you have? Are there different ways of accomplishing our goals?"

When Riedel heard the questions Gates had posed, he wondered what the hell was going on. Just six weeks earlier, he had completed the strategy review, the president had given his speech and Gates had embraced it fully. Were they starting over again?

Petraeus was in Washington that day to attend a National Security Council meeting on terrorist detainees. He watched the press conference on television. As Gates and Mullen were speaking, Petraeus stood to go answer some e-mails. He agreed with the change, but a member of his staff reported that he looked "ashen." McKiernan had been his immediate superior during the 2003 invasion of Iraq. Generals were expendable. Center stage one day, gone the next.

A week later, Obama met for 10 minutes in the Oval Office with McChrystal.

On the choice of McChrystal, Obama later recalled to me, "Well, it was ultimately my decision." But he was relying on Gates's and Mullen's judgment. "They felt that the best person to do the job at this stage was General McChrystal," Obama said. "You know, I had not had a person-to-person conversation with him."

"Did you have any feeling you're picking your Eisenhower, to a certain extent, for your war?" I asked. "Did you feel you were sufficiently involved in that decision at that point, picking your Eisenhower?"

Obama challenged the comparison. "A, I don't want to analogize myself to FDR," he said. "B, I don't want to analogize the Afghan effort to World War II."

"But it is your war," I said.

"But what I will say is," the president said, "is that given the time frames we were operating under, it was important for me to satisfy myself that this was the best person we had available."

Lute understood the rationale for installing McChrystal. But the addition of 21,000 troops included a Marine brigade of 9,000 that McKiernan was dispatching to Helmand province. Less than one percent of the Afghan population lived where the Marines were going. Lute asked McChrystal, How high would the cost be to pull those Marines out and commit them to Kandahar, the cradle of the Taliban movement?

It would be crippling, McChrystal said, because it would break the confidence with the Afghan people in Helmand.

So the Marines stayed. They had sacked the Afghanistan commander but kept his plan.

On May 26, 2009, one of the most sensitive reports from the world of deep intelligence appeared in the TOP SECRET/CODEWORD President's Daily Brief. Those who wrote the PDB had learned to craft careful headlines that did not sensationalize their findings, and in some cases even downplayed them. The headline on this item read, "North American al Qaeda trainees may influence targets and tactics in the United States and Canada."

This report, and another highly restricted one, said that at least 20 al Qaeda converts with American, Canadian or European passports were being trained in Pakistani safe havens to return to their homelands to commit high-profile acts of terrorism. They included half a dozen from the United Kingdom, several Canadians, some Germans and three Americans. None of their names was known.

DNI Dennis Blair thought the reports were alarming and credible enough that the president should be alerted. He personally edited the PDB each night before briefing it to Obama the next morning.

Rahm Emanuel summoned Blair to his office in the corner of the West Wing after the al Qaeda report had been briefed.

"Why'd you put that in the PDB?" he asked.

"This is a threat to the United States," Blair said. "I'm worried about it, and I think you ought to know."

"What can we do about it?" asked the ever practical Emanuel.

"I can't tell you anything to do right now," Blair answered. "If we knew more about it, we would've caught them. But maybe there's some defensive actions we can take."

"You're just trying to put this on us, so it's not your fault," Emanuel retorted.

"No, no," Blair replied, "I'm trying to tell you. I'm the president's intelligence officer and I'm worried about this, and I think I owe it to him—and you—to tell him."

Blair was insulted. The White House chief of staff was not only accusing him of a brazen act of ass covering but of ducking responsibility. Blair viewed his willingness to bring bad news as a strength, a sign of loyalty. He was accepting responsibility. The warning was an important reminder that a domestic terrorist strike was one of the greatest threats to the country, its economy and Obama's presidency.

Though toned down, the item echoed the notorious PDB headline given to President Bush a month before the 9/11 terrorist attacks that said, "Bin Laden Determined to Strike in U.S." An inescapable part of Bush's legacy was that he had not acted quickly or seriously enough against the terrorist threat.

"Wow," Blair thought as he left the White House, "we come from different planets on this one."

Increasingly, he saw a fault line in the administration. Emanuel's "us" meant Obama and his team of political advisers in the White House. The military leaders and former four-stars, such as Jones and himself, were outsiders.

Over the next several months, separate FBI investigations led to the arrest of two U.S. residents who had been trained by al Qaeda or an affiliate in Pakistani safe havens. The first FBI investigation, called Operation High Rise, was triggered by a single alert Central Intelligence Agency analyst examining intercepts. On September 19, 2009, agents arrested Najibullah Zazi, 24, in Denver. He was an al Qaeda operative who was planning to detonate up to 14 backpack bombs aboard New York City subway cars.

A tip from British intelligence launched a second investigation called Operation Black Medallion. Chicago resident David Coleman Headley, 49, was arrested for plotting a terrorist attack in Europe. His business partner ran an immigration and travel agency, which had an office in New York's Empire State Building. That gave him 24/7 access to the building that was possibly the most iconic terrorist target in Manhattan.

Blair figured the U.S. had dodged two bullets because of a single CIA analyst and British intelligence. Was there a third terrorist in the United States, as suggested by the PDB?

Soon, new intelligence showed that some 100 Westerners, including many with U.S. passports or visas, were being trained in Pakistani safe havens. U.S. intelligence had lost track of too many of those people. Al Qaeda had adapted since the 9/11 attack that had killed 3,000 people. It was now aiming for smaller operations that might only require one man and one bomb.

When I later asked the president about these intelligence reports, he said, "I won't get into the weeds on this."

But he added, "What you've seen is a metastasizing of al Qaeda, where a range of loosely affiliated groups now have the capacity and the ambition to recruit and train for attacks that may not be on the scale of a 9/11, but obviously can still be extraordinarily . . . One man, one bomb . . . which could still have, obviously, an extraordinary traumatizing effect on the homeland."

On Tuesday June 2, Stan McChrystal sat down in a wood-paneled Senate chamber for his confirmation hearing. He had deep-set eyes, jutting ears, straw-colored hair and practically no trace of fat. In his prepared remarks, McChrystal suggested that the president might need to send even more troops to Afghanistan.

"A key component of resourcing is people," he told the Senate Armed Services Committee, "and more than 21,000 additional U.S. military personnel will have deployed to Afghanistan by October of this year. You might properly ask if that is enough. I don't know. It may be some time before I do."

The media did not seem to pick up on McChrystal's meaning, but National Security Adviser Jim Jones did. McChrystal had confirmed what Jones was hearing from his contacts inside NATO. Just three months after the Riedel review, a campaign for more troops by McChrystal and Mullen was underway, though the Pentagon had officially committed to holding forces at the current level for a full year, at which point the new strategy—and the impact of 21,000 more troops—could be evaluated.

Jones called Gates and Mullen into his White House office.

"Hey guys, we just went through this," he said. "We told the president, we won't bother you for another year. Troops haven't even gotten there. We don't have an assessment on how they're doing. And now I'm hearing these drumbeats about more troops or things are going to hell in a handbasket, the situation is critical."

Gates's and Mullen's response was, in essence, this is something we think is coming. We're going to have to deal with it sooner rather than later, because Stan is saying things are going badly.

Jones wanted to put some order to it all, some definition. What he was getting was a cacophony of opinions. Inside the White House, people were assuming that the Pentagon was trying to force the president's hand.

Jones flew to France with the president that weekend for the 65th anniversary of D-Day. During the ceremony, he went to a quiet section of the American Cemetery in Normandy. Standing alone amid thousands of marble headstones, Jones missed the ceremony.

As President Obama spoke, Jones pulled out his cell phone to talk to Gates.

They had gone through the whole Riedel review, Jones reminded him. They had gone through all the numbers, briefed the president and the congressional leadership, and teed up the public. The military had given its advice. Obama had supported it.

"And now we got the new team running around saying, the sky is falling," Jones said. "How do we get this back in the box so that what we said to the president in March doesn't sound like we didn't mean it?"

Jones pitched Gates on a way to defuse the tension. Let McChrystal have two months—60 days—to deliver a commander's assessment of Afghanistan, rather than campaign for more troops behind the president's back.

"Look, it makes perfect sense to me the new commander would come in and make an assessment," Jones said. "He has to—it'll be on his watch. He has to make his assessment. Make an assessment. But let's knock off the chatter, in NATO and other places, before the president has a chance to be consulted. And if at the end of 60 days, he wants to come in and say whatever he wants to say, and you want to back him up, there's a certain logic and order to this. But absent that, this is crazy."

Gates agreed to the plan. McChrystal should put his thoughts down in a written report for the president.

After the ceremony, Jones told Obama about the assessment. The Pentagon is unhappy and McChrystal is worried about Afghanistan, he said.

That next Monday, June 8, Pentagon spokesman Geoff Morrell was asked why the Pentagon had yet to announce any measurements of success for Afghanistan. Instead of answering that question, Morrell seized the moment to announce that McChrystal would lead an assessment to "get a ground-eye view of what's going on" and recommend "what changes in the strategy should be made."

12

For six years both as Marine commandant and NATO commander, General Jones had gone to Afghanistan to make his own assessments. He suggested to the president that he go again, evaluate how the strategy was working and send a message to the generals on the ground to stop agitating for more troops. Jones wanted to get to General McChrystal early. "Generals always want more force," he said.

Jones invited me to travel with him at the end of June for what would be a six-day trip to Afghanistan, Pakistan and India. I accepted.

Taliban and insurgent attacks in Afghanistan were escalating, reaching an all-time high of more than 400 attacks during one week in May. Though that did not rival the violence in Iraq, which had peaked at 1,600 attacks in one week two years earlier, it signaled an alarming trend.

Jones and a traveling party of about 40, including his staff and Secret Service protection, took off Sunday night, June 21, from Andrews Air Force Base in a giant C-17 cargo plane that can carry 160,000 pounds. The plane came equipped with about 100 standard airline seats and dozens of bunks. Jones occupied a security pod in the center of the cargo hold that contained a well-appointed office and several bunks.

During an hour-long conversation mid-flight, he laid out his theory of the war. First, Jones said, the United States could not lose the war or be seen as losing the war.

"If we're not successful here," Jones said, "you'll have a staging base for global terrorism all over the world. People will say the terrorists won. And you'll see expressions of these kinds of things in Africa, South America, you name it. Any developing country is going to say, this is the way we beat [the United States], and we're going to have a bigger problem." A setback or loss for the United States would be "a tremendous boost for jihadist extremists, fundamentalists all over the world" and provide "a global infusion of morale and energy, and these people don't need much."

Jones went on, using the kind of rhetoric that Obama had shied away from, "It's certainly a clash of civilizations. It's a clash of religions. It's a clash of almost concepts of how to live." The conflict is that deep, he said. "So I think if you don't succeed in Afghanistan, you will be fighting in more places.

"Second, if we don't succeed here, organizations like NATO, by association the European Union, and the United Nations might be relegated to the dustbin of history."

Third, "I say, be careful you don't over-Americanize the war. I know that we're going to do a large part of it," but it was essential to get active, increased participation by the other 41 nations, get their buy-in and make them feel they have ownership in the outcome.

Fourth, he said that there had been way too much emphasis on the military, almost an overmilitarization of the war. The key to leaving a somewhat stable Afghanistan in a reasonable time frame was improving governance and the rule of law, in order to reduce corruption. There also needed to be economic development and more participation by the Afghan security forces.

It sounded like a good case, but I wondered if everyone on the American side had the same understanding of our goals. What was meant by victory? For that matter, what constituted not losing? And when might that happen? Could there be a deadline? What was the role of protect-the-people counterinsurgency, the Petraeus strategy highlighted in the Riedel report but not embraced directly in President Obama's speech?

The next day, Tuesday, June 23, I attended the last 15 minutes of Jones's meeting with President Karzai. Sensitive intelligence reports on Karzai claimed he was erratic and even "delusional." "Off his meds" was a common description, while high on "weed" was a description by others. Jones said that several months earlier President Obama had told Karzai that he must get his act together. Curtailing corruption had to be Karzai's first goal. As I entered the spacious office inside the Arg-e-Shahi presidential palace, Karzai was exceedingly gracious and warm. He wore his signature lamb's wool cap and mentioned right off his familiarity with my book *Veil: The Secret Wars of the CIA, 1981–1987*, about Reagan's CIA director, William J. Casey.

His interest in the CIA did not surprise me, given his brother's ties to the agency.

I asked Karzai what he might do differently if he won a second term as president in the election, which was two months off.

"I would become a figure of unity," he said, casting himself as a statesman. "I would not become a political player. I would not become a member of a party.

"I would bring the U.S. to the table on the peace process with the Taliban. President Obama announced this on March 27, and we haven't seen much movement on this. In fact the United States is dragging their feet."

Jones shook his head, as did the new U.S. ambassador to Afghanistan, retired three-star Army General Karl Eikenberry.

They knew the Taliban currently felt it had the upper hand and would be in no mood to negotiate. But Karzai, as he often did, placed the blame on the Americans.

That night, we flew into the heart of the Taliban insurgency in Helmand province, southern Afghanistan. Here was the war without the filter of a Situation Room briefing. The cool evening air hit my face as the plane's rear loading ramp was lowered. Jeeps, trucks and buses wheeled around the airfield. Flashing lights pierced the darkness to a dizzying effect. The noise and clamor of it all felt surreal, yet the manic scene seemed to unfold in slow motion. All that was missing was the haunting and elegiac theme music from Oliver Stone's movie *Platoon*, Samuel Barber's Adagio for Strings. We boarded a bus to take us from the airfield to Camp Leatherneck. The moment was exhilarating and frightening.

Helmand is the largest of Afghanistan's 34 provinces, but is sparsely populated and accounts for about half of the country's poppy harvest. Locals call the area the Desert of Death because of its scorching heat (up to 116 degrees) and an annual rainfall that averages less than four inches. A strong headwind can pick up the fine dustlike sand in a blast that is blinding and choking.

I was given luxury quarters in an air-conditioned tent with one of Jones's senior staffers. In the middle of the night I awoke in desperate search for a washroom. With no mountains or high ground surrounding the camp, it is supposedly safe from sniper and mortar fire. I wrapped a towel around my waist. As far as I could see, the concrete T-wall shielding the base might be the only option. I stopped there first, but finally found a small washroom a football field away. A sign on the door said, "Commanding General and Master Sergeant Only." I used it anyway, and padded back, anticipating a random shot into the camp, but there was none. I took a sleeping pill, but I would not call the next several hours restful as I lay with my eyes closed. My mind raced. What would it be like to spend a full year here? How do I show reverence for those who did? What were the real dangers? Suppose the commanding general caught me using his toilet? Did anyone understand this war? Why was 12 percent of the U.S. troop presence in an area with less than one percent of the population? What did protecting the population mean here?

During the night, Jones said he had read Gordon Goldstein's book about the Vietnam War, *Lessons in Disaster*, and reached Lesson Three on page 97, "Politics Is the Enemy of Strategy." Goldstein records how President Johnson's focus on winning the 1964 election blotted out any urgency to reconsider the American strategy in Vietnam. "The preemptive concern: win, win, win the election, not the war," recalled Johnson's then national security adviser, McGeorge Bundy.

Some 9,000 Marines, which included forces that President Obama ordered into the war, had built Camp Leatherneck across a hardscrabble plain where there had been desert six months earlier. It is a sprawling encampment of small and large tent-style facilities, canopied warehouses and fenced-in storage areas in the middle of a desolate wilderness 370 miles from the capital of Kabul.

In the morning, the commander, Brigadier General Lawrence Nicholson, a compact and small-framed Marine, stood outside the tents with Jones and several others.

I joined them, and I will never forget what happened next.

"We lost a Marine last night," Nicholson said with stoic regret.

There was a long silence.

Corporal Matthew Lembke, age 22, from Tualatin, Oregon, had both his legs blown off by an improvised explosive device (IED) while on patrol in Now Zad, a ghost town in Helmand that had been abandoned three years earlier. Taliban fighters, land mines and the howls of wild dogs had replaced the 10,000 to 35,000 people who once lived there. The British troops who were previously garrisoned at the site had summarized life in Now Zad for the U.S. Marines by spray-painting onto a wall: "Welcome to Hell."

Lembke was assigned to a company of fewer than 300 that patrolled Now Zad. This was not counterinsurgency. There was no population to protect. It was an aimless stalemate in the town. I asked a number of Marines what had happened. A trusted senior civilian adviser to Nicholson said that not a single member of the Afghan National Army (ANA) had been with the Marine company. Without any Afghans, no one spoke the language, nor could anyone supply the "eyes and ears" for the patrol. "If we had several ANA in Now Zad, we might not have lost that Marine," the civilian said.

General Nicholson echoed this thought to Jones. He said in the six months that he built Camp Leatherneck and brought in the 9,000

U.S. Marines not a single additional member of the Afghan forces was assigned to him. He said he needed "Afghanistan security forces—all flavors," soldiers, police, border guards and other specialists.

Lembke was airlifted out of Afghanistan and later died at Bethesda Naval Hospital in Maryland on July 10. I can only imagine the sense of danger and uncertainty that must have accompanied Lembke and the Marines trying to patrol a ghost town when the mission is to protect and live among people who weren't there. What intelligence did they have about the danger? How many Taliban held the town? How deadly were the Taliban in Now Zad?

No one could answer these questions, which only led to additional questions. Had the military thought through its plan? Did they know what they were doing? This led to the hardest questions of all: What about Corporal Lembke's sacrifice? What did it mean in terms of the overall war effort?

The Oregon governor honored Lembke by ordering the flags at public institutions to be flown at half-mast. Lembke was the 104th Oregonian to die in the Iraq and Afghanistan wars.*

Later that morning, Nicholson led Jones into a makeshift air-conditioned command headquarters for a 30-minute briefing. Nicholson and his senior staff, 20 Marine colonels and lieutenant colonels, arrayed themselves around a table made of new unfinished plywood about the size of three Ping-Pong tables.

Nicholson said that he was fully committed to a protect-the-population counterinsurgency campaign in which "killing the enemy is secondary" and the death of one innocent Afghan could result in the loss of support from an entire village.

"We don't have enough forces to go everywhere," he said, and overall he was "a little light," more than hinting that he could use more troops.

---

*Five months later, December 4, 2009, about 1,000 U.S. Marines, British and Afghan troops swept into Now Zad—a tacit acknowledgment perhaps that back in June the U.S. command did not know the extent of the danger and problem in that village in the rugged valley. On the first day of the offensive into Now Zad, no U.S., British or Afghan deaths were reported, but several Taliban were killed.

"At a table much like this," Jones began, referring without irony to the polished wood table in the White House Situation Room, "the president's principals met and agreed to recommend 17,000 more troops for Afghanistan."

Obama approved that recommendation in February during the first full month of his presidency, Jones reminded them. The deployments included Nicholson's Marines.

Soon after that, Jones said, the principals such as Clinton, Gates and Mullen told the president "oops," we need an additional 4,000 to help train the Afghan National Army.

"They then said, 'If you do all that, we think we can turn this around,'" Jones said, reminding the Marines in front of him how quickly the president approved and publicly announced the additional 4,000.

Now suppose you're the president, Jones said, and the requests come into the White House for yet more troops? How do you think President Obama might look at this? Jones asked, casting his eyes around the colonels in their combat camouflage uniforms. How do you think he might feel?

This question was being asked by someone who was not only the president's national security adviser but also a former Marine commandant.

It was an unusual question. Jones let it hang in the air-conditioned chill and bright fluorescent light. Nicholson and the colonels kept their poker faces, perhaps realizing that Jones was there to answer his own question. Sitting on the side, I thought I probably had never seen so many maintain expressionless stares for so long.

Well, Jones said, after all those additional troops, 17,000 plus 4,000 more, if there were more requests for forces now the president would quite likely have "a Whiskey Tango Foxtrot moment." Everyone in the room caught the reference to the acronym WTF—which in the military and elsewhere means "What the fuck?"—the universal outburst of astonishment and anger.

Nicholson and his 20 colonels sat riveted. Jones had taken them inside the White House to offer a brief glimpse of the commander in chief's perspective. Nearly all were veterans of Iraq and they seemed to blanch at the explicit message that this might be all the troops they were going to get.

It was easy to imagine the dismay that might be conveyed by a "What the fuck?" eruption from the quintessentially calm 47-year-old commander in chief, a man without military experience.

But in case the message was unclear, Jones said that Afghanistan was not Iraq. "We are not going to build that empire again," he said flatly.

Jones met privately with McChrystal, delivering Whiskey Tango Foxtrot in a slightly less confrontational way for the commanding general.

"Put yourself in the president's place," Jones said. "What would you think if you heard all of this coming up in different—public, private, media—forums? This doesn't make sense."

The national security adviser felt the military had already had its opportunity to give its advice during the Riedel review. Not much had changed with regard to the intelligence since then.

McChrystal said Afghanistan was much worse than he had expected. His 60-day assessment would be highly critical. There are good reasons to be concerned, McChrystal warned, and if the situation is not reversed soon, it might be irreversible.

Jones asked politely if McChrystal could provide specific examples that backed up his statements.

McChrystal ran down a litany of problems.

"The number of Taliban in the country is higher than anything I thought," McChrystal said. "There are 25,000."

That figure intrigued Jones. When he had gone to Afghanistan in 2003 as NATO commander, the estimated size of the Taliban was 4,000. Jones concluded that the reason for the substantial growth was the 2006 treaty between Pakistan and its tribes, which cut out a large swath of Pakistan where new Taliban recruits could train without interference.

Graphs of insurgent attacks also reinforced what McChrystal was saying. The number of attacks was approaching 550 a week and had nearly doubled within the past month. IED incidents were also spiking. The roadside bombs were on a pace to kill 50 coalition troops a month, compared to just eight a month at the same point last year.

But Jones remained somewhat skeptical. He wondered if McChrystal was giving the initial response of any brand-new four-star who was flexing his muscles. Jones had anticipated that might be the case, so he simply wanted to impart to McChrystal what the landscape was like in Washington. It was unfriendly to generals asking for more troops.

The new strategy, Jones said repeatedly during the course of the trip, has three legs, each of which he said had to be dramatically improved: 1. Security; 2. Economic development and reconstruction; and 3. Governance by the Afghans under the rule of law.

There had been an imbalance with too much emphasis on the military, he said. Economic development and improved governance by the Afghans needed full attention.

"This will not be won by the military alone," Jones said. "We tried that for six years." He also said, "The piece of the strategy that has to work in the next year is economic development. If that is not done right, there are not enough troops in the world to succeed." The plea for a focus on the long-range efforts to build the government and the economy seemed to be met with shrugs by the military.

Jones heard repeatedly the complaint that Afghanistan and particularly its leader, President Karzai, had not mobilized sufficiently for their own war.

He emphasized that it was a new era, and Obama would not automatically give the military commanders whatever force levels they requested—a frequent practice of former President Bush in the Iraq War.

But Jones said, "The president realizes it's on the razor's edge," suggesting not only a difficult, dangerous time, but a situation that could cut either way. "And he's worried that others don't."

•   •   •

It is 25 minutes by helicopter from Camp Leatherneck to Lashkar Gah, the capital of Helmand province, where Jones met with the leaders of a Provincial Reconstruction Team (PRT), a unit of about 160 British, U.S., Afghan and other civilians and military officers attempting to rebuild the economy, improve security, and foster a responsive and effective government.

The PRT resembled a fortress. Before getting out of the helicopters we were advised to wear protective body armor. Most donned flak jackets and hustled toward the compound, ducking behind buildings to avoid sniper fire. We walked at the fastest clip possible without breaking into a full sprint.

In a meeting, the PRT leaders told Jones that there had been 58 IED attacks during the last week in the province. They stressed that the biggest problem was "Afghan capacity" because the Karzai government was not really committed.

"The only way we will make security work here is to have this gated community," one of the British team leaders told Jones. "More Afghan National Security Force, army and police, is a lot more important than more U.S. troops. If we go into an area without Afghans of any sort, then all they think is here come the Russians again." But the inherent contradiction was that the successful development of Afghan capacity "can only be delivered by the United States."

Jones said President Obama wanted a strategy designed to reduce the U.S. involvement and commitment. The president didn't think Afghanistan should only be an American war, but there had been a tendency to Americanize it. "We didn't consult, we didn't ask, we didn't listen," Jones said of the attitude toward other countries supplying troops. "We basically said, stand aside, we know how to do this. And we and the Brits will do this. The rest of you don't even play. You French guys stay over there. The Germans, you won't fight, so we don't need you." Several in the room laughed at the mention of the Germans. "So what we've tried to do is rebalance the relationships, make people feel like they are contributing, even a small amount, but to make them feel like they're valued and respected. We all know who's going to do the bulk of the work."

Nonetheless, the British leader of the PRT said the key to progress in Helmand was provincial governor Gulab Mangal, who over the previous 15 months had moved on nearly all fronts to modernize, improve governance and reduce corruption.

The British had identified what they call "the golden 500"—government and other officials, beginning with Mangal, they wanted to stay in their positions in Helmand province.

Reliable information in the hands of the U.S. and British showed that President Karzai planned to replace Governor Mangal with a crony of questionable administrative and anti-corruption credentials. To ensure his reelection, one official said, Karzai was cutting deals with a number of unsavory Afghan politicians.

Jones promised to intervene personally with Karzai. As a first step, he called in about a dozen Afghan reporters and sat down on a couch outside the PRT headquarters next to Governor Mangal for a press conference. He praised Mangal, 52, a soft-spoken leader with charcoal-colored hair and a trimmed beard, and said, "I know of no place in Afghanistan that has more potential."

We then flew to Islamabad and stayed two nights at the ambassador's residence, a large and comfortable home. Anne Patterson, a 60-year-old career Foreign Service officer appointed in 2007 by Bush, was a favorite of Obama because, as acting ambassador to the United Nations in 2005, she had done an exceptional job hosting a visit by the then senator. A small, forthright woman, she gave a candid private assessment of the situation. "I worry that all of this is just going to blow up. Zardari doesn't know anything about governing. He will never get out from being Mr. Benazir Bhutto, but he's basically on our side."

Jones met next afternoon with President Zardari, and I joined them for the last 15 minutes. Zardari sat between two photographs of his late wife—one of her campaigning, the other a pensive close-up. His black hair was pomaded to his scalp and his suit had the smart cut of an expensive tailor. He beamed with a wide smile that appeared whenever I asked troubling questions. Zardari acknowledged the influence of the Taliban in Pakistan and said, "It is a thin line to walk with the Taliban. We must walk in small steps."

On relations with India, he took pride in what he deemed a significant liberalizing moment. "I've allowed Indian movies for the first time."

I asked what had caused him over the past six months to view the Taliban as a lethal threat to Pakistan and its government. Zardari claimed this was not a recent transformation for him.

"I've been fighting terrorism for 30 years," said Zardari, who had spent eight years in jail on charges of corruption and the alleged murder of his brother-in-law. "Khalid Sheik Mohammed [the mastermind of the 9/11 attacks] tried to assassinate my wife."

Afterward, Jones and his staff debated whether they should worry more about Pakistan or Afghanistan. Several members of his staff said the chief problem was Pakistan—Zardari's political vulnerability, the continuing dominance of the country's military-intelligence complex, its nuclear weapons, the persistent presence of al Qaeda training camps in the ungoverned regions, and the possibility of a misstep with the CIA drone attacks that could dramatically shift the political calculus.

Jones said that the problem is Afghanistan. That's where the U.S. troops were, approaching 68,000 total, and a presence of that size engaged in combat operations would always be the center of gravity. Afghanistan's troubles were compounded by what he called "the Karzai problem," adding, "He doesn't get it, or he doesn't want to get it." He said that at best Karzai was "mayor of Kabul," and the reach of the national government did not extend much farther than the capital, other than to promote, encourage and facilitate corruption.

"We haven't been tough enough on him, given the sacrifice in lives that we are making," Jones said.

Jones thought that there was another group that President Obama was not tough enough on—his senior White House political advisers, whom he saw as major obstacles to developing and deciding on a coherent policy. This group included Emanuel, Axelrod, press secretary Robert Gibbs, and the two former Senate operatives now placed in the

NSC—Denis McDonough and Mark Lippert. He privately called them "the water bugs," the "Politburo," the "Mafia," or the "campaign set."

"There are too many senior aides around the president," Jones said privately. "They're like water bugs. They flit around. Rahm gets an idea at 10 A.M. and wants a briefing by 4 P.M., and I will say no" because the work can't be done in a day. The water bugs did not understand war or foreign relations, Jones felt, and were too interested in measuring the short-term political impact of the president's decisions in these areas.

He would invite them to strategy briefings on some of these matters but more often than not they didn't show. When he talked with them, they would often invoke Obama, saying, "The president wants this, the president wants that."

At one point, Jones had told Emanuel, "You have enough juice to say it on your own." In the military, the number two to the commander is not supposed to use the boss as the cover for his orders. He is supposed to establish enough authority to issue orders on his own. But Emanuel and the others continued to invoke the president.

Worse for Jones, he often felt sidelined by Emanuel, who would regularly come to the national security adviser's suite and see his deputy, Donilon. So Jones told Emanuel, "I'm the national security adviser. When you come down there, come see me." It got better for a short time, but the practice of visiting only Donilon soon started up again. Jones hadn't realized what a clique the White House was. He concluded that if he had understood that dynamic when he was picking a deputy, he never in a million years would have gone with Donilon.

Jones also was unsure about Gates. The defense secretary tended to hang back, figure out which way decisions were going, where everyone else, including the president, was leaning and then jump that way. So his comments seemed a studied calculation of the likely outcome. The trademark skepticism was often a cover to delay taking a stand.

At first Jones had had a positive impression of Secretary Clinton, but then there was the Zinni incident. Early in the administration, Clinton was looking for somebody to be the ambassador to Iraq.

"Why not Tony Zinni?" Jones proposed. Anthony Zinni was a retired four-star Marine general, like Jones, former Central Command commander (from 1997 to 2000), and later an outspoken critic of the 2003 invasion of Iraq. Jones and Zinni were close friends.

Clinton thought it was a good idea, had an excellent interview with Zinni, and it looked like it was going to happen. Zinni thought he had been offered the job when she told her assistant, "Let's get the paperwork moving." Obama liked the idea and Biden called Zinni to congratulate him, but nothing was announced for several days, so Jones asked Clinton about the status.

"Oh," she said, "we decided on Chris Hill," a former Bush negotiator with North Korea.

"Has anyone told Tony Zinni?" asked Jones.

All he got was a blank look, so Jones called Zinni, who unloaded on his old friend, telling him, "Stick it where the sun don't shine." Jones mentioned the possibility of the ambassadorship to Saudi Arabia, and Zinni blew up even more.

Jones told the president how distressed he was. "We decided and it didn't happen. It changed. No one called Zinni to tell him." It appeared no one was in charge of the process or coordinating it. "It was just chaotic," Jones said. "This has essentially destroyed an important friendship I had."

But the real offense by the water bugs took place during the president's first European trip in March. Jones was on the trip and asked to see the president. "My access was cut off," he said. One of the water bugs said no. Jones couldn't believe it. He was humiliated. Here they were in Europe and the national security adviser couldn't talk to the president?

Jones complained to Emanuel and explained what had happened. He was offended at the personal slight. As a matter of process, it was malfeasance for someone to block the main foreign policy coordinator for the president from advising the president anytime, let alone when the president was abroad. Jones almost threatened to quit, but instead brought up the subject directly with the president.

"This has got to stop," Jones said.

The president calmed him down and promised, "We'll take care of it."

The situation improved with everyone but one—Mark Lippert, his NSC chief of staff and someone so close to Obama that he was like a favored younger brother.

Jones was convinced that Lippert was trying to derail his role in the Obama administration. But the matter would have to wait while Jones built his case that Lippert was engaged in a massive campaign of leaking, regularly providing criticism and derogatory information to other NSC staffers and the media about Jones and his performance as national security adviser.

Back from Afghanistan, Jones reported to the president that the situation was puzzling. There was a disconnect between what they had been told for the past several months and what General McChrystal was now seeing.

"I wasn't sure what was going on," Jones said. "I wasn't sure on the eve of one commander's departure and another one coming in how things could be so catastrophically different."

On the question of how many troops were needed, Jones told Obama, "The jury is still out on this." It might not matter how many troops were added unless the other legs of the stool—economic development and Afghan governance—accompanied them, he said. Without those other elements, Afghanistan would simply gobble up additional troops.

A few days after returning from Afghanistan, I published a front-page story in *The Washington Post* on Wednesday, July 1. The news value of what had occurred was obvious. I was sure the military would not give up on requests for more troops, no matter what Jones had told the generals in Afghanistan.

Headlined, "Key in Afghanistan: Economy, Not Military: Preventing Another Iraq," the article, datelined from Camp Leatherneck, said that Jones had told the U.S. military commanders on the ground that "the Obama administration wants to hold troop levels here flat for now and focus" on a strategy of economic development, improved governance and increased Afghan participation.

The second paragraph said, "The message seems designed to cap expectations that more troops might be coming, though the administration has not ruled out additional deployments in the future." It reported in detail Jones's warning that a request for more troops would likely give President Obama a "Whiskey Tango Foxtrot" moment.

The sixth paragraph stated: "The question of the force level for Afghanistan, however, is not settled and will probably be hotly debated over the next year. One senior military officer said privately that the United States would have to deploy a force of more than 100,000 to execute the counterinsurgency strategy of holding areas and towns after clearing out the Taliban insurgents. That is at least 32,000 more than the 68,000 currently authorized."

In the Oval Office that morning, the president told Jones, Axelrod and several others that it was the precise message he wanted to convey. As far as he was concerned, they had just started to implement the Riedel review and talk of more troops was premature.

At the Pentagon, the reaction was radically different.

"Jim," Admiral Mullen told Jones in a phone call, "you just capped us." By "cap," Mullen meant that Jones had put a limit on how many troops the U.S. would send to Afghanistan.

"No, I didn't," Jones said.

"Bullshit," said the chairman of the Joint Chiefs of Staff.

"I don't think of it that way," Jones said. "My problem with it, as I told you before, is that I think it's not fair to the president to take the decision that he took in March, decide before you ever even got the 21,000 troops there that things are going so bad you need another 40,000 to 80,000."

"That's a cap," Mullen said, unconvinced. The admiral had some sympathy for Jones, who he felt was trying to manage the political pressures that were coming not from the president but from Emanuel, Axelrod, Lippert and Donilon.

But Jones wanted to drive the point home, so that Mullen would stop pushing for more troops until McChrystal's 60-day assessment was finished. "Stick with what you've got because the rest of it is just kind of innuendo and kind of loose talk.

"Mike," he continued, "think very hard about your role in all of this. Because you're on the record as having done certain things, recommending certain things. You got everything you wanted. Now you're on the record of going around NATO and ginning up allies before the president's even agreed on these others, whatever it is you're doing. I'll tell you as a friend, that's a risky position to be in."

Jones thought Mullen understood.

Afterward, Mullen called Petraeus.

"It's a cap," the chairman said.

When McChrystal called Mullen to inquire what the article and Jones's warning meant, the chairman made it clear.

Oh, it was a cap, he said. Clearly, the president was sending them a message. "I get that," Mullen said. "There's no question about that."

Mullen then gave an interview to Ann Scott Tyson of *The Washington Post* and claimed that it was not a cap. McChrystal had been told he had full latitude to make his assessment and say, "Here's what I need," he said. "There were no preconditions. He's been told, 'In this assessment, you come back and ask for what you need.' "

McChrystal spoke with General Lute at the NSC about the pressure on troop levels.

"Look, I haven't even put pen to paper yet in terms of my assessment," McChrystal said. He thought Jones "was on a traveling road show to go out and sort of sense this from the bottom up," not to pass on a message from the White House.

"I don't need the national security adviser coming out here and telling me what to do," McChrystal said.

At his daily briefing, press secretary Gibbs basically backed up Jones. "I think there are several hundred years of evidence that military might alone is not likely to solve all of your problems in that country," Gibbs said. "The onus is also going to have to be on the Afghans to improve their security situation." He added, "But if we don't get good governance and improvement in governance, if we don't get an increase in development and a change in the economy, I think the president and I think General Jones would agree that no amount of troops are going to leave that country in a situation that is sustainable."

Gates was upset. He told his staff that it was probably best to let him, as secretary of defense, handle these communications to the ground commanders through the military chain of command.

Geoff Morrell, the Pentagon spokesman, sent a stern e-mail to McDonough at the National Security Council that in effect said, Don't do this, leave it to Gates.

It was evident that Whiskey Tango Foxtrot was never going to stop the Pentagon and the generals. Rather, WTF was a clarion call to plan, mobilize and launch a counteroffensive. A growing divide existed between the White House and the Pentagon just four months after the Riedel review, when the president had unveiled a new strategy. In a column for *The Weekly Standard*, conservative writer Bill Kristol suggested that Jones was in over his head and that Obama was on the path of a "Whiskey Tango Foxtrot presidency."

13

During the three months after the Riedel review, General Lute was trying to shape the 3 Ds—"disrupt, dismantle and defeat"— into an actual policy for Afghanistan and Pakistan. With Riedel returned to his think tank, Lute was getting back into the game. But working from his catacomb West Wing basement office, he still felt on the outs.

Members of his shop privately described the Obama administration in Afghan terms. "Tribes" populated the presidency, reflecting its divisions. The Hillary tribe lived at the State Department. The Chicago tribe occupied Axelrod's and Emanuel's offices. The campaign tribe at the NSC—led by chief of staff Mark Lippert and strategic communications director Denis McDonough, both former Obama campaign aides—seemed to flaunt their personal relationships with the president and often circumvented Jones as the national security adviser. Lute's team dubbed them the "insurgency."

Lute had been shut out by Lippert. It was as though Lippert suspected Lute of manning a Pentagon outpost deep inside the White House. When Obama visited Iraq in April, Lippert kept Lute in the dark, practically running the trip himself from his BlackBerry.

Lute had lost Iraq from his job portfolio. The three-star Army general was no longer the war czar, having been demoted from deputy national security adviser to coordinator for Afghanistan and Pakistan.

Lute was now drafting the Strategic Implementation Plan (SIP) for executing the Riedel review. This was a chance to reassert himself in the NSC system. Lute felt the plan should correct a flaw in the Riedel review. It had been rushed, in his opinion, a crash project that failed to discuss the "means" to carry out the new Afghanistan and Pakistan strategy. What would it cost in dollars? How many troops might really be needed? How much civilian support was required to improve governance and reduce corruption? What were the timelines? The review didn't have answers. The SIP would.

By mid-July, Lute was reading the final pieces of feedback about the 40-page draft of the SIP. Gates's memo concerned him. The mission in Afghanistan could not be to "disrupt" the Taliban, Gates wrote. This needs to be "defeat."

Lute instantly grasped the magnitude of Gates's recommendation, which had been pushed by the Pentagon for months and exhibited the strong influence of Petraeus and his COINistas, the true believers in counterinsurgency. This single verb reinterpreted the whole Riedel review, broadening the narrow intention of defeating al Qaeda to include the Afghan Taliban. The review had instructed the military to conduct a comprehensive, "fully resourced" counterinsurgency in Afghanistan, but it didn't state the purpose or effects of that campaign. Was it to disrupt, dismantle or defeat the Taliban?

Defeating the Taliban would take more troops, money and time than disrupting would. "Defeat" suggested an unconditional surrender—total capitulation, victory, winning in the fullest sense of the word, utterly destroying the Taliban.

Lute thought this upped the ante. He walked upstairs to see Jones.

"I want to highlight this to you, because it is different and it's significant," he said, explaining Gates's last-minute suggestion. "Of the potential action verbs here, they're boxing, they're designing for themselves the largest mission, the most expansive mission, to defeat the Taliban."

That's not a big deal, said Jones. Verb choice didn't register with him as a first-order concern. Jones was eager to get the implementation plan out, because McChrystal was in the middle of his own review and the SIP was supposed to be his guiding light. As Jones saw it, "defeat" would get the military to take full ownership of the strategy.

Lute next went to Donilon, the deputy national security adviser, who had a more sensitive political ear than Jones.

When Donilon heard it was Gates making the bid, he too said he was okay with the change.

The classified SIP was signed by Jones and sent to the Pentagon on July 17. Paragraph 3A of the SIP began "Defeat the extremist insurgency . . ."

Lute spoke by Tandberg, the videoconference phone, with Petraeus every Tuesday and with McChrystal every Friday. Adding "defeat" pleased both generals. It precisely defined the mission. Petraeus had never gotten anything this exact for Iraq.

But back in Lute's office, one of the Afghanistan directors—one of his own tribe—noted that for a goal this extravagant they should have found an acronym that spelled out GULP instead of SIP.

There was no speech, press briefing, White House statement, news leak or public discussion of this dramatic expansion of the war aims, a classic example of mission creep. The "defeat" mandate sat there as explicit guidance for McChrystal, who as the new commander was asking his own basic questions: What are my orders? And what do I need to carry out my orders?

Richard Holbrooke, the special representative, was pessimistic about the August 20 elections in Afghanistan.

"If there are 10 possible outcomes in Afghanistan," he told the National Security Council over the summer, "nine of them are bad." Holbrooke added, "They range from civil war to irregularities."

But in public, Holbrooke downplayed his concerns, saying at a news conference that he wasn't "unduly upset" by complaints about Afghan voter registration. He then compared the Afghan presidential race to the litigation-prone 2008 Minnesota Senate election, as if to say all political contests had their problems.

As soon as the Afghan polls closed on August 20, there were widespread reports of fraud. Many State Department and U.N. officials in Kandahar had not left their quarters to visit polling centers out of security concerns. Insurgent attacks did not stop the national election, but some international monitors noted that many of the troops added by Obama in February, ostensibly for election security, had deployed to Helmand province, where a sliver of voters lived. The Afghan National Police barred one group of monitors from checking the tallies in Kandahar, the city controlled by Karzai's half-brother, Ahmed Wali. A major backer of one failed presidential candidate lamented to a monitor, "The only reaction to this election is to buy an automatic rifle and prepare for war."

The day after the election, August 21, Holbrooke and Ambassador Eikenberry went to see Karzai in Kabul. The first three hours went fine, until they turned to the future and what life might be like for Karzai if he was reelected.

"Well, I have been reelected," Karzai said.

Eikenberry and Holbrooke noted that all the votes had not yet been counted.

It was settled, Karzai said, it was over.

"Mr. President," Holbrooke said, "what would you do if there was a runoff?" Under the Afghan constitution, if no one received at least 50 percent of the vote, the top two candidates would have to stand in another election.

"That's not possible," Karzai said, his mood darkening. "I know what the people chose. No one wants a runoff. No one. And no one believes in a runoff. No one."

"Mr. President," Holbrooke said, "we're not saying we want it. I just want to know, if no one gets to 50 percent, will you be okay with that? Will you do a runoff?"

"It is not possible," Karzai said.

After the meeting, Karzai called the State Department operations center and said he wanted to talk to Secretary of State Clinton or President Obama.

The president, who was vacationing on Martha's Vineyard, got word of this and reached Eikenberry by secure phone.

"Mr. President," Eikenberry said, "we had this meeting. Karzai's trying to go around us. Karzai thinks we're supporting a runoff. We're not." He explained what had happened, how Karzai had become defensive, insisting a runoff was impossible. "I recommend strongly you not take the call."

Obama agreed. He would stay out of it. Eikenberry and Holbrooke should continue to try to handle Karzai.

Two days later, Eikenberry, Holbrooke and General McChrystal had dinner with Karzai.

"Mr. President," Eikenberry said, "you're not going to talk to the president or the secretary of state. Just not going to. I recommended against it, and here's why. You misunderstood our position. We are not supporting a runoff." The United States was supporting the Afghan constitutional process—whether there is a first-round victory or a runoff. "And that's our position."

The intelligence showed that Karzai was increasingly delusional and paranoid. Even Karzai's own people were telling that to Eikenberry and Holbrooke.

"You guys are opposing me," Karzai answered. "It's a British-American plot."

In August, I asked my assistant Josh Boak, a former *Chicago Tribune* reporter, to conduct background interviews with members of General McChrystal's strategy review team who had recently returned from Afghanistan. We wanted to find out what was happening on the ground. How was the war going? What was working? What wasn't?

The idea behind the team had come in part from Petraeus's 2007 playbook for Iraq. Bring Ph.D. and other think tank experts into a war zone to assess the situation, just as a troubled corporation might hire outside consultants. Part of the strategy was public relations. As scholars at the Brookings Institution, the Center for Strategic and International Studies, the Council on Foreign Relations, the RAND Corporation and elsewhere, these experts regularly churn out books, position papers and op-ed pieces that could help explain any changes in strategy to the public. And once the team's weeks-long stint in Afghanistan ended, individual members could continue to advise the war effort as "Afghan Hands." The 14-person team also included European researchers, military officers and a Pentagon representative.

It was an experienced group of analysts who were willing to challenge the assumptions of high-ranking generals. Josh interviewed half a dozen of them on background to get a sense of what they were seeing on the ground and what they were advising McChrystal (see chapter notes for a list of team members).

McChrystal's staff had hastily organized the review team in June. One member admitted that signing on was an embarrassing confession to the rest of Washington—a city that values being overly busy— of having a blank calendar. Others frantically rearranged their summer schedules.

Many had been to Afghanistan before, yet few felt they had seen the country as it truly was. Their visits were largely confined to military bases, military transports and military PowerPoint slides.

In a windowless conference room at his headquarters in Kabul on June 25, McChrystal gave the team three guiding questions for their review: Is the mission achievable; if so, what needs to be changed to accomplish the mission; and are more resources necessary to complete the mission?

McChrystal told the group to be pragmatic and focus on things that would actually work. He came across as open-minded, one team member said. The four-star general had previously commanded U.S. Special Forces, leading missions into Afghanistan and Iraq that wiped out terrorists and insurgents. He seemed to have arrived at a counterinsurgency strategy by trial and error, after learning firsthand that America could not simply kill its way out of the war.

The review team traveled across Afghanistan on a fixed-wing aircraft over the next several days, visiting cities and bases in the southern and eastern regional commands.

They found that the military understood relatively little about the Afghan people. It could not measure how the Taliban's propaganda campaign of fear and intimidation affected the population. McChrystal could order a counterinsurgency strategy, but many of the soldiers from the 42-nation coalition lived on bases designed to isolate them from average Afghans. The intelligence collection was in shambles. "We could already be losing Kandahar," one team member said, "but we don't know it because we don't have enough contact with the population to know what the hell is going on in the city."

A counterinsurgency plan, in theory, also involved deploying civilian specialists, who as a whole did not exist, at least not in numbers that could be sent to Afghanistan. The specialists had to be passably fluent in Afghan languages such as Dari and Pashto, or discover a reservoir of native translators that billions of dollars and thousands of soldiers had yet to divine. It required a total immersion in Afghan society and tribes. "The kind of COIN doctrine that they're talking about requires a level of local knowledge that I don't have about my hometown," one member said.

The team discovered that some 70 percent of the intelligence requirements were enemy-centric, and some experts said that they had to widen the aperture to focus on the people they wanted to protect. Who are they? Who are their leaders? What do they really want? Security? Jobs? To be left alone?

One senior member said, "What kind of message does it send to the Afghans when Americans are not allowed to travel on foot through an allegedly safe Kabul and the Italians cannot walk on foot through Herat?"

On top of all that, the war was increasingly Americanized. NATO had grown into a fig leaf that gave the cover of an international effort. A team member asked the Dutch commander in the south if the Americans might ask his troops to stay past their scheduled 2010 withdrawal date. "When we told them we were leaving, they said, 'Thank you for your service,' " Dutch Major General Mart de Kruif recalled, as if their departure was welcome.

Some on the review team figured the war could be fully American-ized in a year or two. The last thing U.S. generals wanted was more NATO forces wandering through Afghanistan, requesting air support to attack suspicious-looking Afghans. The Americans would prefer that the NATO allies provided money and trainers for the Afghan se-curity forces.

At the first interim progress review on July 4, the team told McChrystal nothing but bad news. We could run the finest counterin-surgency campaign in world history and still fail because of the weak and corrupt Afghan government, several members concluded.

McChrystal looked as if he'd been hit by a train. "Thanks so much for that," he said.

The general claimed that the U.S. could beat the Taliban with one hand tied behind its back. But the enemy was not the problem, pro-tecting the people was. That's why several team members stressed the importance of intelligence about the population.

The U.S. and its allies must not accidentally kill civilians, even when air strikes were appropriate under the rules of engagement, McChrys-tal said. A smart tactical move that killed an innocent civilian would be a strategic mistake.

"You may be technically right and long-term stupid," McChrystal said.

The next day, the team flew to Herat, the western regional com-mand overseen by the Italian army. From past visits, some on the team knew that the restaurant on base served an amazing lobster risotto. The Italians had sent an Afghan chef to culinary school back in their home country and were flying in the lobsters. The Italians might have been in Afghanistan, but against the principles of counterinsurgency they refused to be of Afghanistan.

The Italian commanding general, Rosario Castellano, an ebullient, muscled paratrooper, told the team his thoughts about McChrystal's inquisitive nature.

"This McChrystal," Castellano said, "he asks these questions. He asks me my name. I say Rosario Castellano. This McChrystal, he asks me, 'Why?' " The new commander questioned everything.

But for the most part, the team seldom got satisfactory answers to its questions. When they asked Castellano how he would use additional troops, the Italian general struggled for 10 minutes and then replied, "This is a silly question."

NATO allies could help train and teach the Afghan police and army, but the impression was that many of the European armies stationed in Afghanistan had not expected to be in combat.

It became painfully obvious how removed the International Security Assistance Force (ISAF), McChrystal's command, was from Afghans the next day in the northern region. Stuck in armored vehicles, the team could only catch periscope-like glimpses of Mazar-i-Sharif's streets through four inches of bulletproof glass and a two-inch-by-four-inch window.

The team was similarly sheltered in Kabul. They stayed in a contractors' compound guarded by Nepalese Gurkhas. The British transported them in two armored Toyota Land Cruisers. Under orders of the British government, they wore body armor, even for the 15-minute ride to ISAF headquarters. McChrystal, despite being the most powerful man in Afghanistan, did not have the authority to tell the British sergeant in charge of the convoy that team members didn't have to put on body armor. Only the British did. It was a sovereignty issue.

The Toyotas raced around Kabul. The drivers honked their horns rather than step on the brakes, madly changing lanes, swerving through traffic and accelerating at every opportunity. The theory was that erratic driving reduced the chances of a roadside attack. Afghans who didn't jump out of the way could be plowed down. After one of the SUVs ran a bicyclist off the road, Andrew Exum, a fellow at the Center for a New American Security and a former U.S. Army Ranger, asked the driver, "What are you doing, man?"

"You can't be too careful. Could've been a bomb, sir," was the response. But this kind of commute left Afghans on the street visibly angry. The team could see how an emphasis on force protection was causing the coalition to lose the Afghan people. Exum wrote a one-pager for McChrystal about aggressive driving and armored vehicles entitled "Touring Afghanistan by Submarine."

McChrystal soon became the chief traffic cop and issued a written directive to all his troops in the theater "to drive in ways that respect the safety and well-being of the Afghan people."

The commanding general seemed to stay calm despite the daily frustrations. If a subordinate officer flubbed briefings at morning updates, he refused to yell as other generals might have. McChrystal did not consider a drop or increase in Taliban attacks to be a reliable measure of progress. During one conversation about a troublesome province, the review team's well-respected coordinator, Army Colonel Chris Kolenda, noted, "You know, sir, violence dropped 90 percent when my battalion was there."

"Chris, violence dropped 90 percent when General Lee surrendered at Appomattox," McChrystal responded.

One outspoken member of the team believed McChrystal should not base his strategy on "what ifs" and "if onlys" as the U.S. had appeared to be doing. What if we increase Afghan forces? If only we can reform Karzai . . . If only we can improve agriculture . . . What if we secure the ring road around the country?

Such an approach was not reality-based. "It was hope-based, which is to say, in wartime, illusion-based," a team member explained to Josh, my assistant.

Some of the team encouraged McChrystal to bargain with the White House, to come in high. But McChrystal was not interested in that. He was prepared to say, as a team member outlined it, "This is what I need. If you don't give it to me, here are the risks. And if you don't give it to me, I won't resign, but I might not win."

The Pentagon received McChrystal's classified assessment of the Afghanistan War on Monday, August 31. Secretary of Defense Gates was responsible for giving a copy to the president. The document was so sensitive that even members of the review team who had helped draft parts of it and held security clearances could not obtain a copy.

Senior Pentagon and administration officials who were familiar with the substance of the report provided a basic overview for newspaper articles printed the next day. *The Washington Post* called the report "a sobering assessment" that is "expected to pave the way for a request for more American troops." *The New York Times* warned, "An expanded American footprint would also increase Mr. Obama's entanglement with an Afghan government widely viewed as corrupt and illegitimate." But the meaning of the report was interpreted and sifted for journalists by their sources. The actual assessment remained confidential, deepening the mystery as to whether the characterizations were fully accurate. What did it actually say?

Mullen revered McChrystal, and had made him director of the Joint Staff—his previous assignment—in part so that the Senate confirmation could wipe away the role McChrystal had played in the cover-up of the 2004 friendly-fire death in Afghanistan of Corporal Pat Tillman, who had left the NFL to be an Army Ranger. McChrystal had signed off on the Silver Star recommendation that suggested Tillman had been killed by the enemy, a choice he regretted.

The issue resurfaced during McChrystal's confirmation hearings for ISAF. McChrystal assured the Senate Armed Services Committee that he had recommended the Silver Star with the best of intentions, but he had been too hasty in the investigative process. "What we have learned since is, it is better to take your time, make sure you get everything right with the award, and not rush it," he told the committee.

When McChrystal's assessment came in, Mullen embraced it.

"Are you worried that you are too invested in McChrystal?" asked Navy Captain John Kirby, Mullen's special assistant for public affairs. Did it appear that the chairman was too pro-McChrystal? "Are you losing your objectivity?" pressed Kirby, who had been with Mullen for the last 10 years. His job was to make sure some of the tough questions got addressed before they were raised in the media. "Suppose you're wrong, and he fails?"

"Then," Mullen replied, "I've got to leave because I put him there."

•   •   •

In August, members of the Senate Armed Services Committee—Senators McCain, Lindsey Graham, Joseph Lieberman and Susan Collins—went for the standard congressional recess tour of the Afghanistan war zone.

McChrystal told them that President Obama wanted to choose from options A, B and C. And that's what he would get, the general explained.

"There's only one option the president should consider," McCain said, "and that's the winning option." This business of multiple options was crap. "Don't water this down. Stand your ground. You go into the president, just tell him, 'Here's how you win.' "

No, McChrystal said, he would provide options.

"You're getting political pressure," McCain said. "They are putting you under political pressure?"

"No," McChrystal said. "I can say what I want."

But McCain would not hear of it. He smelled political pressure coming from the White House.

McChrystal insisted that wasn't so. He walked the senators through how he could use six or seven brigades more, explaining where and how he might deploy them.

Graham was piecing the puzzle together. It was clear that McChrystal was coming in with an assessment that was grim and he was asking for substantially more troops—seven brigades meant tens of thousands of troops, depending on how the enablers were counted.

Graham stayed behind for about 10 days to serve his reserve time as Colonel Graham, though everyone knew his day job. McChrystal briefed him some more, as did the generals with the 82nd Airborne in Regional Command West and the Marines in the south. The briefings troubled Graham. He heard al Qaeda mentioned only once, causing him afterward to write a strong memo and talk with Petraeus and McChrystal.

Their messaging strategy was a disaster, Graham said. "America is worried about al Qaeda attacking," but their briefings were all about the insurgent Taliban. "Americans understand that Taliban are bad guys, but what drives the American psyche more than anything is, are we about to let the country that attacked us once attack us twice? And your briefings have absolutely no emphasis on al Qaeda. This is a huge mistake."

The briefings soon changed. Al Qaeda became part of the regular message.

McChrystal passed word to Gates that he was going to need 40,000 more troops. Gates was stunned. He had been at the CIA in the late 1970s and the 1980s when the Soviets invaded and occupied Afghanistan with 110,000 troops. He was a Soviet specialist and noted that with the advantage of no restraints and no rules of engagement to protect innocent Afghans the Soviets had been unable to win. They had ruthlessly killed perhaps 1 million Afghans, driven millions more from the country and almost destroyed Afghanistan. How could adding more U.S. troops, essentially duplicating the Soviet numbers, get the job done? he asked McChrystal.

The general said his forces would protect the people and demonstrate they were in Afghanistan to help. The Petraeus model from Iraq could be applied to Afghanistan.

After long discussions, Gates found the argument very compelling. "I'll get you as many troops as I can for as long as I can," the secretary told McChrystal. "And you've got battle space over there, and I've got battle space over here." He would have to fight in Washington to get the troops, but he made it clear he would support McChrystal's request for 40,000.

14

Petraeus read a September 2 column by David Ignatius, a columnist for *The Washington Post* and the author of several well-crafted spy novels. He had spent many hours with Ignatius, a skilled reporter who traveled to Iraq, Afghanistan and other hot spots regularly, often with senior military, including Petraeus.

But what was this? Petraeus read an unwelcome headline, "A Middle Way on Afghanistan?" Ignatius trotted out the line that this could be "Obama's Vietnam." He cited the difficulties the British Empire had had despite "all its troops, wealth and imperial discipline." But worse, Ignatius took a swipe at Petraeus's counterinsurgency strategy. "There is little hard evidence that it will work in a country as large and impoverished as Afghanistan. Even in Iraq, the successes attributed to counterinsurgency came as much from bribing tribal leaders and assassinating insurgents." Obama's decision on Afghanistan would amount to a "roll of the dice."

Petraeus was incredulous. In the fight for the hearts and minds of the American public—and the president—the message war was a deadly serious competition. The best way to counter Ignatius was to call the competition, so Petraeus phoned another *Post* columnist, Michael Gerson. He later claimed he was unaware that Gerson had been the chief speechwriter for President George W. Bush and the celebrated author of some of Bush's most saber-rattling post-9/11 speeches.

Rebutting Ignatius's critique, Petraeus told Gerson that adding troops for "a fully resourced, comprehensive counterinsurgency campaign" was the only way. There was no guarantee, he said, the war strategy "will work out even if we apply a lot more resources. But it won't work out if we don't." In no uncertain terms, Petraeus was saying the war would be unsuccessful if the president held back on troops.

Obama and several of his staffers were furious. It angered Obama that Petraeus was publicly lobbying and prejudging a presidential decision. Bush's former speechwriter must be a go-to guy for Petraeus, already suspect as a "Bush General." As far as Obama was concerned, there were two times in recent history when a president faced major decisions on war—LBJ in 1965 when the Vietnam generals asked for escalation and 2003 when President Bush decided to invade Iraq. Both presidents had failed to drill down into the reasoning, the alternatives and the full consequences. Obama was determined not to repeat that mistake, and a preemptive strike in the public relations war by General Petraeus was distressing.

Denis McDonough read the Gerson column and understood the president's frustration. He thought of how much easier it had been to maintain message consistency in the presidential campaign, where there were fewer players in the know and everyone was united by the goal of electing Obama. McDonough e-mailed Colonel Erik Gunhus, Petraeus's spokesman, to express his irritation. Strategy and resource issues were precisely what the president wanted to debate and consider. It was not helpful to have the combatant commander pontificating in a newspaper about what the strategy must be and the certainty of defeat without the addition of a lot more troops.

Petraeus figured all presidents had a protective inner circle. Before Petraeus had appeared on Sunday morning TV shows, Axelrod participated in a conference call to help shape what the general would say. The suggestions by Obama's senior adviser were often unsophisticated and political. Petraeus told one of his senior aides that he disliked talking with Axelrod, whom he called "a complete spin doctor."

OBAMA'S WARS 159

The general felt as though he had been relegated to the bench by the president. Use me, Petraeus wanted to tell Obama. Use me. Make me part of the team. At one point, he had told Emanuel, "Rahm, I want to win. I can be your lead sled dog here."

"Yeah, okay," Emanuel said. "We're all in this together."

Geoff Morrell, the Pentagon spokesman, weighed in after the Gerson piece, telling Petraeus to stay quiet. The White House was upset because it looked like the generals were trying to box in the president. Morrell asked to be the military's single point of contact for all media interviews, effectively forbidding Petraeus from appearing on the Sunday morning television talk shows anymore. So Petraeus went to ground, but in his ongoing back-channel dialogue with Senator Lindsey Graham he hinted that the South Carolina Republican and some other pro-military senators ought to weigh in publicly.

On the evening of Saturday, September 12, Vice President Biden sat on Air Force Two, studying his notes about Afghanistan and Pakistan. The vice president had flown to Los Angeles to raise funds at a Beverly Hills luncheon for Senator Barbara Boxer and, separately, eulogize two firefighters who had died in the recent California wildfires.

Joining him was Tony Blinken, his national security adviser, so that they could prepare for the first of several three-hour NSC sessions to discuss and debate the McChrystal assessment. Gates had proposed the meetings. The first one was scheduled for the next morning.

Biden had spent five hours hashing out an alternative to McChrystal that he dubbed "counterterrorism plus." Instead of a troop-intensive counterinsurgency, the plan focused on what he believed was the real threat—al Qaeda. Counterterrorism put an emphasis on shutting down terrorist groups by killing or capturing their leaders. Biden thought al Qaeda could be deterred from returning to Afghanistan without having to embark on the costly mission of protecting the Afghan people.

Al Qaeda, he reasoned, would always take the path of least resistance and not come back to its former home as long as:

1. The U.S. maintained at least two bases—Bagram and Kandahar—so Special Operations Forces could raid anywhere in the country;

2. The U.S. had enough manpower to control Afghan airspace, and the enemy was nowhere close to contesting that;

3. Human intelligence networks inside Afghanistan provided targeting information to Special Operations Forces; and

4. The CIA's elite, 3,000-Afghan-strong Counterterrorism Pursuit Teams (CTPT) could move freely.

Afghanistan only had to be a slightly more hostile environment for al Qaeda than Pakistan ("one Predator tougher") for them to choose not to return.

Biden was sold on counterterrorism plus. Obama needed a guide. The president had a mere four years in the Senate. Biden had 35. He believed the military could not push him around, but they could roll an inexperienced president. Biden went to Obama.

You know these guys, the president said. Go after it. "Push."

Obama later explained to me that he had encouraged the vice president to be an aggressive contrarian. "I said, Joe, I want you to say exactly what you think. And I want you to ask the toughest questions you can think of. And the reason is, is because I think the American people are best served and our troops are best served by a vigorous debate on these kinds of life-or-death issues. I wanted every argument on every side to be poked hard. And if we felt a little give there, we wanted to keep on pushing until finally you hit up against something that was incontrovertible and something that we could all agree to. And so in that sense I think Joe served an enormously useful function." At no point, Obama said, did he believe that Biden pushed too hard.

"Personal Observations on Afghanistan," Jones wrote as a heading in his black Moleskine-style notebook. The national security adviser was composing his ideas and questions for the review sessions.

"We're about to change the strategy before evaluating the product of the first decision." That was the crux of the problem. It was crazy to not evaluate the results of the Riedel strategy before making a shift, but here they were.

"Is Pakistan the main effort? Really, should it be?"

In terms of endgame, Jones wrote, "What is good enough?" Outright victory might be out of reach, so they had to find something else. In other words, don't let the perfect be the enemy of the good. Was the U.S. military aware of what good enough meant?

The U.S. had been playing an unsuccessful game of "Mother may I" with both Karzai in Afghanistan and the Pakistani leadership. The U.S. had a right to make some demands, given the investments made in lives and money. Presidents Bush and Obama had been embarrassingly tolerant for too long.

Jones was sure that the best answers, if there were any, would come from a review that adhered to the formal NSC system. Procedure and protocol mattered to the retired Marine general.

Citing the botched attempt to close Guantánamo, he had once told Obama, "Every time you go outside the box—the National Security Council process—we lose." The president seemed to agree.

"Thanks for coming in on a Sunday morning," Obama said as he gathered a small group of his most senior national security team in the Situation Room on September 13. All the main players were there, except for Petraeus, who had not been invited, and CIA Director Panetta, who DNI Blair had kept out.

Burrowed in the windowless room and its black leather seats, the group was missing part of a warm fall day. Obama had read McChrystal's 66-page classified assessment, which said that without more forces the war "will likely end in failure" in the next 12 months. It was an unnerving declaration, but he was far from convinced.

"We have no good options here," the president said, making it clear he would not automatically accept the general's, or anyone's, solution. "We need to come to this with a spirit of challenging our assumptions.

I'm a big believer in continually updating our analysis and relying on a constant feedback loop. Don't bite your tongue. Everybody needs to say what's on their mind. Lots of young men and women out there are making tremendous sacrifices."

The president turned the meeting over to Dr. Peter R. Lavoy, the deputy for analysis in the Office of the Director of National Intelligence. An expert on nuclear proliferation, Lavoy speaks Hindi, Urdu and French and has a Ph.D. in political science from Berkeley. He is the DNI's top authority on Pakistan. Such meetings usually begin with an intelligence update.

"Al Qaeda's embattled," Lavoy said. The drone attacks and other counterterrorist operations had bin Laden and his organization hurting, beleaguered but not yet finished. Al Qaeda has a tenuous foothold in Afghanistan—20 to 100 people there at the most. So Pakistan instead has become the epicenter of their fight. And because of its weakened condition, al Qaeda has grown more dependent on local extremist groups for support.

"They're the leech riding on the Taliban, and strength for the Taliban gives strength to the leech riding on it," Lavoy said. For example, the Haqqani network, a Taliban ally with compounds in Pakistan's tribal areas, is very important to al Qaeda's survival. While the Taliban and al Qaeda have different goals, their senior leadership—meaning Mullah Omar and bin Laden—probably remains pretty close. But the Taliban now needs al Qaeda less than al Qaeda needs the Taliban.

The Taliban does see itself as winning in Afghanistan, which gives a boost to al Qaeda, Lavoy continued. And as long as the Taliban believes it's winning, it also has little incentive to make peace with the Karzai government. Taliban leader Mullah Omar has a good, adaptive command structure out of Quetta, Pakistan. The whole Taliban insurgency is designed to outlast the coalition of U.S. and international troops.

Lavoy's boss, DNI Dennis Blair, stepped in to explain why the Pakistani government had not been more helpful in rooting out the different Islamic groups.

"Pakistan thinks about the U.S. role in Afghanistan in the context of its relationship with India," Blair said. It was the cliché that Pakistan's obsession with its mortal enemy, India, caused the nation to harbor terrorists.

Obama then recognized Biden, who offered a prelude to his thinking. "There's a fundamental incoherence in the strategy" for dealing with Pakistan, the vice president said. "What Pakistan doesn't want, as a matter of faith, is a unified Afghan government that is led by a Pashtun sympathetic to India" like Karzai. So for Pakistan, supporting the Taliban "is a hedge against that.

"But our policy is designed to strengthen a Karzai government and to wipe out the Taliban," Biden said, indicating that it was impossible to win over the Pakistanis completely. "My hunch," he added, "is that the Pakistanis have concluded that we cannot afford to leave" Afghanistan now. Essentially, American policy reinforces Pakistani hedging in a self-defeating cycle, causing Pakistan to aid the Afghan insurgency that the U.S. is trying to beat.

Gates then brought attention back to Lavoy, asking, "What's the impact on al Qaeda central in the region as compared to its position globally?"

"Al Qaeda is coming under pressure worldwide," Lavoy said, "so to justify its leadership role in the global jihad, it's aligning itself with this nexus of militant groups and its role" against the U.S. and NATO forces in the region "as the defining piece of its mission."

"Given it's on the defensive in the wider struggle," asked the president, reframing Lavoy's argument, "they can and are using our presence in Afghanistan as a motivation and ideological underpinning of its effort. True?"

"That's true," Lavoy answered. "Al Qaeda's goals, in order, are: one, preserve the safe haven in the FATA, and, two, advance the goals of global jihad by taking the fight to Afghanistan and Pakistan. So to do that, they question the legitimacy of the Karzai government."

Lavoy continued, "Pakistanis would prefer a Taliban government to a broad-based multiethnic government [in Afghanistan]. As long as they think the Taliban can come back, they will not break with the Taliban. They currently believe the circumstances are such that the Taliban can come back."

The analysis seemed to endorse the conclusion in McChrystal's assessment that the Taliban held the momentum.

Obama had questions he wanted answered more concisely. Can al Qaeda be defeated and how? Do you need to defeat the Taliban to defeat al Qaeda? Can a counterinsurgency strategy be effective in Afghanistan given the capacities of the Afghan government? What can we realistically expect to achieve in the next few years? What presence do we have to have in Afghanistan in order to have an effective counterterrorism platform?

Secretary Clinton then offered an overview of the diplomatic and political context. It would likely be September or early October, she reported, before the Afghan elections were finalized. "Karzai is currently at 54 percent. Nevertheless, there might be enough fraud that legitimacy would definitely be in question." If enough ballots were eliminated for fraud, Karzai might fall below 50 percent and there would be a runoff election. A second round of voting, she said, "by the same token, is also fraught with peril.

"The second question," Clinton said, "is whether we should be associated with an effort toward reconciliation." Could something be worked out with the Taliban? "What would we demand of it, and who will have a role in it?" Which Taliban should the U.S. negotiate with? Moderates? Mullah Omar? What role would Karzai have?

Holbrooke interjected, "The Karzai meeting this morning was hot."

Eikenberry added, "It's starting to dawn on him that this is a very different American administration." Abdullah Abdullah, Karzai's main rival in the elections, he added, "won't go quietly but he does recognize privately that he would lose in a second-round" runoff election.

Gates introduced the McChrystal assessment. "The elements associated with the strategic decision you put in place earlier are only now coming into focus," he said, referring to the March Riedel report, the decisions and the president's speech. "Resources are just getting into place. McChrystal's assessment is the first chance to review that."

Gates said McChrystal's troop request needed more work, so it had not yet arrived.

McChrystal is proposing four big changes, Gates said, "Accelerate the ANSF [Afghan National Security Forces] training. Prioritize governance. Enhance programs for reconciliation and reintegration. And there's got to be a geographic concentration of our efforts."

The "geographic concentration" line caught Jones's attention. He thought the military leaders were talking as though the entire Afghanistan War could be won in the south. Jones believed that was just flat wrong, but he did not interrupt.

"I believe the strategy is the right one, but it is under-resourced," Gates continued. "It's premature to discuss resources until we have a very clear sense of how we tie the McChrystal approach to al Qaeda, how we deal with corrupt and predatory Afghan governance, how we change the subject from nation building to capacity building and how we address Pakistani unwillingness to take on the Pakistani Taliban," also known as the TTP.

Mullen then briefed the group on the McChrystal assessment from a pack of PowerPoint slides entitled "Sunday Small Group, 13 September 2009." He covered the four points from the report that Gates had made, adding, "Governance is at least the same threat, if not the greater threat, than the Taliban themselves."

When Mullen concluded, Biden was the first to speak. "This isn't an easy call. The military's done a hell of a job. But a nationwide, re-inforced counterinsurgency will only expand costs and demand extra resources. So is there not a more efficient way to go about this?"

They then attempted to address the question: Who are al Qaeda's extremist allies? That was the language in the Riedel review that had been open to interpretation.

"I think we have to focus on the threats to us and our allies and our interests," the president said, emphasizing a narrow definition, "not just any piece of any insurgency in Afghanistan."

"That's right," Gates said, "we have to focus on those groups that have the capacity to threaten us, our interests, our overseas presence, or our allies."

"I want to say six things," Biden said. He was learning to edit himself, but he still could be verbose and some in the room seemed to tense up. During one President's Daily Brief in the Oval Office, Biden apparently had disagreed with an intelligence conclusion and merely, without elaboration, shouted out one word—"Wrong!"—and left it at that. He could not be that abrupt this morning.

"This is the most consequential decision we'll make," Biden said, "so we need to make sure we understand the ramifications, or other concerns. Do we have the balance right between Afghanistan and Pakistan?" He noted that the allocation of "resources was currently 30:1—Afghanistan to Pakistan." Shouldn't the focus be Pakistan? he asked.

"Two, what is the most effective way to do what this says?" he asked, pointing to his copy of the McChrystal assessment.

"Three," Biden asserted, moving from questions to firm declarations, "the premise of the counterinsurgency strategy is flawed. There's a balloon effect. We squeeze it, and it pops out somewhere else. Are we prepared to go to other countries where al Qaeda can pop up?

"Four, the prospects for counterinsurgency are dim. We are in our seventh year of this war, and even when successful, counterinsurgency takes seven to 10 years, historically. Even if it were doable, McChrystal says he needs the will and ability to provide for the Afghan people by, with and through the Afghan government. They would need an effective government presence in 40,200 villages in Afghanistan.

"Fifth point, the alternative isn't to leave." The real alternative was "counterterrorism plus," a shift to an emphasis on Pakistan, al Qaeda and training more Afghan forces.

"Six," the vice president said, "it's not that the counterterrorism plus strategy has been tried and failed. We've not tried a fully resourced anything in Afghanistan, let alone one that does exactly what I say we need to do."

Biden then moved to the morning's intelligence briefing, disputing the claim that al Qaeda and the Taliban were so intertwined and so intermingled that the success of one meant the success of the other.

"No, they're actually very distinct," Biden said. "We're assuming that if al Qaeda comes back into Afghanistan, where it wasn't, it would be welcomed by the Taliban. Is that a correct assumption? We have no basis for concluding that."

The vice president then talked about the hierarchy inside the Taliban. It is not a "monolith," he said. There are several levels of organization. It had hard-core believers at a senior level, at best 5 or 10 percent, who need to be defeated. Then there was a middle group of people, perhaps 15 or 20 percent, who had different reasons for being committed. Maybe they were more persuadable, but it wasn't clear. And about 70 percent of the Taliban were foot soldiers, who were only there because it was a way to put food on the table or to deal with getting foreigners out of the country. These were illiterate, uneducated kids who were given a rifle and told to point it in that direction.

"We have to differentiate," Biden said. And the major differentiation is that the hard-core Taliban leaders—the ones causing the most headaches in Afghanistan—are all in Pakistan.

Bottom line, Biden said, it didn't necessarily matter what they did in Afghanistan. "If you don't get Pakistan right, you can't win," he said, addressing the president. If you do what McChrystal wants and adopt his strategy, "You own this war."

"I already own it," Obama said.

What was unsaid, what everyone knew, was that a president could not lose—or be seen to be losing—a war.

After a pause, Obama attempted a summary. "We're going to have to work through five areas," he said, posing a series of unanswered questions. "What are the opportunity costs, given the finite resources?" Were other national interests being overlooked because of the focus on this? It was a radical change from Bush, who was all in, win at all costs. Obama was proposing they consider other national priorities. "Is pursuing a broader counterinsurgency the best way to advance our core goal?" And because that goal is defeating al Qaeda in order to protect the homeland, did we really have to win a civil war in Afghanistan?

"Two, we've got a very real problem with corrupt governance, and I don't see how you get around that if you go with counterinsurgency.

"Three, Pakistan. I'm not persuaded that executing counterinsurgency in Afghanistan gets Pakistan to move in the right direction. How do we change Pakistan's calculus? It's not even clear that Pakistan would accept our increased resources." Obama said he thought some of the points the vice president had raised were valid.

"Four, how do we get good intel and targeting with a smaller presence on the ground?

"Five, when we approached the new strategy, we said we'd need a year. Where did this accelerated timetable come from?" The strategy from the Riedel review was supposed to be assessed after a full year—in March 2010—but it was only September. This sudden sense of urgency was unexpected. "Why do we have to make an accelerated decision?" he asked.

It was the core question and no one answered him.

Gates addressed the question of opportunity costs from a military perspective. "Given the drawdown in Iraq," he said, "we could increase troop numbers in Afghanistan without impacting the dwell time at home." Dwell time refers to time at home base.

Admiral Mullen concurred.

"We're going to need another session," Obama said. "We're just scratching the surface here. This discussion has also clarified our core goal, highlighting the fact that we have done a disservice to McChrystal by not making that very clear to him." The Strategic Implementation Plan (SIP) was the origin of that problem. At Gates's urging, it said that goal was to "defeat" the insurgency, the broadest and most difficult task.

"Is there any confidence in our capacity, in a three-year time frame?" the president asked. That was how much time was left in his presidential term. Anybody who has any confidence in our capability to build anything of consequence in three years has not really explained their case, he said. It was a direct shot at the military.

"What happened in Iraq?" he asked of counterinsurgency's most recent test case. Was the surge plus the Sunni Awakening, when tribes left the insurgency and joined the government, a strategic decision? There had been sufficient infrastructure in Iraq for that decision to have coherence, he said. "We have to make sure that there's similar infrastructure in Afghanistan. I do recognize that it would be difficult to execute a counterterrorism plus strategy without a good foothold in Afghanistan. That intuitively makes sense, because without it you're not going to get good intelligence."

Referring to the next session, he said, "I want to start with Secretary Clinton on the Pakistan/al Qaeda question, and have a discussion about a realistic end state in that."

The president then doled out homework assignments. This meeting had concentrated on the McChrystal assessment. He wanted to take a step back.

"We're going to begin with interests," Obama said, "and then figure out what it is we want to accomplish, how we're going to do it and eventually get to resources. We don't want to talk about troops initially."

I don't even want to see the troop request that McChrystal's preparing, Obama said. It would only obscure the debate he wanted to have about their real "interests."

Holbrooke left the Situation Room thinking that some of the real issues had not been discussed at all. The March Riedel report was flawed. Riedel had presented it in a one-hour Air Force One meeting alone with the president. No one else had been there—not Jones, not Donilon, not Emanuel, not himself. There was no note taker. Four or five people should have been on that plane and in the meeting.

In the Bush administration one of the problems had been the very private sessions that Bush had with Vice President Cheney, who could present his arguments and whisper in the president's ear. Cheney's ideas did not have to be tested, and they were given undue influence.

Holbrooke blamed Jones, who he thought was weak and not proactive enough in protecting the president. He was not the counterweight to Gates, Mullen and Petraeus he was supposed to be.

More importantly, Holbrooke believed the Riedel report and the Sunday meeting had not acknowledged a central truth: The war—or the American role in the war—would not end in a military victory, but nearly all the focus had been on the military. There had been little discussion of reconciliation—how the warring parties could be brought together diplomatically. That might be far off, but it had to be planned. How could the Taliban insurgents be lured off the field? Maybe it was a fantasy. But they had to sincerely try.

The Saudis were already acting as secret intermediaries with elements of the Taliban, but the White House was not seriously engaging the issue. This was the only end for the war in Holbrooke's estimation. How could they not at least consider it?

Holbrooke largely agreed with Biden. He saw the vice president emerging as the administration's George Ball, the deputy secretary of state who had opposed the Vietnam escalation. But the length of Biden's presentation undermined his message, Holbrooke told others.

Like Biden, Holbrooke believed that even if the Taliban retook large parts of Afghanistan, al Qaeda would not come with them. That might be "the single most important intellectual insight of the year," Holbrooke remarked hours after the first meeting. Al Qaeda was much safer in Pakistan. Why go back to Afghanistan, where there were nearly 68,000 U.S. troops and 30,000 from other NATO counties? And in Afghanistan, the U.S. had all the intelligence and surveillance capability, plus the capability to dispatch massive ground forces, not just Special Operations Forces but battalions of regular troops and the CIA's 3,000-man pursuit teams.

Astonishingly to Holbrooke, that key insight had neither been in Riedel's report, nor had it been discussed that Sunday morning. Where was the no-holds-barred debate? The president had told them not to bite their tongues. Holbrooke had to bite his because he worked for the secretary of state, who was unsure of what course to recommend. But where were the others?

Petraeus had not been invited to attend the White House meeting. Instead, the CentCom commander was in Tampa, conducting a halftime reenlistment ceremony at the Buccaneers-Cowboys football game. He thought his exclusion from the meeting was ridiculous. Petraeus was the combatant commander in Afghanistan and Pakistan and recognized as the father of modern counterinsurgency—the strategy under review.

He received a synopsis the next day, Monday, September 14, from General Lute, who had attended. They spoke at 8:30 A.M. for half an hour on a secure personal Tandberg video. Petraeus agreed that Pakistan was important but not all-important. What they did in Pakistan also depended on what they did in Afghanistan.

For Petraeus, war was about initiative and momentum. Regaining the initiative on the ground in Afghanistan was crucial, as was regaining the initiative inside the Situation Room. With one session down, he believed that Mullen was all in on McChrystal's approach and that Gates was increasingly persuaded.

In the message war, Petraeus had allies outside the administration who shared his beliefs and trusted his judgment. On Monday, September 14, a long op-ed appeared in *The Wall Street Journal* written by Senators Graham, Lieberman and McCain. Under the headline "Only Decisive Force Can Prevail in Afghanistan," the senators said they would stand with Obama if he gave McChrystal what the general said he needed. They did not disclose that McChrystal had told them he would need seven to eight brigades. Echoing Petraeus, they wrote, "More troops will not guarantee success in Afghanistan, but a failure to send them is a guarantee of failure."

15

Admiral Mullen appeared before the Senate Armed Services Committee for his confirmation hearings for a second two-year term as chairman on Tuesday, September 15, two days after the first strategy session. He had carefully drafted a three-page opening statement and gone over it with Navy Captain John Kirby, his public relations assistant. He would try to preempt any questions in the opening.

Knowing the sensitivity of the troop issue, Kirby had sent a copy of the statement to McDonough at the White House, drawing attention to the line that said McChrystal's strategy of a properly resourced counterinsurgency *probably means more forces.*

As all nominees do, Admiral Mullen had promised to give the committee his honest conclusions and not hedge his testimony. It was not unusual for the Pentagon to give the White House a heads-up about what senior officials planned to tell Congress, but Kirby was effectively asking for approval.

McDonough okayed the statement. The "probably" made it ambiguous enough. More forces could be interpreted as the almost inevitable addition of more U.S. troops for training the Afghan army.

But when Obama heard about Mullen's testimony, he let his staff know how unhappy he was. Mullen was publicly endorsing the McChrystal strategy. "The Taliban insurgency grows in both size and complexity," he had told the senators. "That is why I support a properly resourced, classically pursued counterinsurgency effort." Had Mullen ignored what Obama said just two days earlier? Had the president not told everyone, including Mullen, that none of the options looked good, that they needed to challenge their assumptions, and they were going to have four or five long sessions for debate? What was the president's principal military adviser doing, going public with his preemptive conclusion? The chairman was poking his finger in the president's eye.

Later that day around 6 P.M., Pentagon spokesman Geoff Morrell was waiting in the lobby outside the White House Situation Room when Emanuel and Tom Donilon emerged from the NSC principals meeting. They were furious.

The president is being screwed by the senior uniformed military, they told Morrell. The generals and admirals are systematically playing him, boxing him in.

Filling his rant with expletives, Emanuel said, "It's bullshit that between the chairman and Petraeus, everybody's come out and publicly endorsed the notion of more troops. The president hasn't even had a chance!"

Morrell realized that Mullen could have ducked the controversy at his hearings with a simple feint: "My job is to be the principal military adviser to the president of the United States and secretary of defense, and I owe them my counsel first and privately before I offer it to you all. I am happy to come back at a later point and give you what I offered . . . but I don't think it's appropriate to share it with the committee before."

Morrell concluded it was all part of Mullen's "compulsion to communicate," to enhance the prominence and stature of the chairman's position, after it had been emasculated by his two predecessors in the Rumsfeld era. The chairman had a Facebook page, a Twitter account, YouTube videos and a Web site called "Travels with Mullen: Conversation with the Country."

Mullen himself then stepped into the lobby and discovered that he was the topic of a heated powwow. Jones joined them.

Emanuel and Donilon attempted to tone down their approach by asking him, How are we supposed to deal with this? You did this, what should we say?

"It's going to be the lead story on all the evening news," Emanuel said. "It's going to be double black headlines above the fold on every single newspaper."

As they were standing there, McDonough passed by. Mullen looked at McDonough as if he, the NSC chief of staff, would come to his defense. But McDonough continued on without a word.

Mullen was surprised they were giving him hell. The fears about headlines were overblown. The White House knew in advance what he was going to say. No specific troop number was in his testimony. He had been as amorphous as he could be. At his confirmation hearing, he must tell the truth. And the truth was that he embraced the general notion of a counterinsurgency. "That's what I believe." What was his alternative?

Why use "probably"? Donilon asked pointedly. Wouldn't "I don't know" have been better?

Mullen let them seethe. "I just took it," he said later.

"Mullen: More Troops 'Probably' Needed," read the headline at the top of *The Washington Post* front page the next morning.

Afterward, Jones called Mullen to ask how he was doing.

"I don't know, you tell me," the admiral replied.

"Losing altitude," Jones said.

Obama asked retired General Colin Powell, the former secretary of state and chairman of the Joint Chiefs, to come for a private meeting in the Oval Office on September 16. A nominal Republican, Powell had given Obama an important endorsement during the presidential campaign. Nearly 25 years older, Powell had 35 years in the U.S. Army, and many had thought he would be the first black president. But Powell had chosen not to run in the 1990s, even when his poll numbers had skyrocketed.

"It isn't a one-time decision," Powell told the president about Afghanistan. "This is the decision that will have consequences for the better part of your administration. Mr. President, don't get pushed by the left to do nothing. Don't get pushed by the right to do everything. You take your time and you figure it out."

Also, don't get pushed by the media, he advised. Take your time, get all the information you need and make sure you are absolutely comfortable with where you come down.

"If you decide to send more troops or that's what you feel is necessary, make sure you have a good understanding of what those troops are going to be doing and some assurance that the additional troops will be successful. You can't guarantee success in a very complex theater like Afghanistan and increasingly with the Pakistan problem next door.

"You've got to ensure that you're putting this commitment on a solid base, and the base is a little soft right now," he said, referring to Karzai and the widespread corruption in his government.

During this period, I had been conducting interviews for this book about what McChrystal's classified assessment said. It was the basis for both Petraeus's and Mullen's controversial statements, yet no one outside of a tight-knit inner circle had actually read it. My sources said that McChrystal's analysis addressed a devastating conundrum: eight years of war with little to no progress.

There is a popular impression that insiders with political motivations simply hand over sensitive documents to journalists, with reporters waiting at their desks to be used as the tools of someone else's agenda. No one offered to leak or provide me a copy of the McChrystal assessment. Through several interviews, I developed an understanding that the assessment was filled with troubling news. I used each interview to try to pry out a little more.

In mid-September, after a nearly two-hour interview, I asked one person, "You've got a copy of the McChrystal report here?"

"Yeah, it's on my desk," was the answer, and that person photocopied the report for me.

The person put no restrictions on using the assessment, but the interview had taken place as part of the long-range research for this book. I did not get a chance to read the report until Friday night, September 18.

With a red pen in hand, I went through the 66-page confidential assessment. On the second page of the "Commander's Summary," I underlined a passage I had not anticipated finding: "Failure to gain the initiative and reverse insurgent momentum in the near-term (next 12 months)—while Afghan security capacity matures—risks an outcome where defeating the insurgency is no longer possible." In other words, the U.S. could lose the war by September 2010.

A culture of can-do pervades the U.S. military, and generals rarely talk about the "no longer possible," especially in writing. But this report was sent directly to the secretary of defense. I had to reread the passage, and I put a red check mark by it.

As I continued, it was clear the report was much more than a routine battlefield assessment. There was a desperate urgency to it. *This is a cry from the heart*, I realized. McChrystal said his forces were "poorly configured" to conduct protect-the-population security.

I underlined, "Pre-occupied with the protection of our own forces, we have operated in a manner that distances us—physically and psychologically—from the people we seek to protect." It baldly said that "we run the risk of strategic defeat" because of operations that cause civilian casualties. I circled the notion of "strategic defeat," which could mean losing the war. "Defeat"? Generals just do not normally talk this way.

Then on the fourth page of the report's summary, my red pen darted under a sentence that blew the whistle on McChrystal's own command: "Almost every aspect of our collective effort and associated resourcing has lagged a growing insurgency—historically a recipe for failure" in counterinsurgency. There was that word again, "failure." I then read that the Afghan security force "will not have enough capability in the near-term given the insurgency's growth rate," so he proposed a "bridge capability" of more coalition troops.

Next, the pen went under, "The status quo will lead to failure . . ."

I got the message, and I wondered how this assessment had gone over with Gates, who, after all, had been secretary of defense for the last 20 months—secretary of defense in a losing war, according to Gates's own new commander on the ground.

Gates had told the president back during the first months of the administration, after the president had authorized 21,000 more troops, that he hoped there would be no more troop requests.

Although McChrystal's assessment did not include a troop request, there was definitely going to be a large one. Other sources were telling me it would be 40,000 or more, as a middle option.

"We cannot succeed simply by trying harder," I read. "The entire culture—how ISAF [International Security Assistance Force] understands the environment and defined the fight, how it interacts with the Afghan people and government, and how it operates both on the ground and within the coalition—must change profoundly." Commanders rarely report on the need for "change." Instead, they order it.

McChrystal said that accomplishing his mission required "defeating the insurgency, which this paper defines as a condition where the insurgency no longer threatens the viability of the state." He used some form of the word "defeat" 14 times.

I underscored this sentence: "The weakness of state institutions, malign actions of power brokers, widespread corruption and abuse of power by various officials, and ISAF's own errors, have given Afghans little reason to support their government."

Insurgents had "a Taliban 'shadow government' that actively seeks to control the population and displace the national government and traditional power structures." This was new to me and it indicated that the insurgents had penetrated deeper into the various provinces than I had imagined.

Because of "inadequate intelligence," McChrystal could not say precisely how much of Afghanistan, beyond a "significant portion," was controlled or contested by insurgents. That was a startling indictment of the intelligence shortcomings.

The report went on to describe the three major Taliban insurgent groups that loosely coordinated with each other: the Quetta Shura Taliban, the Haqqani network, and Hezb-e-Islami Gulbuddin. The Quetta Shura Taliban had established an alternative government in direct competition to Karzai's authority. "They appoint shadow governors for most provinces, review their performance, and replace them periodically," the report said. "They install 'shari'a' [Islamic law] courts to deliver swift and enforced justice in contested and controlled areas. They levy taxes and conscript fighters and laborers."

McChrystal laid out his initial plans for an ISAF future offensive, saying that coalition forces would "focus on critical high-population areas that are contested or controlled by insurgents, not because the enemy is present, but because it is here that the population is threatened by the insurgency." He then divided the Afghan provinces into three groups based on the extent of insurgent presence and listed the order in which he might launch an offensive.

The assessment featured a grim four-page appendix on the Afghan prison system, which had become "a sanctuary and base to conduct lethal operations" against the Afghan government and ISAF troops. "There are more insurgents per square foot in corrections facilities than anywhere else in Afghanistan," it said.

Near the end, I read the general's overall conclusion: "Failure to provide adequate resources also risks a longer conflict, greater casualties, higher overall costs, and ultimately, a critical loss of political support. Any of these risks, in turn, are likely to result in mission failure."

By the time I had finished reading, there was little doubt in my mind that the report should be published immediately.

That same Friday night, I e-mailed Marcus Brauchli, who had been executive editor of *The Washington Post* for slightly more than a year, to let him know I had the report and thought he ought to read it. We met at the *Post* the next morning, Saturday. Brauchli read the report quickly and said he thought it should be published at once and in full.

I called my source and asked that the ground rules be changed.

"When my book comes out next year," I said, "this assessment will be such old news, it will not be news at all. It will be irrelevant." It is news now, I said.

After a few questions, my source agreed and I promised to not iden-tify that person in any way.

Brauchli asked me to call both the White House and the Pentagon to explain that we had a full copy and planned to publish it in the next day or two but wanted them to address which parts, if any, should not be made public and for what reasons.

The June 30, 1971, Supreme Court decision on the Pentagon Papers case, nearly four decades earlier and just three months before I joined the *Post*, opened the door for such conversations with the government. In its 6 to 3 ruling, the court essentially said the government could not restrain the press before publication of classified documents, which permitted *The New York Times* and *The Washington Post* to continue pub-lishing the top secret 47-volume Vietnam War study, which showed that the government had repeatedly lied to the public about the war.

Because the government could not legally stop us from publishing the McChrystal assessment, we had the upper hand in listening to ar-guments for deleting passages from the report. For the Pentagon Pa-pers, the *Times* and *Post* did not consult the government in advance. To do so would have alerted the government and likely resulted in a court action to stop publication, which is exactly what the government did in federal court after the initial articles ran. The beauty of the Supreme Court's Pentagon Papers ruling—which forbids prior restraint—is that it encourages us to ask the government for their specific objections to the publication of classified documents.

I reached General Jones by phone on Saturday. He was on his boat in the Chesapeake Bay. I explained that I had the full 66-page McChrys-tal assessment and planned to publish it but wanted to hear from him and the Pentagon first.

"It will make the president's job more difficult," he said. Publica-tion would give "insight to those who are working against us," mean-ing the Taliban insurgents in Afghanistan.

I said I thought it sounded a dramatic alarm from the new commander about the course of the war, and the public ought to be informed. We would not publish the page outlining future operations. We wanted to hear arguments if there were other parts we should consider deleting on national security grounds.

"I'm not thrilled," Jones said. "It is classified." He also noted that he had lots of questions about the report. McChrystal was "a young four-star," Jones said. "He is naive."

I said that on a careful read and reread, I did not see the harm, but we were willing—even eager—to listen to their arguments.

"I have some calls to make," Jones said.

I called Morrell, the Pentagon spokesman, who said, "They want to fight this," and that we should expect to hear from someone soon.

Within an hour, about 2 P.M. on Saturday, Gates, Jones, Donilon, and General Cartwright, the vice chairman of the JCS, were on the phone in a conference call to *Post* editor Brauchli, a *Post* lawyer and myself.

Gates, who was out of town, said he was asking us to hold off on any article or publication of the assessment for 24 hours. Publication, he said, would be "quite damaging to our efforts in Afghanistan and put the lives of our soldiers at risk."

General Cartwright added that the report was "an operational and tactical assessment" and publication would allow "the enemy to see where we were going." He asked me for time to review.

We repeated what I had told Jones about not publishing the page that contained future operations.

Donilon said, "I have not heard an answer to the secretary's request"—that we wait 24 hours.

Brauchli and I both said it seemed reasonable, and Brauchli wanted to know when and where we could hear all their objections. He would withhold publication of the story, he said, but he wanted to make sure we could meet with someone who would have authority to speak for not just the Pentagon but the White House and the intelligence agencies.

We had an appointment at the Pentagon the next morning, Sunday, at 11 A.M.

• • •

We realized that we would have to listen carefully but be on the alert, ready to separate real claims of national security from bogus ones. We were concerned that the administration didn't want this damning report to be published. At a press conference two weeks earlier on September 3, right after Gates received the report, the secretary had said, "I don't believe that the war is slipping through the administration's fingers." The McChrystal assessment contradicted that.

In addition, Obama was appearing on five television talk shows that morning to make a plea for his health care reform. Obviously the White House would not want other news stepping on its message.

On Sunday, Brauchli, Rajiv Chandrasekaran, a senior *Post* reporter who covers the war, and I drove to the Pentagon for the 11 A.M. meeting. Because Gates was away, the representatives from the Pentagon were Cartwright, Morrell and undersecretary of defense for policy Michèle Flournoy. We sat around the conference table in Cartwright's office.

Cartwright, outgoing and exceptionally personable, said there were three major objections—disclosing future operations, intelligence gaps and anything that might compromise McChrystal's ability to work with the Afghanistan government or other international partners.

At the beginning of the discussion, it seemed it was a contest among several on the government side to see who could get Brauchli to agree to redact the most. In all, they raised 14 specific concerns. The first real issue was whether to quote McChrystal saying that he needed more forces in the next 12 months or the war "will likely end in failure." It was his strongest statement. Flournoy argued that publication of the 12-month time frame would allow "the enemy, basically, to kind of hold out" and "redouble" its efforts for just 12 months because it would be taken as an indication that American resolve was limited. She also said that publication of the 12-month limit "if read by the Taliban, could lead to a change of tactics on their part that directly translates into more U.S casualties."

It was a very direct warning.

McChrystal and his team, she said, had been consulted and "They did not want the time frame in there."

I argued that it was McChrystal's core argument and we needed to reflect that.

Brauchli noted that Gates and others had said the United States had about 12 to 18 months to shift the momentum in the war, so McChrystal's use of 12 months was hardly surprising.

Eventually Cartwright agreed and withdrew their objections, but he wanted the last three words redacted from this sentence: "The insurgents control or contest a significant portion of the country, although it is difficult to assess precisely how much due to lack of ISAF presence AND INADEQUATE INTELLIGENCE."

To let the Taliban know we had "inadequate intelligence" would only encourage them and allow them freer movement because of the inadequacy.

Brauchli agreed, saying, "I think on the issues of disclosure of intelligence gaps, I think we'll look favorably on that because I don't think we need to be pointing that out."

The three words were removed.

I thought this was reasonable, but I chose to publish them in this book because the gaps became increasingly obvious. Overall, Brauchli and Cartwright agreed to redact the details of future ops and the three words on the intelligence gap.

We were able to publish about 97 percent of the assessment without any objections from the government, and deliver the conclusions and details in the story. That evening, the Pentagon provided us with a declassified version of the assessment with the agreed-upon redactions.

We returned to the *Post* to edit my draft article for Monday's edition. The headline in the September 21 *Washington Post* the next morning stretched across the top three quarters of the front page: "McChrystal: More Forces or 'Mission Failure.' " The declassified version of the assessment was available on the *Post* Web site. Within a few minutes, *The New York Times* all but copied the story almost paragraph for paragraph.

The Internet lit up with reactions. Retired Army Colonel Pat Lang wrote on his blog, "This highly classified document was artfully leaked by those who wish to 'bulldoze' Obama and Gates into accepting an unlimited commitment to a nation building counterinsurgency strategy in Afghanistan."

Peter Feaver, who had been on George W. Bush's NSC staff, wrote on a blog for *Foreign Policy* magazine, "The domestic political-military stakes have been ramped up considerably with this leak. It is not quite a 3-A.M.-phone-call crisis, but it is probably the most serious national security test the Obama team has confronted thus far."

At the morning press briefing aboard Air Force One en route to Troy, New York, Gibbs emphasized to reporters that McChrystal had yet to ask for a specific number of additional troops.

"We're going to conduct that strategic assessment and do that in a way that lays out the best path forward before we make resource decisions, rather than having this go the other way around where one makes resource decisions and then finds a strategy."

In my interview with the president nine months later, he said the McChrystal assessment was useful because "it clarified a gap in what had come out of the Riedel report.

"I think the Riedel report retained ambiguity about what our central mission was," Obama told me. "It was interpreted by some as an argument for a beefed-up force that was conducting a counterterrorism strategy." With Riedel's emphasis on Pakistan, some, like the vice president, argued that the strategy should focus on the safe havens in Pakistan being used by al Qaeda and the Taliban insurgents. On the other hand, Obama said, it was interpreted by others as a commitment to a full-blown counterinsurgency strategy "as had been classically laid out by General Petraeus." But the president said he was not buying into a full counterinsurgency because that meant "what you're purchasing is responsibility for Afghanistan over the long term.

"And so when the McChrystal assessment comes in," the president told me, "I think at that point what became clear to me was, we've got to get everybody in a room and make sure that everybody is singing from the same hymnal."

16

On September 29, at 1:30 P.M., Jones assembled the principals in the Situation Room for a two-hour discussion before the NSC meeting the next day. He called it a "rehearsal," where they could sharpen their arguments and presentations without the president there. Jones thought several rambled, especially Biden and Holbrooke.

A video of the meeting would probably alarm anyone who watched. Eight years into the war, they were struggling to refine what the core objectives were.

Biden had written a six-page memo exclusively for the president questioning the intelligence reports about the Taliban. The reports portrayed the Taliban as the new al Qaeda. Because the Taliban was taking the fight to the Americans, it had become a brand that drew Arabs, Uzbeks, Tajiks and Chechens who ventured to Afghanistan for their so-called summer of jihad.

In his memo, Biden indicated that, based on the way he read the intelligence reports, the phenomenon was grossly exaggerated. There were perhaps 50 to 75 foreign fighters in Afghanistan at any given time. That was a magnitude of order below the thousands—including a 22-year-old Osama bin Laden—who had flooded the country after the Soviet occupation started in 1979. The vice president did not see evidence that the Pashtun Taliban projected a global jihadist ideology, let alone designs on the American homeland.

It had already appeared in the news that McChrystal was going to ask for about 40,000 troops. The number was being debated on live television before it was being discussed in the Situation Room.

At 3 P.M. on Wednesday, September 30, Obama sat down for the second meeting of the Afghanistan-Pakistan strategy review. This was a larger group than the first session, about 18 people. Petraeus was in attendance this time. It was clear to everyone in the White House that he had to be there because any decision reached without him would be suspect.

The media debate about Afghanistan had become polarized, a choice between a massive troop influx and a complete withdrawal.

"Is there anybody who thinks we ought to leave Afghanistan?" the president asked.

Everyone in the room was quiet. They looked at him. No one said anything.

"Okay," he said, "now that we've dispensed with that, let's get on."

One note taker circled what he had written: "POTUS says take off the table the notion that we're leaving Afghanistan." POTUS is short for president of the United States.

But Obama also wanted to steer away from Afghanistan as best he could for the rest of the session.

"Let's start where our interests take us, which is really Pakistan, not Afghanistan," he said. "In fact, you can tell the Pakistani leaders, if you want to, that we're not leaving" Afghanistan.

With that out of the way, Lavoy, the DNI's deputy director for analysis, began his intelligence briefing, clarifying the dynamics between al Qaeda, now primarily in Pakistan, and the Taliban. Al Qaeda was the direct threat to the United States, Lavoy said.

The significance of the Taliban, added DNI Blair, was that it was an extremist movement allied to al Qaeda that was succeeding. Providing it was winning, the Taliban was happy to have al Qaeda at its side.

But it was vexing to distinguish perfectly among the Taliban, al Qaeda and other groups, Blair and Lavoy said. As McChrystal's assessment had noted, the Haqqani network drew foreign money and manpower "from its close association with al Qaeda and other Pakistan-based insurgent groups." Its links with al Qaeda could foster an environment for other associated extremist movements "to reestablish safe havens in Afghanistan."

Al Qaeda would return to Afghanistan under two conditions, Lavoy said. The Taliban had to control the country again, or control areas beyond the reach of U.S. and NATO ground forces. And, the security situation in the ungoverned areas of the FATA in Pakistan would have to become too dangerous for al Qaeda. Despite the frequency and success of CIA drone attacks in the FATA and the Pakistani military taking actions against its own branch of the Taliban, there was no evidence that al Qaeda was migrating back to Afghanistan. Why would they? It was still safer for them in Pakistan.

Obama laid out his ground rules for the rest of the session.

"I really want to focus on the issue of the U.S. homeland," he said. "I see three key goals. One, protecting the U.S. homeland, allies and U.S. interests abroad. Two, concern about Pakistan's nuclear weapons and stability. If I'm just focused on the U.S. homeland, can we distinguish between the dangers posed by al Qaeda and the Taliban?"

Biden picked up on the cue—skipping the third goal about Pakistan-India relations—and asked, "Is there any evidence the Afghan Taliban advocates attacks outside of Afghanistan and on the U.S., or if it took over more of Afghanistan it would have more of an outward focus?"

No evidence, Lavoy said. Biden had scored a significant point.

The president returned to his previous train of thought and said, "Changing the Pakistan calculus is key to achieving our core goals."

The U.S. was in the throes of deciding whether to send more troops into the Afghanistan War, yet the safety of the nation hinged on Pakistan.

Obama said that there was a military assumption that a lasting presence in Afghanistan would stabilize Pakistan. What was the basis of that? he asked. Why wouldn't the opposite happen?

Petraeus spoke up. A little more than a month ago, he had met in Pakistan with General Kayani, head of the Pakistani army, whose influence and power were increasing. For two hours, Petraeus sat with a map as the Pakistanis walked him through their plans and operations. Their calculus was changing, as they now factored in extremist terrorist groups such as TTP. That Pakistani branch of the Taliban had used suicide bombers against government targets and earlier in the year had controlled the area near Tarbela, where Pakistan stored some of its nuclear arsenal. The Pakistani military had already launched a ground operation in Swat and was about to do the same in South Waziristan. That was an encouraging sign.

McChrystal then delivered a presentation on what he called "The Pathway" to his initial assessment, outlining how he had arrived at what he thought were his missions and how he assessed his ability to accomplish them.

"Okay," Obama said, "You guys have done your job. But there are three developments since then. The Pakistanis are doing better, the Afghanistan situation is more serious than anticipated, and the Afghan elections did not provide the pivot point hoped for—a more legitimate government. And now we have to make some decisions."

They turned to a chart from McChrystal that listed extremist threats—al Qaeda, the Taliban and other groups. Could some be isolated, and should the administration worry only about those that posed a threat to the homeland?

Biden and deputy national security adviser Donilon voiced skepticism that the symbiotic relationships among them meant the United States had to go after all of them.

The vice president felt he should correct the analysis by Lavoy that, if able, al Qaeda would likely return to a Taliban-controlled Afghanistan.

"We hear that from some in the intelligence community," Biden said, "but it seems to me much more ambiguous. First of all, would al Qaeda go back if it deemed it was unsafe to operate in Afghanistan? Probably not. Second, Pakistan's a much more connected country from which to operate, so it clearly prefers that. And then more important, as I said earlier, there are real questions about whether the Taliban would welcome al Qaeda back, since association with the group carries with it a real security threat to Afghanistan."

Biden then devoted the rest of his monologue to the assumption also challenged by the president, the idea that as goes Afghanistan, so goes Pakistan.

"I think it's exactly the opposite," he said, "that what happens in Afghanistan may have some impact but it won't fundamentally change the outcome in Pakistan. There are many different issues and factors influencing the direction Pakistan takes. Afghanistan's one, but only one of them. But conversely, when it comes to Afghanistan, the role Pakistan plays is determinate, and particularly if it continues to harbor the leadership of the Afghan Taliban and give them the sanctuary, it's impossible to succeed."

It was about an hour and 45 minutes into the meeting and Secretary of Defense Gates had said nothing.

"Bob," Obama said at one point, leaning back in his chair, "I'd love to hear what you're thinking. I know still waters run deep. What's on your mind?"

"I'd like to think about broadening the top priority beyond the homeland to include our interests abroad," Gates said, "key allies, partners, our forces overseas around the world. The focus is al Qaeda and the degree to which al Qaeda would be empowered by a Taliban success. If the Taliban make significant headway, it'll be framed as the defeat of the second superpower. I don't see the chance of real reconciliation until the Taliban is under pressure. Al Qaeda likely would stay where they are in the FATA if the Taliban took over, unless pressure in the FATA reaches a critical point." Supporting Lavoy from the previous session, Gates said, "But we should recognize that al Qaeda is a leech on the Taliban and to the degree that the Taliban is successful, helps al Qaeda."

Obama turned to another metaphor to explain one step America had to take: "We need to drain the swamp and reduce the appeal of violent extremism to young Muslims. We need to elevate our public affairs and our civilian affairs.

"The Pakistan core goal is right," the president said. That goal was to eliminate the al Qaeda safe havens, so chasing the Taliban might be a distraction to that. "If there is an opportunity cost in order to go after the Taliban, it might not be a wise move to go after the Taliban."

This sounded alarm bells for Gates, Mullen, Petraeus and McChrystal. There wasn't much the president could say that could be more disturbing to the military. His statement seemed to question the very wisdom of the war in Afghanistan.

But before any of the military leaders could respond, Biden interrupted to push for a counterterrorism strategy that would involve fewer additional troops. Some leaders in the region, the vice president said, had concerns about the growing U.S. military presence, or footprint, in the Middle East and South Asia. He was referring to Egypt's President Hosni Mubarak and Saudi Arabia's King Abdullah.

Petraeus responded, "Those are the same ones that had a concern about our footprint in Iraq as well, and that was disproved." He reminded them that the biggest of the big ideas in his CentCom strategic assessment from earlier in the year was that combating terrorism required "a whole of governments" approach. This meant the U.S. could not go it alone but had to work with the governments of other countries such as Egypt and Saudi Arabia. In fact, at a speech up the road at the National Press Club the week before, Petraeus had lauded the Saudis' help against al Qaeda.

McChrystal then chimed in to assist his boss and contradict Biden's belief that counterterrorism automatically involved a smaller footprint than counterinsurgency.

"Counterterrorist decapitation"—capturing or killing terrorist leaders—"doesn't work unless it is enabled by effective counterinsurgency," he said. "They complement each other."

Petraeus took them back to Iraq once more. "We killed Zarqawi in Iraq," he said, "probably the best, most competent, charismatic leader in al Qaeda overall, in terms of real battlefield leaders, and the violence continued to go up." Zarqawi's death in June 2006 did not bring peace or stability. Special Operations were commanded at the time by then Lieutenant General Stanley McChrystal.

Sitting on the sidelines, Axelrod was not surprised that Petraeus kept referring to Iraq. He was "Mr. Counterinsurgency," as Axelrod privately called him. Axelrod had been told that Petraeus's *Counterinsurgency Field Manual* had become a hymnal for young Army officers, who were promoted if they mastered its songs. Mr. Counterinsurgency believed he could simply take his Iraq model on the road. Axelrod thought Afghanistan would be exponentially more demanding than Iraq—different mix of population, different culture, low literacy rate, tough terrain. As an expression of his absolute confidence in Obama, Axelrod thought the president was well aware of all of this and understood the region and its history. Despite Obama's youth and lack of experience, Axelrod believed the president was such a fast learner that he could be a counterbalance to Petraeus.

Toward the end of the meeting, Secretary Clinton asked, "How would additional forces be used?" Where would the troops go? Would they be trainers? How many enablers? How would the lessons learned from Iraq be applied?

Donilon, the deputy national security adviser, then listed the information they would try to get and questions they would address in deputies committee meetings. "We'll refine the intel products," he said. "We'll reconsider the goals. Who are the extremist allies? Does the Taliban have to be defeated?"

"What does it mean?" the president asked, breaking in. "Address what it means to break the Taliban momentum. Do we really need to get to the Taliban to degrade al Qaeda? We've made progress against al Qaeda despite the lack of momentum against the Taliban."

Yes, sir.

Petraeus left the meeting troubled by the unfolding narrative. Progress was being made against al Qaeda with the drone strikes in Pakistan, yet Pakistan was emerging as the necessary war. And accordingly, Afghanistan, his counterinsurgency war, was becoming the secondary war.

The highest-level intelligence analysis had never provided a conclusive argument for acting in Afghanistan now. But there was a compelling argument that if the tide of the war was not stemmed, the Afghan government's decline would be inevitable. It might be a slow death. It might take a decade. But there would be a point where the decline would become irreversible, when sending in another 50,000 troops or more would not help. And a completely destabilized Afghanistan would sooner or later destabilize Pakistan. And so the question for the president and his team was: Could the United States take that risk?

After the September 30 meeting, the president asked Gates for a copy of McChrystal's troop request. McChrystal's basic recommendation of 40,000 had already leaked, but there was an extraordinary amount of secrecy surrounding the document itself. To prevent further leaks, a limited number of copies were available and handling them was severely restricted. The 11-page document, dated September, 24 2009, was classified SECRET/NOFORN. Entitled, "Resourcing the ISAF implementation strategy," it did not leak.

It was six months later when I had a chance to review the document, which a source for this book provided to me. The contrast to McChrystal's Afghanistan assessment astounded me. They seemed to share an author in name only. Bureaucratic phrases and eye-glazing sentences replaced the impressive candor from the assessment.

McChrystal listed three troop options:

1. 10,000–11,000 to mostly train the Afghan forces;

2. 40,000 for a counterinsurgency;

3. 85,000 for a more robust counterinsurgency.

Finally at the end, McChrystal got to his bottom line:

"Professional Military Judgment: Thus after careful military analysis of the current situation, I recommend the addition of four combat brigades with enablers"—or 40,000.

In essence, McChrystal said, give me 40,000 more troops and I'll try my damnedest.

Around that time, the CBS show *60 Minutes* aired a prerecorded interview with McChrystal, who said he had only spoken with President Obama once in the last 70 days, and that was by secure video. His answer made the commander in chief look oddly removed from the war. The bloggers pounced and the president was criticized in a *New York Times* article. The White House decided to arrange a meeting with the general. Obama was flying to Denmark to pitch Chicago as the host of the 2016 Olympics and McChrystal was scheduled to be in London, where Jones assumed he was on a rest-and-relaxation trip.

But McChrystal had come to London for a reunion with British Special Forces who had fought in Iraq. An invitation to address the International Institute for Strategic Studies, a think tank, had also come in and Mullen told him to accept it.

"Obviously, you need to be careful," Mullen said.

Every three-star who made four-star has had to grow, Mullen later reflected. McChrystal's challenge was that he would have to grow on a world stage.

During McChrystal's October 1 speech at the institute, he stuck to his assessment that only a counterinsurgency strategy could work. He declared the importance of resolve and warned of the demoralizing impact of uncertainty.

McChrystal tried to joke with the audience about his speech. "If this works according to my plan, it will totally exhaust your appetite for this issue and I will leave the room to wild cheers and lucrative job offers. If my plan fails, as most of mine do, I will be happy to field any questions."

It was a discordant start by the commander of a major war five months into his assignment, talking about lucrative job offers and failed plans.

After his prepared remarks, he was asked if a limited, scaled-back effort to go after the terrorists could succeed. His answer was unequivocal. "The short answer is: No. You have to navigate from where you are, not where you wish to be. A strategy that does not leave Afghanistan in a stable position is probably a shortsighted strategy."

He said he had been encouraged to state his case bluntly in his confidential assessment. He praised the process of Washington deliberations, but laughed when he said he might not always be free to speak out, adding, "They may change their minds, and crush me someday."

McChrystal's comments marked a seminal moment for the White House staff. What better proof that the military was on a search-and-destroy mission aimed at the president? Emanuel, Donilon and McDonough were furious. Even Jones was shocked. "It was another Whiskey Tango Foxtrot moment," he said. Was it possible that having led a sheltered existence in the secretive Special Operations Command left McChrystal this ignorant of public relations?

Already on his flight to Denmark, Obama said, "We got to stop this. This is not helping."

McChrystal told Petraeus, "I know I screwed this up. I'm going to lie low." Petraeus had previously hoped everything between the White House and the military had calmed down. He passed word to Gates, who told the president that McChrystal knew the speech had been inappropriate.

Obama and McChrystal met aboard Air Force One in Denmark the next day for 25 minutes. Neither dwelt on the speech, but both acknowledged that it wouldn't happen again.

McChrystal stood by his written 66-page assessment but added, "Mr. President, you describe the mission and we'll do whatever we need to carry it out."

By both accounts, there were no fireworks or rebukes. Obama was controlled. When the president returned home, he told Axelrod and Gibbs, "I like him. I think he's a good man." McChrystal was the right man for the job, he said, but added that the output they got from the military had a lot to do with the input given by the civilian commanders, Gates and himself. McChrystal's mission was circumscribed and limited to Afghanistan, Obama noted, but as they were learning, the real problems stemmed from Pakistan.

Colin Powell, the former chairman of the Joint Chiefs, who as a young officer had worked with McChrystal's father, Major General Herbert J. McChrystal, Jr., e-mailed McChrystal recommending that it was time to lower his profile.

The president had already agreed to 21,000 more troops and a request for 40,000 more was on its way. This was probably one of the biggest shocks a president could receive, hauntingly reminiscent of the June 7, 1965, request by General William Westmoreland for 41,000 more troops in Vietnam. In his 1995 book, *In Retrospect*, Robert McNamara called Westy's request a "bombshell" that "meant a dramatic and open-ended expansion of American military involvement. Of the thousands of cables I received during my seven years in the Defense Department, this one disturbed me most. We were forced to make a decision."

Facing an unexpected and stunning strategic request was not where Obama had planned to be in the fall of the first year of his presidency. On top of that, the military was out campaigning, closing off his choices, and the White House was losing control of the public narrative.

Obama vented to Emanuel, Axelrod and Donilon. He became the most impassioned with Donilon, the national security staffer with whom he spent the most time. By one account, Donilon told a colleague that the president was stabbing his finger at his deputy national security adviser's chest so much that he almost had a bruise there.

Obama wanted to know how he had arrived at this place. Why did I give them the troops in February? Those troops haven't gotten there yet. They're about to ask for a game-changing number and they're going to the public and leaking it to trap us.

Donilon unloaded on many people at the Pentagon, invoking the president's name and insisting Obama wanted this fixed immediately. He was a lawyer with one client—the president. But instead of absorbing Obama's frustration, he was a pure transmission belt for it. He took the heat from the president and retransmitted it, eliciting sniping that Donilon didn't have the broad experience needed for the sensitive White House position and lived in a lawyer's bunker. Donilon had not even visited Afghanistan. He had no feel for the situation on the ground or for the military. He had hosed down Pentagon officials and in the process come close to endangering his relationships with some of them, including Gates.

Jones was dumbfounded by McChrystal. How could he give such a speech and answer so categorically while the president sought alternative strategies? The whole thing amazed him, particularly after the White House had scolded Mullen and Petraeus for their comments weeks earlier.

The national security adviser told Gates that McChrystal's speech was an over-the-top moment and the president had demonstrated a lot of restraint.

"You've simply got to stop this," he said, "or the president is going to have to fire somebody."

A frustrated Gates said he thought he had taken the necessary steps, including issuing guidance to prevent incidents like this from happening.

Jones thought this was not a matter of guidance but of common sense, which was sadly lacking.

Furious, he also called Admiral Mullen, McChrystal's biggest booster. "I don't know what you guys are doing," he said. McChrystal's speech was either "insubordination or stupid." It read like a direct challenge to the president.

"It is a firing offense, but McChrystal won't be fired because we need him," Jones said. Referring to Mullen and Petraeus, Jones said, "One of you is going to get fired and I'm going to recommend it." Repeating his previous warning, Jones said, "You're losing altitude."

It had largely been a one-sided conversation with Jones. Mullen had gotten little chance to talk. One of his responsibilities as the Joint Chiefs chairman was to prevent a breach between the president (and his senior civilian staff) and the uniformed military. Mullen knew that such a breach, even short of firings, could be catastrophic. His job entailed protecting President Obama from the military, which had enormous stature with the public. But it also meant protecting the military from the president, who after all was the commander in chief. The relationship was not heading in the right direction.

Was Jones speaking for the president? Were his comments—threats really—the eruption of a retired four-star offended by his peers? Or was Jones trying to protect and insulate the president? Jones had been hired as a counterweight to Gates and the Pentagon brass. Was he trying to protect himself?

When Mullen and Gates met with Obama for their next weekly meeting, the president raised McChrystal's remarks.

This was something that really put me in a box, Obama said, and I don't like being boxed in.

"It will never happen again," Mullen said. "It was not intentional."

Obama felt disrespected and trapped. The White House saw the speech as a scheme on the part of McChrystal, Mullen and Petraeus.

"We didn't do that," Mullen tried to reassure him. "We would never do that intentionally."

Jones had been dealing with his own turmoil inside the NSC for several months. A giant thorn in his side had been Mark Lippert, the 36-year-old who had parlayed his three years as Obama's Senate foreign policy aide into an appointment as NSC chief of staff. Jones believed Lippert was leaking derogatory and defamatory information about him to the media and undermining him inside the White House. Jones had had a couple of come-to-Jesus meetings with him, but to no avail.

Lippert, a Navy Reserve lieutenant (junior grade) intelligence officer, had deployed to Iraq during the presidential campaign, but he remained as tight as ever with Obama. The president called him "brother." It was a proximity and comfort—even friendship—that Jones did not have with Obama. He had surveyed the daily schedule of Steve Hadley, his predecessor as national security adviser. Hadley often spent six hours or even the whole day with President Bush, much of it for routine meetings and phone calls.

Jones did not want to be seen as hovering around Obama. But his low-key, low-profile approach appeared to verify the whisper campaign that portrayed him as an out-of-touch national security adviser who only worked 12-hour days when many of the younger staff stayed in their West Wing offices until late at night. The criticism had grown so intense among some blogs and foreign policy publications that Jones gave interviews to reporters from *The Washington Post* and *The New York Times* in early May.

The resulting articles failed to halt the whisper campaign. On June 11, Fox News reported that Jones was not up to the job, saying, "One NSC staff member claimed that Jones is so forgetful that at times he appears to have Alzheimer's disease." An outraged Jones kept the notes of the broadcast in his office.

Jones finally went to talk to Emanuel about the leaks he believed were coming from Lippert.

"When I heard it three times, I ignored it," he said. "Then four, five, six times. Longtime friends said that someone was providing this, and they said they can't say who but his initials are M.L." Emanuel had to find Lippert another job.

"You'll have to talk to the president," Emanuel said. "This is his guy."

In July, Jones laid out his case to Obama and others. All seemed to agree that it was rank insubordination. Obama promised to move on Lippert.

"I will tell him," Obama told Jones.

It took more than two months. On October 1, the day of the McChrystal speech in London, the White House press secretary issued a three-paragraph statement that Lippert was returning to active duty in the Navy. The statement made it sound as though this had been Lippert's choice.

"I was not surprised," Obama said in the statement, "when he came and told me he had stepped forward for another mobilization, as Mark is passionate about the Navy."

Jones was quoted as saying, "Mark has been vital to building a strong and revitalized National Security Council, ready to address the myriad challenges we face in the 21st century. I'm confident that Mark will continue to serve his nation in the United States Navy with the same commitment and sense of patriotism that we benefited from here in the White House. I congratulate him on this new post."

Jones was also contemplating who might succeed him as national security adviser. He was thinking about an exit strategy. His deputy, Donilon, had become indispensable. The lawyer was an office junkie, staying later, reading more and generating the agendas and memos and tasking orders like no other. He was on track to lead some 147 deputies committee meetings that year—occasionally two or three a day. These were often sophisticated reviews of policy, intelligence and in-depth backgrounders.

Jones was impressed, but he also resented the close relationship that Donilon had with Emanuel, Axelrod and some of the others. He still chafed that the main pipeline continued to be Emanuel–Donilon, who were like two tuning forks—when one vibrated, so did the other.

In good Marine Corps tradition, Jones believed that all key subordinates were entitled to a performance evaluation. He called Donilon into his office.

"I will leave at some point," Jones said, suggesting it might be sooner rather than later. He had always tried to set up a successor in his previous jobs, he said. "Maybe you're my replacement, maybe not," but let me give you my sense of where you stand, what you're doing right and what you may be doing wrong.

Jones praised his substantive and organizational skills, and told Donilon that he was indispensable to the president, the principals—including Jones—the whole interagency and NSC staff. But Donilon had made three mistakes. First, he had never gone to Afghanistan or Iraq, or really left the office for a serious field trip. As a result, he said, you have no direct understanding of these places. "You have no credibility with the military." You should go overseas. The White House, Situation Room, interagency byplay, as important as they are, are not everything.

Second, Jones continued, you frequently pop off with absolute declarations about places you've never been, leaders you've never met, or colleagues you work with. Gates had mentioned this to Jones, saying that Donilon's sound-offs and strong spur-of-the-moment opinions, especially about one general, had offended him so much at an Oval Office meeting that he nearly walked out.

Third, he said, you have too little feel for the people who work day and night on the NSC staff, their salaries, their maternity leaves, their promotions, their family troubles, all the things a manager of people has to be tuned into. "Everything is about personal relations," Jones said.

On Friday, October 2, Gates invited Pakistani Ambassador Haqqani to the Pentagon for one of their periodic lunches.

Haqqani felt upbeat as he strolled through the Pentagon's outer E-Ring hallway. There was progress on so many fronts. In the next few weeks, the Pakistani army would move into Waziristan, an offensive President Zardari had pushed for. Since he had lost support by being pro-American, Zardari thought he could gain support by being tough on the Taliban.

Haqqani's relationship with Gates, as with other important Washington figures, was carefully nurtured. He had known the defense secretary for more than two decades.

They sat in the secretary's private dining room, with its view through bulletproof glass of the Potomac River. An assistant defense secretary joined them to take notes.

As the president had suggested two days before, Gates had an explicit message for Haqqani.

"We are not leaving," he told Haqqani, asking him to note that in his cable to Islamabad. "We are not leaving Afghanistan. How many more troops to put in and for what purpose, that is the question. What kind of troops and for what purpose? There is no interest whatsoever in reducing the number of troops already present in Afghanistan."

Haqqani unfurled a shopping list of gear and vehicles that the Pakistani military needed. Congress had given them the equivalent of a Pentagon gift card, approving a $400 million fund in May to pay for improvements to Pakistan's counterinsurgency arsenal.

Haqqani scrolled through the must-haves. Cargo helicopters, Beechcraft 350 aircraft, unmanned aerial vehicles, night vision devices, IED jammers, aviation maintenance support, communications monitoring equipment, frigates and P-3C Orion airplanes to conduct maritime surveillance. This could all help with the Pakistani army's upcoming offensive against the Taliban in South Waziristan.

Gates instantly okayed almost everything on the list but chose to be noncommittal on the frigates and P-3C Orions. They would have little use in the landlocked tribal areas where the Taliban and al Qaeda were.

With the buying spree out of the way, Haqqani brought up the $1.6 billion that America owed the Pakistani military for conducting operations along the Afghan border. After 9/11, the U.S. set up an expense account for Pakistan and other countries called the Coalition Support Fund. It reimbursed allies for their assistance, although a scathing 2008 report by the U.S. Government Accountability Office said the U.S. could not verify more than $2 billion in Pakistani claims. The new $1.6 billion had steadily accumulated between May 2008 and March 2009. For Pakistan, the tab was equal to more than 30 percent of its defense budget, according to CIA estimates. Haqqani pressed for the money and Gates promised to look into it.

17

Jones called the principals together for a meeting on Monday, October 5, to rehearse for the next NSC meeting. Debate went again to the question of who the primary enemy was.

"We're just parsing this distinction between the Taliban and al Qaeda too much," Petraeus said in frustration. "The Taliban is almost becoming a new extremist brand itself."

"The Taliban and al Qaeda are together when they're winning," DNI Blair said. He didn't have to add the subtext: The Taliban were winning. "They can't be split apart except when under pressure."

The U.S. ambassador to Pakistan, Anne Patterson, was on a secure video screen. She said that al Qaeda, the Taliban and all the groups were "mutually reinforcing."

There were questions about the prospects for a Taliban takeover of Afghanistan.

"If we left," Petraeus said, it would happen "pretty, pretty quickly."

Gates said that they had to realize that Afghanistan carried a unique symbolism for the jihadist movement. "This was where the jihad was born."

"We're struggling to separate groups that are relatively linked," CIA Director Panetta said.

The logic went like this: A victory for the Taliban counted as victory for al Qaeda, so the U.S. couldn't walk away from Afghanistan.

But Jim Steinberg, Clinton's deputy, didn't see it quite that way. "What do we have to do to win the war?" he asked. "How much do we have to win the war against the Taliban?"

No one answered directly, but Peter Lavoy went back to his usual argument, "Were the Taliban perceived to be winning in Afghanistan, that would be a boost to militants worldwide."

Eikenberry, on secure video from Kabul, supported that line of reasoning. But as a practical matter, he said, "We should distinguish between the Afghan and Pakistan Taliban. Getting Pakistan to move against the Afghan Taliban would help enormously." While Pakistan moved against its own Taliban, the ISI still had contacts with the Haqqani network and other affiliates of the Afghan Taliban as part of its hedging strategy.

Mullen reinforced Gates's point that the Pakistan-Afghanistan border area was the epicenter of terrorism. He also parroted Petraeus's warning against making too many distinctions among the groups.

Clinton saw little ambiguity. "The Taliban are linked to al Qaeda," she said firmly. "The Riedel core goal and supporting objectives were correct and proper. We don't need to change those to discuss the level of effort in Pakistan and Afghanistan. The debate is about whether we need to conduct a fully resourced, comprehensive counterinsurgency campaign and massive aid to Pakistan."

That's not exactly the debate, Petraeus thought. First and foremost, it's about what the reality is on the ground in terms of these groups. Everything else would come out of that.

Lute reminded Clinton of the context for McChrystal's counterinsurgency strategy. "You know, the implementation plan signed by General Jones told the field to defeat the Taliban, because of the assumption that that is what is required."

The Jones directive had said the core goal was to "defeat the extremist insurgency," meaning the Taliban.

Donilon said, "You have to give meaning to the phrase." The question after two hours of discussion was still whether they had to defeat the Taliban to achieve the core goal or could they disrupt or degrade them until the Afghan National Security Forces were ready.

Petraeus was sure that it would be difficult if not impossible to build the Afghan security forces in a challenging security environment. He had seen that in Iraq. It was the reality on the ground. But he would have to wait to make that point.

Clinton and Gates went off to George Washington University for a roundtable discussion, where they were interviewed by then CNN correspondent Christiane Amanpour. They had dinner at the Blue Duck Tavern afterward, where they seemed to agree on what should be done with Afghanistan and troop levels. Gates and Clinton would be a team inside the Situation Room, a formidable one.

At 2:30 P.M. on October 6, Obama met in the State Dining Room with a bipartisan group of about 30 congressional leaders. It was a chance to update them on the strategy review.

Representative Eric Cantor, the Republican minority whip, offered his party's support. "If you decide to move forward, we'll be with you," said the congressman from Richmond, Virginia.

Obama said that he appreciated the gesture. "I can't help but notice that when the supplemental came up," he said, referring to the May request for $94.2 billion for the Afghanistan and Iraq wars, "that support wasn't as forthcoming. I don't remember that bill sliding through the House. So I'm glad to hear that it's here today."

A number of legislators criticized the counterterrorism approach that Biden had been advocating. They interpreted it as a way to reduce the U.S. presence. Troops had to be on the ground, they said, winning popular support and developing human intelligence. None of this could be done from offshore or from the air.

"Let's just be clear," Biden said after hearing three versions of this complaint, "that I'm not, and nobody else who's participating in these meetings is, advocating a strictly counterterrorism policy that would be carried out by a few Special Forces at night with some drones."

"Look, guys," the president interjected, "nobody's talking about leaving Afghanistan."

McCain said, "I hope the decision won't be made leisurely," adding that he respected that the decision was Obama's as commander in chief.

"John," Obama replied, "I can assure you I'm not making this decision in a leisurely way. And you're absolutely right. This is my decision, and I'm the commander in chief."

What a bracing moment, thought Axelrod.

"Nobody," Obama continued, "feels more urgency to make this decision—but to make it right—than I do."

Petraeus and Senator Lindsey Graham had one of their regular conversations that same day. The general had come to admire the Republican's ability to navigate Washington. He considered Graham to be a brilliant and skillful political chess player. But Graham's comments a few days earlier on *Fox News Sunday* were not helping.

The senator had quoted McChrystal as saying that without reinforcements the U.S. would not defeat the Taliban. Eight Americans had just been killed in Afghanistan, Graham said. "The president has a window of time here to seriously deliberate, but it's running out. And what you saw yesterday is exactly what awaits this country—our troops cannot change momentum. They're sitting ducks. They need to be reinforced."

Petraeus told Graham, You're kind of taking some of Stan's statements out of context. "Stan doesn't want to be pitted against the president," he said. "Stand down, ratchet it down a little bit."

Graham saw the wisdom in this. He didn't want to inflame the situation more than McChrystal's London speech already had.

"If I were the commander in chief, I wouldn't have appreciated that," Graham said. "And Stan, I don't think, meant it. He's just, he sees what's coming. What happened Saturday, with the eight deaths, more of that's coming."

Petraeus agreed that something had to be done. He said he thought Gates was with him on troop levels. The military chain—Gates, Mullen, Petraeus and McChrystal—would not break ranks in the Situation Room.

In the course of their conversations, Graham offered Petraeus some thoughts on how to deal with the crucial number of troops.

"If there is a number in your mind below which we can't succeed," Graham said, "don't ever create a scenario where that thought is lost. They can ask you for 20 options and you can give them 20 options, but one thing you've got to say, 'This is the fail-safe line right here.' "

Graham continued, "If you're not strong on this, they're going to water it down, because that is their instinct, to water it down." He recommended giving some leeway, so it would be okay if Obama didn't pick the exact number. "But if you show any weakness here," he added, if a lower number "becomes attractive in any way, shape or form, you're in trouble."

Graham, the Air Force Reserve colonel, advised the general, "I'm a politician. I know exactly how to create back doors for myself. Every good politician always has a back door. The day that you get an issue where there's no way out is when you're dangerous to yourself and others." Help the president, Graham said. "You're doing him a service by really making it difficult."

Petraeus said he did not want to make it easy or hard on anybody, including the president. "I am going to just give my best professional military advice, period."

Yeah, of course, Graham understood. "One thing the president does not ever need to lose sight of: We've been in Europe for 60 years and Japan, all these countries. Nobody gives a shit. It is casualties." Americans being killed and wounded on a regular basis were what mattered. "Go in with the biggest punch you can go in with, and change the dynamics on the ground in terms of casualties."

Petraeus said they needed 40,000 more U.S. troops, but his fail-safe number would probably be 30,000.

Around this time, Mullen also paid Graham a visit. Perched on the couch inside the senator's office, the admiral said to not worry about how much time Obama was taking to make a decision.

"I just want you to know, Senator Graham, that we're having good discussions," Mullen said. "We don't think it's taking too long."

Graham decided to back off and during his next major television appearance he said that the quality of Obama's final decision mattered more than the quantity of time spent making it.

Both Obama and Emanuel believed Graham was their most reasonable Republican ally, but he had given Petraeus what might be the most crucial advice for securing what the military wanted—not to budge from a bottom-line number.

On Wednesday, October 7, Jones invited Clinton and Gates into his White House office for a private meeting. The president was not happy. The sessions so far had exposed a simple fact: They had not found a way to articulate why the United States was in Afghanistan. What were America's interests?

They had to find a better way to explain. It was not entirely a public relations gloss they needed, but that was part of it. The initial cause of the war was crystal-clear—retaliation for the September 11, 2001, terrorist attacks and the successful effort to deny al Qaeda a safe haven in Afghanistan. But the war had ambled along somewhat aimlessly, under-resourced for eight years.

The discussion brought into relief, once again, just how unconventional this war was. Fixing the Afghan government was central to the mission if the U.S. was ever going to get out.

Yes, Gates said, they had to focus on governance—the Afghan national government, the provinces, the local districts and the tribes. They had to help the ministries of the central government that were worth supporting, he said. Afghanistan had to get beyond its failed-state status—a giant task.

All three admitted that they were being dragged down with terms like counterterrorism and counterinsurgency. The public didn't under-

stand what those words meant. There were too many labels. They also
agreed that McChrystal's mission had to be reframed with realistic
goals and time limits.

They also skirted the troubling question: What precisely were they
trying to do?

Later that day at 3:30 P.M., Obama gathered his team for a three-hour
review and discussion of Pakistan.

Lavoy again began by summarizing the intelligence picture. Pakistan suffered from the enduring we're-with-you, we're-not-with-you
schizophrenia, the continuing dominance of the military-intelligence
complex, and President Zardari's political weakness.

The consensus inside the intelligence community was that Afghanistan would not get straightened out until there was a stable relationship between Pakistan and India. A more mature and less combustible
relationship between the two longtime adversaries was more important than building Afghanistan, Lavoy said.

Lavoy revisited the Bush years. "We had engaged Musharraf as
though he was Pakistan, which he was." But with Musharraf out of
office and living in London, the U.S. still had not done enough to
build relations with other political entities. Deep Pakistani mistrust of
American intentions persisted.

Mullen pointed out that the robust military-to-military programs
with Pakistan had grown to nearly $2 billion a year for training, equip-
ment and other enterprises. Relations were getting better. The admiral was spending a lot of time with General Kayani, improving trust
between the countries.

The real issue was whether U.S. soldiers could conduct operations
on the ground in Pakistan. That had traditionally been the red line,
but it was the crux of the problem that had to be solved. If they wanted
to go to the center of gravity to solve the security problem, that was
what they would have to do. But no one raised that issue that day.

Panetta passed around a list proposing the expansion of ten CIA
counterterrorist activities. Adding more Predator drones inside Paki-

stan was one. Another was increasing the size of the areas in which Pakistan permitted drone strikes. There were also suggestions for opening new facilities in Pakistan, working through the ISI to develop more sources within the tribes and embedding U.S. military advisers in Pakistani operational units. Most of the activities would be carried out with Pakistani consent.

Let's do it, Obama said, approving all the actions on the spot. It was unusual to get an immediate order from the president, particularly since the review sessions had been, up until that point, all talk and no decisions.

Sorting out the budget for how much was being spent on Pakistan was difficult. Jones jotted a note to himself to get a sense of the outstanding requests for resources and equipment in both the white, open world and the black, covert world.

The president returned to India. "We need to move aggressively on India-Pakistan issues in order to try to reduce the tensions between the two countries."

Secretary Clinton addressed the consequences of not engaging with the Pakistani public for the past several years, contributing to America's unpopularity there.

"There hadn't been much public diplomacy in recent years," she said. The history of the United States abandoning the region after the Cold War still hung over everything.

Meanwhile, "the U.S. relationship with India is growing steadily," she said, which to say the least was characterized as a negative in Pakistan. When the Pakistani media ran negative stories, there was not enough pushback. Where was a "counter-propaganda plan?" she asked.

"There's been lack of sufficient funding, people, concepts, structures and authorities," said Petraeus, chuckling. "Other than that, we're doing great."

For much of the Bush presidency, U.S. policy had coddled Musharraf and disregarded the 170 million people in Pakistan. Clinton wanted a decision on multiyear, civilian assistance for Pakistani infrastructure, energy and agriculture, in addition to media outreach.

Biden spun a hypothesis about how a Pashtun leader in Afghanistan influenced Pakistan. It contained enough what ifs that some in the room were quickly confused. Petraeus later told others that the vice president tended to get lost in his own verbiage, erecting strawman arguments that he could then easily demolish.

The session was grinding to a halt. Obama read through a list of specific questions about how to convince Pakistan that it was in their interest to change.

"There's no clear answer yet with regard to what induces Pakistan to make a strategic shift in our direction," he said.

"Why can't we have straightforward talks with India on why a stable Pakistan is crucial?" Obama asked. India is moving toward a higher place in its global posture. A stable Pakistan would help that.

Among his other questions were: Would the addition of U.S. troops in Afghanistan make Pakistan more or less cooperative? Because of Pakistani corruption, is there a way to funnel U.S. aid directly to the people for whom it's intended?

Speaking by video, Ambassador Anne Patterson tried to address the aid question. "We need to give Pakistanis some control over projects, although mobilizing the civilian sector would be a good thing to do."

Obama ended by saying he wanted to improve the U.S. image in Pakistan.

In one discussion about the tensions between Pakistan and India, Holbrooke introduced a new angle. "There's a global warming dimension of this struggle, Mr. President," he said.

His words baffled many in the room.

There are tens of thousands of Indian and Pakistani troops encamped on the glaciers in the Himalayas that feed the rivers into Pakistan and India, he said. "Their encampments are melting the glaciers very quickly." There's a chance that river valleys in Pakistan and perhaps even India could be flooded.

After the meeting, there were several versions of one question: Was Holbrooke kidding?

He was not. Holbrooke subsequently detailed his concerns in a written report. The diplomat—sensing he was on the outs with Obama—was trying as hard as he could to say something distinctive that would impress the president. He had talked about tripling the number of civilian experts in Afghanistan to 1,000 by the end of the year, calling it "the biggest civilian surge in history." And Holbrooke had routinely cited what he considered to be major progress in restoring Afghanistan's agricultural economy. Donilon eventually had to tell him to give the NSC something more than a list of activities and issues. The president wanted a comprehensive strategy from Holbrooke's office, Donilon said.

It wasn't until well into the Obama presidency that Holbrooke learned definitively how much the president didn't care for him. When the president had announced Holbrooke's appointment a couple of days into the administration, the two had a private moment.

"Mr. President, I want to ask you one favor," Holbrooke had said, expressing gratitude for the highly visible assignment. "Would you do me the great favor of calling me Richard, for my wife's sake?" It was her preference. She disliked the name "Dick," which the president had been using.

At the ceremony, Obama referred to Holbrooke as "Richard." But later, the president told others that he found the request highly unusual and even strange. Holbrooke was horrified when he learned that his request—which he had repeated to no one—had been circulated by the president.

Petraeus thought the back-and-forth at these sessions was useful on some level, but it was dragging on. Intellectual exploration had its limits. Sensing the drift at the meeting, he wrote optimistically in his small black notebook: "There will be a recommitment to Afghanistan."

18

McChrystal finally had a chance to present his troop options to principals only—Obama was not present—at 10:30 A.M. on Thursday, October 8. His face, earnest and somber, appeared on one of the flat-panel monitors hanging on the Situation Room wall. It was 7 P.M. in Kabul.

His briefing contained 14 slides.

The general stuck to his main point: Conditions inside Afghanistan were much worse than he had anticipated and only a fully resourced counterinsurgency would remedy things.

Jones interjected testily that there were essential questions that had not yet been answered. The U.S. still had a long way to go on managing the Afghan-Pakistan border. He circled and starred in his notebook, "It will be impossible to implement *ANY* Afghan strategy that does not address the safe havens in Pakistan."

What about the will of the Afghan security forces to fight? Jones asked. What about the will of the Afghan people? What about the potential for reforming local, regional and national governance? They were kidding themselves if they thought adding troops was the solution.

"The plan is not executable without change in governance—fundamental changes," Jones said.

McChrystal listed his three options. The first called for 10,000–11,000 troops, mainly for training the Afghan security forces. The middle one would add 40,000 troops for protecting the population, while the last one would double that to 85,000 for the same purpose.

Each option was illustrated on a map of Afghanistan filled with blue bubbles, or "inkblots," over the areas where the troops would be stationed. The bubbles grew larger and more numerous as the numbers increased.

None of the blots spread along the border with Pakistan. It was blank space, open country for the Taliban insurgents. The missing bubbles underscored a fundamental weakness in the plan, Jones thought. There's a mismatch between our core objectives and our understanding of the troop request as it currently exists, he wrote in his notebook.

And even with 85,000 more troops—apparently an overshot to make the 40,000 seem more appealing—the U.S. could only protect 60 percent of the population. A full counterinsurgency was impossible with these options. So how could McChrystal presume to "defeat" the Taliban?

The "defeat" goal had been nagging nearly everyone, including Holbrooke, who didn't consider it necessary or achievable. He had chastised McChrystal about this the other day.

What did defeat mean? Holbrooke asked again.

It means degrade, McChrystal said, stopping the Taliban from taking over substantial parts of the country. This was a major tweak of the definition, which had previously been interpreted as destroying the Taliban, almost literally obliterating them.

So, Clinton asked, if the mission is reduced to degrade, can you do it with fewer troops?

"No, ma'am," the general said. He was sticking to 40,000.

Obama awoke that next morning to learn that he had been awarded the Nobel Peace Prize. The president called his foreign policy speechwriter Ben Rhodes, who was now the NSC director of strategic communications. Could Rhodes help fashion a few words?

The 32-year-old Rhodes called his lunch date to cancel. Before entering the world of politics, the native of Manhattan's Upper East Side had aspired to write novels. He had published one short story, "The Goldfish Smiles, You Smile Back," about an office worker who climbs the corporate ladder thanks to his exceptional note taking. "My notes are so impressive that they have taken on the form of ideas . . . I capture other people's words in a manner that not only organizes them, but inserts a clarity and purpose that was not present in the original idea," reads one passage in the story. Rhodes basically did a similar thing for the president, recording Obama's thoughts and words before enhancing them with additional "clarity and purpose."

Obama appeared at a podium by the Rose Garden at 10:30 A.M. His sentiments were grounded in hard realities, rather than the idealism of many other Nobel laureates.

"We have to confront the world as we know it today," he said. "I am the commander in chief of a country that's responsible for ending a war and working in another theater to confront a ruthless adversary that directly threatens the American people and our allies."

It was a revealing turn of phrase. U.S. troops weren't fighting in Afghanistan. They were "working" in a "theater."

The full NSC session with the president was scheduled for 2:30 that afternoon. It was their fourth meeting. Petraeus had flown in from his hometown of Cornwall, New York, where a road had been named for him the day before.

The president opened the meeting by asking everyone to tell him what they thought should be done with the war.

As usual, Lavoy, the soft-spoken DNI expert, was up first. He had been gaining immense credibility with most in the room. Some even seemed to anoint him as the review's oracle. Lavoy was very good, but others believed that no group charged with such immense responsibility should rely too heavily on one person, no matter how informed he might be, particularly when most of them knew relatively little about Pakistan.

Pakistan was obsessed with India, Lavoy reminded them again. The Indians have a $1 billion aid program in Afghanistan, for example, that the Pakistanis think pays for intelligence. Each year, a thousand Afghan agricultural students study in India. The Pakistanis say that means a thousand spies. According to the CIA, it probably only meant a few spies. The Pakistanis also thought the head of Afghan intelligence, Amrullah Saleh, who had been with the Northern Alliance, an ethnic Tajik pre-9/11 group that fought the Taliban, was an Indian agent.

There also was concern that India funded separatist movements in various regions of Pakistan, most notably among the natives of Baluchistan, the same desolate province where some of the Afghan Taliban were camped.

Lavoy said that the Pakistanis were accommodating the U.S. to a degree, but they had continuing reservations about American commitment. They know they're indispensable to us and our effort in Afghanistan. Pakistan has changed its behavior because of U.S. counterterrorist actions and, more importantly, by actions of extremists against the Pakistani government. This has led to the political and popular support for Pakistan's recent military operations in the tribal areas.

The Pakistanis, however, Lavoy said, see some risks to a larger U.S. military involvement in Afghanistan. Taliban fighters and refugees entering Pakistan help extremists in Pakistan justify their own attacks in the name of religion.

Afghanistan and Pakistan have contradictory interests, Lavoy continued reminding them. While Karzai wants increased U.S. and NATO presence, Pakistan would view a strong Afghan national government as aligned with their archenemy, India, thereby basically surrounding and isolating Pakistan. The Pakistanis, especially the army and the ISI, worry about having too many U.S. troops. Karzai worries about having too few.

Citing sensitive intelligence, he said, Pakistan was making a half-hearted effort against the insurgents, all the while allowing safe havens for al Qaeda. To make matters worse, the intelligence suggests that money alone won't influence the Pakistanis to do more because they're probably getting payments from other countries with competing interests, like Saudi Arabia and China.

I've been up at night reading the intelligence reports, Obama said at one point. On one early page, it said—as Lavoy had noted—that Pakistan was overwhelmed with concern that the United States would pull out of Afghanistan and the region as it had done before.

Much later, Obama said, the report warned that Pakistan dreaded having a large Afghan army on its border that might be in an alliance with India. One of the U.S. objectives is to build that army.

How do you explain the contradiction? Obama asked. What exactly was Pakistan worried about—too much or too little? "What am I to believe?"

Mr. President, they're both true, Lavoy answered. That was the nature of Pakistan. Clinton, Holbrooke and Gates all said that they basically agreed with Lavoy. There was abundant evidence for both cases. Holbrooke later told others he saw the president playing a lawyer's game. Any lawyer could spot a surface contradiction.

Next, McChrystal made a 30-minute, 14-slide presentation of his assessment and troop options that had been rehearsed the day before.

When he got to the slide stating the goal—to "defeat" the Taliban—there was now a little blue box off to the side of the chart. It read, by defeat, we mean that the Taliban no longer would be an effective threat to the Afghan government, that they could not succeed as an insurgency.

Reversing himself from his position at the rehearsal, McChrystal said that if the mission is modified, then the request for resources would be different. But he presented exactly the same options—10,000–11,000, 40,000 and 85,000.

McChrystal emphasized the importance of training the Afghans. The army and police should have a combined strength of 400,000 by 2013. The 400,000 target had originated during the Riedel review in March. The Afghan army currently had about 100,000 soldiers, while the police totaled about 80,000—a more than doubling would be required.

Ultimately, Afghanistan can only be stabilized by the Afghans, McChrystal said. Improved governing and dealing with corruption were also key.

His pitch for a counterinsurgency was textbook. The objective of a 400,000-man Afghan security force corresponded perfectly with the preferred counterinsurgency ratio of 40 to 50 people for each soldier or policeman. But some felt McChrystal diminished the quality of his presentation by using the charts, PowerPoint slides and maps as a crutch.

The question was put to McChrystal: If you're doing a population-centric strategy, General, why the discrepancies between where the people live and where you have or want to commit troops? Not all of the bubbles overlapped with the population density map.

McChrystal said they had to have forces in the production centers and around the lines of communication. If they did not connect the population centers, they would be like Fort Apache—vulnerable islands out there by themselves.

Lute wondered why the president did not pursue things further by asking McChrystal to compare all the ink spots to the population density. And to ask questions like, Why do you have all this blue on this map? Why do I need to buy all this? Why are some areas along the Pakistani border not blue?

Biden began a cross-examination. "As I hear what you're saying, as I read your report, you're saying that we have about a year," he said. "And that our success relies upon having a reliable, a strong partner in governance to make this work?"

Yes, sir, McChrystal said.

Biden then addressed Karl Eikenberry, the retired three-star general who was ambassador to Afghanistan and appearing by videoconference. He had graduated from West Point a year before Petraeus. Fluent in Chinese, he had a hard-charging reputation. Serving under him was like an apprenticeship with a pirate captain, according to former junior officers. Eikenberry had served as the military commander in Afghanistan for 18 months from 2005 to 2007. Obama picked him to become ambassador the previous January, despite the rarity of having a retired general in the post.

Instead of calling Eikenberry "Ambassador," the vice president said, "General, in your estimation, can we, can that be achieved in the next year?"

No, sir, Eikenberry said, because that kind of reliable, strong partner did not exist in Afghanistan.

Eikenberry gave a pessimistic 10-minute summary of his views. He agreed with the assessment that the situation was deteriorating and more resources were needed, but a counterinsurgency strategy was too ambitious and would edge into nation building—a massive undertaking that could be a dramatic overreach.

In counterinsurgency, he said, "We talk about clear, hold and build, but we actually must include *transfer* into this," Eikenberry said. The "transfer" was how the U.S. would get out and that required a reliable partner, which was not currently the case.

Are we aligned with the Kabul government? he asked. We assume yes. "I would challenge that assumption," he said. They were severely hindered by Karzai's weakness as president, the absence of a strong central government.

"Right now we're dealing with an extraordinarily corrupt government." All this, he added, is "depressing and discouraging." The Kabul mansions belonging to senior Afghan officials had only become more ornate since he had last been in the country as the military commander.

There are limits on what we can do in dealing with corruption, he said. They had to be realistic.

"The Afghans think we're there because we have to be there, so they don't have to pay attention to what we want them to do," the ambassador said. He had almost said it was hopeless.

He said they had to think through the political and psychological implications in neighboring Iran and Pakistan of adding more troops into Afghanistan.

"Before looking at resources," Gates said, "we've gotten ourselves wrapped around three options." There was: 1. Counterinsurgency, which has come to mean nation building; 2. counterterrorism, which people think means missiles coming from a ship in the ocean; and 3. the counterterrorism plus proposed by the vice president. There obviously are more than these options, Gates said.

The goals that we have set out were right but, "we frame this in a way that is too ambitious." The objective that we have is right—defeating the Taliban. But then, "What do we mean by defeating the Taliban?"

Gates was elaborating on the box McChrystal had added to his slide about the U.S. goals in Afghanistan.

"The Taliban will probably be an element of the political fabric going forward," Gates said. "On the security side, we have to deny the Taliban the ability to hold 'consequential lands and territory.' " Especially, in the south and east of Afghanistan.

A key was denying the Taliban access to cities and driving down violence to a point where the Afghan National Security Forces can handle it.

"We need to redefine the goal," Gates said. "Not to destroy the Taliban—that sets a bar we probably can't achieve." He was retreating from his insistence in the implementation plan that summer that they "defeat" the insurgency.

The U.S. has probably been trying for more than is achievable, Gates said. Good governance is contrary to Afghan history, so the focus should instead be individual ministries that matter. He offered his opinion of Karzai's government, "This group is way beyond the pale in terms of corruption.

"We've talked the talk on corruption, but we've never exercised serious leverage." Once the election is resolved, the U.S. should be willing to hold back on funds.

"We need a new compact that says there won't be one dollar that will go to a corrupt minister, but we'll support those who do the right thing," Gates said.

The secretary of defense recapped. They needed to reframe an alternative to counterinsurgency or counterterrorism. Any final strategic plan should deny the Taliban the ability to occupy and control territory—his new standard—but facilitate the reintegration of the Taliban with the government and improve governance.

As usual, Petraeus had written out a summary of what he wanted to say before the meeting—all aimed to illustrate the dire situation and underscore the urgent need for adding forces.

He seconded Gates, "We're not going to defeat the Taliban," but we do need to deny them access to key population areas and lines of communication to "contain" them.

"If we don't reverse the downward spiral on security, we will enter a *security death spiral as we had in Iraq*.

"We learned in Iraq"—muted groans from some—"that as violence gets worse, first the local police and then other forces become increasingly challenged."

Security, which he felt had not been fully explained, was the cornerstone for all other progress in Afghanistan. Without it not only would advancing the Afghan security forces be impossible, but the development of local governance and the reintegration of reconcilables would be highly unlikely. People were too afraid with all the killings and bombings to take the necessary steps, finding it easier instead to submit to the Taliban shadow governments.

"I can understand the reluctance to commit more forces until the political situation in Kabul is sorted out," Petraeus said, "but time is of the essence. We have to break the Taliban momentum and regain the initiative."

He pulled out all the stops. "This is important, not just physically, but morally as well. Struggles like these are contests of will. I do think the objectives that we have discussed are important, not just for Afghanistan but for the region, NATO and the United States. And I would contend that we recognize that we don't know how long it will take to sort out the political situation and need to be sober about that fact, as Karl has noted.

"I understand the government is a criminal syndicate," he said. "But we need to help achieve and improve security and, as noted, regain the initiative and turn some recent tactical gains into operational momentum. I strongly agree with Stan's assessment and recommendation, albeit with some clarification," about the Taliban. "Secretary Gates will provide my formal comments with the chairman and JCS endorsement early next week."

Biden broke in for a question. "If the government's a criminal syndicate a year from now, how will troops make a difference?"

No one recorded an answer in their notes. Biden was swinging hard at McChrystal, Gates and Petraeus.

"What's the best-guess estimate for getting things headed in the right direction?" he asked. "If a year from now there is no demonstrable progress in governance, what do we do?"

No answer.

Biden tried again. "If the government doesn't improve and if you get the troops, in a year, what would be the impact?"

"The past five years are not heartening," Eikenberry answered, "but there are pockets of progress. We can build on those." For the next six to 12 months, he said, "We shouldn't expect significant breakthroughs."

Biden admired Eikenberry and privately showered him with his highest accolade, "a goddamned stand-up guy."

19

It was the secretary of state's turn at the October 9 meeting. "Mr. President," Clinton began, "the dilemma *you* face . . ."

On the back bench, press secretary Gibbs noted that she said *"you"* as if there was only one person in the boat and she and the others were at a pleasant distance. To Gibbs, it seemed as though Clinton was opining from afar. Memories of the vicious scrap and deep hostility from the Democratic presidential primaries lingered inside the White House, at least for former campaign aides like Gibbs and Axelrod.

Clinton's use of *"you"* also floored Holbrooke, since she should have said "we" to underscore and even trumpet her team-player status. Holbrooke suspected the Obamaites would recognize the *"you"* as distancing on the part of the secretary of state. He held his tongue as Clinton spoke, because interrupting her would be unforgivable when she was in full flower like this. It was "a Freudian giveaway," Holbrooke later told others. The only question was whether it was conscious or not. Whatever it was, he thought Clinton felt detached from both the policy and the process. And the more hawkish her position, the more she came under suspicion from White House staffers loyal to the president.

The *"you"* was a formulation used by others. And it was a matter of fact that the decision was Obama's, so the word was correct.

But Gibbs's and Holbrooke's reactions revealed how raw the emotions were running.

Clinton said the dilemma was which should come first—more troops or better governance? "But not putting troops in guarantees we won't achieve what we're after and guarantees no psychological momentum. Preventing collapse requires more troops, but that doesn't guarantee progress."

She tipped her hand further. Afghans had to feel safe before their governance could improve. It was the same logic as Petraeus's argument that she had seemed to challenge in earlier meetings. Obama "must move on more troops.

"In the absence of a troop commitment, can we achieve our goals in Afghanistan and Pakistan?" she asked. Answering her own question, Clinton said, "The only way to get governance changes is to add troops, but there's still no guarantee that it will work."

Clinton then rattled off the reasons why there was no guarantee. If there is a troop commitment, what size? How to coordinate with Pakistan? How to support reintegration and how to conduct partnering? What's the most effective way forward with the Afghan leadership?

"These are all difficult, unsatisfactory options," she said. "We do have a national security interest in ensuring the Taliban doesn't defeat us. The same with destroying al Qaeda, which would be difficult without Afghanistan. It's an extremely difficult decision, but the options are limited unless we commit and gain the psychological advantage."

Admiral Mullen echoed the other hawkish comments, saying that Secretary Gates's reframing of the objectives was correct. "Security is achievable, but time does matter." In his opinion, the training of a 240,000-man Afghan army in "three to five years is reasonable."

"Possibly we'll see by the end of next year if this will work," Mullen added. "The urgency is there. Psychologically, this is huge. NATO's commitment and future are in the balance."

•   •   •

DNI Dennis Blair suggested that domestic politics might be a problem. It would be tough because of casualties, he said. Last month had been tough—40 killed, double the rate of the year before.

"Will this be worth it?" he asked. "The answer is, people will support it as long as they think we're making progress." For the first time, the president would have a strategy developed by his full war cabinet, and we'll be able to tell the American people what we're doing, he said.

What they could not do, CIA Director Panetta said, is accept the status quo. "You can't leave." And, he agreed, "You can't defeat the Taliban." They were not talking about a Jeffersonian democracy in Afghanistan, said Panetta, who saw this as a basis for narrowing the American mission and accepting Karzai despite his flaws.

"That leaves you to a targeted mission: to battle against al Qaeda, ensuring no safe havens," Panetta said.

We have to work with Karzai, he went on, sounding like Karzai's case officer. The CIA had been in alliance with the Karzai family for more than eight years. A narrower mission still meant securing population centers and pursuing the Taliban. They had to continue targeting Taliban leaders, he said. But the major question was: "Within one year, can we turn the momentum around?"

Susan Rice, the ambassador to the United Nations, spoke next. A former Rhodes Scholar who was a top Obama foreign policy adviser during the 2008 campaign, Rice had been something of a prodigy in Bill Clinton's administration, serving at 33 years old as the assistant secretary of state for African affairs.

"I have not made a decision yet personally," Rice said. She believed improved security in Afghanistan was necessary to defeat al Qaeda, since the relationship between al Qaeda and the Taliban was intertwined and the two groups couldn't be separated.

Rice drew attention to the Afghanistan-Pakistan border, which had a minimal U.S. and NATO presence in the McChrystal plan. There are possible safe havens there, she said.

More actions were needed against corruption, "including possibly Karzai's brother," she continued. While others had stressed security, Rice believed that the U.S. strategy should emphasize an anti-corruption campaign.

"If the government removes the worst actors, then our investment may yield dividends."

The president picked up on the problem with the bubbles on McChrystal's map. At one point, he noted that the blots didn't encompass all of the country. Other than a few bubbles, their locations were not necessarily connected to where Afghans lived. One hugged the Iranian border to the west. Based on the counterinsurgency manual ratio of one member of the security force for every 40 to 50 people, Obama noted that would require a total U.S., NATO and Afghan security force of 500,000 to 600,000 to be at Iraq levels.

"Sir," Petraeus said, holding both his hands high in the air like it was a stickup, "I'm not out there telling people this is like Iraq."

But the president had made a dispiriting observation for the COINistas. These numbers were not in the realm of the possible. Petraeus's major concern was that this would be a rationale for shortchanging any counterinsurgency strategy.

Stan's recommendations, Holbrooke said, are good for one country dealing with one issue. You were given the task of Afghanistan, he addressed McChrystal, but your responsibility ends at the border. The resource request did not take into account Pakistan or terrorists coming into Afghanistan from Pakistan.

"If I were fully convinced that there were no other questions, this would be a good request," Holbrooke said. "But I have concerns." He noted that General Pasha, Pakistan's intelligence chief, explicitly opposed having more American troops in Afghanistan.

The two weakest links were corruption and the Afghan police. "Our presence is the corrupting force," Holbrooke announced. All the contractors for development projects pay the Taliban for protection and use of the roads, so American and coalition dollars help finance the Taliban. And with more development, higher traffic on roads, and more troops, the Taliban would make more money.

He expanded on his concerns about the Afghan police. Over the next three years, the training command planned to grow the Afghan forces to 400,000—160,000 policemen and 240,000 soldiers. Holbrooke felt the police numbers were phony and getting phonier, so he had dispatched some of his staff to Afghanistan to look into things. About 80 percent of the Afghan police force was illiterate. Drug addiction was common. And many police were "ghosts" who cashed paychecks but never showed for duty.

Holbrooke opened one of the briefing folders that had been passed out to everyone before the meeting. He pulled out the documents from McChrystal about the Afghan police.

The yearly attrition rate was more than 25 percent, a figure that exceeded the number of new recruits. With the recruitment levels McChrystal projected, the size of the police force of roughly 80,000 would actually shrink. Doubling it to 160,000 would be mathematically impossible.

"It's like pouring water into a bucket with a hole in it," Holbrooke said.

"Richard," McChrystal answered, "you're absolutely right. And that's why we have to lower the attrition rate."

Holbrooke said that in 2006 he had visited a police center in the western Afghan city of Herat. Two months ago, he returned to the same center. Though everyone said it was much better, he found it hadn't changed at all.

"The police are the weak link," he said, and the Afghan policy was only as good as its weakest link.

The muddle on the Afghan presidential elections, Holbrooke said, has hurt U.S. credibility. Almost two months after the vote, Afghans had yet to see final certified results.

Yes, he said, we need more troops. The question was how many and how to use them. We need a significant increase in training personnel, but more forces may result in more dependency.

Like the others, Holbrooke was heavy on diagnosis but light on solutions. Several note takers had learned to do the same thing when Holbrooke embarked on his discourses. They set down their pens and relaxed their tired fingers. The big personality had lost its sheen. He was not connecting with Obama.

"What are we trying to achieve?" asked John Brennan, 55, the deputy for counterterrorism and a former CIA operative who had spent most of his career on Middle Eastern countries. "The security decisions here will be in play in other areas too."

Brennan's head, as well as Blair's and Panetta's, would be on a pike if there was another successful terrorist attack in the United States. Stopping that attack was his main concern and the focus of his professional life.

Why are we contemplating this in Afghanistan? Brennan asked. He could not realistically envision a fix.

"If you're talking about a completely uncorrupt government that delivers services to all of its people, that end state won't be achieved in my lifetime," Brennan said. "That's why using terminology like 'success,' like 'victory' and 'win,' complicates our task."

He said they needed to identify milestones that would measure progress in Afghanistan and align the resources with those milestones. There are very few al Qaeda in Afghanistan. The intelligence analysis indicated the Taliban might not even want al Qaeda back if it reestablished control of the government. Hosting al Qaeda had cost the Taliban Afghanistan in 2001. Why would al Qaeda want to go back to Afghanistan, where the U.S. and NATO already had 100,000 ground troops?

No, Brennan said, they needed to think about places like Yemen and Somalia, which are full of al Qaeda. And al Qaeda is taking advantage of these ungoverned spaces where there is little or no U.S. troop presence. There were larger issues in this decision that had to be considered in a global context.

"We're developing geostrategic principles here, and we're not going to have the resources to do what we're doing in Afghanistan in Somalia and Yemen," Brennan said.

Afghanistan was a small piece of real estate, the counterterrorism chief said. His worry was the rest of the world.

The clock read 5:05 P.M. They had been meeting for two and a half hours.

"I think these meetings have resulted in a useful definition of the problem," the president said, "and that redefined efforts against the Taliban are helpful and that a good definition is emerging." But they were not there yet, he said, adding that he appreciated the late hour for those in Pakistan and Afghanistan, where it was past midnight.

"We won't resolve this today," Obama said. "We've recognized that we're not going to completely defeat the Taliban, which we all agree on. Bob's summary, I think, was clear-eyed and achievable." The trouble, he said, with the ill-defined notion of defeating the Taliban, which would be hard to achieve, was "We need something that can be in our sights."

"Second," the president said, "I'm not of the view that we can simply leave. To the extent that we define counterinsurgency as population security as opposed to a high Taliban body count, that I can embrace and I think it's sound. We need to determine how broad or narrow the scope of that objective is, though." They would debate that further.

Obama said he thought the basic inkblot strategy was sound. But they needed more work on defining what those key areas were.

"If I ordered in 40,000 troops, that would not be sufficient for a counterinsurgency strategy for the entire country. So we need to find some key strategic areas to deny the Taliban a foothold and give ourselves a platform to achieve our goals."

Grappling for consensus, he noted the general agreement on the difficulty of defeating the Taliban and the importance of protecting Afghans.

"The fact that we agree on these pillars of a strategy belies the notion of huge divisions among the team here and it provides a basis for moving forward," Obama said, overlooking substantial disagreements. Biden and Brennan, for example, were not on board.

But several issues remained for the president that had to be addressed in the next sessions.

"Are the Afghan government's interests aligned with ours?" On some topics they may not be aligned, he said. There are significant questions about corruption, about dependency.

"On training Afghan troops, are they invested in the strategy we described?" Obama said. "We need to ramp up in a way that we can envision an exit strategy in a meaningful time frame. It's not enough to have trainers if the Afghans don't know why they're fighting. They need to be invested in success." The Afghans were not fighting with the same commitment in their own country as "our kids," he said. "They need to be fighting for something."

As he did at these sessions, the president had a notepad. In very neat, small writing, he would list five or six phrases from the discussion. It was a way for him to exercise control, set the agenda at the end of these meetings by asking questions from his notes.

"Can we get them to a point that will enable us to extract two, three, four years from now?" Obama asked.

Also on his question list was, "Why should Karzai change?" Without giving Karzai the right incentives to reform, the U.S. would be stuck tending to the country for him.

"So the question is: We can clear, hold and build, but how can we transfer?" he asked. Is the strategy sustainable over time? "We've put a lot of lives and money in Afghanistan." Just to put the timeline question in human terms, he added, "I don't want to be going to Walter Reed and Bethesda eight years from now." These were the military hospitals filled with those wounded in the wars.

"It will be tough for our allies," Obama said, as well as the American public.

The key piece for any eventual drawdown, as the president saw it, was reintegration. Not all members of the Taliban were glad to have hosted al Qaeda. Some Taliban warlords were obsessed with tribal matters. They had neither the wherewithal nor the desire to crash airliners into American skyscrapers. Ending the war would involve getting the less zealous Taliban to support the Afghan national government and move to neutral.

"How can we peel off the folks who are fighting against us?" Obama said. That was what Petraeus had done in Iraq.

"Given how much we spend on civilian aid and assistance, we need to make sure we have the right strategy for spending," he continued. That went to the matter raised by Holbrooke that foreign aid money could be a corrupting influence in Afghanistan.

He returned to the question of timetables, another big debate from Iraq.

"I'm always wrestling with this issue," Obama said as he weighed the pros and cons out loud. A timetable could send a message that all the enemy needed to do was run out the clock.

"We don't want our enemy to wait us out, but we also need to show some"—and he lapsed into a worn phrase from Vietnam—"light at the end of the tunnel."

"We can't sustain a commitment indefinitely in the United States," he said. "We can't sustain support at home and with allies without having some explanation that involves timelines."

The word "timeline" was a red flag for the military. They already planned to protect Afghans, train the Afghan security forces, and help straighten out the Afghan government. The president was now saying all that had to be accomplished on a deadline. For the military brass, it is an axiom that war does not take place on anyone's schedule.

"How could we ramp up as recommended and have an exit strategy within a reasonable time?" Obama asked. "How do we get to transfer starting eight years after the fact?"

During this period, Obama said that they had all talked about Afghanistan "from here forward," as though the war was starting anew and the past could be sidestepped.

"We should understand as we talk about this that the American people don't see this as beginning now. Right?"

No one disputed that.

"Their memories of this extend eight years back," he continued. Then there was the Iraq invasion. "The endeavor in Afghanistan, in their mind, did not begin in the last six to eight months."

Underscoring the earlier questions about where McChrystal placed bubbles on the map, Obama repeated, "We're not sending enough troops for a countrywide insurgency. We have to ask hard questions about where we're doing population security. Is it in the south? Are there some bubbles in the north?

"Finally, Pakistan is publicly saying they're opposed to more troops," Obama said. "If the neighbor says that, what does that say about their buy-in?" If he added troops, he said they had to carefully explain to the Pakistanis what it meant.

Biden seconded the president. "We paid a price for pressing the pause button," he said. "Everyone agrees that were we to be seen as losing Afghanistan, that would be a victory for al Qaeda and help jihadist recruiting." But, returning to the dividing line in the room, he worried about making an additional commitment without having the ability to assure any progress in governance.

"We're not leaving," Holbrooke said, bolting in as the meeting approached the three-hour mark with the president having given his summary and intent on winding down. He said the civilian programs in place are beginning to produce results. "I'm concerned about setting timelines. This is a long war. It will be longer than Vietnam.

"If it is important, and it is, then we must make a commitment. But we must ensure it's sustainable."

The president took over.

"We won't get any more bites at this apple," he said, adding as if speaking to himself, "it's been useful to discuss but we have to make a decision."

But the serious sticking points of Afghan governance and Karzai had yet to be settled.

"You do have one bite at the apple," Petraeus said, almost pleading. "Make it one that can make a difference. Try to avoid leaving a position that requires us to come back. But I do recognize we have to be able to say by the end of 2010 whether it's working."

Rahm Emanuel made a rare comment about how to convey the severity of the U.S. conviction that Karzai must put good people as governors of the 34 provinces.

Nurtured as a political operative in the Chicago political machine, Emanuel was comfortable with sending Karzai the equivalent of a dead fish with an imperial wrapping.

"Tell him we're going to put our own governors in if we have to," he said.

The president ignored that impractical, if not impossible, suggestion.

"I'm not an advocate of the timetable," Obama said, "but it will come from the Hill." A Democratic Congress would insist on a timetable, he said, even though Congress had shown itself unable to set a timetable for Iraq, the much more unpopular war. The Iraq timetables had finally been set by the Bush and Obama administrations.

"We have to show a plan that will actually enable us to show progress," the president continued. "These conversations are helpful, and I see conversions" since the first meeting in September. They were coming together, he insisted. "We all looked around and admired the problem. Now it's time to make some decisions."

Obama looked around the room as he made one last comment.

"I appreciate not reading about the meetings in *The Washington Post*," he said.

Jones wrote in his black book that the Afghan National Police have "always been weak and remains a critical failure." Not just a problem, but a "failure."

The president was not completely satisfied with the meetings thus far. One day during this period, Obama was walking toward the Oval Office with Gibbs. The inertia of the debate and boilerplate statements bothered him. He was tired of hearing about how everyone recognized the challenges—Afghanistan had been under-resourced, needed more troops, required a better government. Most of the principals were reiterating what they said in their reports.

"People have to stop telling me what I already know," he said. "And we have to get to the point where we hear some information about what people want to do."

Holbrooke went back to his office at the State Department, where his small staff had been complaining that they were up all night drafting analysis papers that went unread.

"There's one person in the room who reads them," Holbrooke told them, "and that's the man they are intended for." The sleepless nights were worth it and they should prepare another package of reports for the president.

20

General Lute was trying to get the Pentagon to evaluate counterterrorism plus (CT plus) as an option. It was Biden's idea and it meant adding CT forces to hunt the Taliban and other forces to train the Afghan army and police. Exactly how many troops were needed for that? Could CT work?

CT involved precise lethal attacks, generally on a person, a small group or a single building. It usually required fewer troops than protect-the-population counterinsurgency, which was one of the reasons why it appealed to the vice president.

An NSC memo was sent to Gates, who passed it along to McChrystal. The Afghanistan commander responded with a cursory two-page paper saying that CT wouldn't work. Successful CT depended on the density of conventional forces used in a counterinsurgency. Those conventional forces gathered intelligence from the bottom up through Afghan villagers and by interrogating low-level insurgents. That intelligence let CT forces know whom to target, attack and kill. Without the strong human intelligence available only through counterinsurgency, CT would be ineffective.

Biden was not convinced. There were already 68,000 U.S. troops in Afghanistan who could do counterinsurgency and develop the intelligence for CT.

"Why don't we just apply more CT forces?" Biden asked at a meeting with Tom Donilon, General Cartwright and his national security adviser, Tony Blinken. They could disrupt the Taliban, keeping the insurgents off balance to make sure they couldn't take over the country, Biden said.

"I'm not a military guy," Biden said. "Here's how I would approach this strategically, but we need a military plan." He needed detailed analysis and numbers.

"We'll provide that," said Cartwright, the vice chairman of the Joint Chiefs of Staff.

Those three words marked the beginning of one of the worst times in his 38 years of military service. A small fireplug of a man, Cartwright, 60, a Marine fighter pilot, was known in the White House as Obama's favorite general. The president frequently dealt with him on sensitive code word JSOC operations and other Special Access Programs because Chairman Mullen was traveling. Obama wanted to approve and stay informed about these operations, so the two had spent a fair amount of time together.

Before becoming vice chairman, the second highest ranking military officer and a member of the Joint Chiefs of Staff, he oversaw airspace and missile defense as head of the U.S. Strategic Command. Cartwright doubted that an increase of 40,000 troops would pay off in the ways advertised. In his view, counterinsurgency could not work if the borders were not controlled. The Afghanistan-Pakistan border was notoriously wide open. Taliban fighters could cross into Pakistan to "rest, relax, and rearm" before returning to Afghanistan to kill Americans.

Cartwright also believed that the president was by law entitled to a full range of options.

The vice chairman phoned Blinken.

"I tried to flesh out what you guys have put on the table," Cartwright said. He had run the numbers, done the analysis. Would Blinken like to go over it?

They met in Blinken's second-floor office at the Eisenhower Executive Office Building. Cartwright sketched out his plan. The problem with counterinsurgency was that the military had to concentrate its troops and resources in one area until the Afghan forces could take over, whenever that might be. With U.S. troops confined to an inkblot—a bubble—the enemy had the freedom to maneuver outside that bubble. Taliban insurgents had the advantage of being able to take whacks constantly at stationary American forces, which gave them the initiative. The bubble strategy also let the Taliban have potential safe havens in parts of Afghanistan where coalition forces were not located.

Instead of the options McChrystal proposed, the U.S. could send in two Special Forces brigades, totaling 10,000 troops. Those CT forces could outmaneuver the Taliban. Rather than sitting there protecting people, these troops would engage and kill the enemy.

"We can sort of use their tactics against them," Cartwright said.

The U.S. could send another 10,000 trainers to prepare the Afghan forces to take over the areas already secured by the U.S. and its allies. That would free coalition troops to either expand the inkblots or start new ones. It was a combination of counterinsurgency and counterterrorism. Or put simply, a hybrid option, requiring only 20,000—half CT, half trainers.

From that sketch, Blinken wrote a memo for the vice president. Blinken and Cartwright also outlined the hybrid option for John Brennan, the president's counterterrorism adviser.

Biden shared the memo with the president and explained his thinking. A hybrid approach would let the military demonstrate whether counterinsurgency worked in parts of Afghanistan before the U.S. committed to it for the entire country.

"Shouldn't our focus be on proving our concept before we double down on it?" Biden said.

But there was a glitch. Admiral Mullen despised the hybrid option. He did not want it discussed and debated at the White House. So he barred it from leaving the Pentagon.

"We're not providing that," Mullen told Cartwright.

"I'm just not in the business of withholding options," Cartwright responded. "I have an oath, and when asked for advice I'm going to provide it." Under the law as a member of the Joint Chiefs of Staff, he was empowered to give independent military advice to the president, even if it differed from the chairman's. And the law said that the chairman was obligated to submit any alternative advice "at the same time he presents his own advice to the president, the National Security Council, or the secretary of defense."

The relationship between Mullen and Cartwright had been tense. It just got much worse. Some senior civilians in the Pentagon thought they were barely on speaking terms.

Jones thought the option should possibly be considered, but Cartwright had basically circumvented the chairman and the military hierarchy. The national security adviser spoke with him for more than an hour to see if there was some way to smooth over the disagreement. Mullen was still the boss. Going around him even at the vice president's request was risky. It put Cartwright in an awkward position. This wasn't how the system was supposed to work. There had to be a process. Jones too was appalled by Mullen's inflexibility, but there had to be a way other than going against the chairman to get the option heard.

"At the end of the day," Cartwright told Jones, "it's my job. It's what I signed up to do. I'm going to give them options if they ask. I'm one of the Joint Chiefs, that's the oath."

Jones knew it well. As Marine commandant for four years, he too had been one of the chiefs.

"I'm not uncomfortable," Cartwright said. "I got it that maybe I'm not in the mainstream here." But Biden's notion of a hybrid option with 20,000 was not crazy. It might be the right answer. How could they be afraid of presenting the president with choices? Mullen wasn't a war fighter, Cartwright noted. He hadn't done this stuff before. He had never been in combat. So Cartwright said he was going to stand his ground.

"I understand where you are," Jones said. "I don't disagree with you."

It was the president who could circumvent the system. When he learned of the option, Obama instructed Gates and Mullen that he wanted the hybrid option presented to him.

At a principals meeting without the president, the DNI analyst Peter Lavoy was beginning to display a level of confidence that some found high-handed.

"The whole world is waiting to find out what happens in this room," he said.

"That's not right," Jones angrily interjected. "Don't say that. The world has to participate in this." Afghanistan was a NATO operation and 41 other nations were involved. U.S. allies should be consulted. "We've got to get more out of NATO," he said. "And the world shouldn't wait for us."

"Jim," said Blair, Lavoy's boss, "when did NATO ever lead if we don't lead?"

The two started to argue, and Clinton and Holbrooke stepped in, saying the U.S. should have a rollout plan to explain the president's eventual decision to everyone—first NATO and the allies, of course, and Congress and the public.

The principals' afternoon rehearsal on Tuesday, October 13, was mostly devoted to civilian efforts in Afghanistan.

We will know the election outcome in a few days, Holbrooke said. It was possible that Karzai might not have to compete in a runoff, since his rival, Abdullah Abdullah, was willing to have some kind of coalition government.

But Holbrooke wasn't entirely sure about Karzai. As the election drama played out, Holbrooke had warned others that the Afghan president was threatening to reject the commission's finding that he received less than 50 percent of the vote. How could you give troops to Afghanistan if the government had lost its democratic legitimacy? That would play right into Taliban propaganda.

Holbrooke said more emphasis should be placed on the provincial and district-level governments instead of Karzai and the capital in

"To quote a famous American," President Barack H. Obama told the author in an interview on July 10, 2010, "'War is hell.' And once the dogs of war are unleashed, you don't know where it's going to lead."

1

2

Vice President Joseph R. Biden opposed General McChrystal's request for 40,000 more troops, saying that progress in Afghanistan depended on reducing corruption. "If the government's a criminal syndicate a year from now, how will troops make a difference?"

3

James L. Jones, national security adviser, thought the Afghan War was central to international stability. "If we don't succeed here, organizations like NATO, by association the European Union, and the United Nations might be relegated to the dustbin of history."

4

Hillary Rodham Clinton, the secretary of state, endorsed the military's position during the Afghanistan-Pakistan strategy review. "If we don't come with an approach close to this, we shouldn't even try, because we'll just be wasting time, lives and money," she said.

5

Robert M. Gates, the secretary of defense, said during an Afghanistan-Pakistan strategy review session, "We should have a plan that says 18 to 24 months. We will begin reducing our forces, thinning them out." Obama seized on this statement to set July 2011 as the date they would begin reducing U.S. forces.

Rahm I. Emanuel, Obama's chief of staff, saw the Afghanistan War as "political flypaper" and thought the military was boxing Obama in with public statements. "It's bullshit that between the chairman [Admiral Mullen] and Petraeus, everybody's come out and publicly endorsed the notion of more troops. The president hasn't even had a chance!"

David M. Axelrod, the president's senior adviser, was wary of Hillary Clinton, Obama's chief rival in the presidential campaign. When Obama said he was considering her for a top cabinet post, Axelrod asked, "How could you trust Hillary?"

Robert L. Gibbs, White House press secretary, said the July 2011 date Obama had announced to start drawing down U.S. forces in Afghanistan was etched in stone, and he had the chisel to prove it.

9

Thomas E. Donilon (far right), the deputy national security adviser, wanted to make sure the military understood and carried out the president's specific orders, so he worked with Obama to develop a six-page "terms sheet" detailing Obama's final orders.

10

John O. Brennan, the deputy national security adviser for counterterrorism, questioned ambitious plans for Afghanistan. "If you're talking about a completely uncorrupt government that delivers services to all of its people, that end state won't be achieved in my lifetime. That's why using terminology like 'success,' like 'victory' and 'win' complicates our task."

Army Lieutenant General Douglas E. Lute, Obama's coordinator for Afghanistan and Pakistan, told the president he didn't have to send 30,000 more troops because there were too many risks with the new strategy. "It still smells to me like a gamble," he said. "You shouldn't base this on sort of an unexpected windfall of luck."

Bruce O. Riedel, a former CIA analyst, was brought in to lead the early 2009 review of the Afghanistan-Pakistan strategy. He told the president that Pakistan was the central problem and al Qaeda remained as dangerous as it had been on September 10, 2001.

13

Benjamin Rhodes (left), deputy national security adviser for strategic communications, drafted the president's Afghanistan speeches. Denis McDonough (right), a former Obama campaign aide who became chief of staff of the National Security Council in October 2009, was one of the president's most trusted advisers and attempted to enforce message discipline.

14

Mark W. Lippert, a key Obama foreign policy aide from Obama's Senate days, became National Security Council chief of staff. He left the White House after Jim Jones, the national security adviser, complained Lippert was trying to undermine him.

15

Antony J. Blinken, the vice president's national security adviser, was skeptical that the U.S. could succeed in Afghanistan and helped design an alternative to the military's strategy. "I don't know if they can ever pull this off," he said while visiting the war zone in early 2009. "How do you leave?"

16

Dennis C. Blair, who served as director of national intelligence until Obama fired him in May 2010, lacked the authority to challenge the CIA. "I think the CIA is fundamentally an organization that's like a really finely trained, not very smart, dangerous animal that needs to be controlled very closely by adults," he said.

17

Army General David H. Petraeus served as the commander of Central Command and then replaced General McChrystal as the Afghanistan commander. He said privately, "I don't think you win this war. I think you keep fighting. . . . This is the kind of fight we're in for the rest of our lives and probably our kids' lives."

18

Navy Admiral Michael G. Mullen, chairman of the Joint Chiefs of Staff, was a tireless advocate for McChrystal's request for 40,000 more troops. When asked what he would do if McChrystal failed, Mullen said, "Then I've got to leave because I put him there."

19

Marine Corps General James E. Cartwright, vice chairman of the Joint Chiefs of Staff, drafted a 20,000-troop option requested by Vice President Biden. When Chairman Mullen refused to provide it to the White House, Cartwright said, "I'm just not in the business of withholding options. I have an oath, and when asked for advice I'm going to provide it."

In July 2008, then Senator Obama and General Petraeus, then Iraq commander, ride together in a helicopter there. Obama recalled telling Petraeus, "I expect you, as the commander of our forces in Iraq, to ask for everything you need and more to ensure your success. That's what you owe the troops who are under your command. My job, then, which in some ways is more difficult, is I've got to choose. Because I don't have infinite resources."

Army General Stanley A. McChrystal got 30,000 of the 40,000 troops he requested, but Obama later fired him because of derogatory comments the general and his staff made about civilian leadership in a controversial June 2010 *Rolling Stone* magazine article.

Leon Panetta, director of the CIA, told others that "no Democratic president can go against military advice, especially if he has asked for it. So just do it. Do what they said." He said the decision should have been made in a week.

Michael McConnell, a retired vice admiral who was director of national intelligence in the Bush administration, told President-elect Obama that sensitive intelligence was good on targets in Pakistan and Afghanistan. "They talk, we listen," he said. "They move, we observe. Given the opportunity, we react operationally."

Michael V. Hayden, a retired Air Force general and outgoing director of the CIA, warned that drone strikes against terrorists in Pakistan were not a long-term solution. "Unless you're prepared to do this forever," he told chief of staff Rahm Emanuel, "you have to change the facts on the ground."

24

25

Richard C. Holbrooke, special representative for Afghanistan and Pakistan, never made a personal connection with the president. A pessimistic Holbrooke concluded on the eve of Obama's decision to add 30,000 troops, "It can't work."

26

Karl W. Eikenberry, a retired Army lieutenant general who was the U.S. ambassador to Afghanistan, questioned a troop increase, alienating the military hierarchy.

27

Afghan President Hamid Karzai (left) was considered an unreliable partner by U.S. officials. "He's on his meds, he's off his meds," U.S. Ambassador Eikenberry said. Pakistani President Asif Ali Zardari (right) told the CIA to aggressively attack top al Qaeda leaders in his country. "Kill the seniors," he said. "Collateral damage worries you Americans. It does not worry me."

General Ashfaq Kayani, chief of staff of the Pakistani army, refused to take on all of the extremist Islamic groups in his country. Kayani had other priorities. "I'll be the first to admit, I'm India-centric," he said.

Senator Lindsey O. Graham, a Republican from South Carolina, advised General Petraeus on how to argue for more troops in Afghanistan. "If there is a number in your mind below which we can't succeed," he said, "don't ever create a scenario where that thought is lost. . . . One thing you've got to say, 'This is the fail-safe line right here.'"

The October 9, 2009, session of the Afghanistan-Pakistan strategy review, held in the White House Situation Room. Clockwise from President Obama: Retired General Jim Jones; Hillary Clinton; U.S. Ambassador to the United Nations Susan E. Rice; retired Admiral Dennis Blair; Leon Panetta; Richard Holbrooke; General David Petraeus; Tom Donilon; Rahm Emanuel; Admiral Mike Mullen; Vice President Joe Biden. Pictured on the video screens are retired General Karl Eikenberry and General Stanley McChrystal (left) and U.S. Ambassador to Pakistan Anne W. Patterson (right).

"We can absorb a terrorist attack," President Obama told the author. "We'll do everything we can to prevent it, but even a 9/11, even the biggest attack ever, that ever took place on our soil, we absorbed it and we are stronger. . . . A potential game changer would be a nuclear weapon in the hands of terrorists, blowing up a major American city."

Kabul. Success for McChrystal depended on at least a minimum level of governmental competence.

The top three priorities—in terms of civilian effort—were agriculture, education and reduction of poppies, Holbrooke said. Pursuing all three would undermine support for the Taliban.

Jones wrote in his notebook, "But the big question is, what can you do in a year?" That was the problem with how Holbrooke approached his job. He talked about long-term initiatives when things in Afghanistan had to be turned around immediately. Restoring Afghan agriculture might take a decade of harvests.

The NSC meeting with the president on Wednesday, October 14, was scheduled for 9:45 A.M.

Donilon asked, "What are the prospects we can get a credible Afghan government in place in five years?"

No one answered.

Obama emphasized that transfer was the key. What was the prospect of getting to "Bangladesh-level" corruption? The term meant the U.S. might have to tolerate the inevitable "bakshish," the small cost-of-doing-business bribes that were part of Afghan culture. Clinton, Holbrooke and the intelligence chiefs, Blair and Panetta, all agreed that out-of-control corruption was the main problem.

The president turned to reconciliation and reintegration.

"Are we able to make arrangements with local leaderships that are legitimate and can help repel the Taliban? Do we have a plan to interact with local tribal leaders who are credible, so that as long as the central government isn't repressive we can repel the Taliban?" I haven't seen a plan that achieves that, he said.

"How do we transfer?" he continued. "Are there existing structures that we can work with? My working premise is that we can't be the sheriff in every town, so are there local partners that can do that? Are we in a position to strengthen something legitimate that already exists that doesn't require a constant ISAF presence? Is there an elite that allows Afghans to take control of their government without us having to administer it?"

Eikenberry tried to field the barrage of questions.

"Based on past policies, Karzai has a compact with foreign governments and not his own people," the ambassador said. The challenge was not just Karzai's relationship with the United States, but with the rest of Afghanistan that could partner against the Taliban.

Petraeus reminded everyone that a "transfer" was not the same as a withdrawal. There would still be an American presence in Afghanistan. With transfer, you don't "hand off," he said, you thin out.

Gates attempted to answer the president's questions.

"Our chance of success is about narrowing our focus and narrowing our mission," he said. "No government in Central Asia is a democracy and delivers services well. We can't aim too high. How can we reempower local Afghan leaders? The key is to blend with local Afghan culture and not to impose Western democracy."

The conversation moved to how adding troops would contribute to growing the Afghan forces, and whether there would be enough trainers to speed the transfer. Ambassador Rice asked for the ratio of U.S. trainers to Afghans.

There may not be enough trainable forces, Biden pointed out.

Obama had specific questions. How much are Afghan troops paid? the president asked. Would we be better off having fewer, better-trained soldiers that were paid more? What about the possibility of creating Afghan Special Forces units that were highly trained and better paid?

As the negotiator famous for the treaty ending the war in Bosnia and Herzegovina, Holbrooke had been pondering ways to bring a peaceful settlement to this war. He saw reconciliation and reintegration as distinct. Reconciliation was esoteric, an iffy high-level treaty with Taliban leaders. Reintegration occurred down at the local level in villages and towns, possibly financed by the U.S. military's discretionary Commander's Emergency Response Program.

As an ongoing reconciliation effort, the State Department had a secret compartmentalized operation to negotiate through Saudi Arabia with elements in the Quetta Shura, the central Afghan Taliban organization that is based out of Pakistan. Its leader, Mullah Omar, had threatened to kill anyone who talked to the Saudis or Karzai's people.

Several years earlier, Karzai had written to the Saudi king and asked him to set up back-channel talks. The people the Taliban sent were repudiated by Mullah Omar. At least three rounds of talks took place, but the bona fides of the Taliban representatives remained in question. No American official had ever talked directly to a Quetta Shura Taliban representative.

Near the end of the meeting, Obama called on Petraeus. The president had previously asked the general for a briefing about what his experiences in Iraq might say about the prospects of reconciliation in Afghanistan.

Actually, I've written this out in a document, Petraeus said. He had passed out copies of a memo around the table that was entitled "Lessons on Reconciliation."

This surprised Chairman Mullen.

What memorandum, Dave? he asked.

The memorandum that the secretary of defense cleared, Petraeus said.

Gates sat there, not moving a muscle.

There was an awkward moment of silence.

"Okay, well," Mullen finally said, "let me . . . I didn't know about this memo." He added that the service chiefs hadn't seen this memo either.

When Mullen needed reinforcements, he often invoked the chiefs, as though they acted as a unitary body. But the chiefs were more like the Supreme Court, full of dissenting opinions.

By law Petraeus, as a combatant commander, reported directly to Gates. Their arrangement was that Mullen, who only had a communications, oversight and advisory role, would be kept up to speed.

Mullen passed a private note to Petraeus, who read it, folded it and put it aside as he gathered his thoughts.

"I'd like to withdraw this memo," he announced. "Could everyone give it back to me?"

The memos were collected.

That was odd, Jones thought. You don't see that every day. Right in front of the commander in chief, two four-star officers had openly exhibited their internal tension.

For veterans of internal White House and national security power politics, it was a bizarre vignette to savor. But it was also disturbing. The president had asked Petraeus about reconciliation and Mullen had effectively put his foot down in defiance of a presidential request. To many, it made the chairman of the Joint Chiefs look small and petty. It also revealed another dysfunctional relationship. Holbrooke, who dealt extensively with both men, believed that this was more than a rivalry, that the two "hated" each other.

"I'll just describe this to you," Petraeus said, once most of the memos were back in hand. He then began his briefing.

At least one copy never made it back to Petraeus. The secret document contained three major sections, each broken into bullet points. The first section was, "Factors that enabled reconciliation in Iraq."

This section noted the importance of the U.S. showing resolve:

- "A sense by the [insurgent] Sunnis that coalition determination was firm and that the insurgent groups were not going to prevail over coalition and Iraqi forces."

At the time, Sunni Muslims in Iraq were also beginning to reject the foreign insurgents and had a political alternative to the violence:

- "Sunni weariness of insurgent activity.

- "Disenchantment with foreign leadership of [al Qaeda in Iraq].

- "Rejection by Sunnis of the extremist ideology, oppressive practices and indiscriminate violence of AQI and the Sunni insurgent groups.

- "The presence of an Iraqi political process that had a degree of legitimacy."

The second section was called, "Factors that enable reconciliation not present in Afghanistan." It revealed how arduous it would be to bring parts of the Taliban into the fold of the existing Afghan government. In sharp declarative sentences, it detailed how almost none of the positives from Iraq existed in Afghanistan:

- "The Taliban and other insurgent groups believe they are winning, not losing.

- "There are questions about coalition resolve.

- "The political process lacks the relative legitimacy of that in Iraq.

- "Insurgent leaders and members are largely indigenous, not foreign.

- "The Taliban provides better governance, security and dispute resolution than does the government of Afghanistan in some areas."

The third section, "Actions that could facilitate reconciliation/reintegration in Afghanistan," indicated there was one way to overcome these problems. The overarching solution reflected the counterinsurgency doctrine of its author, Petraeus:

- "Commit to providing the resources needed to accomplish our objectives in Afghanistan, including securing the main population centers.

- "Develop the nuanced understanding of local situations necessary to identify reconcilables and irreconcilables.

- "Craft individual approaches for individual areas."

"Now we have a pretty good idea of what the reality is," the president said. He did not have to add that it was grim. "At the next meeting, we need to move towards options and decisions." The review had been going on for more than a month.

•   •   •

The meeting ended around 12:45 P.M. Petraeus and Mullen went to the Pentagon. Starting at two, Mullen was leading a four-hour war game that was supposed to test the impact of different troop levels, especially McChrystal's request for 40,000 and the Cartwright-designed hybrid option of 20,000.

DNI Blair had suggested it in September. The retired admiral was enthusiastic about the benefits of such exercises, having served as the director of the Joint Staff war-gaming agency in the early 1990s. In that post, Blair had read through the old Vietnam studies known as the Sigma Series. He found them heartbreaking. The games had correctly forecast the flaws in the Vietnam strategies but the military had ignored them. Blair thought a war game analysis might appeal to Obama intellectually.

Lute had been invited to the game, but he proposed an NSC boycott.

"We should not participate in this," he said. "First of all, we don't need the war game. I can tell you what the answer's going to be. So I'm not spending a day over there in the Pentagon drinking lousy coffee to get to the self-evident conclusion."

The game would be a sham to bolster the case for the 40,000, Lute said, expressing the increasing skepticism that the military leaders had closed their minds. "If State and DNI and NSC participate in this war game, we're going to give it the legitimacy that it does not deserve."

But State and DNI were participating.

The code name for the game was "Poignant Vision." Instead of the classic opposition forces model—in which red and blue teams respond to each other move after move—it was more a seminar in which Mullen posed a series of questions. What would be the impact if the Taliban got surface-to-air missiles? What if the Pakistanis squeezed major supply routes into Afghanistan?

Petraeus noted that a normal war game model was designed for conventional force-on-force conflict. He knew of no way to war-game counterinsurgency, which included so many other social variables. And in the discussion during Poignant Vision, he made it clear he didn't believe that adding 20,000 troops for an expanded counterter-rorism strategy would work. Mullen agreed.

But Cartwright recognized that some kind of counterterrorism component would be needed. A counterinsurgency fixed troops in one location where the enemy could keep thwacking away at them. Their flanks would be vulnerable.

No one disputed that.

Having more CT forces roaming the countryside would enable the U.S. to go after the Taliban more aggressively, Cartwright said. He thought the war game showed the hybrid option was still viable.

Blair, who was more steeped in these issues than any of them, thought Poignant Vision didn't go beyond a normal staff analysis. This kind of game did not come close to producing a definitive conclusion.

"Well," Blair said at the end of the day, "this is a good warm-up. When is the next game?"

But he realized that Mullen and Petraeus had no intention of tak-ing the issue further.

21

On Tuesday evening, October 20, Axelrod and Gibbs were out enjoying a steak dinner when Axelrod's BlackBerry went off.

The Washington Post and ABC News were running a poll about the president the next day. Axelrod read the e-mail out loud.

"Drop for Obama in Afghanistan, Few See a Clear Plan for the War," was the headline. "Barack Obama's ratings for handling the war in Afghanistan have dropped sharply, with Americans by two to one saying he lacks a clear plan there. The public itself is divided on how to proceed, torn between the difficulties of the war and the threat of Taliban or al Qaeda–backed terrorism."

Axelrod took a breath. The public didn't distinguish between the Taliban and al Qaeda. That might be part of the problem. There were nuances in this decision. The first part of the review had been about distinguishing between the groups. Axelrod knew that voters didn't tolerate nuance—Obama's specialty—from politicians.

"Forty-five percent now approve of the president's handling of the situation," he continued, "down 10 points in a month, 15 points since August and 18 points from its peak." The drop was mostly attributable to the loss of Republican support.

Axelrod said he was neither jolted nor surprised. They had a monumental communications task in front of them for the president.

"At the end of this process," he said, "it's going to be incumbent on him and on us to explain our decision in very clear terms so that people understand what we're doing and why. . . . The politics of taking our time to make a decision are absolutely fine. But the problem is we have to make a decision. . . . And any decision we make is going to be difficult."

CIA Director Panetta, who had served 16 years as a congressman and then as President Clinton's budget director and chief of staff, saw that Obama was facing a huge political reality. He told other principals, "No Democratic president can go against military advice, especially if he asked for it." His own recommendation would be, "So just do it. Do what they say." He repeated to other key White House officials his belief that the matter should have been decided in a week. But Obama never asked him about it, and he never volunteered his opinion to the president.

The long hours in the strategy review were taking their toll on a number of participants. Several times, Emanuel just stood up and started walking around the Situation Room and gesturing with his arms, nervous energy practically shooting out of him. Some found it entertaining. Others found it distracting. But no one else had the leeway or self-confidence to behave this way at a presidential meeting. Donilon called it "adult-onset Attention Deficit Disorder."

Former Vice President Dick Cheney tore into the Obama strategy review at a Wednesday, October 21, ceremony where he accepted the "Keeper of the Flame" award from the Center for Security Policy.

"The White House must stop dithering while America's armed forces are in danger," Cheney said.

At the White House press briefing the next day, Gibbs shot back at the vice president as the one who dithered. "I think it's a curious comment, given—I think it's pretty safe to say that the Vice President was for seven years not focused on Afghanistan," he said. "Even more curious, given the fact that an increase in troops sat on desks in this White House, including the Vice President's, for more than eight months, a resource request filled by President Obama in March."

Gibbs's comments angered Pentagon spokesman Geoff Morrell. The White House seemed to forget that the same troop request had also sat on Gates's desk. In their effort to fire back at Cheney, they were firing at the same defense secretary they oftentimes propped up as validation for their decisions.

At yet another NSC principals meeting, Hillary Clinton turned to the secure video screen showing Admiral Mullen, who was on a five-day goodwill trip to Japan and South Korea.

"I just talked to our civilian chief in RC South, Frank Ruggiero," she said. In June, Ruggiero had become the head of U.S. Provincial Reconstruction Teams in southern Afghanistan. He was stationed at the Kandahar airbase, yet he could seldom wander far from it.

"He's only been in the city twice, and he had to go in an MRAP every time," Clinton said. "And yet, we have 8,000 troops in the Kandahar area and we had only 800 a few years ago." She had identified a big problem: with 10 times more troops, security didn't seem to improve.

It was no secret that the fate of the war might rest on Kandahar, the wellspring of the Taliban movement. When Kandahar had fallen on December 7, 2001, the first phase of the war ended—the Taliban regime had been overthrown. But despite the presence of extra troops in Kandahar province, the top U.S. civilian had to be chauffeured in a heavily armored vehicle.

"How come the whole city is out of our control?" Clinton asked.

That's why McChrystal needs more troops, Mullen answered.

The intelligence about Kandahar showed that the Taliban already controlled Loya Wiala, a sprawling refugee neighborhood north of the city center that the Americans called "District 9." Other parts of the city were in the hands of Karzai's corrupt brother, Ahmed Wali, who feuded with rival tribes for power.

A survey of the Kandahar population commissioned by the Canadian Department of Foreign Affairs and International Trade contained the depressing observation that some locals felt safest by bribing the Taliban: "Many city residents believe that currently the most effective protection against the Taliban insurgents is not the number of police or international forces, but the payment of protection money, a practice that is already widespread. This demonstrates that the operational radius of the Taliban insurgents already reaches into the very heart of the city." The survey was later heralded in a report co-written by Army Major General Michael Flynn, McChrystal's intelligence officer, as a model for U.S. intelligence in Afghanistan.

According to some intelligence analysis, Kandahar was susceptible to a mass uprising that might resemble the 1968 Tet Offensive in Vietnam, a public relations disaster and psychological crossroads in that war. Watch Kandahar, the intelligence warned. It could be more important than Kabul, the capital.

On Friday, October 23, Jones reviewed the unfulfilled troop requests for Afghanistan that had stacked up before Obama became president. It showed that not only President Bush but Gates had punted for years. The inflexibility of the Pentagon brass—especially Mullen and McChrystal—during the review sessions offended Jones.

Once, he half jokingly said to Mullen, "Listen, my impression is we could tell you your mission is to guard two Quonset huts in Afghanistan, and you'd say 40,000."

Mullen laughed. "Yeah, we heard you," the chairman said. "But it's 40,000."

Obama wanted to meet next Monday and hear the bottom-line recommendations from his top advisers.

Writing in longhand, Jones said that McChrystal should be "provided with four brigade combat teams, per his request. Two brigades should be provided by the United States. A third should be provided by the Afghanistan National Army and a fourth brigade to be provided through the NATO coalition."

He figured this was where the president was heading—about 20,000 U.S.—but by dressing it up with a brigade each from the Afghans and NATO it would look like McChrystal was getting what he requested. Jones thought it might be a good compromise. He was seeking what he called the "sweet spot."

Jones typed his recommendation into his computer that Saturday. But he never formatted it for the meeting, or printed it out. It stayed on the hard drive, never to be sent to the president.

Months after the review ended, Jones admitted, "I should've sent it, in retrospect. But it was moving that way, I thought."

Clinton's deputy at State, Jim Steinberg, had privately told her he was worried they were on the path to another Vietnam. There was an "open-endedness" to the mission, and he worried that McChrystal would again be back asking for more troops. Seek more clarity about where this is going, he urged.

Holbrooke also gave his advice to Clinton in confidence.

I will support you in any position you take, because you're my boss, he told her. But you need to know my actual views. I'm against the full 40,000. The military has not made the case. Instead, let's send 20,000 and put the other half on standby status so they can be deployed later if necessary.

She listened to Steinberg and Holbrooke, but that was all.

The Situation Room had lots of empty chairs around the table at 11:30 A.M. on Monday, October 26. Mullen's chair was vacant. Petraeus was in the Central Asian country of Tajikistan. No uniformed military had been invited. The back bench seats were also vacant. None of the White House regulars were there—not Axelrod, not Gibbs, not Rhodes, not McDonough, not Lute. They had not been invited.

After nearly six weeks of meetings, the president had called this meeting to ask Gates and Clinton to present their recommendations.

I would like to make a decision before I leave on my Asia trip in two weeks, Obama said. The announcement of the decision could come later, but he wanted to get the decision locked down.

His assessment of the choices was not reassuring. "We don't have two options yet," he said directly. "We have 40,000 and nothing."

No one could dispute that. Obama said that he wanted a new option that week. He had in his hand a two-page memo sent the day before by his budget director, Peter Orszag, projecting costs for the Afghanistan War. Under McChrystal's recommended strategy, the memo said the cost for the next 10 years would be $889 billion, nearly $1 trillion.

"This is not what I'm looking for," the president said. "I'm not doing 10 years. I'm not doing a long-term nation-building effort. I'm not spending a trillion dollars. I've been pressing you guys on this."

Gesturing to the McChrystal assessment, the troop request, and the Orszag memo, he added, "That's not in the national interest." The president had talked about opportunity costs before. Spending $1 trillion on Afghanistan would come at the expense of other priorities—domestic programs or lowering the deficit.

The first "flaw in Stan's proposal," he continued, was that there was no international element to it. McChrystal's request was for a brigade of about 10,000 every three months over the course of a year. The fourth U.S. brigade would replace the departing troops from the Netherlands and Canada.

Gates said that it could be a challenge for NATO to fill that fourth brigade. The administration could go back to these countries with a full-court press to get them to maintain, if not increase, their troop presence. But since that was a year off, they didn't have to decide on a fourth brigade right now. It could be held in abeyance.

"Yes," Obama said, "this needs to be internationalized. That's one of the big flaws in the plan that's been presented to me." Overall, he said, they needed evaluation points, the ability to test if any addition of force was working.

If more troops were added, Gates said, they could do an evaluation after 12 to 18 months. "At that point," he said, "it's either working or it's not working. You should be able to transfer after that period."

Obama seemed to like the word "transfer." He said there needed to be a focus on counterterrorism training and accountability, ultimately turning over the security elements to the Afghans.

"The presentation that's been given to me is very different than the surge," Obama said, referring to Bush's decision to send 30,000 more troops to Iraq in 2007. Did they not need to consider a surge-type option in Afghanistan to break the insurgency momentum?

Obama then raised McChrystal's request that they train the Afghan National Security Forces up to 400,000. This was based entirely on the so-called counterinsurgency math that one soldier or policeman was required for every 40 to 50 people in the general population (400,000 plus 148,000 U.S. and NATO troops fulfilled the ratio for an Afghan population of 28.4 million). That was literally the extent of the analysis, the president complained, and there seemed to be a degree of automatic piloting to it.

Gates didn't object. "The goal of 400,000 Afghan National Security Forces is neither necessary nor desirable," he said.

On the troop request, Gates said he basically supported the full McChrystal request, but the fourth brigade should be held back for now.

The president summarized what Gates had said. They would measure whether it was working in 12 to 18 months. "We don't need the fourth brigade. We might not need the full 400,000, and we can look at a more measured growth of the ANSF. And we could surge to break the momentum but not stay in a long-term COIN strategy."

It was Clinton's turn. They should give McChrystal what he wanted, she said, but she agreed they could wait on the fourth brigade. Her recommendation seemed closer to the original McChrystal request than Gates's.

"On the civilian side," she added, "we need some realism."

They all agreed there was lots of work to do with Karzai.

Jones said that he did not think the military had proven its case for the troops, and suggested they should send all the trainers—the 11,000 that McChrystal requested—and the enablers.

In terms of brigades, Jones thought the one for Kandahar should be sent right away. Kandahar was the most critical city in the war. Three of the four major population centers were firmly in the hands of the Afghan government. All but Kandahar. Lose it and the country would be split, the war could be over, he said. But given the long lead time for the other brigades—one brigade a quarter as McChrystal had requested—the final decision on the other brigades could wait. Jones also said that McChrystal was overly focused on the U.S. role, the troops for southern and eastern Afghanistan, and was overlooking the role of NATO forces in the rest of the country. He thought it possible to get 5,000 more troops from the NATO countries.

Obama indicated he was not ready to make a decision. "We don't have an end state," he said. "I don't see it clearly. There are no guarantees of progress in any short period of time. The plan is too open-ended. There is neither victory nor defeat in 10 years."

He was envisioning an option that would be a surge of forces that lasted less than a year. Everyone, he said, should go back and think some more. He wanted to schedule a meeting with the Joint Chiefs of Staff to hear their ideas.

Gates said he had two disagreements with the uniformed military. One, was over the application of the word "defeat" to the Taliban. That was not possible, so they should use "degrade." His second disagreement was over the term "fully resourced counterinsurgency." That couldn't be done either.

I want a realistic ramp-down of troops, Obama said, to an equilibrium that is manageable and a better-described closure.

Jones wrote in his black book, "McChrystal's plan does not address comprehensive turnover in a rational way."

Obama asked Gates, Do you really need 40,000 to reverse the momentum of the Taliban?

Before Gates could answer, Obama said, "What about 15,000 to 20,000? Why wouldn't that do it?" He repeated that he wasn't buying into a $1 trillion, 10-year counterinsurgency strategy.

"I want an exit strategy," the president said.

•   •   •

Nearly everyone could see that by supporting McChrystal, Clinton was joining forces with the uniformed military and the secretary of defense, diminishing the president's running room. She had reduced his cover for any decision with significantly fewer troops or a softer policy. It was a definitive moment in her relationship to the White House. Could she be trusted? Could she ever truly be on the Obama team? Had she ever been? Even though her electoral future seemed circumscribed, politicians know that anything can happen. They generally play for themselves. Gates believed she was speaking from conviction.

The next day, October 27, Jones sent a formal tasking memo to Gates requesting him to present a plan with the attributes that had been discussed with the president, one that brought the troops in faster.

Jones and Donilon were sure the president wanted clarity, and the lessons from Iraq and Gordon Goldstein's book about Vietnam, *Lessons in Disaster*, showed that a president had to have precision on military matters of this consequence. Absent clear recommendations and decisions, the military would tend to do what they wanted to do. Clarity would have to be forced on them.

Having watched the sessions for more than a month, NSC chief of staff Denis McDonough thought the process was turning into a disaster, veering out of control in a way that would make it difficult ever to get consensus.

It did not take long for a number of the like-minded to get together. Biden and Blinken were also worried, as were Tom Donilon, General Lute and John Brennan.

These six—Biden, Blinken, Donilon, Lute, Brennan and McDonough—had a series of off-line meetings. It was a powerful group, close to Obama in different ways, a balance to the united front put up by Gates, Mullen, Petraeus, McChrystal and now Clinton. Lute liked to call their sit-downs "breakout sessions"—small, informal get-togethers after the large NSC meetings. There was about half a dozen of them, in Lute's office, Brennan's, Donilon's—even one at the vice president's residence.

"Where are we headed?" Biden asked at one. "What's going on here, guys?" The vice president said that he still didn't think the president had to do the 40,000. The cost was too high and the prospects for success too low. How could they get his counterterrorism plus option on the table to give it the proper airing it deserved?

Just before midnight on Wednesday, October 28, Obama boarded the presidential helicopter on the White House lawn for a 45-minute flight to Dover Air Force Base in Delaware to observe the arrival of the bodies of 18 Americans killed in Afghanistan. He told aides he wanted to see for himself the solemn ceremony in which the cases carrying the bodies were transferred out of the plane to a van. He wanted to meet with the families of the fallen. I want to see how hard this is for them, he told one aide.

At 12:30 A.M. Thursday the helicopter landed at Dover next to the giant C-17 cargo plane. The large cargo hold in the back was open, but Obama could not see the 18 flag-draped coffins inside. A car brought him to the chapel where 60 family members waited. Their loved ones had died that week, and their shock and sorrow were fresh.

"I'm so sorry," he said as he approached each group. He put his hands on shoulders, gently patted backs, hugged and embraced the young ones. "How grateful . . . The nation is grateful. . . . You're in the prayers of every person in this country and in the prayers of Michelle and me."

The motorcade returned him to the hulking, gray C-17. He walked up the back ramp to the line of cases. At each one, he stopped, said a small prayer and placed a presidential coin.

For nearly two hours he stood in his long overcoat in the cool darkness and watched as a six-person Army unit wearing fatigues, black berets and white gloves transferred the individual cases from the plane to the van. It was all done with precision. The units had regular prac-

tice because Dover was the main point of entry for the nation's war
dead. By 4 A.M. the ceremonies were complete. The president thanked
everyone, slipped back in the helicopter, switched off the overhead
light. No one said a word during the 45-minute flight to the White
House.

22

Around 1:30 P.M. on Friday, October 30, Obama called the Joint Chiefs to the White House. This was not just a matter of checking another box on the way to making a big decision. The president was in a desperate search for another option.

For the past two months, the uniformed military—Mullen, Petraeus and McChrystal—had been locked into counterinsurgency and 40,000 troops. But the individual service chiefs had yet to be consulted for the review.

As the heads of the Army, Navy, Marine Corps and Air Force, the chiefs recruited, trained, equipped and supplied the forces to combatant commanders like Petraeus and their subordinate ground commanders such as McChrystal. Neither Petraeus nor McChrystal attended the Friday meeting, because both were in Afghanistan and were junior in rank to the chiefs. But in the tangle of all things military, the chiefs were not in the chain of command. They had been largely sidelined since the strong JCS chairmanship of Colin Powell 20 years earlier. George W. Bush had used the chiefs to provide perfunctory opinions after he had made his decisions.

Nonetheless, the chiefs had an almost mythic lore in military history. George Marshall had been the powerful Army chief of staff during World War II. On the other hand, the reputation of the chiefs had suffered dramatically after their spineless performance during the Vietnam War, when they failed to give honest guidance to President Johnson as documented by Army Brigadier General H. R. McMaster's 1997 book, *Dereliction of Duty*.

"I have one option that was framed as three options," Obama told the chiefs. "I want three real options to choose from." It was an unusual appeal for help from the chiefs.

"I'm committed to making this a unified effort" a success, he continued. "This is America's war, but I don't want to make an open-ended commitment." They had all read McChrystal's assessment and his troop request. The objective of this meeting was to get unbiased views on alternatives, the president said, and the costs associated with any other options.

Biden added, "If it isn't working, you should be prepared to say so."

Just to be clear, the president said, "The goal is to defeat and dismantle al Qaeda," the central threat. But the goal in Afghanistan is to "disrupt the Taliban, weaken them so that the Afghans can handle it."

Marine Commandant General James Conway addressed the over-riding allergy the fighting man has to prolonged missions that go beyond defeating an enemy. Conway, burly and blunt-spoken, had commanded 60,000 troops for two combat tours in Iraq. It was a masquerade for a Marine to act like a social worker, in his opinion. A Marine was a killer. I recommend, Mr. President, he said, "don't subscribe to long-term nation building."

Obama could not agree more.

"The Good Lord is working against us in trying to do any kind of nation building there," Conway went on. "There are things we couldn't fix in our lifetime. We have to train the forces and hand it over."

Gates offered what sounded like a partial rebuttal, saying that he had little confidence in a civilian surge or in serious governance reforms by Karzai.

General George Casey, the Army chief of staff, who had commanded the forces in Iraq for two and a half years during some of the darkest days, said that the scheduled withdrawal in Iraq would permit the Army to contribute the necessary units for a 40,000-troop ramp-up in Afghanistan. Casey, however, was a skeptic about large troop commitments in these wars. In his view, the key in both Iraq and Afghanistan was a quick transition, getting out while helping the people to govern and protect themselves. But, he said, the 40,000 plan was an acceptable global risk for the Army. With the anticipated Iraq withdrawal, Casey said he would have forces available in case there was another crisis.

Assess for me, the president asked, the impact of "disrupting" the Taliban in Afghanistan.

As evidence of how much the Joint Chiefs were out of the loop, Casey said even though he had heard the president describe the mission as "disrupting" them, he still understood the mission to be to "defeat" the Taliban. McChrystal's resource request was premised on that.

"When you defeat the insurgency, that's a tall order," Casey said. "It's going to take some time. But if you take defeat away and make the mission disrupt the insurgency, that's a different matter."

"What Stan concluded," Obama said, "is in terms of the Taliban, using the word 'defeat' is probably overambitious. Disrupt the Taliban, control their momentum, keep them from establishing a platform that can be used, destabilizing efforts."

Casey indicated he was glad to hear that. "It is not possible to defeat the Taliban in the classic sense. It would be like defeating Hamas," the Palestinian movement governing the Gaza Strip that the U.S. classifies as a terrorist group.

The mission was "disrupt," the president said.

"Well, that would make a difference," Casey said.

Obama wanted him to elaborate.

"There's a big difference here, Mr. President," Casey said, "in terms of the number of troops that are required."

General Conway agreed with Casey. The chief of naval operations and the Air Force chief of staff had little to say, noting that whatever the decision in Afghanistan, the impact on their forces would be minimal.

Chairman Mullen had listened as Casey and Conway undermined his argument for the 40,000. He defended that option by trying to alleviate what had to be one of Obama's concerns.

We won't ask for more troops again, the chairman promised.

It was a cap. There was no doubt. Mullen, who had objected to suggestions of a cap by Obama that summer, had just offered one of his own. "Bingo!" thought Biden.

The president said he wanted more options, but they had to be affordable and executable. He didn't want to be boxed in by huge costs and manpower increases.

"We need a sustainable effort that the country can absorb," he said. "We need to be hardheaded about an exit strategy."

After the meeting, the president expressed appreciation for Casey and Conway, telling his aides that he thought they had stepped up with advice based on his mission definition, not the one to which Mullen, Petraeus and McChrystal were still clinging.

On October 30, Gates sent Obama a two-page SECRET memo: "Attached is our response to the 27 October NSC request asking DOD to develop alternative option to General McChrystal's force option two, Tab A."

Under the heading, "Alternative Mission for Afghanistan," the secretary of defense wrote, "Implementing this alternative mission will require an extended surge of three U.S. combat brigades plus enablers (30,000 to 35,000 in additional troops)."

It was an easy calculation for Gates. At least 5,000 couldn't get to Afghanistan for about a year, so why should the president have to make that decision right away? Also, he believed they could get 5,000 or more from the allies. In another way, Gates had found a "sweet spot," as suggested by Jones—something between 20,000 for the hybrid option and McChrystal's 40,000.

On the second page, Gates backed off from his summer position that the goal was to "defeat the extremist insurgency." He now called for "disrupting and degrading the Taliban"—a much less ambitious undertaking. "Our counterterrorism forces," he wrote, "will continue to degrade the Taliban by conducting sustained operations against their command and control and facilities networks."

• • •

During a principals meeting in early November—more than six weeks into the strategy review—Ambassador Eikenberry made a long presentation on why a COIN strategy relying on a large infusion of U.S. forces was unlikely to work. He voiced worries about the costs, an overreliance on the U.S. military, increased Afghan dependency, the unreliability of Karzai, and the high attrition and low recruitment rates of the Afghan forces, weaknesses that he said were so great that the Afghans would not be able to take over in 2013 as outlined. More U.S. troops would not end the Afghan insurgency as long as the Quetta Shura Taliban and the Haqqani network had sanctuaries in Pakistan.

Donilon found the arguments persuasive. "Why don't you develop that?" he said to Eikenberry. "Put it in a cable and send it."

Jones agreed, and Eikenberry promised he would.

Holbrooke was waiting at the Four Seasons restaurant in Manhattan for Petraeus. Both had by coincidence delivered lunch speeches in separate private rooms of the famous restaurant. They had urgent business to discuss. A cable had arrived from Afghanistan that morning, Friday, November 6.

The U.S. ambassador to Afghanistan had sent Secretary Clinton a cable outlining his "reservations about a counterinsurgency strategy that relies on a large infusion of U.S. forces." Eikenberry's concern was that they had not studied every alternative. The proposed troop increase could "bring vastly increased costs" and "an indefinite large-scale U.S. military role" in Afghanistan, the presence of which would "increase Afghan dependency" and deepen the military involvement in a mission that could not be won solely by military means. Eikenberry suggested that the bell curve charts of troop deployments were "imprecise and optimistic."

As he waited for Petraeus, Holbrooke took a call from Mullen. The chairman of the Joint Chiefs was as angry as Holbrooke had ever heard him.

"What has gotten into Eikenberry?" Mullen said.

"You knew his views."

"Not like this," Mullen said. "This is a betrayal of our system."

Eikenberry had not given Petraeus and McChrystal the courtesy of a heads-up about the cable, which had been requested by Donilon and Jones.

When Holbrooke told Petraeus the contents of the cable, Petraeus went ballistic.

The top American diplomat in Afghanistan had just isolated himself from the military and alienated his counterpart—McChrystal. One of the essentials in counterinsurgency was cooperation between the civilian and military leadership. That had just been blown to pieces.

At another principals meeting about a week later, on Monday, November 9, they honed in on McChrystal's plan for the Afghan National Security Forces to be increased to 400,000. That was a total of 240,000 for the army (nearly tripling from 92,000) and 160,000 for the police.

"We need to plan for 400,000 ANSF," Petraeus said, "not something fuzzy" as had been suggested in an NSC staff memo that had been circulated before the meeting. This was a long-term project, he said, and decisions in advance would allow them to order equipment, mortars and artillery, build infrastructure and refine the training. If you don't know where you're going, any road will take you there, he thought, and he wanted the road to be clearly laid out.

Mullen endorsed the idea, while Gates, who did not believe 400,000 was necessary, simply remarked that "having an end state out there is good."

For Jones, this sounded like the same kind of empire that had been built for Iraq—precisely what he was sure the president did not want for Afghanistan. But Jones left it to the vice president to intervene.

"Is that doable?" Biden asked. On the army side, current training of new recruits was about 2,000 a month. At that rate, it would take six years, assuming no attrition, and attrition was high. On the police side, it was worse—they were regularly losing more than they were gaining.

The military leaders would not give up the 400,000 number, as if it was written in holy text. As they became increasingly dogmatic, Biden unloaded. Without the president at the meeting, the vice president felt he could speak even more freely, and he became "apoplectic," in the words of one participant. The vice president thought the 400,000 target was hollow, the same kind of BS number that had been presented by Rumsfeld during the Iraq War. He attempted an aggressive interrogation, but Petraeus and McChrystal stuck to their arguments. It was not just planning. Petraeus and McChrystal said they had to create a training system including schools, buildings, recruiting teams, manuals, personnel and the whole infrastructure to be effective. This could not be a fly-by-night operation. It had to be long-lasting.

Petraeus's attitude was, hey, I've done this before. He had headed the training command in Iraq for about 15 months beginning in 2004. *Newsweek* had put him on its cover when he took over that command, asking in its headline: "Can This Man Save Iraq?"

The implied question bouncing around the Situation Room was: "Can this man save Afghanistan?"

McChrystal continued to push hard on the 400,000 target in a follow-on meeting with the president.

How much would it cost? Obama asked.

At another meeting, the numbers came back. The president expressed sticker shock. "Let me get this straight," he said. "So our ticket out of here are these guys? And if we sign up for this, we're signing up for a build price of $55 billion just to get out of this, and then an annual bill of $8 billion indefinitely. What's magic about 400,000? How'd you get to 400,000?"

Donilon, Lute and the NSC staff asked McChrystal and his staff about the math. The short answer was that this came out of the tired standard COIN ratio of one counterinsurgent for every 40 or 50 people. But the ANSF target was flawed; the insurgency wasn't on a national scale. It was mostly limited to an area of the country nicknamed Pashtunistan. Only about 42 percent of the Afghan populace was Pashtun. So for example, they would not have to worry about the Taliban in the Tajik areas—at least 27 percent of the total population—because the Taliban would not survive in those areas given the deep hostility the Tajiks felt for them.

"The police aren't working," Lute told the president. "We're being fed a pack of bullshit." He suggested that Obama press on the issue.

What's the risk you can achieve these numbers with high quality? Obama asked at another meeting.

For two meetings, McChrystal was not able to answer. So Lute added it to the question list for the next session.

Moderate risk for the Afghan army, McChrystal finally answered, but "high risk" for the Afghan police.

"Guys," the president asked, "what evidence is there that this is necessary or doable?" No one had a good answer. This seemed to be a turning point for Obama. The 400,000 goal did not fit with his evidence-based reasoning. It was a pipe dream illustrated with charts and abstract ratios.

"This presentation strains credulity," Obama said. He would not authorize such an extravagant plan. The military should instead develop ANSF goals on a year-by-year basis. It was as flat a no as he had given, and a clue that he did not believe the Iraq model would fit Afghanistan.

It was a somber flight back for Gates from the November 10 memorial service for the 13 people killed at Fort Hood, Texas, in a shooting by U.S. Army Major Nidal Malik Hasan. Geoff Morrell, the Pentagon press secretary, noticed Gates was jotting some notes for the next meeting with Obama.

"Are you going to use that in a meeting?" Morrell asked.

"Yeah," Gates said.

"We should clean that up for you, you know?" Morrell said. The handwriting was sloppy, and there were little arrows and marks on the sheet of paper. "Get it tidy, you know?" The Pentagon prided itself on neatness.

"Absolutely not," Gates said with a touch of indignation. He was spending countless hours thinking long and hard. "This is my work and I want that perfectly clear to everybody involved," he said. "This is my thinking. This is my analysis. This is my determination." He was doing his own homework and wanted people in the Situation Room to know. "It's not staff work."

Jones worried that DNI Blair was edging too much into policy advice and proposed dropping him from the strategy review session.

But if Blair was dropped, they would also have to exclude Panetta. The president wanted Blair out, so both intelligence chiefs were not invited to the remaining review sessions. Jones told them that everyone now understood the intelligence picture and they were no longer needed.

Blair, for one, was baffled. And Panetta, who was in charge of the secret CTPT army of 3,000 in Afghanistan, would have no role in the troop debate.

23

About noon on Veterans Day, Wednesday, November 11, the president and his wife, Michelle, stepped out into a cold rain at Arlington Cemetery. They walked around Section 60, where the dead from the Iraq and Afghanistan wars are buried. One writer christened it "the saddest acre in America." Obama moved down the aisles of small white headstones to greet the relatives and friends of those lost in battle. Heavy raindrops gathered in his hair, on his face, and on his black overcoat. New graves were being dug in the damp earth.

Pentagon spokesman Geoff Morrell often worked with televisions blaring in the background, watching the ambient screens as a driver might scan the road for oncoming traffic. He was poised to respond to the slightest departure from Gates's orders that the military lie low during the review.

Around 2 P.M. on Veterans Day, Morrell heard CNN announce an exclusive interview with General Petraeus. No one from the Pentagon or military was to go on television, not even for helping an old lady cross the street.

"I want you to see the humanity in a leader who lives his commitment to his troops," said CNN anchor Kyra Phillips. "And because of that commitment, one soldier lives today."

The camera showed Dave Petraeus in the White House briefing room. Whoa. Hold up. No one had told Morrell about this. Could it have been previously taped? Nope, this was a live feed. Right from inside the West Wing, right in the middle of the strategy review.

Petraeus spoke about First Lieutenant Brian Brennan, who had barely survived when his Humvee tripped a 44-pound roadside bomb in Afghanistan a year and a half before. The explosion shredded his legs, which were both amputated, and left him comatose with a brain injury at Walter Reed. On July 4, 2008, Petraeus had visited Brennan. His body lay motionless on the hospital bed, his eyes open but unable to register those around him. And that was when Petraeus—in the glowing words of the CNN anchor—did something "no family member or doctor could," something "miraculous."

Brennan had served in the 506th Infantry Regiment, the unit made legendary as the "Band of Brothers" who parachuted into Normandy on D-Day in World War II. Petraeus reminded Brennan of the regiment's motto, "Currahee." There was a brief flicker of life from the soldier. Petraeus decided to try again, along with his sergeant major, counting to three and then shouting, "Currahee!"

Like Lazarus, the young soldier awoke. His head and thighs pumped in the air after hearing that familiar Cherokee word. "Currahee" meant "stand alone." Brennan recovered, walked again, and, inspired by General Petraeus, started a foundation to help injured veterans.

The CNN anchor noted that in less than 10 minutes Petraeus would step into the Situation Room for the eighth meeting of Obama's war council. Would Obama approve the additional 40,000 troops requested for Afghanistan? she asked.

"That's up to the president, obviously," said Petraeus, the White House emblem visible over the shoulder of his dress greens. "And again, our job is to provide him our best professional military advice."

The anchor weighed in with one last question for the general. Would he run for president in 2012? Some Republicans had suggested he would make an outstanding candidate.

"I'll close it right here, right now in the CNN newsroom," Petraeus said. "I will remind you of the great country song that used to ask, 'What about "no" don't you understand?' "

Morrell was livid. What part of "no" had Petraeus not understood? He was not supposed to be doing interviews with anyone, not about Afghanistan and Pakistan, and definitely not about Oval Office ambitions. The general should have been unmistakably aware of this after his September comments about the need for a counterinsurgency to a *Washington Post* columnist had enraged the president.

Morrell later phoned Colonel Erik Gunhus, Petraeus's public affairs officer.

"What the fuck?" he said.

It's a Veterans Day double-amputee-feel-good-story, Gunhus said.

"You motherfucker," Morrell shouted into his phone. He could recognize another chapter in Petraeus's endless campaign of self-promotion. Dave, the miracle worker, heals the sick. And he had chosen to talk about it—from all places—at the White House, moments before a meeting with the president.

"Why didn't I know about CNN?" Morrell demanded.

But unbeknownst to Morrell, Gunhus was with Petraeus, and he handed his cell phone to the general.

Gunhus should keep you in the loop, Petraeus acknowledged. But perhaps, he continued, the Pentagon should not try to muzzle its Cent-Com commander.

"When are you going to realize I do these things all the time and I know how not to make news?" Petraeus said. "I can help the cause and explain."

"Sorry I'm late," Obama said as he walked into the Situation Room for the eighth strategy review meeting. He added sarcastically, "I was busy reading about what we're doing in *The Wall Street Journal*."

The *Journal* story quoted "a senior military official" who said the president was about to be presented with a new option for 30,000 to 35,000 troops. The article did not reveal that this was the Pentagon's response to the October 27 memo from Jones. Obama was angry. It was more of the leaking that Gates and Mullen had pledged to stop.

More troubling was that they were still wrestling with the basic questions: What is the mission? What are we trying to do? What are the objectives? For what purpose? Session after session, these questions remained at the heart of it, yet they had not been answered after nearly two months of work. The experienced Obama watchers from the presidential campaign could see that he was very frustrated and, for him, almost on edge.

Admiral Mullen started off with a PowerPoint presentation titled "CJCS Brief to the President, November 11." The slides made a psychological warfare argument, a primer on the centrality of resolve to show that war was very much a mind game. The cheerleading message emphasized the importance of commitment, which was what they wanted to convey to the Afghans. And while Mullen didn't say it, showing commitment started at the top with the president. In counterinsurgency, people have to believe they are more secure. This was right out of Petraeus's playbook—perception often ruled.

"Resolve is a force multiplier," Mullen said, and would "have a vital psychological impact."

His brief continued, "Resolve will be a signal to many stakeholders." Demonstrating it will reduce "Taliban momentum" and "influence how the Afghan people view their future with the government.

"It will impact continued NATO and coalition commitment and it will encourage the Pakistanis to continue their counterinsurgency effort on their side of the border.

"It also has a potential to produce political and diplomatic effects that will drive reintegration and reconciliation and negate any requirement for additional force"—presumably beyond the 40,000—"by creating a sense of inevitability." Overall this is "a significant opportunity to impact their strategic calculus."

Jones suggested they were getting somewhere with these discussions.

"Our goal," he said, implying a consensus, "is to deny the Taliban the ability to threaten to overthrow the Afghan state and provide safe haven to al Qaeda. It is not to defeat or destroy the Taliban. The military objectives will be limited only to levels necessary to attain this goal."

"I hope we don't expand this goal," Biden said.

"We've got to deny the Taliban the ability to take over the country," Gates said.

"To be more specific," Petraeus said, "we have to deny them access to and the ability to control the major population centers, the production centers and the lines of communications."

In a more general way, he added, disrupting the Taliban was insufficient. Throwing them off balance was not enough. It sounded temporary. The time when the Afghans could manage security was a long time off. So the goal had to be to deny the Taliban access to the population.

"More than disruption is required," McChrystal said, agreeing with his boss.

Gates agreed with his generals.

Biden questioned them, Was it really necessary?

"The key," McChrystal said, "is stopping their momentum and securing sufficient amounts of the population and lines of communication." His force level option of 40,000, he said, "does not fully resource a counterinsurgency." The 85,000 force level got closer, but they had agreed that the military just did not have that many troops available.

Petraeus and McChrystal seemed to be pushing hard to migrate the conversation back to "defeating" the Taliban. The principals had already decided against defeating the Taliban in a traditional sense, yet the generals were making the case that disruption was inadequate.

"Let's see if we can reconcile Joe's concerns and Dave's concerns," the president said.

Gates said it seemed more a drafting problem with the language than a real disagreement. "We want to provide the time and space to stabilize the country and build forces to resist the insurgency."

Obama stepped in to halt the discussion. "It's going to be disrupt. And this is my definition of disrupt: to degrade capacity to such an extent that security could be manageable by the ANSF. Disrupt doesn't mean scatter, it means degrade their capacity." He preferred the description of securing substantial portions of the population—though not all of it—and the lines of communication.

Biden wondered if it was possible to accommodate the Taliban the same way Hezbollah had been in Lebanon. The extremist party had become part of the democratic process by winning seats in parliament.

"The key point Joe's trying to make," Obama said, "and I want to agree with, is we're not trying to achieve a perfect nation-state here. We don't have the resources to do that."

"No one disagrees," Gates said. "There has to be reintegration, reconciliation. But we just have to define—with precision—the point at which the Taliban threatens the effort."

McChrystal insisted that they had to secure the major population centers.

"It'll take 18 to 24 months to know if this is working or not working," Mullen said. He had added six months to Gates's 12 to 18 months. "Disruptions are not enough."

Had Mullen not been listening? No one said anything, but it was a direct contradiction of the president's declaration that it was "disrupt." Mullen then reiterated, "We must reverse the momentum."

The constant refrain about "momentum" was the military's way of saying they were losing. "The 40,000 is the best opportunity to protect the population," Mullen added.

"We should have a plan," Gates said, "that says 18 to 24 months we will begin reducing our forces, thinning them out. And that puts a marker on the wall for the Afghan leaders."

This was an electric, pivotal moment for the president. Gates had said in 18 to 24 months they would begin reducing or thinning out U.S. forces. That would be the start of the exit strategy that Obama so clearly wanted. But the president pushed further. Why not just commit to 25,000 and then another brigade could be added after that if necessary? "Could we order in two brigades and then go from there? Why does it have to be all in now?"

That had been discussed in Iraq, Gates and Petraeus said. Dribbling them out would just create more news and questions about whether a certain X number of soldiers would be added at various intervals—all creating great expectations, doubt and more headlines, making it look like they were losing and had to ask for more.*

The question, most agreed, was what would send the strongest message to Karzai and create the most leverage?

Biden read some quotes from a cable that had been sent in by Ambassador Eikenberry—including questions about whether Karzai was the right partner and whether 40,000 troops would do much good. These were the arguments Donilon had asked the ambassador to develop.

Eikenberry wrote, "The proposed troop increase will bring vastly increased costs and an indefinite, large-scale U.S. military role in Afghanistan, generating the need for yet-more civilians. An increased U.S. and foreign role in security and governance will increase Afghan dependency, at least in the near-term, and it will deepen the military involvement in a mission that most agree cannot be won solely by military means."

In a follow-up cable, Eikenberry recommended that instead of approving the 40,000, "the White House could appoint a panel of civilian and military experts to examine the Afghanistan-Pakistan strategy and the full range of options." The panel would then meet and deliberate through the end of the year.

Petraeus thought it was laughably late in the game for all this. Though these were reasonable concerns, he felt they had all been asked and answered.

Mullen was still livid at Eikenberry and shocked the cables had not been given to McChrystal in advance.

Turning to immediate business, Mullen then laid out a set of options with the new fourth alternative—the hybrid option developed by Biden and Cartwright that the president had insisted the military include. This final presentation of options had been worked out in very

---

*At the end of 2006 when Petraeus had been the commander-designate for Iraq he insisted that President Bush make an up-front commitment to send five brigades, saying, "Don't bother to send me to Iraq if you're only going to commit to two brigades."

close-hold discussions via secure video or secure phone with Gates, Petraeus and McChrystal:

- Force Option 1 was 85,000—this was an impossible number, Mullen said; everyone had agreed forces at that level were not available.

McDonough thought it reflected poorly on the military that Gates, Mullen, Petraeus and McChrystal would put an option before the president two months into the deliberations that they thought was not realistic.

- Force Option 2 was 40,000, which McChrystal and the military felt provided the best opportunity to protect the population.

- The new Force Option 2A was 30,000 to 35,000 in an extended surge of 24 months that Gates had proposed in his October 30 memo. *The Wall Street Journal* had it right. This included three combat brigades, required a specific appeal to NATO for a fourth brigade, and "accepts additional risk in developing local security forces." The fourth U.S. brigade from Option 2 would be held in abeyance, allowing Obama to decide on it in December 2010.

- The hybrid option was 20,000, or two brigades, primarily to disrupt the Taliban with counterterrorist strikes and train the Afghan forces. This was the proposal brought from the October 14 war game by Vice Chairman Cartwright, who had worked it up with the Joint Staff at Biden's request. Mullen presented it without much enthusiasm.

Petraeus was quite exercised. He found the 20,000 option more than disquieting. It was a repudiation of his protect-the-people counterinsurgency. It should not even get serious consideration. Worse, in the desperate search for options this hybrid "throwaway" seemed to be getting some support.

"You start going out tromping around, disrupting the enemy, and you're making a lot of enemies," he said. "Because all you're doing is moving through, trying to kill or capture bad guys who will fade into the woodwork, and then you leave. And so what have you accomplished?" Alienating the population—the opposite of the counterinsurgency goal—would not really result in any damage to the enemy because "there are not targeted operations."

Petraeus continued, "This is not a stiletto, this is a chainsaw." And you have the small-unit, quick-reaction forces from the Joint Special Operations Command "that are doing the stiletto operations, very precise, highly enabled, lots of support and enablers and ISR [Intelligence, Surveillance and Reconnaissance] and all kinds of intelligence fusion centers supporting them and everything else. These are conventional forces that can't be enabled anywhere near the same way. There's just a limit to how many precise targets you have at any one time anyway. And so you're essentially going out, just trying to put sticks in hornets' nests and see what happens. But what you do is you just stir things up.

"We can't use two brigades to disrupt the enemy," he went on. "We are going to increase the number of JSOC elements and we will have, within them, a small disruption force."

Petraeus turned back to Mesopotamia.

"We did this in Iraq. We actually used a battalion in Iraq from the 82nd Airborne that was specially trained and enabled and equipped in the summer of 2007, called Task Force Falcon. And it would go out, but it had all the enablers of a JSOC operation. But it would go into an area where we knew there were bad guys, and it would basically flush them out so that the other JSOC forces could then pounce on them. But they were very, very carefully supported operations because you can get in real trouble out there, and you've got to have a lot of assets available in case they really end up hitting something big. You could do them at night when you could have AC-130s [gunships] and all of the other enablers that we could bring to bear that the enemy just couldn't match." He explained how they could only use a company of several hundred soldiers at a time for these operations.

And that had been done during the really dark days of Iraq in areas that were in the grip of the enemy, where the U.S. could attack without having to worry about protecting the population.

They would adopt a concept like that for Afghanistan, supported by intelligence and other enablers and backup. But a Task Force Falcon kind of operation couldn't be done with a brigade—which was at least three times the size of a battalion—because of the amount of helicopters and intelligence needed. Petraeus's bottom line: You can't do counterterrorism with infantry brigades. He also cited the Poignant Vision war game, which he said showed that 20,000 wouldn't work. Relying on the war game was highly misleading and a real stretch. It implied there had been some serious, neutral analysis. The war game had actually been a lot of discussion, and the only two people who might have explained this—DNI Blair and General Cartwright—were not there.

"So," Obama said, "20,000 is not really a viable option?"

That was correct. Gates, Mullen, Petraeus and McChrystal went further, saying the words a commander in chief never wants to hear. If they only got 20,000, they would not be able to accomplish the mission now described by Jones as "denying the Taliban the ability to threaten to overthrow the Afghan state." Besides, CT was already a component of their strategy. They planned to increase the counterterrorist forces the next summer under a campaign plan for the secret Task Force 714.

"Okay," Obama said, "if you tell me that we can't do that, and you war-gamed it, I'll accept that."

Later Biden got a report on the war game, and he told the president that the claims made by Mullen and Petraeus were "bullshit." It was impossible to reach those conclusions that such an exercise could show counterinsurgency plus would not work. Biden thought the president saw through the war game.

In my interview with the president, Obama did not indicate he was aware that the results of the war game had been misrepresented to him. "The decisions that I ultimately made were not based on any particular war game," he said.

At another point in the meeting, the president asked, "If Stan needs to get to 40,000, why does that all have to come from us? Why can't part of that come from NATO?"

The military answer was that NATO troops didn't always have the same capabilities ours had. What was left unsaid was the simple fact that there was an increasing Americanization of the war. Troops from each of the NATO countries operated under their own rules of engagement and had to answer to their own defense ministries, giving McChrystal less control over them than the absolute authority he had over U.S. forces. This disjointed structure violated one of the first principles of war—unity of command.

But some of the proposed 40,000 were going to be used for training and security that NATO troops could handle, Obama noted. "I want to include a NATO brigade as part of the 40,000," he said.

Petraeus seemed fixated on preserving the third brigade. Gates had already effectively given away the fourth brigade. Now the third was in jeopardy. "Stan needs this brigade in order to be able to plan," Petraeus said, "to set his plan for the next couple of years."

Petraeus was thinking in timelines, but so was Obama.

The president held up a green-colored graph labeled "Alternative Mission in Afghanistan" showing the projected deployments like a slow-rising mountain that peaked at 108,000 U.S. troops after the 40,000 were added in the next 15 months. The mountain then gently slid back down to the current 68,000 over six years.

"Six years out from now, we're just back to where we are now?" said Obama in mild disgust. "This just gets me back to where we are today six years from now. I'm not going to sign on for that."

It was a clear rebuke to the military, across the board. Two months of work. And the president had only begun.

Earlier, he had had a private talk with Donilon and Lute, who told him the Pentagon wasn't stretching itself. Here was the glaring contradiction: The military said the situation was so serious that it might fail in 12 months, but they wanted to deploy 40,000 more troops in what amounted to 15 months. The Pentagon and its military leaders could come across as organized, thoughtful and hard-charging, but, Donilon and Lute had told him, they needed to be probed.

At the meeting, Obama said, "Look, here's the deal. I don't know why it takes us this long . . . I don't know how I'm going to describe this as a surge?"

He turned to Petraeus. "Dave, why does it take so long to get these troops in there? How long did it take in Iraq?"

"We built it from January to June, 2007," Petraeus answered. So it took six months to move in 30,000 troops and then begin a gradual off-ramp."

"Why is this going to take longer?" Obama asked. His tone had turned to interrogation.

Petraeus explained the differences between landlocked Afghanistan, where supplies had to be trucked through mountain ranges on limited and dangerous roads, and Iraq, which had better roads and access to a port along the Persian Gulf.

"I know it's not the same as Iraq," Obama said. "I know this is a very different country. So I'm not saying it'd be the exact same plan as Iraq, but I am looking for something that is a surge to create the conditions for a transition." The president was looking to the military to provide much more than a way into Afghanistan. He also wanted to find a way out.

"If we went faster," Obama continued, "wouldn't it have a bigger effect on the politics of the country?" He pointed to the slow-rising graph showing the projected addition of force into Afghanistan. "You've got to move this to the left. If it's as grave as we know it is, why are we waiting until 2011 to be at the maximum?"

Obama held the chart and waved it as if it were a piece of damning evidence in a courtroom. "Where we are now," he said, pointing to the current 68,000, "is above where we were when we came in." That had been just 35,000. "Five years from now we're only where we are now," he said. The chart showed the force level at about 68,000 then. Under this plan he would have more troops in Afghanistan when he left office—whether after one or two terms—than when he took office. And the United States would only get down to 20,000, as he put it, "after my presidency."

Rhodes passed McDonough a note saying: More troops in Afghanistan in 2016 than when he took office!

Obama was almost fretting. "A six-to-eight-year war at $50 billion a year is not in the national interest of the United States." That was what was before him. The entire timeline from deployment to drawdown was too much. "Actually," he continued, "in 18 to 24 months, we need to think about how we can begin thinning out our presence and reducing our troops. This cannot be an open-ended commitment."

Petraeus then boldly declared that he thought they could get all the troops in by the first half of next year.

The president took another look at Mullen's four options.

"So let me get this straight, okay?" Obama asked. "You guys just presented me four options, two of which are not realistic"—the 85,000 dream and the 20,000 hybrid. Of the remaining two—the 40,000 and Gates's 30,000 to 35,000—he noted their numbers were about the same. "That's not good enough." And the way the chart presented it, the 30,000 to 35,000 option was really another way to get to the full 40,000 because there would be a decision point for the fourth brigade in a year, December 2010. So 2A is just 2 without the final brigade? he asked.

"Yes," said McChrystal.

Two and 2A are really the same, Obama said. "So what's my option? You have essentially given me one option." He added sternly, "You're not really giving me any options. We were going to meet here today to talk about three options. I asked for three options at the Joint Chiefs meeting." That was some 10 days earlier. "You agreed to go back and work those up."

At one point Mullen said, "No, I think what we've tried to do here is present a range of options, but we believe that Stan's option is the best."

But, Obama pressed, you haven't really made them that different. It was silent in the room, and there was a long pause.

"Well, yes, sir," Mullen finally replied. He later said, "I didn't see any other path."

It was as if the ghosts of the Vietnam and Iraq wars were hovering, trying to replay the history in which the military had virtually dictated the force levels. This was the second lesson from Gordon Goldstein's book about McGeorge Bundy and Vietnam: "Never Trust the Bureaucracy to Get It Right."

The president repeated that he wanted the graph moved to the left. Get the forces in faster and out faster. "You tell me that the biggest problem we have now is that the momentum is with the Taliban, and the reason for this resource request is that the momentum is with the Taliban. But you're not getting these troops into Afghanistan" for more than a year. "I'm not going to make a commitment that leaves my successor with more troops than I inherited in Afghanistan.

"We have a government with a serious dependency issue," Obama said of Afghanistan. "If I'm Karzai, this looks great to me, because then I don't have to do anything.

"It's unacceptable," he said. He wanted another option.

"Well," Gates finally said, "Mr. President, I think we owe you that option."

It never came. I later pressed the president twice about what happened and why. He finally acknowledged that he personally had to help design a new option. "What is fair is that I was involved," Obama said. "I was more involved in that process than it was probably typical."

Afterward, Petraeus immediately got on the secure video with his logistics team, which moves troops and supplies in and out of war zones.

"Okay," he said, addressing them fondly as "Logistics Nation," his term for the team headed by Major General Ken Dowd, who was the combatant commander's supply officer. "I've just written a check and I need you to help me cash it."

"Hooah, sir!" Dowd said, using the universal military expression that means anything and everything except no.

Petraeus said that he had told the president they could get all the troops and equipment on the ground in Afghanistan by the first half of 2010. "We really need to drill this absolutely in every respect. Where can we shorten timelines?" It was a matter of squeezing everything.

So it was back to the drawing board for the military as Obama went off on a 10-day trip to Asia. On the way over, he phoned Gates from a secure line on Air Force One.

"Bob, I just want to go through what we talked about," he said, and repeated the elements of the new option he was looking for.

"That's what we're working on," Gates promised.

Later, Obama expressed his frustration to his top advisers. The military was "really cooking the thing in the direction that they wanted." Once they got around to dealing with enablers and the flexibility that the military would want, the choice would be between 40,000 and 36,000, he said.

It was laughable. "They are not going to give me a choice."

What also really set off the president was that the military wanted to leave more than 100,000 troops there for years. "I'm not going to leave this to my successor," and the military plan "compromises our ability to do anything else. We have things we want to do domestically. We have things we want to do internationally."

The open-ended, perpetual commitment of force in Afghanistan is wrong for our broader interests, Obama said. First, it would increase the dependency of the Karzai government, which would be happy to have us there forever to do the hard things. Second, it doesn't address corruption and it reinforces the Taliban's talking point that we will permanently occupy the country. So, he said, the task of balancing the military imperative with all of this was going to be his.

"If they tell me these are the resources that they really need to break the Taliban's momentum then we need to do that" in some form. "But I have to figure out a way to make this option aligned with what I feel are the strategic interests that we have in Afghanistan." And they are limited. He was going to have to begin to map some way out.

Obama indicated that he had wanted the strategic review to be as prolonged as it had been in order to get away from the events of the early fall when the McChrystal assessment had been published and McChrystal had given the London speech. These events had created the appearance that the military was boxing him in. Obama said he wanted his final decision to be based upon his consultation with the military and not something that was forced upon him. He had to get himself and the country out of that box. War could not suck the oxygen out of everything else. Some of it had to do with the nature of wars that had the U.S. fighting local insurgencies. There were going to be no victory dances in the end zone. One of his problems with Bush had been the constant talk of a victory that was not attainable.

Obama had campaigned against Bush's ideas and approaches. But, Donilon, for one, thought that Obama had perhaps underestimated the extent to which he had inherited George W. Bush's presidency— the apparatus, personnel and mind-set of war making.

After the November 11 meeting, Mullen and Lute talked privately.

"Mr. Chairman," Lute said, "the president really wants another option. This is not a wild hair by the VP. This is, he's serious about this. There's no question. Look, he really expects a paper here. We've got to have this analysis." Gently he added, "You're on the hook. The president's going to call on you."

Mullen wasn't acting as if he felt any pressure. Lute was astonished.

Three days later, Mullen and the Joint Chiefs of Staff produced the latest version of the secret graph entitled "Alternative Mission in Afghanistan."

It was a source of the president's mounting frustration. Under this revised plan, an imaginary dotted line showed a drawdown beginning—possibly—in 2012, the year he would be running for re-election. The current level of 68,000 would not be reached until the spring of 2013, according to the chart. Then the shift to an "advise/ assist" mission would begin to take place. But according to the chart, it would only happen if four "key assumptions" were realized, none of which the strategy review had suggested were likely. The assumptions were that the Taliban would be degraded to "manageable" by the Afghans, the Afghan security forces would be able to secure the gains from the U.S. surge, the sanctuaries in Pakistan would be "eliminated or severely degraded," and the Afghan government could stabilize the country.

The chart projected some 30,000 U.S. troops in Afghanistan into 2015. In my interview with the president, I said that based on the chart someone had suggested "No Exit" as the title of this book.

Obama disagreed. "You don't know the ending," he said. "Because there is going to come a point in time in which the United States' combat function in Afghanistan will have ceased."

The president did not say when that might be.

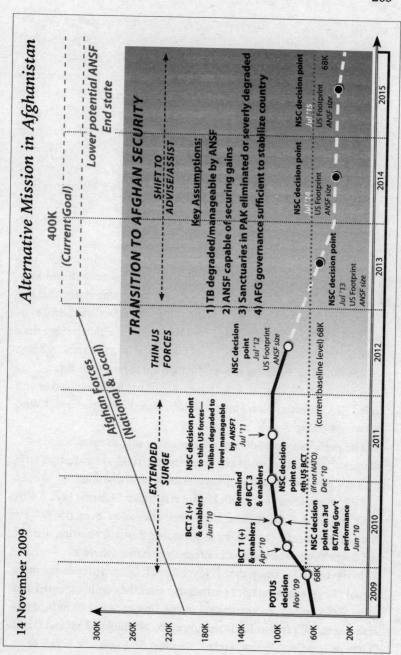

Alternative Mission in Afghanistan

14 November 2009

24

Despite the CIA's love affair with unmanned aerial vehicles such as Predators, Obama understood with increasing clarity that the United States would not get a lasting, durable effect with drone attacks. "I don't think anybody believes that we'll have much more than a disruption effect on al Qaeda," said Lute, "and its associates by doing it from the air or by doing sort of the high value target hit list."

Still, Emanuel showed an intense interest in the drone strikes and called CIA Director Leon Panetta regularly with one question: "Who did we get today?"

The president wanted to move the Pakistanis to bring some semblance of law and order to the ungoverned tribal areas and go after al Qaeda and the Taliban more aggressively on the ground.

"We've got to get to that Pakistani risk factor," Obama said. "Why don't we send a delegation, high-level delegation over there?" He reached out directly to Pakistani President Zardari, drafting a letter and dispatching Jones and John Brennan to hand-deliver it.

In the two-page letter, dated November 11, Obama proposed a more formal "long-term strategic" partnership over the coming months and years. Referring to "recent arrests in the United States of individuals with ties to militants in Pakistan," meaning Najibullah Zazi and David Coleman Headley, Obama wrote, "we must find new and better ways to work together to disrupt their ability to plan attacks." In an unmistakable reference to the ISI-supported terrorist group LeT, he said that using such "proxy groups" would no longer be tolerable.

Obama made an unusual appeal to the widower of the assassinated Benazir Bhutto in the private letter, which was not intended to become public. "I know that I am speaking to you on a personal level when I say that my commitment to ending the ability of these groups to strike at our families is as much about my family's security as it is about yours."

He proposed an escalation. "If your government will match my gesture, I will commit my government to deepening and broadening our work together, particularly in the area of counterterrorism cooperation, with the goal of defeating al Qaeda, TTP, LeT, the Haqqani network, the Afghan Taliban" and others.

Jones and Brennan flew to Pakistan, presenting the letter to Zardari on November 13. "Pakistan is the epicenter of the strategic review," Jones said. The president was elevating the importance of Pakistan. Jones said the region would now be called PakAf instead of AfPak.

This distressed the Pakistanis, who responded that the inversion might suggest that Pakistan was the main problem. That would not be positive, nor would it be in the spirit of the proposed partnership, they said.

Jones said he understood, and the name change was not made.

Brennan, Obama's trusted counterterrorism adviser, said that during the past several months, U.S. law enforcement agencies had discovered at least two individuals who had been trained in terrorist camps in Pakistan, and he cited the cases of Zazi and Headley. They had been very close to developing attacks in New York and Europe, Brennan said. They had been uncovered by the U.S. and foreign intelligence services.

"It is difficult," Jones said solemnly, "to imagine the consequences to our relationship had they been successful."

This was both a plea and a warning. If a destructive attack originated from Pakistan, there would be a response from the U.S.

Jones's message also was that Pakistan could get virtually anything from its wish list of weapons, trade deals and money if it agreed to go along with the partnership. He believed that no country could refuse such an offer from the United States.

And it was not as though the U.S. was seeking the kind of presence in that country as it had in Afghanistan, or for that matter Germany and Japan. "We are not asking for bases in Pakistan," he said at one point.

On November 17, Tony Blinken met with Pakistani Ambassador Haqqani. Blinken said that despite the impressive Pakistani efforts in Swat and Waziristan there was still concern about the ISI and some terrorist groups. "There is appeasement one day, confrontation another day and direction a third day," he said.

And that same week, Panetta visited Islamabad for meetings with Zardari and other top officials.

"The United States," the CIA director said, "expects Pakistan's full support as al Qaeda and its affiliates are common enemies." This cooperation, he added, was a matter of Pakistan's own "survival."

Panetta noted that the command and control for the Taliban was in the Pakistani city of Quetta. Intelligence showed that bombs were being made there. "They are taken across the border and blowing up Americans," Panetta said. "We have to go after this."

The CIA had a secret base in Quetta, but the Pakistanis tried to keep the CIA people on the base. They did not allow them much access around the city, arguing that they would be spotted too easily because many had white skin. The CIA people felt almost as if they were under house arrest. The CIA argued it could assert a lot more pressure on the Taliban senior leadership if they could be seen as running agents in Quetta. It would demonstrate that the Taliban had been penetrated, a message the CIA wanted to send.

The CIA team did have kill-capture authority on Mullah Omar. But because of the large population in Quetta, drones would not be very effective. Thus—and this was the bottom line—there was a need for "joint ISI-CIA operations on the ground," Panetta said. This would be a big step that would involve more CIA covert teams inside Pakistan.

The Pakistanis balked at the joint operations, but were soon granting visas for more CIA people to enter Pakistan. For example, a January 18, 2010, request for 36 CIA people was soon approved, and CIA deputy director Steve Kappes personally asked for 10 more visas on April 19, 2010.

Later in November, Zardari answered Obama with a wandering letter that the White House concluded must have been composed by a committee dominated by the Pakistani military and ISI. It wallowed in the impact of three decades of conflict in Afghanistan: "We continue to suffer. Pakistan continues to bleed." The letter did not directly refer to India, but its subtext lurked behind many paragraphs. "Our security is fragile," it said, "due to a fast evolving imbalance in the conventional field." The Swat operation "cost Pakistan nothing less than US $2.5 billion.

"Here I must draw your attention to a proxy war against Pakistan, now in full swing," Zardari wrote, "in which neighboring intelligence agencies"—read India—"are using Afghan soil to perpetrate violence in Pakistan." The letter insisted the Pakistan contributions to the war on terror "against al Qaeda and Taliban are second to none." Instead of accepting or rejecting the offer for a strategic partnership, Zardari—or the committee—said it was being given "my highest consideration."

There was a lot of head-scratching at the White House over this. It was decided to take it as a yes, and soon the Pakistanis learned that U.S. military Special Operations Forces were rehearsing attacks into the tribal areas of Pakistan. At a dinner with Ambassador Haqqani, DNI Blair said the two countries had to get over their mutual distrust as he pressed for the strategic partnership. Or, Blair said, "we will have to do what we must to protect U.S. interests." In other words, go it alone.

There was another side to the tough talk. As a result of nearly endless policy discussions in the White House, Jones, Donilon, Lute and others had repeatedly asked: How are we going to get these guys in

Pakistan to change? For the moment, they knew this was the wrong question. Pakistan was not going to change. The Pakistanis were hardwired against India. Let's quit banging our heads against that wall and accept it.

Pakistan would be at such a disadvantage in a conventional war with India, which had a two-to-one advantage in troops, that it had relied on two asymmetric tools—proxy terrorism through LeT and the threat of nuclear weapons. As a result, Pakistan did not want to be pressed to halt their production of fissile material for more nuclear weapons.

Jones tried to convey to them: We've come to the conclusion that after years of trying, we're not going to change your strategic calculus. It's yours. We accept it and want to understand it better. You get to be the Pakistanis in this relationship, while we get to be the Americans. We're not going to try to be both.

DNI Blair believed the Pakistani policy was deeply flawed because it was based entirely on carrots. There were no sticks.

Al Qaeda and the Taliban in the safe havens were having a field day in his opinion. "Those tribes in that territory are trading ideology, leadership, explosives, logistics, money, suicide bombers," Blair told a colleague. "And so Haqqani, TTP, even LeT, al Qaeda don't much care if they blow up a bunch of people in Pakistan, India, Afghanistan or the United States. It's all a touchdown, a good thing."

The Pakistani leadership had claimed their government was so weak that it might collapse if the U.S. used any sticks. They were basically saying, "You don't want us falling apart, do you? Because then all hell will break loose."

Blair figured it would take about ten minutes of good, honest discussion at a National Security Council meeting to sort out what the real leverage was on Pakistan. Suppose the president asked in earnest, "What do you think you could do?"

If asked, Blair maintained he would have said, "We could conduct some raids across the border, we could bomb" the extremist groups inside Pakistan.

The president and others then would have asked, of course, "Denny, what would be the consequences of that?"

"I think Pakistan would be completely, completely pissed off and they would probably take actions against us," he would recommend, "but they would probably adjust. And depending on which raids, which things, I think we might be able to get away with it."

In Blair's view, the Oval Office and Situation Room conversations were artificial. Obama, like all presidents, wanted harmony. If there was anything other than that, it would get out that there had been a knockdown, drag-out fight in the Situation Room and the president would look like he had lost control of his team. Blair believed the debate had a hollowness to it. The president asked good questions but quickly exhausted the wisdom of those in the room. Instead of a real in-depth discussion, there was a scripted feel. Prior to meetings, someone in the NSC trying to control the agenda would call Blair and say, "Denny, you have five minutes for the intel update."

Blair realized that Jones had no control over the place. Donilon and Brennan had direct access to the president, so they didn't have to go through Jones. There were at least three national security advisers—Jones, Donilon and Brennan. But Denis McDonough also had his own turf, so he was a fourth. And Emanuel also tinkered in policy and acted at times as a fifth.

"It's the goddamnest thing I've ever seen," Blair said.

After meeting up with the rest of the presidential entourage in China, Jones requested permission from Obama to go back to Washington several days early to work on the strategy review.

Obama had one important thought. He had realized that the key to holding the national security team together was Gates. My goal is to keep Gates, he told Jones. I do not want to break with the secretary of defense.

The president told me this was not an exact quote, but it reflected his view. "What is absolutely true is that my relationship with Bob is sufficiently close," he said, "and my respect for the job that he's been doing is sufficiently high that I would take his views very heavily into account in any final decision that I made. Partly because I'm asking him to execute" the final decision.

"I'm not sure if he considers this an insult or a compliment, but he and I actually think a lot alike, in broad terms." The president said he understood that Gates had to be a voice for the military. "Now, he has a different job than I do. And part of the job of secretary of defense is tending to a particular constituency within the Pentagon."

After returning from Asia, Obama called his national security team together again at 8:15 P.M., Monday, November 23, for an unusual evening meeting.

"Final decision in the next couple of days," he promised.

Gates had written a memo to Obama summarizing the six primary military objectives in Afghanistan that incorporated comments from the agencies.*

Obama said he agreed with the less ambitious, more realistic objectives. Although the military leadership had previously argued that "defeating" the Taliban was necessary, the word was missing from the memo. The U.S. now planned on "disrupting" and "degrading" the Taliban.

The president explained that these objectives should be met on a much shorter timeline than what the Pentagon initially recommended, saying the troops would start thinning out after July 2011—the time frame Gates had suggested in their last session.

"If people don't think this realistically can be done in this time

---

* 1. Reversing Taliban momentum.
  2. Denying the Taliban access to and control of key population and production centers and lines of communication.
  3. Disrupting the Taliban outside secured areas and preventing al Qaeda from regaining sanctuary in Afghanistan.
  4. Degrading the Taliban to levels manageable by the Afghans.
  5. Increasing the size and capacity of the Afghan security forces.
  6. Building the Afghan government, especially in key ministries.

frame, they need to speak now," he challenged. Our goal is to stabilize population centers and then transition to Afghan forces. "It's not perfection. If you don't think we can do this, you need to speak up now. This is not going to be the five-year time frame that had originally come in." You have to understand if this time frame is not realistic, one will be imposed on us, so we need to have a realistic time frame. We need to understand with precision what we're trying to do. "If this two-year time frame for accomplishing these goals is not possible, I want to hear it now."

Obama wasn't expecting a model outcome in Afghanistan, though he was demanding precision from his advisers and military leaders. There would be no extended surge that lasted long enough for the Afghan National Security Forces to reach 400,000 and fulfill the counterinsurgency ratios suggested by the Pentagon.

"We do not need perfection," Obama said. "Four hundred thousand is not going to be the number we were going to be at before we started thinning out."

Clinton seemed to be almost jumping in her seat, showing every sign she wanted to be called on. But Jones had determined the speaking order and the secretary would have to sit through Biden's comments. Her desire to speak and disappointment at having to wait was noticeable to several on the back bench.

Biden had issued a response memorandum that took the president up on his offer to question the strategy's time frame and objectives.

As he began, Petraeus felt the air go out of the room.

First, Biden said once again, he wasn't sure if the 40,000 was politically sustainable. I still have serious questions about the viability of the elements of a counterinsurgency strategy. Eikenberry's cable raises questions. We should prove the concept before we go any further. What about competing needs for State Department personnel elsewhere? What about doing more for Pakistan? He said he thought the Pentagon's plan was putting the counterinsurgency cart before the troop horse. Is the civilian surge going to be adequate? How much will it cost? This will limit flexibility in foreign and domestic policy, he said.

Clinton then got her chance. "I wholeheartedly endorse the approach," she said, "and think it can make a difference. We spent a year waiting for an election and new government. The international community and Karzai all know what the outcome will be if we don't increase the commitment."

The status quo was totally unacceptable, she said. "What we're doing now will not work." The plan was not everything we all might have wanted. "But we won't know if we don't commit to it. The six operational objectives are good and linked.

"I endorse this effort," she said. "It comes with enormous cost, but if we go halfhearted we'll achieve nothing. We must act like we're going to win."

It was a version of one of her sayings from when she had been first lady in the White House that she still used regularly—"Fake it until you make it."

She continued, "If we don't come with an approach close to this, we shouldn't even try, because we'll just be wasting time, lives and money." The plan—Gates's six objectives and McChrystal's request for 40,000—meant they would "have a fighting chance to be successful." She rapped her fist on the table.

Petraeus was blown away. What a persuasive, powerful and magnificent performance, he thought.

"This outcome really matters," Gates said next. "We're not winning. I endorse this." But doing a full assessment in six months, in July 2010, was too early. "Our forces will just be taking hold; international forces arriving; civilian surge is taking hold; Karzai's appointments and recruiting of ANSF still taking hold. We should wait until December 2010" for the full assessment.

That was an appealing date on the political calendar—one month after the November midterm elections. Postponing a formal assessment until then might keep Afghanistan out of the election debate. It was like throwing Emanuel, Axelrod, the political team and the president a bouquet of flowers.

On the question of the third brigade, Gates said, "I believe we should approve it up front. It doesn't give big leverage anyway. Holding it in abeyance will complicate Stan's campaign planning. We'll do everything we can to meet the timelines, getting the third brigade on the ground ASAP. That's what'll help get conditions for success. So, formal report in July 2010 on progress, major reassessment in December 2010. Approve three brigades." He said he agreed with Clinton that July 2011 is when they could begin to make transitions and thin forces. Their tag team approach was evident and formidable to many in the room.

Mullen, calling in from Geneva, Switzerland, by videoconference, strongly endorsed the plan, saying they needed the forces as rapidly as possible. He said he believed that counterinsurgency would work and agreed on the timelines presented by Gates. Mullen acknowledged that developing the Afghan security forces did have risk, but they had to get the trainers on the ground and do everything possible to get on with it. "I'll know whether the strategy is working in July 2011," if we'll be winning or losing.

At one point, facing the bloc lining up for the 40,000, the president interjected, "I don't want to be in a situation here where we're back here in six months talking about another 40,000."

"We won't come back and ask for more troops again," Mullen said, repeating his pledge from the October 30 meeting with the chiefs and making an important concession.

"Mr. President," Petraeus began, "we will support your decision." The military was not self-employed, Petraeus noted, but was trained to take orders. Everyone in the military swore an oath to "obey the orders of the president of the United States." It was an oath he knew by heart and repeated several times a week at soldiers' reenlistment and promotion ceremonies.

"We will support you at the end of the day," Petraeus said. "We will also provide our best professional military judgment right up until the point that you make a final decision."

After declaring his unconditional loyalty, he said his military advice was that they couldn't do it with less than 40,000.

"You've got one bite at this apple," Petraeus continued. "It ought to be a decisive one. I agree with the secretary and chairman that a two-part decision on the third brigade is unwise. Not sure what's achieved by withholding the third brigade, but it does create issues for our military campaign plan." July 2010 is probably too soon to conduct another review, he said. "Best course of action is a single-deployment decision with possible off-ramps rather than on-ramps." In military terminology, this meant the president could decide later not to deploy some of the forces.

Petraeus said he strongly supported an energetic effort to get more from NATO, but he said that 10,000 troops from the allies would not be as useful as 10,000 American troops.

"Be careful how you characterize our NATO allies," Obama said sharply. "We need them. They will be useful in this coalition."

"The objectives are good, as defined," Petraeus said. The July 2011 goal is fine on the thinning of our forces, but the military advice, he said, would be for conditions-based transitions because that gives the president more flexibility.

"Just as a point," he added, "Pakistan is achieving progress. It is tough, but we need to keep pushing to support them." Petraeus repeated for emphasis, "I will support your decision, be part of the unified effort."

Turning to the Afghan security forces development, he agreed with McChrystal that it would take time—"2013 at the earliest and it is high-risk, but we need the additional U.S. and ISAF forces to create space and time for ANSF development. It can be done with the right number of forces and resources. Have to convince the ANSF and people that it can be done, and to convince the Taliban they'll lose."

Because Mullen was out of the country, General Cartwright was the acting chairman of the Joint Chiefs and was relaying the opinion of the service chiefs. He got to the crux of things by addressing an issue that had yet to be discussed at the meeting.

"We have to be flexible," Cartwright said. "We've got to be prepared to listen to the commander on the ground."

In response to the president's request for a speedier troop deployment, the Pentagon had sent SECRET backup documents to the White House and the principals that front-loaded the deployment schedule.

The first round would be 18,000 troops, instead of the 10,000 in the original McChrystal plan.

Cartwright said the last deployment was so small that it provided no additional leverage over Karzai, even though the four blocks of granite had essentially said that the troop number was a way for Obama to show resolve and influence the Afghan government.

"It's not the number of troops," he said. "It is how quickly we can get our troops in." The idea was to create a shock with so much force. "Getting troops in quickly and the 18-to-24-month time frame is leverage." The length of the surge was what mattered in changing Karzai's behavior.

This was a sharp contradiction of what the president had heard so far and he seemed to agree with it.

"Mr. President, I shared the option with the chiefs before I came over," Cartwright said. "And the chiefs said to me that there's leverage in your plan at the front and at the back. The fact that you get more in sooner and you've made clear that they're coming out at the end increases your leverage on the Afghans." It would send the message "I'm not an occupier—that there is a date certain that I'm going to start to change the character of my relationship here." The message was that Afghans would have to assume more responsibilities.

Cartwright realized that by disagreeing with the chairman and then invoking the rest of the JCS he was really sticking it to Admiral Mullen.

Instantly, McDonough realized that this was the option that the president had been looking for. It was all about "leverage" on the Afghans, their leader, Karzai, and others. McDonough was struck that Cartwright was representing the consensus of the chiefs, and they clearly saw the heart of the matter—time frame not number of troops. In contrast, all Mullen did was channel the views of McChrystal.

Axelrod and McDonough were convinced that this was a decisive moment in the debate, and they admired the way Cartwright seemed to blast through the smoke.

"We should announce a total number of troops and not detail the force mix," Cartwright continued. Instead of talking about brigades, the president should set a total number of troops and let McChrystal decide the makeup of the forces, he said.

Budget director Peter Orszag, who had been invited to the meeting, said there was a significant chance of having to submit a supplemental funding request to Congress.

Holbrooke said he supported Clinton's view and agreed strongly that since July 2010 was only seven, eight months away, it was too soon for a big evaluation. He said they should be careful on topics like "eliminating" corruption because that was not possible. He said he didn't think they had enough leverage over Karzai. They must maintain the focus on Pakistan, he said.

Speaking from Pakistan, Ambassador Anne Patterson said the most important element was to show resolve and assure Pakistan that the U.S. would not leave a mess on its doorstep. They had to remove uncertainty about American intentions in order to deal with the negative press within Pakistan. "They're making progress against the internal extremists, and we're making progress against al Qaeda, but it will be frustrating. The sooner we get going, the better."

Eikenberry, by video from Kabul, said they needed to remember that the Taliban was going to continue to be a part of the political fabric. Second, he said it was a fact that "a lot of our risk comes from the governance side, not the security side." And the governance issues needed to be dealt with no matter what was decided regarding troop numbers. While they did require more forces to build the ANSF, what was needed was a settlement within the Pashtun community. He pointed out that Karzai didn't feel he was necessarily fighting a war against the Taliban.

Brennan said, "The counterterrorist program will continue regardless of the decision on any of these military options." Adding troops would be basically irrelevant. He was very skeptical of making a five-year investment in counterinsurgency, indicating he doubted it was worth the blood and treasure with respect to the goals. In his view, the focus should be on training the national army and police in order to turn the war over to the Afghans. They had the plans and platforms in place to carry out the counterterrorism mission. "It will take a generation to develop an Afghanistan that can achieve modest governmental goals and consolidate these gains." He underscored the importance of the operations in Pakistan, Yemen and Somalia.

As Petraeus heard Brennan's argument that the focus should be on training the Afghan army and police, his thoughts went straight to what had happened in Iraq. There had to be a level of security and safety first—something provided by having more boots on the ground—before local security forces could take over.

Donilon tried to summarize. "We are not accepting the argument in this discussion that to defeat al Qaeda means we would have to do a long-term counterinsurgency strategy to defeat the Taliban," he said. "To do a counterinsurgency strategy to defeat the Taliban would take a trillion dollars and six to eight years." The deputy national security adviser felt that Petraeus and his "ilk" had repeatedly argued for counterinsurgency during the past three months. But Donilon wanted to reiterate that the cost of this approach was not in the national interest. A nationwide counterinsurgency was a seam in the proposed strategy, a crack in the strategy that Donilon felt had to be continually addressed. The key difference between what had been proposed and what the strategy would ultimately be, Donilon believed, was that it would not be a full-scale counterinsurgency.

"People have to be comfortable with the decision that in 18 to 24 months we would begin the downward slope so at the end of 2012 we would be at pre-surge levels," he said. He did not mention it, but the deadline, 2012, was the year Obama would almost surely seek reelection.

Donilon pointed out that everyone also needed to be comfortable with having fewer than 400,000 combined Afghan army and police. Moving up the deployment of a NATO brigade combat team by a year to August 2010 would provide more force than McChrystal had requested in his original request.

There were hard choices with the Pakistani safe haven issue that had yet to be fully addressed, Donilon said. And within the next six months, they had to have a clear path toward dealing with that particular problem.

Rahm Emanuel talked about the difficulty of passing supplemental funding through Congress. "We would need the support of the American people to undertake this project," he said. With the options favored by the military, Emanuel explained that the U.S. commitment would effectively triple in one year.

This got the president's attention. "I've been very careful to not interject domestic politics into this discussion to date," Obama said. "Rahm, as a good chief of staff, has just raised this question. It behooves us to ask it. I'm not being flip, but what would happen, what would you do if Congress refused to fund the 40,000 troops?" That scenario was highly unlikely. If a Democratic president wanted to send 40,000, the Democratic Congress would no doubt go along. If it didn't, the Republicans would certainly provide the votes. But it was a way of asking what they would do if the president did not approve 40,000.

Obama seemed to turn to Petraeus, but the general didn't answer.

He's punting! McDonough and Rhodes concluded. Petraeus was passing the question to McChrystal, they thought. Donilon figured that Petraeus wouldn't want this option considered.

"I'm committed regardless," McChrystal said. "I haven't developed this in detail, but what I would do is go to Plan B. It would be to pull back to key population centers, to train the Afghan security forces, and to continue to target key sanctuaries, including trying to remove sanctuaries in Pakistan."

Cartwright said that would be the Plan B, which was essentially the hybrid option of 20,000 additional troops, including trainers and counterterrorism assets, that he had developed for Biden.

"Just real quick," Eikenberry said. "That's right. You focus on the Afghan National Security Force development as your ticket out, and speed up reintegration."

Donilon, McDonough and Rhodes thought Plan B didn't sound half bad. It was pretty good, plausible. Here again was an option the military had never offered, another viable alternative that the president had been waiting to receive from the Pentagon.

Petraeus now had an answer to the question about what would happen if the 40,000 were not funded or somehow they did not get them.

"You would see the spots on the map that we control—and that the Afghan government controls—slowly recede," he said. "What you would have is a recipe for a slow loss." Without a secure country, it would become more difficult and more important to improve the ANSF. "But you've got to recognize the enormous risk and how difficult it is to develop ANSF if the security situation's deteriorating."

The president attempted to sum things up. "At the end of two years," he said, "the situation may still have ambiguous elements. We'll have cleared and held areas, security will be improved, there will be more ANSF. It won't be fully there yet. Taliban momentum will be broken. Political environment will be complex. Some progress there in the economy, but not as much as we'd like. And basically, we'll have to ask, is this good enough?

"If anybody has additional comments," he said, "they should get them to me." Obama added, "I'm inclined to agree with the notion that we announce the third brigade. I'm more inclined to off-ramp rather than on-ramp. But if we are not seeing progress, we could off-ramp.

"Okay, thanks everyone. We need to get a decision. I'll be working through the weekend on this and I'd like to be able to have a decision early next week."

On Tuesday, November 24, Biden called Petraeus, who was on a plane heading to the USS *Nimitz*, the aircraft carrier that was in the theater supporting the war. Petraeus was going to spend Thanksgiving on the ship.

Just want to confirm that you are okay with the 18-to-24-month timeline, Biden said. Obama was likely to set a specific date—July 2011—to begin the drawdown. Biden wanted to make sure the most visible general would not balk.

Roger, Petraeus said. He concluded that the president and vice president were wondering if the military would support the decision.

•   •   •

When Petraeus passed through Washington during the next week or so, Cartwright tried to review the hybrid option with him.

"Let's talk about this," he said. "What's the problem?"

Petraeus said he did not want to discuss the matter.

"I'm taking your lessons here," Cartwright said, noting that it was straight out of Petraeus's Iraq playbook to get the surge of troops in fast and also expand counterterrorist operations. "What's wrong with this plan?"

"You don't understand," Petraeus responded, shutting the door on further discussion.

Cartwright had thought for a long time that he was a lone military voice howling into a strong wind, but he was surprised that Petraeus was unwilling to have a frank conversation.

Gates spoke with Cartwright at this point. He wanted to figure out how to have a recommendation that did "not break the internal coalition" among the uniformed military. Cartwright thought of their discussion as a negotiation, but it almost approached an argument.

The secretary of defense said he wanted 35,000 troops, the high end of his Option 2A.

The vice chairman said he was in the 25,000 area, up 5,000 from the hybrid option.

25

At about 2:30 on Wednesday afternoon, November 25, the day before Thanksgiving, the president and his chief of staff met in the Oval Office with the White House national security team—Jones, Donilon, McDonough and Rhodes, the foreign policy speechwriter.

Obama said this was the most difficult decision he had faced—and he looked like it was.

He unspooled what was on his mind, offering some conclusions, expressing some uncertainty, and outlining specifics to Rhodes for the upcoming speech. He said he was "inclined to go with the 30,000" troops, yet he didn't sound like this was final.

"This needs to be a plan about how we're going to hand it off and get out of Afghanistan," Obama said. "Everything that we're doing has to be focused on how we're going to get to the point where we can reduce our footprint. It's in our national security interest. There cannot be any wiggle room. It has to be clear that this is what we're doing."

There were uncertainties, he said. "As we describe this to the American people, they're not as interested in things like the numbers of brigades. It's the number of troops. And I've decided on 30,000." It was the lowest number in Gates's Option 2A, which had been submitted three weeks earlier. Obama now sounded more certain on that number. "We should make clear that this is not the Iraq debate. We're not talking about setting a date for removing our troops and lessening our commitment. We're talking about identifying the time frame for transition" to the Afghan security forces.

"And we also need to make clear that we're going to have interests in Afghanistan that are enduring, in terms of counterterrorism and governance, assistance." Focus on training also, he said. "I want to emphasize the speed with which we're doing things. Faster in, faster out."

In an unusual move, he said, "I want everybody to sign on to this—McChrystal, Petraeus, Gates, Mullen, Eikenberry and Clinton. We should get this on paper and on the record." With the president speaking as if there would be a signed contract, some had the mistaken impression that he wanted actual signatures on a document.

"We're not going to be precise about the speed with which we're winding down," Obama said. They would just identify the point of transition—July 2011. In a shot right at Petraeus, he said, "Avoid the counterinsurgency language in public." The language he wanted to use was "target, train and transfer."

He reiterated that he was out-of-hand rejecting the McChrystal proposal to train the Afghan security forces up to 400,000. "We're not going to set targets unless we're going to meet them." He added that on the price tag, "We shouldn't low-ball the price in our estimates. We should be as clear as we can, when we can, about how much this is going to cost.

"We shouldn't be belligerent in how we talk about this," said Obama, who had been offended by Bush's "bring 'em on" talk and the early Bush rhetoric of getting bin Laden "dead or alive." He added, "We need to set public expectations that this is going to be difficult and it's going to take time."

Donilon asked about Pakistan. Exactly how were they going to explain that the safe havens there would no longer be acceptable? It could not be framed as a declaration of war inside Pakistan. This was a tricky problem.

"We need to make clear to people that the cancer is in Pakistan," Obama said. "The reason we're doing the target, train and transfer in Afghanistan is so the cancer doesn't spread there. We also need to excise the cancer in Pakistan." But the fuller explanation would not—could not—be in the speech because these were covert drone attacks and other clandestine operations. "We also have to connect this to our counterterrorism efforts in the homeland."

Turning to the governments of Afghanistan and Pakistan, he said they had to make it clear they "are both supportive of this and will get into the fight. That this is an opportunity for them to increase their partnership."

Obama said the speech should address the underlying purpose of these decisions. "The reason we're doing this is to create the space for the training and partnership with the Afghans to work." It was a surge intended to get the United States out.

Donilon said that not everything was resolved. The Pentagon was now raising another troop request that had been overlooked during the deliberations. It was for 4,500 more "enablers"—logistics, communications and medical personnel—and it had been pending since summer. As best he could tell, some of those enabling functions were built into the request for the large brigades. I'm not impressed that they have made a good, strong case that these 4,500 enablers are necessary for those brigades, Donilon said.

"That's basically taking it up to 40,000?" the president asked.

"Yes."

"I'm done doing this!" Obama said, finally erupting. "We've all agreed on a plan. And we're all going to stick to that plan. I haven't agreed to anything beyond that."

The 30,000 was a "hard cap," he said forcefully. "I don't want enablers to be used as wiggle room. The easy thing for me to do—politically—would actually be to say no" to the 30,000. Then he gestured out the Oval Office windows, across the Potomac, in the direction of the Pentagon. Referring to Gates and the uniformed military, he said, "They think it's the opposite. I'd be perfectly happy—" He stopped mid-sentence. "Nothing would make Rahm happier than if I said no to the 30,000."

There was some subdued laughter.

"Rahm would tell me it'd be much easier to do what I want to do by saying no," the president said. He could then focus on the domestic agenda that he wanted to be the heart of his presidency. The military did not understand. "Politically, what these guys don't get is it'd be a lot easier for me to go out and give a speech saying, 'You know what? The American people are sick of this war, and we're going to put in 10,000 trainers because that's how we're going to get out of there.'

"And the military would be upset about it," the president added.

It was apparent that a part—perhaps a large part—of Obama wanted to give precisely that speech. He seemed to be road-testing it.

Donilon said that Gates might resign if the decision was only the 10,000 trainers.

"That would be the difficult part," Obama said, "because Bob Gates is . . . there's no stronger member of my national security team."

No one said anything more about that possibility.

"I'm just going to lay it out," the president said, returning to the path they had supposedly agreed on for the 30,000. Overall, he said there were five points he wanted to underscore for how they all would talk about the decision.

"We need to emphasize this is an international effort," he said. "We need to emphasize we're getting troops in faster and getting them out faster. We need to emphasize the training of the Afghans. We need to emphasize the need to beat back the Taliban's momentum, and we need to emphasize that this will help us improve Afghan governance."

The speech "should be very sober but not depressing." He said again that he didn't want to use the word "counterinsurgency," but just talk instead about security for the Afghan population centers. The terms counterinsurgency and counterterrorism had become caricatured, he felt, code words for nationwide security versus pulling back and firing missiles from ships and drones.

Full counterinsurgency was not possible, yet it had become a Republican mantra. "Here's the part of it that I agree with," he said. "In order to have successful training of these security forces and to blunt the Taliban's momentum, you need to secure enough population centers to create space for that training mission to succeed."

He repeated that he wanted a decision memorandum that everyone would have to follow.

"We're not going to do this unless everybody literally signs on to it and looks me in the eye and tells me that they're for it." The president was as animated as most in the room had ever seen him. "I don't want to have anybody going out the day after and saying that they don't agree with this." No more gentlemen's agreements. The lawyer in Obama would attempt to deter revisionism with a written document.

Addressing Rhodes, he began to sketch the case he wanted to make in his speech.

"We need to remind people why we went into Afghanistan in the first place," he said. "We need to tell the story of how we got up to where we are today. I want to make the point that this is the epicenter of violent extremism." The speech should describe how he believed in the mission in Afghanistan and the need for additional resources.

"People think that this is some kind of numbers game," the president said. He repeated what he had said two weeks earlier during a review session. If I was not convinced this was necessary, he said, "going to Dover, another night in Dover, would be enough for me to just say the hell with this, and let's get out of there." A version of that should be in the speech, Obama said, to show it had been hard to make this decision, and how deep his conviction was.

The president also wanted to stress that an international coalition supported this war. It was not just an American war, and any increase in force would be accompanied by an increase from the NATO allies. He also said he had to be specific about the July 2011 date for beginning withdrawal.

Biden had suggested a long section on Pakistan, but they had to be careful. Much of that would be on the covert side and involved classified forces. All hell would break loose if the president announced that safe havens were no longer acceptable, and he was going after them with U.S. ground combat forces—Special Operations or CIA paramilitary teams. Crossing the border, even with Pakistani acquiescence, was dicey.

"You know what?" Obama said. He had outlined the Pakistan problem already in March. "We did that the first time. We've made it clear to people. They'll link it, but this speech is about Afghanistan. Americans are really concerned about our troops in this speech."

The president repeated that he had decided on the 30,000-troop option and that should be in the speech draft, he said, adding a caution. "There's a chance the decision could change," he said. "We may need another speech."

Obama called Rhodes back to the Oval Office shortly after the meeting.

"One other thing," the president said, "I want to say in the speech why this is not Vietnam, why this is not Iraq." He wanted to say that in Afghanistan, unlike Vietnam, the United States had 41 nations supporting the war as coalition partners. And it would be useful to remind people that the 9/11 attacks were orchestrated by al Qaeda, which had sanctuary in Afghanistan. Tell the whole story from 9/11. It was not like Iraq because we weren't attacked from there and there is no threat to the homeland from Iraq. Yet, he said he wanted to acknowledge that Iraq's security and stability had improved.

Of both Vietnam and Iraq, he said, "We've had wrenching debates about these issues as a country. But we need to move beyond relitigating those debates. We need to celebrate the heroism and courage of our troops without glorifying war.

"We need to convey the extent of the threat and the fact that these dangers still exist," he directed. The tone ought to be "clear-eyed and resolute with a clear focus on our interests, that we've not overexpanding or moving beyond those interests.

"Give it some lift that we've carried a special burden since the time of FDR. We have not always been lauded as a consequence. We've made some mistakes, but we've underwritten the architecture of national security with the service and sacrifice of our young men and women and our taxpayers.

"Extremism will be a long struggle," he said. "In many ways, it's more complicated than simply dealing with nation-states, because you're dealing with disorderly regions.

"Our motivations are the same as they were over the last 60 years, which is that we don't seek world domination or occupation." He said he thought that the lives of our children and grandchildren would be better if other people's children and grandchildren had better lives.

Expressing some frustration, he noted, "Our entire national policy can't just be focused on terrorism." There were 6 billion people in the world with a vast range and diversity of concerns, and we also had to be focused on our own economy because it's the foundation of our strength in the world. "We can't lose sight of that, and we have too much in recent years."

Finally, the president added, "The American people are idealists, but they also want their leaders to be realistic. The speech has to convey that."

Obama had met that week with House Speaker Nancy Pelosi, who was later quoted in *The Washington Post* as saying there was "serious unrest" among Democrats over the possibility of voting to spend billions more for the Afghanistan War. It was the most difficult vote she could ask her fellow Democrats to cast. On a conference call with bloggers, Pelosi said, "We need to know what the mission is, how this is further protecting the American people and is this the best way to do that, especially at a time when there's such serious economic issues here at home."

Later on Wednesday, Obama held his regular weekly meeting with Gates in the Oval Office. The room is so well lit, bright with no shadows, that it has a stark feeling. It is assuredly a setting for business.

Everything was winding down for the Thanksgiving holiday. They had completed nine often grueling sessions on the strategy review, and it was clear to everyone, including Obama, that Gates needed some final decisions soon. Since Mullen was traveling to Geneva for an unannounced meeting on strategic arms reductions, Cartwright, the vice chairman, was attending in his place. Jones also joined.

The president said that he had arrived at the number. Under the redefined mission, he said, the best I can do is 30,000.

Cartwright was not surprised. It had a perfect symmetry—right between the McChrystal 40,000 and the hybrid 20,000. But it was also between the 35,000 that Gates had most recently been seeking, and the 25,000 that Cartwright had thought was about right.

Here is why it will be 30,000, the president added. The financially hard times were real, as they all knew. Obama said he wasn't going to support an open-ended commitment. In addition, he was not going to do nation building or pursue a full counterinsurgency strategy. Already, he and Bush had committed 33,000 troops more in one year.

Jones was still amazed that the military had not provided a real assessment of how the hell those 33,000 were doing, and they still wanted another 40,000. A cynical person would think you can't be serious. A cynical person, Jones thought, would say, "Whiskey Tango Foxtrot."

The country would not support business as usual in Afghanistan, Obama said. "This is what I'm willing to take on, politically." The very best was 30,000, he repeated.

Gates had worked for seven other presidents. Each had his own decision-making style. Assertions and conclusions were often floated, sometimes emphatically, sometimes tentatively. It wasn't evident what this meant.

"I've got a request for 4,500 enablers sitting on my desk," Gates said. The requests for force had been stacking up since September when they began the review. "And I'd like to have another 10 percent that I can send in, enablers or forces, if I need them. If I need mine-clearing units or more medical personnel, support people."

"Bob," the president said, "30,000 plus 4,500 plus 10 percent of 30,000 is"—he had already done the math—"37,500." Sounding like an auctioneer, he added, "I'm at 30,000."

It was an extraordinary moment. He had never been quite so definitive or abrupt with Gates. When Obama spoke at the meetings, it had often been questions or summaries. "I'm at 30,000.

"I will give you some latitude within your 10 percentage points, things that you might need in the future," but under exceptional circumstances only. "But I'm not getting to 37,500," Obama said emphatically. "I might as well go to 40,000."

"Can you support this?" Obama asked. "Because if the answer is no, I understand it and I'll be happy to just authorize another 10,000 troops and we can continue to go as we are and train the Afghan national force and just hope for the best."

"*Hope for the best*," the condescending words hung in the air.

Gates said that he would support 30,000. Yes, he could go along.

Cartwright signed up as well. He realized that the president had given a shot across the bow—take it or leave it. Clearly, the vice chairman of the Joint Chiefs concluded, the president had picked 30,000 in order to keep the family together.

The auctioneer had closed the bidding. The president had decided.

As a Thanksgiving tradition, Biden and his family rented a house in Nantucket.

There was no good option that would guarantee success, the president told him by secure phone. "We were dealt a very bad hand," Obama lamented again.

Biden said it would not be that bad if the Karzai government fell.

No, Obama said, the downside was too great, and he was going with 30,000.

Biden wrote a long-hand memo to the president. "It's not the number, it's the strategy," he said, and sent it on secure fax to Obama. In the course of the holiday he faxed half a dozen handwritten memos to Obama, underscoring that theme and urging that the president incorporate five points into his final decision:

1. No full counterinsurgency;

2. No nation building;

3. Focus on al Qaeda;

4. The military can occupy only what they can transfer to the Afghans; and

5. The goal is to "degrade" the Taliban with eventual reconciliation in mind.

He also pressed Obama not to buy in to the extravagant goal of building a 400,000 Afghan security force.

26

On the morning of November 27, Obama again invited Colin Powell to the Oval Office for another private talk. The president said he was struggling with the different points of view. The military was unified supporting McChrystal's request for 40,000 more troops. His political advisers were very skeptical. He was asking for new approaches, but he just kept getting the same old options.

"You don't have to put up with this," said Powell, a former chairman of the Joint Chiefs. "You're the commander in chief. These guys work for you. Because they're unanimous in their advice doesn't make it right. There are other generals. There's only one commander in chief."

When I asked the president about this advice, he said, "General Powell and I talk. And I consider him a friend. And since he's now out of that building [the Pentagon], every once in a while I'll check in with him. I'll leave it at that."

"Why are we having another meeting about this?" the president asked that day after Thanksgiving as his White House national security team filed into the Oval Office—Jones, Donilon, Emanuel, McDonough, Lute and Colonel John Tien, an Iraq combat veteran and former Rhodes Scholar on the NSC staff. "I thought this was finished Wednesday."

Donilon and Lute said there were open questions from the Pentagon. Were the enablers already authorized?

No.

What does the 10 percent apply to?

The 30,000, an exasperated president said, and that's it. "Why do we keep having these meetings after we have all agreed?"

Well, we're still working with the military on these questions.

The president said he had reached agreement with the secretary of defense—why was there still a debate? That should have ended it. But the Pentagon was not used to or comfortable with being held to such precise standards.

The Pentagon seemed to be reopening every question. Donilon started ticking them off. Most came by phone from Mullen or the JCS staff, though Donilon and Lute were also talking with General Cartwright and Michèle Flournoy, the undersecretary for policy.

Like what?

Well, the estimate that they could get all the 30,000 troops into Afghanistan by summer.

"We didn't come up with that," the president said. "Petraeus told us that."

Now the Pentagon was saying they were unsure.

"It wasn't us that concocted . . ." the president said.

The Pentagon was also questioning the withdrawal date of July 2011. At one point earlier, Gates had said he preferred six months later—the end of 2011.

"I'm pissed," Obama said, but he didn't raise his voice much. That was their date as well, he said. It was actually on the chart they briefed to us—the one with the longer trajectory. They identified it as the point when Afghans would be able to take the lead and responsibility in certain areas. Was this a negotiating tactic or what?

It seemed every issue was back up for discussion, negotiation or clarification. Obama said he was ready to go back and just give them 10,000 trainers. That would be it.

This was a contest that pitted the president against the military establishment. Donilon was stunned by the political power the military was exerting. But, he reasoned, the White House had to be the long-distance runner in the contest. From studying Vietnam and George W. Bush's Iraq War, he knew one common theme was miscue after miscue. Presidents being surprised, presidents not getting into the details enough, presidents not being clear about what they wanted, presidents not understanding the implications of seemingly simple decisions.

Jones left the meeting and spoke with Mullen, who was indeed saying that getting the 30,000 there might take longer than the end of the summer. McChrystal had been told he could decide which units composed the 30,000. Not surprisingly, he wanted units from the legendary 101st Airborne Division, the "Screaming Eagles" that Petraeus had commanded during the 2003 Iraq invasion. These units would not be ready until September.

No, Jones told him, it would really not be a good idea to go back to the president now and say it couldn't be done. Assertions had been made. The president wanted everyone to keep his word. In essence, this was military advice Obama didn't want.

"Got it," Mullen said, disappointed that Jones, a retired four-star, didn't seem to comprehend.

In the Oval Office, Obama continued with Donilon, Lute and the others. The meeting went on for hours, almost the entire day, as they tried to nail down the president's orders. They had all read *Lessons in Disaster*. One of its conclusions was that Johnson failed to translate his Vietnam decisions into specific orders for the military.

Obama began to dictate precisely what he wanted, composing what Donilon called a "terms sheet," making it similar to a legal document used in a business deal. He took Gates's memo and agreed that the strategic concept would be to "degrade" the Taliban—not dismantle, not defeat, not destroy. He pasted Gates's six military missions from the memo into his own orders. The six military missions involved reversing the Taliban momentum and then denying, disrupting and degrading them.

As the contest went on through the afternoon, the Pentagon civilians and the Joint Staff had an ever expansive view of the strategy, seeking to broaden it.

"You can't do that to a president," Donilon kept saying. That was not what Obama wanted. He wanted a narrower mission.

But the push continued.

Put in restrictions, Obama ordered.

Donilon tried, but back it would come from the Pentagon with more, not less. One addition had to do with messaging to al Qaeda.

"We're not going to do it," the president said when he received word.

Donilon felt like he was rewriting the orders ten times, and he finally told the military interlocutors that the president only wanted matters directly related to the goal. "If you guys have a bunch of other bullshit you want to do," he said, the president would not accept it.

Say it directly, Obama dictated. In final form, his orders said that the military mission "will be limited in scope and scale to only what is necessary to attain the U.S. goal." Period. It couldn't be clearer. When all the words were filtered and reworked, he had two goals—defeat al Qaeda and degrade the Taliban.

But expansive, protect-the-population counterinsurgency ideas and side missions kept coming from the Pentagon.

No, Obama said. Again, he would say it directly, dictating the line, "This approach is not fully resourced counterinsurgency or nation building." It couldn't be clearer, and he couldn't be more emphatic.

Still, some were clinging to the original McChrystal request for 40,000. It was as if no one had ever told them no.

No, Obama said. On the troop number, he was picking the low end of Option 2A, the proposal for 35,000 to 30,000. It was 30,000. Let's be clear, he said. He had picked Option 2A with "the narrower mission and the express tighter timeline." He was sticking to July 2011. It was not just to begin withdrawing U.S. forces, but on that date "we will expect to begin transferring lead security responsibility from these forces to the ANSF," he dictated.

In case anyone did not understand the big change, he said for the terms sheet, "In July 2011, we will assess progress nationwide and the president will consider the timing of changing the military mission." The mission would not grow. It would only contract.

Around dinnertime—after nearly eight hours of wrangling and clarifying with the Pentagon—Obama went over a final draft, dictating and crafting the language.

"Maybe I'm getting too far down in the weeds on this, but I feel like I have to," he said. The president polished the document until 9:15 P.M.

When he was done, the orders were typed out, six single-spaced pages. That's what he would issue, he said. His decision wasn't just going to be a speech or a general sense on the numbers game of 30,000. It would be this directive. And everyone was going to read it and sign up. That was the price he would exact, the way he would end the contest—for the moment, at least. Because, as they all knew now, the contest, like the war, would probably not end, and the struggle would continue.

Among the most top secret elements were not only stepped-up CIA drone and other attacks against al Qaeda in Pakistan, but the president's directive that McChrystal increase the tempo of counter-terrorism attacks against the Taliban inside Afghanistan.

In some respects, McChrystal was the perfect wolf in sheep's clothing. After years as Special Forces commander (JSOC) in Iraq, no one in the U.S. military knew more about these operations than he. Now McChrystal was the Afghanistan commander who had embraced the kinder, gentler protect-the-people counterinsurgency, putting limits on combat operations in order to reduce Afghan civilian casualties and even instructing his forces on the road to treat Afghans with respect.

But under the radar, McChrystal had his own wolf, Vice Admiral William H. McRaven, a Navy SEAL, who had taken command from him of the Joint Special Operations Command in June 2008. The scale and lethal intensity of McRaven's attacks in Afghanistan was at a level almost unimaginable to anyone without TOP SECRET CODEWORD clearances. The "jackpot rate"—when the strikes got the intended target—had jumped from 35 percent to 80 percent. Slapping a table for emphasis on each word, one senior civilian official with those clearances said, "Every single night they are banging on these guys with a pace and fury that is pretty impressive." And the 18 months to July 2011 would give the special operators time and space to disrupt, degrade and perhaps in a significant way decimate the Taliban insurgency. It might give new meaning to the word "degrade."

Obama's strategy was built on the idea that the time, space, intensity and success would allow the politics to come together. At least that was his hope.

Word circulated in the highest reaches of the Pentagon that the decision was about to implode. The Pentagon was saying that the secretary of defense thought he had received permission for the 4,500 plus the 10 percent.

Obama thought he had been clear, so he made it clearer and talked to Gates about 7 P.M. "I thought we'd straightened this out on Wednesday," he said, obviously bewildered. He hated wasting time, and this was to him a complete rehash. But Donilon and Lute wanted absolute clarification.

How many times did he have to say it?

The number was 30,000, the president said, and the overall deal was that the 10 percent of that 30,000 was only for exceptional circumstances. But the 4,500 enablers would have to be part of the 30,000. It would have to be built into or come out of that 30,000 somehow, but it was not on the table. Period. His number was 30,000. It was a hard cap.

Later that night, Obama gave a final read of his six pages of orders. The relitigation and debate were over. "I'm comfortable with this decision," he said. "I'm comfortable with the way that it's been set forth here. I'll call Bob tomorrow, I'll call Hillary, and we'll have them in tomorrow or Sunday and I'll go through it with them face-to-face."

Donilon felt that the document was an assertion of presidential and civilian control of the military. The uniformed military had had too much of a say in the later years of the Bush presidency. The embodiment of that was Dave Petraeus, who, with his team, had made important and sound decisions in Iraq beginning in about 2007. But a lot of poor decisions had been made before that by Bush and others in both Iraq and Afghanistan. Petraeus had been engaged in damage limitation. To Donilon, President Obama was trying to ensure that his administration was not engaged in damage limitation five years from now. No nationwide counterinsurgency in Afghanistan was necessary to protect the United States.

The question Obama had attempted to answer was: How do you draw down, his ultimate goal, in the face of a serious and deteriorating situation? The answer was they had to break enemy momentum and then leverage that by going faster in "an extended surge."

27

Saturday, November 28, was another day for the devoted at the National Security Council staff, including Tom Donilon and Doug Lute. They realized they probably should have been out doing something else on the weekend after Thanksgiving, but the strategy review was the all-consuming center of their universe. So the two were there at the White House sharing their frustrations. The president and all of them were being rolled by the military, they agreed. No matter what questions, leading or otherwise, the president or anyone asked, the only viable option was 40,000 U.S.

"How many of these guys who are pushing that option are going to be here to see the effects by July of 2011?" Lute lamented to Donilon.

They ticked through the list.

"There's no chance in hell Petraeus is going to be in CentCom until the summer of '11," Lute said.

Mullen's second two-year term as chairman would almost be up, so he would be heading out too.

"McChrystal's probably rotated out," Lute said. "He says he's willing to stay three years but my guess is that probably won't happen."

Gates, they noted, had only planned to stay for the first year of the administration, so he would almost certainly be gone.

"So," Lute summarized, "the bottom line is, you're left with the president standing here, owning this thing that these guys sold to him but who have since exited stage right." He added, "Everybody else is going to have their White House commission hanging in their den."

"My God," Donilon said, "what are we getting this guy into?" The president would be the one left when the bill came due in 2012, the year he would be running for reelection. The bill was not only in terms of money but in terms of results. What could they accomplish by 2011 or 2012?

The president was not going to get any relief that Thanksgiving weekend. The debate was still going on—in his house and in his head. He met in the Oval Office with Emanuel, Donilon, Lute, Brennan and Colonel Tien that Saturday for a kind of rump session. Clinton, Gates and Jones were away or had out-of-town guests for the Thanksgiving weekend.

Obama sounded like he was back to tentative on the 30,000 troops with the beginning of the withdrawal in about 18 months, July 2011. "This is the way I'm leaning," Obama said, adding sharply, "but the door is not closed. I got Rhodes writing two speeches. And I want to hear from you guys one last time."

Donilon and Lute said the backers of the 40,000 would likely not be around in July 2011, but Obama would be.

The president simply took it in.

Colonel Tien was junior in rank, so he spoke first. There are thousands of active duty colonels in the American military and it was unusual for one to be able to advise the commander in chief directly, particularly just before a defining decision.

"Mr. President," Tien said, "I don't see how you can defy your military chain here. We kind of are where we are. Because if you tell General McChrystal, I got all this, I got your assessment, got your resource constructs, but I've chosen to do something else, you're going to probably have to replace him. You can't tell him, just do it my way, thanks for your hard work, do it my way. And then where does that stop?"

The colonel did not have to elaborate. His implication was that not only McChrystal, but Petraeus, Mullen and even Gates might go—an unprecedented toppling of the military high command. Perhaps no president could weather that, especially a 48-year-old with four years in the United States Senate and ten months as commander in chief.

Lute could see the president had reached a fork in the road and was pausing.

"Mr. President," Lute said, "you don't have to do this. I know you know this, but let's just review the bidding here. How do we think things are going to look in July of '11?"

Lute told Obama he saw four main risks in the ongoing war. First there was Pakistan, the heart of many of the problems without solutions in sight. Two, governance and corruption in Afghanistan—huge problems with no practical fix readily available. Three, the Afghan National Security Forces—army and police—could probably not be cured with a massive decade-long project costing tens of billions of dollars. Four, international support, which was in peril.

"These are cumulative risks," he said. The risk in one increases the risk in another. "You can't look at these in discrete bites and say, well, with Pakistan, I can take a few mitigating steps" to reduce the risk. Each of the four risks overlaps and reinforces each of the others. The Afghan governance and corruption problem, for example, made the security force problem worse, and vice versa.

"So when you look at these discretely," Lute continued, "like we did in the review, Mr. President, you might be left with the impression we can manage this risk. But I would offer you another model. That is, look at them as a composite. Look at them as a set, and then you begin to move, in my mind, from a calculated risk to a gamble."

Lute did not have to add that gambling was no way to make policy. "When you look at all the things that have got to break our way," Lute added, "I can't tell you that the prospect here for success is very high. And if you add those risks up and ask me where I think we'll be in July 2011, sort of your big decision point, I'm telling you I think that we're not going to be a whole lot different than we are today.

"I'm sure there are going to be political consequences that other people appreciate better than I do.

"It still smells to me like a gamble," Lute said. "You shouldn't base this on sort of an unexpected windfall of luck." He had the floor and was comfortable giving bad news to presidents, so he drove his point home. "We want to get from here to there, but, my God, you know, the Himalayas, you know, the Hindu Kush, is between here and there. How in hell are we going to do this?"

It was a telling moment. Was the general a pessimist? Or a realist?

"Yeah," the president said graciously, indicating that he did not disagree. "Thanks for being candid. It can't be easy for you to come in here and tell me that. Basically, we're going to have to execute our heart out to make this work." The July 2011 date, he said, was the key.

His new strategy and approach was different from the "all in" Bush model. "This is not as much as it takes for as long as it takes, but that we are going to have a turning point here and it's going to be July of 2011."

From his frequent private discussions with Brennan, Obama knew his counterterrorism chief's views. Brennan opposed a large troop increase.

Donilon agreed about the risks, calling them "key dependencies"—success would depend on all these working one way or another.

"We're just taking on a lot," Donilon said. "If you ask yourself where are we going to be in December 2010"—a year out from then when the president planned follow-up review—"or go another six months, July 2011, and the answer's going to be we're not a whole lot different than we are today." In other words, there could not be that much improvement in 12 months or 18 months, he said. The war, he said, would still be precarious "because of these four risk factors, which look hard to mitigate." He asked bluntly, "How do you mitigate any one of those?"

Neither the president nor anyone else had an answer for the short run.

Donilon said the fundamental issue was the new strategy with 30,000 troops. "Then the question is, why did you do this?" he asked. Why was there a need for a big surge in troops? The best answer Donilon had was that the U.S. needed to be in a position to deliver a big punch to stop the Taliban's momentum and give the Karzai government a chance. It would create more space to continue executing counterterrorism operations. This would demonstrate resolve to Pakistan, or so the idea went.

"I didn't come in with a blank slate," Obama had said to his team at one point. Afghanistan had drifted for too long, the victim of a poor military strategy and being under-resourced. He had inherited a war with a beginning and middle, but no clear end.

After the meeting, Lute and Tien went downstairs together.

"Well, you know," Lute said, "giddy up."

They laughed slightly, recognizing that it looked like a decision.

"This is what you work for," the three-star general (West Point 1975) told the colonel (West Point 1987). "You work your butt off, you get an opportunity to have a small group discussion with the president of the United States on the eve of a big decision, and all you can say is, Did you get a chance to say what you wanted to say?"

Lute felt that the military establishment was really rolling the president, though he didn't want to assign motives. It wasn't deliberate on McChrystal's part. As far as Lute could tell, McChrystal didn't have a conspiratorial bone in his body. If there was someone trying to roll Obama, it was Petraeus. But he had done so subtly and with a light touch, Lute believed. On the other hand, Mullen had failed to maintain the integrity of the process, which required the serious presentation of something other than the one recommended option. He adamantly wouldn't budge and give a hard look at alternatives. To Lute, Gates also had failed to expand the horizon of alternatives for the president, which in his view was the job of the secretary of defense. The secretary was supposed to give his own advice and bottom-line recommendation, but he was also supposed to be the final window into the larger world of choice for a president. Because a president did have choices, and in this case his had been significantly limited, perhaps to the disadvantage of all.

Lute thought Gates overly deferential to the uniformed military. The secretary of defense is the president's first line of civilian control.

If the secretary did not assert civilian control at his level and say, wait a minute, then it got bumped up to the president to do it. Gates didn't serve the president very well, Lute felt, and his practice of holding his cards close—being so quiet, so subdued—wore thin. And then writing a personal memo to the president about the issue of whether the goal should be to "defeat" the Taliban or to "disrupt" them. Gates had, of course, created a new definition, to "degrade" the Taliban. Though the president had accepted the new definition, the personal memo defied and circumvented the rigorous process of the strategy review. It was a process on which Obama, at the very least, had staked his standing and reputation as commander in chief, and, at most, his presidency. And Gates was playing the role of the new Cheney—whispering confidentially in the ear of an inexperienced commander in chief. It gave him extraordinary leverage.

For his part, Donilon was hugely skeptical of the entire uniformed military chain of command. McChrystal was hardly an innocent. He took command, got out first by writing his long, classified assessment, staking his ground and then hiding behind the uniform and the flag. Petraeus and Mullen had joined in after that.

"I want to have a meeting Sunday," the president told Biden by phone. He would call the whole national security team to the Oval Office and give them his terms sheet and orders.

"Mr. President," Biden said, "I want to meet you before you go in."

"No," Obama replied.

"I'll meet you in the residence."

"No, no, we're fine."

28

Biden left Nantucket early on Sunday, November 29, for the White House, where he waited in the portico that connects the residence and the Oval Office. He was taking a chance because the president at times got mad at him when he pushed too hard.

When Obama came down from the residence and saw Biden, he started laughing.

"What you're about to do is a presidential order," Biden advised. It was not a continuation of the debate anymore. "This is not what you think. This is an order." If he didn't stick to those orders, there was no exit. Without them—and this was his main argument—"We're locked into Vietnam." It might not work, and by next December it might be clear. "You may get to the point where you've got to make a really tough goddamned decision, man."

"I'm not signing on to a failure." Obama said. "If what I proposed is not working, I'm not going to be like these other presidents and stick to it based upon my ego or my politics—my political security."

"This is what I'm going to announce," the president said, handing out copies of the six-page terms sheet at 5 P.M. In additional to Biden, Obama had brought in his military team of Gates, Mullen, Cartwright and Petraeus. Jones and Emanuel joined them in the Oval Office. Several seemed surprised to find the president had outlined the exact decisions in writing.

Obama allowed time for everyone to read it.

"There's going to be a hard-and-fast 30,000-troop surge," the president said. In December 2010—a year from then—there would be an NSC-led assessment to see what was working and what was not. "In July 2011, we're going to begin to thin out," he said. There would be a drawdown of forces.

Obama turned to Gates, "I agree we won't know exactly what to do by December 2010. I will wait until July 2011 to determine only one thing though." That would be the slope of the thinning out. He raised his hand high and with it drew the slope of an imaginary graph heading way down.

"In 2010 we will not be having a conversation of how to do more," Obama added. There would be no repeat of what had happened that year. "I will not want to hear that we're doing fine, Mr. President, but we'd be better if we just do more. We're not going to be having a conversation about how to change . . . unless we're talking about how to draw down faster than anticipated in 2011."

This was a redefined mission, the president said, with a narrower focus. "This is neither counterinsurgency nor nation building. The costs are prohibitive." Focus was to be on developing the Afghan government and security force capacity. This was designed to give Afghanistan a chance and provide McChrystal with new resources and some flexibility.

"It can't be an open-ended nation building, unrealistic nation building endeavor," he said. "It's not a full-blown counterinsurgency strategy, but obviously has many elements of a counterinsurgency strategy."

They would do annual targets for the increase of the Afghanistan security forces, not the 2013 target of 400,000 that McChrystal had requested. The president said he would not commit to the 400,000.

Turning to Petraeus, he said, "Don't clear and hold what you cannot transfer. Don't overextend us.

"This represents a strategic modification of what Stan drew from the Riedel report and the Strategic Implementation Plan."

He was approving 30,000 U.S. troops plus 10 percent more or 3,000 which Gates could send if there were exceptional circumstances. "There won't be universal applause on Capitol Hill," he added. Everyone knew that the Democrats were going to be the biggest naysayers, and the Republicans the biggest supporters.

"Many of my political advisers will not be overly happy with this," he said.

"There's going to be tough, tough fighting in the spring and summer," he added. "We anticipate a rise in casualties."

If you have any personal misgivings or any professional doubts about what we're about to do, tell me now, because I need to hear it, he said. "If you don't think this is the right approach, say so now. The only alternative is just to go with trainers"—the 10,000 to 11,000 option that in the military's judgment carried the most risk.

"Here's what I need you to do," the president continued. "I need you to tell me now whether you can accept this. And if you can't, tell me right now. If you can, then I expect your wholehearted support. And that includes what you say in public, to Congress, and internally to your own organizations."

Obama then turned to Mullen, who would be appearing before congressional committees soon. "When you go up and testify," the president said, "you have an obligation to say what you think. I'm not asking you to change what you believe, but if you do not agree with me, say so now."

There was a pause.

"Say so now," the president repeated.

"I fully support, sir," the chairman said, adding that "internal deliberations have been internal. Internal discussion wouldn't be part of, certainly, the public record or anything." None of them would speak about it. He seemed to be saying he had not leaked information about the strategy review sessions and would not testify about them. "Testimony will fully support what you've said here, Mr. President. You need not worry about this." Mullen then complimented the decision. "This does give us a shot at turning things around."

Petraeus had privately concluded that the terms sheet, though a little heavy-handed, was not just to get clarity, but to show the president was in control. When he later learned the president had personally dictated the orders, he couldn't believe it. "There's not a president in history that's dictated five single-spaced pages in his life. That's what the staff gets paid to do."

However, the military was getting almost everything.

"We support you," Petraeus said. "What matters is the sheer number of troops. We'll do repackaging of forces to ensure three combat brigades in the package" even though some of the 4,500 enablers might have to come out of the 30,000. "We're all now committed to this. We'll do everything possible to get the troops on the ground as rapidly as possible and to enable, ultimately, the transfer to begin in July 2011."

The general shifted into cheerleading mode. "We need to link arms now and pull forward." He cited an editorial in one of the newspapers quoting a local Afghan leader saying that security is the mother of all development.

Petraeus recommended that the transition of security tasks to the Afghans be "conditions-based," determined by what was happening on the ground, though he added, "I do think some transfer can take place by July 2011." He also said, "We will push as rapidly as possible to deploy" and get the new forces there as fast as possible.

Next, Obama turned to Emanuel, who privately had called the war "political flypaper"—you get stuck to it and you can't get unstuck.

The chief of staff said he was worried about the cost, noting that he had recently worked hard just to find a few hundred million dollars for an important program. "This could cost $30 billion" more, he said. "You know, this is a big deal." He agreed they needed to stay linked together. "You've got to just go forward now," he told the others, making it clear he was unhappy with the outcome. "Now, we've got a decision, and we've got to go forward."

The president next asked Jones, who simply said he supported the decision.

Gates then said, "This came out about where I thought was right. What we laid out in late March, in retrospect, was too ambitious. The timelines are about right, in terms of the assessment"— December 2010 for a serious evaluation "and then beginning transition in summer 2011. We have a strong case . . . I'm sure Congress will support us."

Biden said, "As I see it, this is not a negotiation. I fully support. I view this as an order from the commander in chief." This was a mission change. "If this is not perceived as a change in mission, we cannot justify why we spent months working on this.

"The context for this is that this is necessary to defeat al Qaeda and support the effort in Pakistan. We can't lose sight of Pakistan and stability there. The way I understand this, Afghanistan is a means to accomplish our top mission, which is to kill al Qaeda and secure Pakistan's nukes. We must be making progress separately against al Qaeda and separately in Pakistan."

Yes, the president agreed. The main pillar of this would be top secret and not be made public. That pillar was that safe havens for al Qaeda in Pakistan or elsewhere would no longer be acceptable. He was already expanding the mission against the main enemy and planned to intensify it with both the military and CIA. He wanted to send a message to Pakistan that the United States was committed, and address the real threat to the homeland and U.S. interests.

After the 9/11 attacks, President Bush had developed the so-called Bush Doctrine that said in responding to terrorist attacks, "We will make no distinction between those who planned these acts and those who harbor them." Obama was not going to wait for an attack. They were going after the sanctuaries with a vengeance.

"Okay," the president said, "the process has been very useful. This is an order. We'll all be united." He planned to unveil the new strategy on Tuesday night at West Point, he said.

Gates said, "You sound the bugle Tuesday night, Mr. President, and Mike"—the chairman—"and I will be the first to charge the hill."

They all walked out of the Oval Office. Everyone seemed supportive. They were going along, but did anyone truly believe?

Unlike Lute, Donilon thought Gates had navigated the divide between Obama and the uniforms pretty well. The secretary of defense had to keep the trust, confidence and loyalty of the uniforms and balance that with the president's vision. It looked as if Gates had been able to deliver unanimity and Obama would not have to deal with military leaders saying they couldn't do it or, worse, have a bunch of resignations.

The president then went down to the Situation Room with Biden and Jones for a secure videoconference with McChrystal and Eikenberry to review the terms sheet, which had been sent to them.

"Gentlemen," Obama began, "I want to be clear about what we are not doing. This is not a nationwide counterinsurgency strategy." Such a strategy would not be sustainable with the American public, he said, it would break the budget, and it would leave the Afghan government more dependent on us. The cost of Stan's plan might be up to $1 trillion.

"No way," the president said.

We have to break the momentum of the Taliban, he said. The terms laid out in the sheet would give the time and space for the ANSF growth. "We need to send a message of resolve to the region." But above all, he said, "We're not making Afghanistan a long-term protectorate.

"The first reassessment will be in December 2010." That would be used to reach a conclusion about the pace of thinning out forces the next year. "This assessment will not result in holding the numbers we now have or adding numbers. It will only be about the flexibility in how we draw down, not if we draw down.

"We are not going to do 400,000 [ANSF]," Obama said, "but we'll train as many as possible. We still will have a big problem getting this through Congress.

"Everything is calibrated on us thinning out. . . . Stan, if this were

2003, maybe we could do a counterinsurgency strategy. Maybe I would have done that, but it's 2009 and we're long past that point.

"Even with a narrower mission and less resourcing, there is still no appetite here for us doing this. I hope you understand that. So there cannot be any dogfights between you, Petraeus, Mullen and Biden, and that includes you, Karl." Addressing Eikenberry, he said, "If this is not the case, I will go with" the 11,000 trainers only. He said he wanted them to understand precisely what he was saying. "Messaging in the next two weeks is going to be critical."

"Mr. President," McChrystal said, "I think I've got it. But I need clarification on the size of the ANSF. Mr. President, what is the target? I need more clarity for the Afghans. They're going to want to know what is the actual number."

"You'll give yearly goals for two years," Obama said, "and keep working on developing the cost for the next decade for the Afghan National Security Forces." Train as many as possible, he said. "I'm not going to micromanage this." But there was no longer a target of 400,000.

Eikenberry said he fully supported the decisions but saw three risks—Pakistan, the Afghan forces and governance. "What kind of security guarantees can we offer beyond two years?" the ambassador asked.

The president asked the NSC staff to get talking points from McChrystal and Eikenberry that he could present to Karzai in a secure videoconference. Finally, he directed that the principals have a series of meetings to develop the strategic framework for relations with Pakistan.

As they all knew, the Pakistan problem was not just a matter of protecting the homeland and destroying al Qaeda. There was always the prize: bin Laden. "We've found the hornets' nest," Jones said later. "We're poking at it from different ways. The bees are swarming but the queen is still there."

That Monday morning, the president met with his White House national security staff. He had several changes to the draft of his speech and the tone was different from his secret orders. "The days of providing a blank check are over," the speech said, but the reference was to Karzai and not the military.

He wanted a three-part argument: troops, civilian surge and Pakistan. There was nothing explicit about limiting the mission.

I went back and read Eisenhower's famous farewell speech about the threat of the military-industrial complex, Obama said. The speechwriters had given him a copy in a packet as he was also preparing his Nobel acceptance speech.

He said everyone focuses on the military-industrial complex part, but to him the most interesting quote was Eisenhower's statement about the need to find a reasonable equilibrium between defense needs and the other vital functions of government: "Each proposal must be weighed in the light of a broader consideration: the need to maintain balance in and among national programs."

"I want you to put that quote in the speech," Obama told Rhodes. And he wanted to say that the loss of balance was one of the mistakes made in recent years. Military might and national security were dependent on the economy, which needed major attention.

Copies of the latest draft were sent to Clinton and Gates.

Robert Rangel, Gates's Pentagon chief of staff, called Rhodes because the secretary was concerned about the rigid July 2011 date to begin withdrawing some forces. Gates wanted to make sure the decision to draw down was based on something. He proposed adding a phrase saying that any withdrawal would take into account "conditions on the ground."

Rhodes went to Obama, who approved the change. That was what they had done in Iraq, and the president seemed to like the flexibility and the ambiguity.

Clinton, who had been at Karzai's November 19 inaugural, wanted the speech to underscore a lasting commitment to both the Afghan and Pakistani people.

Obama agreed to add those points.

•   •   •

On the morning of Tuesday, December 1, before the speech, Jones repeated his lingering concerns to an associate in his office. He was still
worried that they had not evaluated the 33,000 already ordered in by
Bush and Obama. "One of the weaknesses in the demand, I think, for
more troops, was we got 33,000 flowing in there this year and no real
assessment yet as to how the hell they're doing."

It had been a real roller coaster, Jones felt. "It was raw," he said.
"There were some raw emotions out there.

"It just frayed. There are people here whose background is politics,
so they look at everything in political terms. . . . The hard part was to
not let the political interpretation of everything we decide drive the
train: If you can't sell it politically, you can't do it."

"We're going to get our asses kicked for a while here," Axelrod said six
hours before the speech. "There's going to be a lot of turmoil politically around this. We've got to strap on our armor here."

Biden believed the president had put a stake in the heart of expansive counterinsurgency. His orders, in Biden's view, formed a new
strategy to stabilize Afghan population centers, such as Kabul and
Kandahar, to prevent the Taliban from being able to topple the Karzai
government. The military felt they had outsmarted the president and
had won, but he believed that the president had prevailed.

Petraeus saw it differently. Counterinsurgency was alive and well.
The core of the decision was 30,000 troops to protect the population.
All the issues about what the strategy wasn't—not fully-resourced
COIN, not nation building—were just words. The reduction from
40,000 to 30,000 allowed the president to save face. It wasn't ideal,
but McChrystal could get 10,000 from NATO and other countries. If
the president had told him at the beginning that it would come out
with this strategy and 30,000 troops, Petraeus would have taken it in
a second.

Petraeus said privately, "You have to recognize also that I don't
think you win this war. I think you keep fighting. It's a little bit like
Iraq, actually. Iraq is a bit of a metaphor for this. Yes, there has been

enormous progress in Iraq. But there are still horrific attacks in Iraq, and you have to stay vigilant. You have to stay after it. This is the kind of fight we're in for the rest of our lives and probably our kids' lives."

Perhaps the most pessimistic view came from Richard Holbrooke. "It can't work," he said.

29

The White House stage-managed the West Point speech, making sure that key members of the national security team would be in the audience. Clinton and Gates had to testify before the Senate Armed Services Committee the next morning, but their government planes would not be allowed to fly into Andrews Air Force Base when the president was departing or returning. So the whole team flew with Obama on Air Force One, then transferred to a helicopter for the 10-minute ride to the West Point campus.

When security officials heard that Obama, Clinton, Gates, Mullen and Jones were traveling together, they complained that one broken hydraulic line could have wiped out the entire brain trust.

Obama, wearing a dark suit, white shirt and red-striped tie, stepped to the podium at the United States Military Academy's Eisenhower Hall Theatre at 8:01 P.M. on December 1. It was the speech the president and Rhodes had worked on for days, long on history, short on rhetoric and anticlimactic. He announced he was sending 30,000 more U.S. troops.

"I make this decision because I am convinced that our security is at stake," Obama said. "In the last few months alone, we have apprehended extremists within our borders who were sent here from the border region of Afghanistan and Pakistan to commit new acts of terror. And this danger will only grow if the region slides backwards, and al Qaeda can operate with impunity."

The plan was for Afghanistan to eventually stand on its own two feet, so the U.S. could "begin the transfer of our forces out of Afghanistan in July of 2011," he said. Without irony, Obama held up what was happening in Iraq as a model. "Just as we have done in Iraq, we will execute this transition responsibly, taking into account conditions on the ground." There was no talk of victory or winning.

He ended the 34-minute speech by addressing the divisions over the war.

"It's easy to forget that when this war began, we were united—bound together by the fresh memory of a horrific attack, and by the determination to defend our homeland and the values we hold dear. I refuse to accept the notion that we cannot summon that unity again."

Although most news coverage focused on the 30,000 troops, the headline in the next day's *New York Times* was: "Obama Adds Troops, but Maps Exit Plan."

The day after the West Point speech, Clinton and Gates appeared before the Senate Armed Services Committee to testify on the new plan.

Many Republicans, especially Senator Lindsey Graham, were troubled by the president's July 2011 deadline to "begin the transfer of our forces out of Afghanistan." Someone practically had to be a lawyer to figure out what it meant.

Was this an absolute deadline? Graham asked.

"I think the president, as commander in chief," Gates said, "always has the option to adjust his decisions."

"So it is not locked in that we're going to be withdrawing troops in July 2011?" Graham asked. The pace of withdrawal "or not withdraw at all" would be decided later? "Is that correct?"

"The president always has the freedom to adjust his decisions," Gates answered. "It was a clear statement of his strong intent."

"Okay," Graham said, and he turned to Clinton, who was in the witness chair next to Gates. "Have we locked ourselves into leaving, Secretary Clinton, in July 2011?"

"I do not believe we have locked ourselves into leaving," she said. The July 2011 date was a "signal" that the United States "is not interested in occupying Afghanistan . . . in running their country, building their nation." The transition to the Afghanistan forces would "be based on conditions" on the ground.

Later that day, Graham was in the Oval Office. The president wanted support from the moderate Graham on the closing of the prison in Guantánamo.

Graham told the president that he thought the decision to put some of the 9/11 suspects, including the alleged mastermind, Khalid Sheik Mohammed, in civilian court was a strategic blunder. "I don't know if I can," Graham said. As he was leaving, he mentioned that the president's West Point speech was good. "But tell me about July 2011? Is it a goal, which I would share, or is it a withdrawal date no matter what?"

Obama didn't answer immediately.

"Let me tell you what Secretary Clinton said," Graham explained, standing at the Oval Office door. "She said it's a policy based on conditions."

"Well," the president said, "if you'd asked me that question, what I would say is, 'We're going to start leaving.' I have to say that. I can't let this be a war without end, and I can't lose the whole Democratic Party."

"Mr. President," Graham said, "let's just don't let that statement get so much attention." That rationale for why the deadline existed would make it difficult for the president to have Republican support.

"This is tough," Obama replied, repeating his concern. "I can't lose all the Democratic Party. And people at home don't want to hear we're going to be there for ten years."

"You're right," Graham said. "But the enemy is listening too."

"Thank you," the president replied.

•   •   •

Later, at the White House press briefing, Chip Reid, the chief White House correspondent for CBS News, asked Gibbs if July 2011 was the beginning of withdrawal or just a goal?

Gibbs did not have a complete answer, so he went to see the president.

As Reid reported on the CBS blog *Political Hotsheet*, "Gibbs then called me to his office to relate what the president said. The President told him it IS locked in—there is no flexibility. Troops WILL start coming home in July 2011. Period. It's etched in stone. Gibbs said he even had the chisel."

Graham called General Petraeus and went over what had happened, including the etched-in-stone-by-chisel statement from Gibbs.

"Oooohhh," Petraeus said, "hadn't heard that before. That's a problem. You need to fix that."

"Why do I need to fix it?" Graham asked.

"I'm not so sure I'm the one that needs to bring that up," Petraeus replied. He would let "Gates and Clinton deal with this one."

Gates went to Afghanistan and declared, "We're in this thing to win." Discussion of July 2011 seemed to fade, letting Obama have it both ways. July 2011 was a date with some meaning and none at all.

At a December 13 regional security conference hosted by the London-based International Institute for Strategic Studies, Petraeus gave his interpretation of President Obama's West Point speech. He noted, "In July 2011, we will begin—and I stress the word begin—to draw down our forces in the process whose pace depends on the security conditions on the ground. . . . This does not mean we will 'race for the exits' in 2011—far from it."

In their regular talks, Lute pushed Petraeus. The three-star general felt close enough to the four-star Petraeus that he would usually insert a "sir" early in the conversation and then drop the formality.

Lute thought the four risk factors or "key dependencies," as Donilon called them, loomed large.

"Sitting here," Lute said to Petraeus, "this is how this looks. What am I missing? What makes you so cocksure that you can defy these kinds of risk factors and produce?"

Petraeus said they did not have to defy all those risk factors. Progress could take many forms. There was another risk—the battlefield. In Iraq it had been the most visible differential. Provide security and the other risks would be reduced. Violence would drop and the country would appear more stable. "All we have to do is begin to show progress," Petraeus said, "and that'll be sufficient to add time to the clock and we'll get what we need."

"That's a dramatic misreading of this president," Lute said. Obama hadn't even uttered the word "counterinsurgency" in his speeches and opposed the idea of a long-term commitment. "I don't think he's into that."

Lute wondered how the president had packaged this for himself. He surmised the following: The president had fast-forwarded and figured it would most likely be ugly following July 2011. Obama had to do this 18-month surge just to demonstrate, in effect, that it couldn't be done. The surge would be expensive, but not so much that the country could not absorb it. Obama would have given the monolithic military its day in court and the United States would not be seen as having been driven off the battlefield. The only way Lute could explain the final decision was that the president had treated the military as another political constituency that had to be accommodated. "Because I don't think the review adds up to the decision," he said.

Lute thought the president could have reasonably said to Gates, we just committed 33,000 troops this year. When you can show me it is working, then I will double down. As I read it, there's nothing about the situation that is so imminently deteriorating, so dramatically deteriorating, that we don't have time to prove that we know what we are doing. That would have been a more prudent approach, Lute believed. And wasn't it incumbent on them to be as sure as possible that they knew what they were doing?

• • •

Mullen heard though his sources at the White House—JCS chairmen have their sources too—that Lute believed the strategy would not work. Given their frequent contact, Mullen thought Lute might have told him his views.

It upset Mullen, who shared his disappointment in their Friday afternoon Tandberg video session after the West Point speech.

Lute's relationship with the chairman had been tense. He had agreed to take the job as war czar in 2007, after Gates promised that he would be taken care of later with an important assignment from the JCS chairman. When Pete Pace left and Mullen became chairman, the job of taking care of Lute fell to him. Mullen had offered Lute several jobs that were hardly plums, so Lute had declined them. He planned to retire out of the White House assignment.

Lute believed Mullen resented the fact that Jones, a retired four-star, and Lute, an active duty three-star, were giving Obama regular military advice. Mullen was supposed to be the principal military adviser to the president.

Lute was also convinced that Mullen had consumed the COINistas' Kool-Aid without understanding it. As a naval officer, Mullen's head was on the bridge of a capital ship drinking coffee, shouting out rudder orders and "More coffee!" He had not done an independent, sober, clear-eyed analysis of what was being sold. He thought his job was to endorse the work of his subordinates. Mullen didn't do much homework and hadn't dug into the details of what they were doing. "That's a recipe for quagmire," Lute said. "That's a recipe for disaster in this business."

On the Tandberg that afternoon, Mullen and Lute agreed that now that they had a policy decision, they would have to implement their butts off to give it the best chance.

Mullen decided to be frank. "The secretary and I believe you weren't always helpful in the course of the review," he told Lute.

"I hope the president doesn't have the same view," Lute responded.

• • •

Gates planned to go see the president to say he wanted to leave soon. In a December meeting, the president, however, said, "I'd like for you to stay on through the full term, but I know that's asking too much."

Caught off guard, Gates felt preempted. It got under his skin. The full term meant another three years. They began negotiations, and Gates thought the president sounded like a rug merchant.

"I can commit to you for another year," he finally said. That meant he would stay until January of 2011, just a month after the first serious reevaluation of the new strategy, but six months before the beginning of some kind of withdrawal in July 2011. Gates said he would be willing to revisit the issue the next year to see if he would stay longer.

On Christmas Day 2009, a 23-year-old Nigerian named Umar Abdulmutallab attempted to detonate a bomb sewn into his underwear on a flight from Amsterdam to Detroit. The bomb fizzled, igniting but not exploding. The plane landed safely with 300 on board. On vacation in Hawaii, Obama blasted what he called "systemic" intelligence failures.

The president directed Brennan to examine what went wrong and write a report. As a deputy national security adviser, Brennan reported directly to the president on terrorism. He was known as "The Answer Man" because he worked so hard, read raw intercepts, and talked directly to foreign intelligence services and chiefs. Because the failed bomber had come from Yemen, Brennan had spoken with its president, Ali Abdullah Saleh. But Brennan's closeness with Obama also caused DNI Blair and others in the intelligence bureaucracy to see him as the competition.

Two weeks after the failed Christmas bombing, around 11 A.M. on Thursday, January 7, 2010, Brennan handed Blair a copy of the report hours before the president planned to make a statement and release it.

"This is the first time I have seen it," Blair said with some dismay, "and you've got the president going on in three hours?" He read the report quickly.

"This is wrong," he said. The draft report placed far too much blame on lower-level analysts, simplifying a problem that was vastly more complicated. "I can't support this."

He was quickly hustled into the Oval Office to see the president.

"What's the problem?" Obama asked.

"This is incorrect," Blair said, holding a copy of the report. "If I'm asked whether I agree with this report, I will say no." In military parlance, Blair was throwing his admiral's stars on the table. It was an act of protest that implied a threat to resign. If a Senate committee asked whether he agreed with the report, he said, "I'll tell them no."

Blaming lower-level analysts was a dodge, Blair said. Everyone had screwed up—DNI, CIA, NSA, FBI, the State Department, the National Counterterrorism Center (NCTC), which was supposed to connect the dots scattered among the agencies, and even the White House. There had been clear, multiple warnings in their reports, intelligence systems and computer networks.

"Well," Obama said, "I thought I've been a pretty stand-up guy on this thing. I didn't fire you."

Blair was tempted to say, "Go ahead." Instead, he said, "There's leadership responsibility for this, and I'm willing to take it.

"It's not just the analysts' fault," he said. The Christmas Day bomber previously had been in Yemen, where he had contact with the branch of bin Laden's group called al Qaeda in the Arabian Peninsula (AQAP). Earlier intelligence had focused solely on that branch conducting terrorist acts inside Yemen. "We did not pay sufficient attention to them being able to send an attacker against us."

Yet a few months ago, Blair said, one significant intelligence report stated that an AQAP leader—an American-born cleric named Anwar al-Awlaki—was trying to find, recruit and train converts for attacks against Western targets outside Yemen. Jihadist groups that had concentrated on their own countries were now actively plotting against the U.S. homeland.

"Nobody paid any attention to it," Blair said. "So shame on leadership, including me." In addition to these shortcomings, Brennan's report contained too much sensitive intelligence.

Brennan had acknowledged that he let the president down, but he was steaming with anger. He was following the al Qaeda threats out of Yemen. Being second-guessed about his report made him bristle.

Obama summoned Gibbs, the press secretary.

"This is not right," the president said. "Can we put off the press conference?"

"No, we can't," Gibbs said. They had told the news media that the report would come out at 2 P.M.

"Put it off an hour," the president directed, "and Blair, you go down with Brennan, and work with him. See if you can change the report to something you can accept."

Blair was annoyed that the priority was sticking to the messaging schedule. Nonetheless, he descended to the Situation Room with Brennan to edit the report.

The final six-page report was vague, repetitive, disorganized and obviously hurried.

After it was released and the president spoke, Gibbs apologized to the press for the delay. "As you know," he said, "declassifying a highly complex document takes some time, and we wanted to get that right."

On January 12, a devastating earthquake struck Haiti. Leading the U.S. relief was Air Force General Douglas Fraser, head of the Southern Command. Early in the effort, Donilon raced into Jones's office. It was an example of how Donilon made impulsive statements and snap judgments.

"We've got to relieve General Fraser for cause," Donilon said. "He's incompetent. You won't believe how slow they are getting relief down there."

"Calm down," Jones said. "You've got to realize that SouthCom— do you even know where it is? SouthCom is always at the bottom of the resource list. They get the last helpings from the military pie. They're always shortchanged. I know Fraser. He's a good guy. He'll straighten this out. It's going to take longer than we would like."

Fraser, whose command is based in Miami, was not relieved. More than 20,000 U.S. troops were in Haiti by the end of January.

The Pentagon also had concerns about Donilon. When criticism of Jones had reached a high-water mark the previous year, Gates had decided to publicly embrace him. "I think of Jim as the glue that holds this team together," Gates told *The Washington Post*'s David Ignatius, whose "Jim Jones's Team" ran prominently on the op-ed page.

Gates did this in part, he told an aide, because he did not think Donilon would work out as Jones's successor. Gates felt that Donilon did not understand the military or treat its senior leadership with sufficient respect. The secretary later told Jones that Donilon would be a "disaster" as Obama's national security adviser.

In February, when he had some time to reflect on the strategy review, Donilon thought it was one of the rare examples in recent American history where a president had fully understood the contours of a national security decision.

Obama doesn't "contemplate losing," he told others. "His life experience teaches him that if he applies himself, and you're patient and you're relentless—and you're correct—that you'll succeed."

But Donilon's professional frustration with Jones was growing. With Jones booking substantially fewer hours than his deputy, NSC staffers observed that Donilon was doing one and three quarters of a job, working long days and weekends, rarely seeing his family and not taking physical care of himself.

If Obama wanted something followed up after meetings, he turned to Donilon, not Jones. Donilon was the go-to guy, answering the calls that came from the Oval Office. He moved at 100 miles per hour, while Jones ran at 35 and got lapped a couple of times. Donilon was both the victim and beneficiary of Jones's limited definition of his job. He showed both pride and resentment in his expanded role, telling friends he'd never been happier but at times erupting from the stress.

While looking at a Holbrooke memo one day, he lashed out, "This is fifth-grade work. My fifth-grade son wouldn't do work this bad."

Donilon had studied his history, poring over and absorbing what he felt were the mistakes in Vietnam and Iraq. In neither of those wars had the president been precise in his instructions. Obama had fixed that with the terms sheet, which Donilon considered to be a historic document and model for presidential decision making.

The troop surge was part of a reallocation of the nation's resources, which after the 24-month "punch" into Afghanistan could be directed away from the war. At the same time, Donilon felt the U.S. was battering al Qaeda far more than the Bush administration ever had in terms of tempo, tools and global scope.

Donilon hashed out most matters at the deputies level, while the principals working with Jones met rarely and often only to rehearse the monthly reviews before an actual NSC meeting with Obama. When Jones was abroad for the president, however, Donilon would not host a principals meeting in his absence. He might be the de facto national security adviser, but Jones had the accounts with the key principals—Clinton and Gates.

In 40 years in the Marine Corps, Jones had always found a way to connect with the boss. That was not the case with Obama, whom he found cerebral and distant. Jones had never really been invited into the inner circle of Emanuel, Axelrod and Gibbs—and now Donilon. With those aides holding so much control, Jones felt as though he couldn't be in charge. He planned to leave office around the start of 2011.

Jones had several get-togethers and meals with Pakistani ambassador Haqqani, hoping to work out a deal.

"We are a nation of rug merchants," Haqqani said, trying to explain his country without disparaging it. "That's our origin historically. So have you ever tried buying a carpet in Iran or Pakistan?"

Over the years, Jones had bought many rugs during his trips abroad.

"The guy starts at 10,000 and you settle for 1,200," Haqqani went on. "You guys have no idea of the proportionality, you know? So be reasonable, but never let the guy walk out of the shop without a sale. Do a sale. So our side now, we've asked for the moon, but we'll get something. We're getting our stuff. We'll get our helicopters, which the army needs to go into North Waziristan."

At another meeting with Donilon and Lute present, Jones asked, "What would it take to get you guys to focus on our concerns without you guys totally giving up whatever your obsessions and concerns are?"

Economic aid and more military capability, the ambassador said. "Give us a little bit of respect. Don't humiliate us publicly."

Jones made it clear that the United States wanted real support on counterterrorism—more CIA, more Special Operations inside Pakistan. How could the U.S. really get that?

"A man who is trying to woo a woman," Haqqani said, was the best analogy. "We all know what he wants from her. Right?" The man wants one thing; he wants to make love. "But she has other ideas. She wants to be taken to the theater. She wants that nice new bottle of perfume. If you get down on one knee and give the ring, that's the big prize. And boy, you know, it works."

Turning to Donilon and Lute, Jones said, "We have to figure out a way of giving these guys the ring."

"The ring is, by the way," Haqqani said, "recognition of Pakistan's nuclear program as legitimate. That is going to be the ring."

But Pakistan already had nuclear weapons and acknowledgment by the U.S. was not going to get them to change their behavior.

30

Petraeus met for two hours on Saturday, April 3, with Derek Harvey, his trusted intelligence adviser and the director of CentCom's Afghanistan-Pakistan Center of Excellence, the organization that Petraeus had founded to gather and analyze intelligence in Afghanistan with a homicide detective's rigor.

Harvey drew one of the most pessimistic pictures possible of the war. "Our political and diplomatic strategies are not connected to our military strategy," he warned. "It is not going to work. We're not going to achieve the objectives that we've set out for ourselves. We can get to a point of some transient stability and the appearance of success that will not be enduring, that might provide a window for us to withdraw, and to keep things steady for the next three or four years. But inevitably, it will result back to the Great Game," the 19th- and early-20th-century struggle for dominance in Central Asia.

Pulling no punches, Harvey listed the likely long-term outcome: "malign actors, disrupted, ineffective, collapsing government in Kabul; a reemergence of violent extremist groups and safe havens." In other words, a complete return to a pre-9/11 environment.

Was Harvey sure? Petraeus asked.

Harvey said that McChrystal did not have a plan to moderate, adjust and change President Karzai's behavior. The Afghan government had to improve if the campaigns in Marja and Kandahar were to succeed. Once the coalition forces cleared the Taliban from each of those places, a competent government needed to be in place to prevent the Taliban from returning. The default move by McChrystal and his command was deferring to Karzai and equating the president to the entire Afghan government. That was wrong.

What are the options? Petraeus asked.

The strategy of supporting the Karzai government was counterproductive, Harvey said. Looking at cease-fire options or reconciliation with the Taliban, "When you peel it back, there's nothing there. And we're being played in a rope-a-dope manner by various elements at different tiers of the Taliban." For insurgents who want to put down their arms and help the government, there was no place to go, no organization in place. The guidance to the U.S. forces said to turn these people over to the government. "This is exactly who these people are in opposition against, even if they're not fighting actively." The Karzai government was despised.

Harvey said there were missed opportunities coming from the Karzai reelection fraud that previous August. Karzai had largely gone unchallenged by the U.S. afterward, and his victory was sealed when his opponent dropped out of the runoff election. "We are so dependent upon Karzai," Harvey said. "His weakness becomes a strength. And sometimes you have to break china to make real progress. There was a real opportunity to shift the dynamic there on the ground. It would've been costly and painful in the near-term."

By not holding him accountable after the election, "what we've done is make Karzai even stronger in the process. He's a very strong president in a weak system, and we've assumed for too long that he's a weak leader in a weak system and we don't have any other choice. That is wrong. He's a strong leader, tactical in orientation, with poor management skills.

"The outcome of the elections is we made him stronger and contributed to his tendencies that we don't want to contribute to. . . . He's already getting everything he wants."

On the ground, he said, McChrystal's forces had not finished clearing key areas. "The enemy is just beginning to adapt," Harvey said. Assassinations by the Taliban had gone up, as had IED attacks. The Taliban continued to intimidate other Afghans trying to work with the U.S., by dropping short notes on the front seat of a car: "Stop taking the money. Don't go to these meetings." Or when an Afghan's son shows up four hours late from school, the note read: "Next time it'll be his head." One incident like that gets magnified a hundredfold as people talk about it, repeating the story in coffee shops and the market, Harvey said.

He had some 89 intelligence analysts in Afghanistan doing the same kind of detailed, methodical work he had personally done for Petraeus in Iraq. One harsh reality was that the Taliban senior leadership thought they were okay, even with the surge of 30,000 more U.S. troops.

As a concrete measure, Harvey had a 12-step plan for dealing with Ahmed Wali Karzai, the president's half-brother, who controlled parts of Kandahar. The plan was designed to get control over his roadside extortions and kidnappings, and go after his private security firms. Harvey's bottom line: Someone would have to get really tough, but that wasn't happening.

On April 16, the president met with the NSC for the monthly Afghanistan-Pakistan update. McChrystal had committed his forces to clearing and holding operations because the ANSF weren't ready to hold the territory themselves. It was bogging down the model of clear, hold, build and transfer.

The president asked about the recent Marja operation in Helmand, where coalition troops were holding after the offensive had been launched in February. "Are we on timeline?"

Yes, sir, the military said.

Hey, Obama asked, by the way, what about the areas we cleared in the summer of 2009? Now, those were in Helmand too?

Yes, sir.

Where would you put us on the clear, hold, build, and transfer model in the places south of Marja? These were the districts of Nawa and Garmsir.

We're holding, the military said, our forces are fixed there.

How about the 25,000 U.S. troops in the east? the president asked. They had been there for years. Where are they on the clear, hold, build and transfer model?

They are still holding, sir.

Any of them close to transferring?

Not a single one, sir.

The model had become clear, hold, hold, hold, hold and hold. Hold for years. There was no build, no transfer.

Petraeus said they were misconstruing the approach for beginning a transfer. First, July 2011 was more than a year off. "It's not hand off, it's thin out," he said. The "advise and assist" mission ordered by the president last year meant partnering with the Afghan forces, working together, joined at the hip. That involved a gradual transition, eventually shifting from U.S. to Afghan forces in the lead. "Then we recede and then we thin out our numbers."

They were still in the early stages, said Petraeus, who felt the situation was sobering but, as always, not disheartening.

No one in the meeting pushed it further and asked, When would the transfer begin? When would the U.S. forces be able to get out completely? What made anyone think that the United States could go down to the Taliban heartland in the south and achieve an outcome different from the one in the east?

Before the president's Thursday, May 6, secure video with McChrystal for the 90-minute monthly review, Donilon and Lute had been conspiring to raise the prominence of Kandahar, because they felt the counterinsurgency mission there would fail. The operation to gain full control of the city was beginning that month.

It was impossible to escape the conclusion that Kandahar would be a litmus test for the war. The city was the iconic center of the Taliban.

Mullah Omar had ruled from there. If "Pashtunistan" were a country, Kandahar would be its capital.

Donilon and Lute had prepared questions for the president to focus the meeting on Kandahar. Since it was going to be the test case for 2010, the questions included: How are we doing? How is Kandahar going to change the complexion of the war in the next six months?

McChrystal presented a map of Kandahar and its suburbs that attempted to lay out the tribal dynamics. It was a crazy quilt of overlapping colors that resembled a piece of modern art. The legend for the 20 tribes was as big as the map itself. It would almost require a Ph.D. in Afghan culture for an American to comprehend. The Taliban lived this, putting the United States at a strategic disadvantage.

The slide also had mug shots of some three dozen political power brokers in Kandahar, attempting to outline the current balance of power. Some were known to aides in the room—the provincial governor, Tooryalai Wesa, and Ahmed Wali Karzai, the president's half-brother. But most were not. A spaghetti soup of dotted lines, dashed-dotted lines and double-dotted lines reflected what were believed to be the relationships and tribal loyalties. Some are Barakzais, others such as Karzai are Popalzais, and on and on. Some of the narcotics kingpins were listed.

President Obama's body language was like a flashing neon sign. He crossed his arms, crossed his legs and literally pushed away from the table, distancing himself from what was up on the wall. He leafed through his briefing papers, full of loaded questions from Donilon, Lute and the NSC staff. One item was, "I got the diagnosis of the problem, and I see what you're prescribing for a cure, but the two don't connect. The dots don't connect." Why?

Perhaps it was too stark and confrontational. He didn't ask it.

The president reflected on the Kandahar map and the power broker chart.

"This reminds me of Chicago politics," Obama said. "You're asking me to understand the interrelationships and interconnections between ward bosses and district chiefs and the tribes of Chicago like the tribes of Kandahar. And I've got to tell you, I've lived in Chicago for a long time, and I don't understand that."

McChrystal quipped, "If we're going to do Chicago, we're going to need a lot more troops."

Much laughter. When everyone settled down, he added, "We're not going to make Kandahar a shining city on the hill."

McChrystal had presented snapshots of the main players in Kandahar. There were no full answers to the questions such as, who's beholden to whom? Who owes a debt to whom? Who has blood feuds? Where are the real alliances? Where are the intermarriages? What could be changed? And when?

Petraeus had just returned from southern Afghanistan. "We did things in Marja that you could not have done two or three months ago," he said. "We walked through the market with the district governor, stopped and ate bread, surrounded by Afghans." He said they did the same thing in Nad Ali and in Kandahar.

Though he had lots of security, Petraeus walked around Marja without body armor, no Kevlar, no personal weapon and a soft cap. He said he felt safer there than walking the markets in Baghdad several years earlier. His bottom line—"progress without question but innumerable challenges."

There were some key tribes not inside the tent with the U.S. and Afghan government, largely because of threats and intimidation by the Taliban, Petraeus said.

The president asked how they would measure success. He said he wanted sustainable progress and was still thinking about the transfer. "Be careful we don't start something for which we don't have resources to enable completion.

"Keep thinking about how we'll know if we're succeeding," the president said, "and when we'll know."

Afterward, the president indicated to several close aides that the briefing had a clarifying effect on him. "What makes us think," he asked, "that given that description of the problem, that we're going to design a solution to this?"

Donilon and Lute had told the president: If you're not fully satisfied with General McChrystal's description here, he will be in Washington next week. You should invite him to come see you and continue this discussion in a smaller, more intimate setting.

In other words, if the meeting had amounted to a "strike one" for the commanding general, the president ought to give McChrystal another swing.

He agreed.

Toward the end of one of the NSC principals meetings without the president, the conversation turned to the challenge of dealing with Afghan President Hamid Karzai. CIA Director Panetta believed Karzai was the kind of individual who would shut down if he felt isolated. Should that happen, the U.S. would never know where the hell he was going to go or what he was going to do.

"It is very important that we be able to have someone who can talk to Karzai, he can talk to, who he trusts," said Panetta, who had an ideal candidate in mind. The new CIA Kabul station chief was the same operative who had saved Karzai's life back in 2001 by serving as a human shield when a bomb dropped near them. But Ambassador Eikenberry refused to let the station chief meet with Karzai alone.

"Our chief of station out there is somebody who saved his life, has a relationship with him, talks to him," Panetta said. "Karzai wants to talk to him. It's really important to give him that access."

Secretary Clinton agreed. She had instructed Eikenberry to let the meetings occur, but he had refused to budge even though he believed everything rode on Karzai being prodded in the right direction.

"We will do that," said Jones. "That has to be done."

Eikenberry was ordered to relent. The CIA could now have private meetings with Karzai when no one else was present.

On May 10, during President Karzai's visit to Washington, McChrystal and Holbrooke had a 45-minute talk.

"Stan, are you really okay with July 2011?" Holbrooke asked.

"I think we can do the job," responded the commanding general, who by necessity was now a professional optimist. "It depends on what we have to withdraw."

But, Holbrooke said, it was not just a matter of withdrawing U.S. and NATO forces but also of transferring the security responsibility to the Afghans.

McChrystal agreed, though he had his own question for the special representative. "Why is there so much skepticism about Kandahar?" As the next big operation, it could be a turning point. But he had found lots of doubters in Washington.

Holbrooke had just spoken with Biden, who was pessimistic and more convinced than ever that Afghanistan was a version of Vietnam. Holbrooke, in a bleak mood himself, asked if there was an Afghan example of "clear, hold, build and transfer" actually happening.

Not yet, McChrystal said.

Was there a way to actually have a transfer? Holbrooke inquired. For example, in the three-month-old Marja operation involving 15,000 U.S., British and Afghan troops, was there a way to take out, say, one U.S. company made up of just several hundred soldiers and transfer their responsibilities to the Afghans? "It would prove the concept," Holbrooke said. "It would prove we are not trapped."

"That's a good idea," McChrystal replied. He paused, and thought hard for a long time. "No, we're not ready yet."

Holbrooke's heart sank. "Transfer" had been a core concept in the president's strategy review going back six months. It was the ticket out. And they couldn't even transfer one company? Marja was a partnering operation, which meant each U.S. unit was supposed to be working with an Afghan counterpart. A senior U.S. commander was working side by side with an Afghan general in a command center.

Marja was a 155-square-mile farming town of 80,000, and after all that work and firepower McChrystal was saying they weren't ready to transfer sole responsibility to a single Afghan company.

•   •   •

That evening, Secretary Clinton hosted a dinner at Blair House across from the White House for President Karzai and several of his top cabinet ministers. Gates, Jones, McChrystal, Lute and Holbrooke attended. In all, only about a dozen sat around the table.

There were the usual tensions, good moments and bad.

How strong is your commitment? Karzai asked at one point.

Gates, as usual, had held back during most of the dinner. But he reminded everyone that he still felt guilty for his role in the administration of Bush senior in 1989 when the United States had pulled out after the Soviet withdrawal.

"We're not leaving Afghanistan prematurely," Gates finally said. "In fact, we're not ever leaving at all."

At least one stunned participant put down his fork. Another wrote it down, verbatim, in his notes.

Though Gates meant a long-term security commitment, not a lasting combat presence, his comment was precisely the kind of soothing reassurance that would only encourage Karzai to leave the security issues to the United States.

On May 11, the president took Donilon and Lute up on their proposal that McChrystal be invited to continue the discussion. Obama assembled a small group in the Oval Office to hear the Afghanistan commander. It included Biden, Gates, Mullen, Jones, Donilon and Colonel John Tien, the NSC Afghanistan director who essentially had a foot in each of the camps. Tien was a COINista at heart because of his experience in Ramadi, Iraq, but he also saw reason for skepticism.

After the session, Lute, who had missed the White House meeting because he had been at the State Department with Clinton and Karzai, caught up with Colonel Tien.

"John," Lute asked, "how did Stan do?"

"Strike two," Tien said.

•   •   •

At Clinton's meeting with the Afghan president, a kind of informal, tea-and-cookies session, Karzai voiced the conviction that the Pakistani ISI played a dominant role in managing the Taliban. The Pakistanis often complained that they never got actionable intelligence about the location of Mullah Omar. Some CIA experts half joked that the Pakistanis only had to ask the ISI case officers who managed the Taliban. "They don't need that from us," one intelligence expert had said. "They could get better information from their case officers."

"Do you really think the ISI could pick up Mullah Omar if they wanted?" Clinton asked.

Karzai reached over and plucked a chocolate chip cookie from its plate. "They could deliver Mullah Omar like I can pick up this cookie," he said.

During that week, Biden invited Ambassador Eikenberry and General Lute over to the vice president's office, where Tony Blinken joined them.

Biden, Blinken, Lute with Donilon, McDonough and Brennan had tried to hold the line against the big troop increase during the strategy review. The six got their traction during the review from Biden. Obama had given the vice president extraordinary freedom and airtime to try to develop the counterterrorism option. They never got a full military analysis of that option, but in the six months since the review, they noted that the Biden pillar—the counterterrorism portion of the decision—was the one that was really producing.

McChrystal had tripled the number of JSOC teams, and the CIA's Counterterrorism Pursuit Teams, the 3,000-strong Afghan paramilitary organization, were having superb results—multiple raids every night around Kandahar, despite the lack of the troop density Petraeus had insisted would be necessary for successful counterterrorism.

I have been focusing on Iraq and other matters, the vice president said. Since it was six months after the president's Afghanistan decisions, he asked, "Where do we stand?"

Eikenberry could have simply said, go back and read my cables about the risks. Instead, he reminded the vice president what an unreliable partner Karzai was.

"He's on his meds, he's off his meds," Eikenberry said, trying to account once again for Karzai's erratic behavior. "They're not producing governance in Marja. And we haven't tackled the hard problem, Kandahar. And now we're saying, essentially, that Karzai's going to produce a political solution for Kandahar. That's completely irresponsible to suggest that," adding, "so basically, we're screwed."

Was there a political solution that would bail them out? They needed a big break, a strategic break. Could Pakistan be the wild card? Could it change its DNA?

Lute thought it was a measure of their desperation that they would even consider looking to Pakistan for luck.

Could Karzai become a new guy? Could the Taliban have an epiphany and change?

The intelligence showed that the Taliban leadership was feeling the pressure of the eight-year war, of living in virtual exile in Pakistan, of living under the not-so-light touch of the ISI. That was wearing thin. Things were closing in on them, like the capture of Quetta Shura Taliban military commander Abdul Ghani Baradar and shadow governors being arrested. The families of the Taliban were also living under the ISI's thumb. It was evident that this safe haven sojourn wasn't all it was cracked up to be. The intelligence showed that the Taliban and their families were effectively asking, Do we have to live under this ISI regime forever? That's not our vision of what this was supposed to be all about. Meanwhile, there was no way Taliban leaders, at least not the meaningful guys, were crossing the border into Afghanistan—or even stepping one foot inside—where the wild-eyed JSOC teams were on the prowl. JSOC was putting the wood to Taliban regulars in Afghanistan. So was there an alternative for the Taliban?

Maybe the landing zone was not through the COINistas' clear, hold, build and transfer? someone asked. Maybe there was an end run, getting some Taliban to reconcile, to break with al Qaeda and provide a bridge back into Afghanistan. Such an effort could not be led by the

United States. They needed to find a philosopher-king. But who? Did such a person exist?

They ruled out Holbrooke. He seemed to need center stage too much and had lost Obama's confidence.

One possible candidate was Lakhdar Brahimi, the elderly United Nations diplomat who had helped engineer Karzai's rise to power after the U.S. invasion in 2001. Could he deliver this? Brahimi was 76, perhaps too old for the monumental diplomatic mission.

The more they looked at it, the more complex it was. The more they stared at the problem and unpacked its elements, the clearer it was that Pakistan held an unhealthy amount of leverage on the whole outcome. Pakistan owned the Taliban. So the Taliban couldn't necessarily deliver themselves.

31

On Friday afternoon, May 14, Brigadier General Lawrence Nicholson, who had commanded the 10,000 Marines in Helmand province for a year, visited Jones and Lute at the White House. He was going to be the military assistant to the deputy secretary of defense, Bill Lynn.

Jones said that the last time he had seen Nicholson he had been in Helmand delivering the Whiskey Tango Foxtrot warning about more troops. And now, he noted with some irony, the WTF vaccination had not only failed, but had the opposite impact—the patient got the disease and, Jones noted with some irony, an additional 30,000 were headed to Afghanistan.

Lute reminded Nicholson of the "clear, hold, build and transfer model" and its importance to the president's orders under the new strategy.

Nicholson indicated he understood this.

"Larry," Lute said, "forget Marja, this year's adventure. Let's go to last year's adventure. So we're now at the 12-month mark. So tell me." The operation into the town of Nawa, which was the brightest light and seemed to have the best prospects for being secured, had been launched in July 2009. "Where are we in Nawa in this four-step model that leads to 'T' transfer?"

"Well," Nicholson said, "we're in the hold/build phase."

Hmmm, said Lute. "So at the 12-month mark, Larry, you're at hold/build. Let me ask you to look into a crystal ball and tell me when are you going to get to 'T'?"

They agreed that it depended on the Afghans, who had to produce the army, police and a government that could take over.

So, Lute asked, when would those Marines be available to do something else? "Like maybe Kandahar? Or go home? Be part of the July 2011 gang?"

"Whoa, whoa, whoa," Nicholson said. "At least another 12 months." And that was for the best district.

"Larry," Lute said, "we try to calibrate Washington's expectations. From clear to transfer is at least 24 months? The 12 months you've just had, and another 12 months? That's not the promise here. We haven't even gone into the suburbs of Kandahar yet, which, by the way, is much more important than where you guys were." Kandahar was much more dangerous. It was where the Taliban was going to make a stand. "They don't care about Nawa. Okay? They care about their iconic center, which is Kandahar."

In Nawa, Lute continued, "this is what right looks like. Well, if right looks like 24 months, if that's as good as it gets, then we can't connect the dots here."

Nicholson said that he also placed extreme caveats on 24 months. "Maybe you can get there in 24 months," he said, "if you can get at the surrounding poppy problem, which fuels the insurgency."

"How the hell are we going to do that?" Lute asked. Even though a blight had recently destroyed 33 percent of the poppy crop, the prospects of really undercutting the insurgency's financing were remote. Despite the Afghan conspiracy theories, the CIA had not, in fact, developed a poppy-eating bug.

Nicholson said the other caution was that they would have to stop the Taliban insurgents from coming in from Pakistan. "If you can control the border," he said.

The Afghan-Pakistan border was like Arizona. There was no control for 100 miles in either direction of a legal crossing point, and no

U.S. or coalition troops were committed to the border. For practical purposes, the Taliban could cross anywhere.

"If Nawa is on—the best case—a 24-month timeline," Lute said, "we're screwed. We're not going to demonstrate progress this year."

Lute probed Nicholson on the force ratios. "So when you went into Garmsir and Nawa, what was the U.S.-to-Afghan force ratio?"

Nicholson said it was about 10 U.S. to one Afghan, making it virtually an all-U.S. operation.

Now, Lute said, for this year's version in Marja, McChrystal was advertising an improvement—just two U.S. battalions to one Afghan battalion, for example. But Lute said when you dug into the numbers, the reality was very different. The Afghan units were composed of dramatically fewer soldiers than U.S. units. And McChrystal was counting the Afghan police, which improved the ratios. But there was a lot of smoke and mirrors. They were recycling the Afghan National Civil Order Police (ANCOP), which was a cut above the normal police, a kind of gendarme force. The ANCOP moved from dangerous trouble spot to dangerous trouble spot. But these ANCOP essentially now say, I signed up to be a policeman and I'm basically the first guy through the door in operation after operation. The gendarme force voted with its feet, and the attrition rate was 75 percent annually. The model was supposed to be just a 15 percent attrition rate.

The other problem was that the ANCOP were in Marja and they were now supposed to go to Kandahar. Who would police Marja?

Astonishingly at the end of their hour-long meeting, Jones said, "That sounds like good progress."

God damn, Lute thought. Had he and Jones been in the same meeting?

Jones later said all the news from Afghanistan was not good, and the war was not like a light switch that could be turned off. "But McChrystal's upbeat," he said.

After the meeting with Nicholson, Lute went back to Colonel Tien and the rest of his team. "Let's start building the scheduled strategic review," he said. "There's no reason building it in November," just a month before it would be due. They could make the slides for the December review now. "I can pretty much predict that Kandahar's going to look a lot like it looks today. There's no reason to work the weekends in November. We might as well just do it during the workday in May and June." He emphasized, "We might as well do this leisurely and get going on it because I can tell you what the outcome's going to look like." The president had directed that the military not go anywhere unless they could transfer in 18 to 24 months, he reminded them. He told them about the Nicholson meeting. "Well, the best case, with big caveats, the guy on the ground is saying 24 months.

"This is a house of cards," he added.

A few days later, Petraeus was flying back from a trip, another in his endless travels, and he came to the rear of the plane to visit with his executive officer and Colonel Gunhus, his spokesman. It was unusual. Normally Petraeus was all work—and some sleep—at the front of the plane. This evening he also had had "some grape," as Gunhus called it, a single glass of wine.

Several days earlier Petraeus had told the Associated Press that Times Square bomber Faisal Shahzad had been a "lone wolf." Shahzad had attempted to set off a makeshift bomb in his SUV, which he had parked by the crowded Midtown Manhattan tourist area on the evening of May 1. The bomb smoked but failed to explode. By calling Shahzad a "lone wolf," Petraeus had meant that he had not operated in the United States with any assistance. But the story read as though Petraeus was contradicting claims by others in the Obama administration that Shahzad had been trained by the Pakistani Taliban (TTP).

Petraeus and Gunhus had prepared a short press release to correct the miscommunication. But first the general had asked Gunhus to contact Denis McDonough in the White House to get his advice. McDonough had said to do nothing, let it blow over, it was not a big deal. This was just short of an order, so the release was not issued. But once again it looked like Petraeus was at odds with the White House. As the plane roared to its next destination Gunhus noted that the White House still had a tendency to leave Petraeus twisting in the wind.

They knock you down every chance they get, Gunhus said.

"They're fucking with the wrong guy," Petraeus said.

To address worries of a nuclear terrorist attack in the United States, Brennan ran a top-to-bottom classified exercise on Tuesday, May 18, testing how the intelligence agencies and federal government would respond. Called COOPEX 2010 (Continuity of Operations Exercise), it was essentially a scripted war game in which terrorists detonated a small, crude nuclear weapon in Indianapolis, taking down several city blocks and killing thousands.

In the hypothetical scenario, the terrorists had access to about 17 kilograms of fissile material. After the Indianapolis blast, enough was left over for a second bomb, which the terrorists planned to set off in Los Angeles.

Obama himself participated, appearing on the secure video with a series of questions. How did this happen? Who most likely did it? Was it state-sponsored? How can we retaliate?

As part of the game, the nuclear material had come from a country much like Pakistan, but the attack was not state-sponsored because that country—just as Pakistan was in some cases—had been fighting the terrorist group responsible for it. No immediate retaliation against the country was deemed necessary.

Each federal department and agency had to weigh in with evaluations and recommendations. The Agriculture Department noted that the price of food was shooting through the roof. Some discussion focused on the demand for services and treatment at Indianapolis hospitals, but no one addressed the question of clean water, one of the major needs after a nuclear fallout. Such an attack would create mass panic and almost unimaginable dislocations in the economy and transportation, making 9/11 look small. But COOPEX 2010 included no discussion of what Congress, the media or 300 million Americans were doing. The attack was presented in a vacuum, as if all those people stayed on the sidelines.

Michael Morell, named deputy director of the CIA a month earlier, raised a different problem. According to his calculations, there was likely enough fissile material for yet another bomb. "We haven't found the third bomb," Morell said.

"Brennan went ripshit," recalled one senior participant. This was designed as a two-bomb scenario, not three. "And he's trying to wrap it up neatly and tidily, but Morell kept wondering if there was a third bomb. What about a third bomb? And they couldn't wrap it up." This participant said the whole exercise was "dumbfounding" and "surrealistic," demonstrating that the administration seemed woefully unprepared to deal with such an attack.

During my Oval Office interview with the president, Obama volunteered some extended thoughts about terrorism: "I said very early on, as a senator, and continued to believe as a presidential candidate and now as president, that we can absorb a terrorist attack."

I was surprised.

"We'll do everything we can to prevent it, but even a 9/11, even the biggest attack ever, that ever took place on our soil, we absorbed it and we are stronger. This is a strong, powerful country that we live in, and our people are incredibly resilient."

Then he addressed his big concern, "A potential game changer would be a nuclear weapon in the hands of terrorists, blowing up a major American city. Or a weapon of mass destruction in a major American city. And so when I go down the list of things I have to worry about all the time, that is at the top, because that's one area where you can't afford any mistakes. And so right away, coming in, we said, how are we going to start ramping up and putting that at the center of a lot of our national security discussion? Making sure that that occurrence, even if remote, never happens."

Obama sent Jones, Panetta and Lute to Pakistan, yet again, for May 19 meetings with the country's leaders. Times Square bomber Faisal Shahzad, a 30-year-old U.S. citizen born in Pakistan, had been trained by the Tehrik-e-Taliban (TTP), the Taliban branch fighting against the Pakistani government.

Jones and Panetta were looking for a breakthrough, hoping this time would be different. It now seemed more likely than ever that a terrorist trained in Pakistan would carry out a deadly attack on U.S. soil. On past trips, they had prodded Pakistan to do more about the safe havens used by al Qaeda, the Quetta Shura Taliban, the Haqqani network and LeT. The Pakistanis had for the past year argued that their main priority was TTP. Now Jones and Panetta would have to try to persuade them to do more about that group.

"We're living on borrowed time," Jones said at the meeting with Zardari and other top Pakistani officials. "We consider the Times Square attempted bombing a successful plot because neither the American nor the Pakistani intelligence agencies could intercept it and stop it." Only luck prevented a catastrophe.

Jones said that President Obama wanted four things: full intelligence sharing, more cooperation on counterterrorism, faster approval of visas for U.S. personnel, and, despite past refusals, the sharing of airline passenger data.

If, God forbid, Shahzad's SUV had blown up in Times Square, we wouldn't be having this conversation, Jones warned. The president would be forced to do things that Pakistan would not like.

"The president wants everyone in Pakistan to understand if such an attack connected to a Pakistani group is successful there are some things even he would not be able to stop. Just as there are political realities in Pakistan, there are political realities in the United States.

"No one will be able to stop the response and consequences. This is not a threat, just a statement of political fact."

Wait a second, Zardari replied, if we have a strategic partnership, why in the face of a crisis like you're describing would we not draw closer together rather than have this divide us?

President Obama's only choice would be to respond, Jones said. There would be no alternative. The U.S. can no longer tolerate Pakistan's à la carte approach to going after some terrorist groups and supporting, if not owning, others. You are playing Russian roulette. The chamber has turned out empty the past several times, but there will be a round in that chamber someday.

Jones did not reveal that an American response could entail a retribution campaign of bombing up to 150 known terrorist safe havens inside Pakistan.

"You can do something that costs you no money," Jones said. "It may be politically difficult, but it's the right thing to do if you really have the future of your country in mind. And that is to reject all forms of terrorism as a viable instrument of national policy inside your borders."

"We rejected it," Zardari said.

Jones begged to differ. He cited evidence of Pakistani support or toleration of Mullah Omar's Quetta Shura and the Haqqani network, the two leading Taliban groups killing U.S. soldiers in Afghanistan.

As a result of FBI interviews done in the United States and other intelligence, Panetta said they had a good outline of the TTP network, showing ties to the Times Square bomber Faisal Shazad. He took out a so-called link chart showing the connections. "Look, this is it," the CIA director explained. "This is the network. Leads back here." He traced it out with his finger for the Pakistani leaders. "And we're continuing to pick up intelligence streams that indicate TTP is going to conduct other attacks in the United States."

This was a matter of solid intelligence, he said, not speculation.

"Just to be clear," the CIA director added, "the Times Square bomber, thank God, did not get enough training." His training in bomb making had been compressed. "But if that had gone off, perhaps hundreds, if not thousands, of American would've been killed." Underscoring Jones's point, he said, "If that happens all bets are off."

"If something like that happens," Zardari said defensively, "it doesn't mean that somehow we're suddenly bad people or something. We're still partners."

No, both Jones and Panetta said. There might be no way to save the strategic partnership.

Jones and Panetta were very specific about the alarming intelligence they had gathered.

The LeT commander of the 2008 Mumbai attack, Zakiur Rehman Lakhvi, who is being held by Pakistani authorities, is not being adequately interrogated and "he continues to direct LeT operations from his detention center," Jones said.

LeT is operating in Afghanistan and the group carried out a recent attack at a guesthouse there. Intelligence also shows that LeT is threatening attacks in the United States and the possibility "is rising each day," Jones said.

The recent attack on Bagram Airbase, Afghanistan, was coordinated with the Haqqani network in Miram Shah, the capital of North Waziristan. "We have intercepts to prove that."

Zardari didn't seem to get it.

"Mr. President," his foreign minister, Shah Mehmood Qureshi, said, "This is what they are saying. They're saying that TTP was involved in this attack in Times Square. They're saying that if, in fact, there is a successful attack in the Untied States, they will take steps to deal with that here, and that we have a responsibility to now cooperate with the United States."

Afterward, the Americans met privately with General Kayani. Although Kayani had graduated from the U.S. Command and General Staff College at Fort Leavenworth, he was a product of the Pakistani military system—nearly 40 years of staring east to the threat posed by India. His training, exercises, maps, intelligence focus and the bulk of Pakistani troops were directed toward India. This was part of a Pakistani officer's DNA. It was hard, perhaps impossible, for a Pakistani general to put his binoculars down, turn his head over his shoulder, and look west to Afghanistan.

Jones told Kayani the clock was starting now on all four of the requests. Obama wanted a progress report in 30 days.

But Kayani would not budge very much. He had other concerns. "I'll be the first to admit, I'm India-centric," he said.

In the meeting with Kayani, Panetta laid out a series of additional requests for CIA operations. He had come to believe that the Predator and other unmanned aerial vehicles were the most precise weapons in the history of warfare. He wanted to use them more.

Pakistan allowed Predator drone flights in specified geographic areas called "boxes." Since the Pakistanis had massive numbers of ground troops in the south, they would not allow a "box" in that area.

"We need to have that box," Panetta said. "We need to be able to conduct our operations."

Kayani said he would see that they had some access.

The Americans pressed on the Haqqani network. The Pakistanis had their 7th Infantry Division headquarters nearby. Why was there little sharing of intelligence?

Kayani did not explain.

Jones and Panetta left feeling they had made only baby steps. "How can you fight a war and have safe havens across the border?" Panetta asked in frustration. The latest intelligence showed trucks crossing the border that were full of Taliban combatants with all kinds of weapons packed in the back. They were being waved through into Afghanistan to kill Americans at checkpoints controlled by the Pakistanis. "It's a crazy kind of war," Panetta said.

The U.S. needed some kind of ground forces, he concluded. "We can't do this without some boots on the ground. They could be Pakistani boots or they can be our boots, but we got to have some boots on the ground." The U.S. quick-strike JSOC units were too visible. The main alternative was a giant expansion of the covert war. His 3000-man Counterterrorism Pursuit Teams (CTPT) were now conducting cross-border operations into Pakistan.

Lute supervised the writing of a three-page trip report to the president that Jones signed. It contained a pessimistic summary, noting first the gap between the civilian and military authority in Pakistan. The U.S. was getting nowhere fast with these guys, talking with Zardari, who could deliver nothing. On the other hand, Kayani had the power to deliver, but he refused to do much. Nobody could tell him otherwise. The bottom line was depressing: This had been a charade. Jones said he was once again alarmed that success in Afghanistan was tied to what the Pakistanis would or would not do. The White House was almost right back to where it had started with Pakistan in 2009.

Second, the report said the Pakistanis did not have the same sense of urgency as the Americans. Should there be another terrorist attack in the U.S., the Pakistanis suggested that something could be worked out after the fact. There were regular terrorist attacks in Pakistan, so they could not understand the traumatic impact of a single, small act on the U.S. homeland. The Pakistanis were making another mistake by applying that same logic to India. They did not comprehend that India might not show restraint if LeT, the group behind the 2008 Mumbai attack, struck there again. Indian Prime Minister Singh, who had barely survived Mumbai politically, would have to respond.

But the Pakistanis also wielded tremendous leverage over the U.S. because they gave tacit approval for drone strikes. Furthermore, the intelligence indicated the Pakistanis believed the U.S. would not jeopardize their relationship because some 70 to 80 percent of the U.S. and NATO supplies for the Afghanistan War came through Pakistan, and there was no way to supply everything by air. The Pakistanis would not even have to close the supply routes, just allow some of the extremists to shut down bridges and overpasses.

The options for Obama would be significantly narrowed in the aftermath of an attack originating out of Pakistan. Before such an attack, however, he had more options, especially if there was a way for Pakistan to make good on his four requests. Some 150 visa applications for U.S. military and intelligence operatives were being withheld that were over six weeks old, and U.S. embassy personnel were now required to renew their visas every 90 days. The Pakistanis were dragging their feet on visas for U.S. personnel to carry out the transfer of equipment that the Pakistani military needed. It was insane, Jones thought.

The easiest accommodation would be for the Pakistanis to share the names of all airline passengers traveling to or from Pakistan. The investigations of the two bombing attempts in New York City by Zazi and Shahzad established that both went to Pakistan for training, but the U.S. government did not have any record of their travels.

The Pakistanis had countered in the past that disclosing airline data would violate their sovereignty. They also suspected it would give the U.S. insight into where their intelligence officers were going. Most ISI agents were flying east to India or Bangladesh, so the U.S. had proposed just getting data on flights heading west to the Persian Gulf, Europe and the United States. But the Pakistanis had stubbornly resisted.

In the event of a terrorist attack, Lute worried that it would be hard for Obama to defend Pakistan because their leaders had refused to do what had been simple and easy, especially on the visas and passenger lists. If two near-misses were the leading edge of a trend, what would it take to wake the Pakistanis up?

When I interviewed President Obama two months after the failed Times Square bombing, he played up Pakistan's counterterrorism efforts. "They also ramped up their CT cooperation in a way that over the last 18 months has hunkered down al Qaeda in a way that is significant," he said.

"But still not enough," I interjected.

"Well, exactly."

32

It had been a rough 16 months for Dennis Blair. The DNI had failed in his effort to name the chief intelligence officer in each foreign capital. The CIA had won and the feud had gone public. Blair had also conducted a nonpublic war against two other sources of power for the CIA. In his view, the CIA was using the President's Daily Brief as a house rag for telling Obama their triumphs—even something as minor as an operation involving three guys and a pickup truck. He edited out these advertisements for the CIA's wares, saying, "I'm not going to give that to the president."

He also went after the CIA covert action programs, attempting to trim them and align them more with overt U.S. policies. "Covert action programs should continually be considered for transition to noncovert activities," he wrote in one SECRET proposal rejected by the White House.

Blair grew so frustrated that at one point he declared, "I think the CIA is fundamentally an organization that's like a really finely trained, not very smart, dangerous animal that needs to be controlled very closely by adults."

By May 2010, President Obama was telling Jones and others, "Isn't it about time to get rid of Blair?" There had been too many fights with the CIA. And Blair had also pushed too hard for a no-spying agreement with the French that Obama and the rest of the cabinet opposed.

Without informing Blair, members of Obama's staff began shopping around the DNI job, talking about it with deputy secretary of state Jim Steinberg, Chuck Hagel, a former Republican senator from Nebraska, and John McLaughlin, a former deputy director of the CIA. When word about this reached Blair, he complained and soon had a meeting with Obama.

The president listed his reasons why the retired admiral was not working out as DNI. Blair responded to them in writing, defending himself and detailing his accomplishments.

After reading Blair's response, Obama phoned him on Thursday, May 20. "I have decided and I'm going to make the change," the president said.

He then offered Blair a face-saving exit. Take your time, weeks, even months, Obama said. Come up with a personal reason or any explanation. He would support any story Blair wanted, the president said. A smooth transition was in everyone's interest. After all, they were at war.

Blair was deeply offended. He wasn't ill. His family was fine. And he had told people he would stay as DNI for four years because part of the problem with the office had been the constant turnover at the top.

"You want me to lie?" Blair asked.

No, Obama said, I didn't mean that at all.

Fire me, Blair basically said.

That's exactly what Obama did.

Within several minutes of the conversation, Jake Tapper of ABC News reported on the network's Web site that Blair was leaving.

About 5 P.M. on June 21, Gates called Jones. "There's an article coming out in *Rolling Stone* magazine that's not very good about McChrystal," he said. It contained some disparaging and mocking comments from McChrystal and his senior staff about administration officials. One unnamed McChrystal aide called Jones a "clown" who is "stuck in 1985."

McChrystal himself was quoted saying that Obama's strategy review was "painful" and "I was selling an unsellable position." Recounting McChrystal's stay in Paris, including a heavy-drinking evening with his wife and senior staff, the article revealed the commanding general as anti-French. Gates said he planned to release a statement reprimanding McChrystal, but hoped to salvage the situation and avoid a setback to the war strategy.

"I'm not sure that goes far enough," Jones said. "This is pretty sensational stuff." The article also quoted unnamed McChrystal aides who took shots at Biden, Holbrooke and Eikenberry.

McChrystal called Biden about the profile. "I have compromised the mission," he said.

He also apologized to Holbrooke and said he had offered his resignation to Gates.

Later that evening the president met with Emanuel and Jones, who recommended that Obama order McChrystal back to Washington. Don't do anything now, Jones suggested, but sleep on it.

Obama agreed and the next morning McChrystal was ordered to return to Washington—a dramatic statement in itself. Jones told Gates that protecting McChrystal was noble. "But you don't want to put yourself between him and the president."

Gates proposed that he issue the first two paragraphs of his statement criticizing McChrystal, and Jones agreed. "I believe that General McCrystal made a significant mistake and exercised poor judgment," Gates said in his statement.

At the Pentagon, Geoff Morrell, Gates's spokesman and confidant, was in agony. It was like seeing a funnel cloud rising for Gates and the whole military establishment. The article would once again expose the messiness and mistrust between the White House and the military. Morrell's job was to quell what he called the "family feud," downplay its significance, respond to protect the military without appearing disloyal to the administration. To get into detail about the rift would only further reveal the divide that he believed was, in part, a consequence of the prolonged AfPak strategy review. The fact was that the White House had its version, claiming that the president had dramatically asserted civilian control while the military version was that it had basically gotten what it wanted. The tensions had abated in public and since gone underground. Now they were headed for another public airing. He tuned into Gibbs's noon press briefing, knowing that the press secretary would be operating under presidential instructions.

"Is removing the general from his position at least an option the president is considering?" one reporter asked.

"I would say all options are on the table," Gibbs replied.

Fair enough, Morrell thought.

"I think the magnitude and graveness of the mistake here are profound," Gibbs said next, shooting way beyond Gates's comment that it was a mistake and poor judgment.

Gibbs reported that Obama was "angry" upon seeing the article and was recalling McChrystal "to see what in the world he was thinking."

"So you're questioning whether or not General McChrystal is capable and mature enough for this job he has?"

"You had my quote right," Gibbs said.

Morrell was sickened. Gibbs was relishing it too much, "like a pig in shit," as he told others later.

The next day Obama accepted McChrystal's resignation, and he proposed that Petraeus take over. Though it would involve a technical demotion because as central commander Petraeus was the boss, it was an idea that would address both the military and political problems. The Iraq hero would come to the rescue of Afghanistan.

Obama met alone with Petraeus for 40 minutes. Obama told me, "Dave Petraeus was the only person who fit the bill."

I noted that it was a demotion.

"He certainly doesn't consider it a demotion," the president said. "I think that Dave Petraeus understands that this is the single most important job that anybody in our military could be doing right now."

At 1:43 P.M. on Wednesday, June 23, the president announced the changes in the Rose Garden. He said he admired McChrystal's "long record of service," "remarkable career," and "his enormous contributions." Pulling out all the stops, the president added, "Indeed it saddens me to lose the service of a soldier who I've come to respect and admire."

He said that Petraeus would "maintain the momentum and leadership that we need to succeed.

"He is setting an extraordinary example of service and patriotism by assuming this difficult post." Calling Afghanistan "a very tough fight," Obama said, "I welcome debate among my team, but I won't tolerate division."

33

In the interview I had with the president on July 10, 2010, Obama offered his thoughts about the nature of war and his efforts to limit and eventually end American's combat role in Afghanistan.

Where would you begin a book—or movie—about your handling of the Afghanistan war? I asked. What would be the first scene?

"You know," he answered, "I'd probably start it back in 2002, when the debate was taking place about the run-up in Iraq. And that was probably the first speech I gave on foreign policy that got a lot of attention."

This was the speech he gave as an Illinois state senator at a rally in Chicago, declaring himself one of the early opponents of President Bush's plan for a war in Iraq. It became famous during the presidential campaign. He said such a war would lead to a "U.S. occupation of undetermined length, at undetermined cost, with undetermined consequences."

Isn't this undetermined cost, time and consequence, I asked, "the nature of all war?"

"You are absolutely right," Obama said. "To quote a famous American, 'War is Hell,' " he continued, referring to the line by Union Civil War General William Tecumseh Sherman. "And once the dogs of war are unleashed, you don't know where it's going to lead. When I entered into office, we had two wars taking place. So once you're in, what you're trying to do is impose clarity on the chaos."

I was struck by the strong language—"Hell" and "the dogs of war" and "chaos." He clearly saw the dark, unfathomable side of war.

"You have an obligation," he continued, "to work over, again and again, your goals, your mission, your progress. Are we staying focused? Are we preventing mission creep? Are we clear about the endgame?" The policymakers had to have extraordinary discipline during wartime, he added. "It entails so much of the country's resources, so much of our blood and treasure, and unleashes so many passions." And he worried about "the ease with which something [war] gets momentum."

"And you can't lose a war or be perceived to lose a war, can you?" I asked.

"I think about it not so much in the classic, do you lose a war on my watch? Or win a war on a president's watch? I think about it more in terms of, do you successfully prosecute a strategy that results in the country being stronger rather than weaker at the end of it?" He noted there would be no formal surrender in either the Iraq or Afghanistan wars.

"It is very easy to imagine a situation in which, in the absence of a clear strategy," he said, "we ended up staying in Afghanistan for another five years, another eight years, another 10 years. And we would do it not with clear intentions but rather just out of an inertia. Or an unwillingness to ask tough questions."

He reaffirmed his timeline—that in July 2011 he would begin thinning out U.S. forces. "Sometime next year we will have been there 10 years," Obama told me. "A decade. By far our longest war. And I think it is part of my obligation as president to look at our efforts in Afghanistan, in the context of all the other issues that face this country and our long-term national security." So his timeline, he said, reminded everyone "there's urgency here," that the international forces would not be there forever. "It forced, I think, our military to think not in terms of infinite time and infinite resources."

The president said his message to the Afghan government was:

"Our commitment to your long-term security and stability will extend for a very long time, and in the same way that our commitment to Iraq will extend beyond our combat role there. But it's time for us to start thinking in terms of how you guys are going to be able to stand on your own two feet."

Near the end of the interview, the president noted that since much of the story had to do with the relationship between civilian leadership and the military, he ought to offer his views.

"I am probably the first president who is young enough that the Vietnam War wasn't at the core of my development," he said. He was 13 in 1975 when the United States finally withdrew from Vietnam.

"So I grew up with none of the baggage that arose out of the dispute of the Vietnam War. I also had a lot of confidence, I guess, coming in that the way our system of government works civilians have to make policy decisions. And then the military carries them out. You know, I don't see this as a civilian versus military situation the way I think a lot of people coming out of Vietnam do. I also don't see it as a hawk/dove kind of thing.

"So a lot of the political frames through which these debates are being viewed don't really connect with me generationally. I'm neither intimidated by our military, nor am I thinking that they're somehow trying to undermine my role as commander in chief."

At the beginning of the interview, which was scheduled for an hour, the president told me, "You're on the clock." He called final halt after one hour and 15 minutes. "That's it, I have to go, all right?"

"Okay," I said. "There are unanswered questions."

"Of course there are," he said, rising from his chair in the Oval Office.

"Thank you, sir."

As we walked out together, Obama said, "Sounds like you've got better sources than I do."

"No, sir."

"Have you ever thought of being the DNI director?" he asked, laughing lightly. "Huh? Or CIA?"

I laughed as well. We shook hands as we entered the small anteroom off the Oval Office. He was wearing informal Saturday clothes— dark olive chinos and a checkered blue shirt with an open collar.

I said I had one more question and handed him a quotation from the World War II history book *The Day of Battle* by Rick Atkinson, a former colleague at *The Washington Post*. I keep a photocopy of the passage in my home office.

Obama stood and read:

"For war was not just a military campaign but also a parable. There were lessons of camaraderie and duty and inscrutable fate. There were lessons of honor and courage, of compassion and sacrifice. And then there was the saddest lesson, to be learned again and again . . . that war is corrupting, that it corrodes the soul and tarnishes the spirit, that even the excellent and the superior can be defiled, and that no heart would remain unstained."

I wanted to ask, *Did war corrupt everyone? Did no heart go unstained?* But the president was obviously in a hurry.

"I sympathize with this view," he said, returning the quote to me. "See my Nobel Prize acceptance speech." The president disappeared back into the Oval Office. No more questions.

I went home and dug out the speech he delivered in the Oslo City Hall on December 10, 2009.

And there it was:

"The instruments of war do have a role to play in preserving the peace. And yet this truth must coexist with another—that no matter how justified, war promises human tragedy. The soldier's courage and sacrifice is full of glory, expressing devotion to country, to cause, to comrades in arms. But war itself is never glorious, and we must never trumpet it as such. So part of our challenge is reconciling these two seemingly irreconcilable truths—that war is sometimes necessary and war at some level is an expression of human folly."

• • •

The Afghanistan War was now in General Petraeus's hands. Jones, for one, knew how bad the situation was and thought Petraeus was probably saying to himself, "What have I gotten myself into?"

If Jones had the job as the new commander, he knew exactly what he would say to Obama after making an assessment: "Mr. President, I think the strategy is correct. But it was predicated on the fact that Pakistan would be coerced into moving more than they have been, particularly with regard to the Haqqani network and Quetta Shura." The Taliban war in Afghanistan was being run from these safe havens. And hundreds, if not thousands, of fighters were pouring across the border. The Taliban was taking full advantage of the safe havens to rest and train fighters before rotating them into Afghanistan for combat. In those circumstances, "You can't win. You can't do counterinsurgency. It is a cancer in the plan."

Petraeus also worried about the sanctuaries in Pakistan, but he saw them as more of a challenge than as insurmountable obstacles. "This is slow, hard, frustrating," he acknowledged to his staff. He said it was "a roller coaster existence." He recalled that President Obama had remarked at one of the strategy review sessions, "I've got political capital I can invest here. I'm going to do it. But it's not a renewable resource."

The general disagreed. He thought that political capital was somewhat renewable. It all depended on progress and everyone—Americans, the NATO allies, the Afghans—having a sense that the mission was doable. "That's the central issue." Endurance and persistence were what mattered.

"It's results, boy," he said in front of one of his colonels. "Stay rucked up, keep putting your left foot in front of your right foot."

But history had its cycles and ironies, he knew all too well. He thought back almost four years to the fall of 2006, when Rumsfeld had called him in to discuss his future. Petraeus had commanded the 101st Division during the Iraq invasion in 2003, then headed the training command there in 2004.

What did Rumsfeld want to talk about? Not Iraq but Afghanistan.

At the time, many thought it was the war the United States was winning. What about Petraeus going to be commander there?

Petraeus resisted, and they didn't work it out. Several months later in early 2007, he was, of course, in command in Iraq. When he arrived there, he was shocked at the level of violence and instability. Those were the darkest, most awful days with Iraq on the verge of civil war. He went out on patrol into the neighborhoods of Baghdad. They were like ghost towns. It was so bad that at one point he went back to his quarters, and with nobody else around, put his head down on his desk in despair. "What in the world?" he thought to himself that day in 2007 and on a number of occasions later. "Why didn't I just take that Afghanistan job?"

GLOSSARY

AfPak Afghanistan-Pakistan, term used to demonstrate that the war in Afghanistan and the al Qaeda and Taliban presence in Pakistan must be addressed with one policy.

ANA Afghan National Army, the army of Afghanistan.

ANSF Afghan National Security Forces, umbrella term for the Afghan National Army and Afghan National Police.

AQAP Al Qaeda in the Arabian Peninsula, a branch of al Qaeda whose members include those active in Yemen.

CentCom United States Central Command, the combatant command located in Tampa, Florida, responsible for the wars in Afghanistan and Iraq.

COIN Counterinsurgency, the doctrine for using military force to protect a local population.

CT Counterterrorism, the operations to capture or kill terrorists, often with small quick-reaction military or intelligence units.

CTPT Counterterrorism Pursuit Teams, 3,000-man paramilitary force of highly experienced and skilled Afghans paid, trained and controlled by the CIA.

DNI Director of National Intelligence, oversees the U.S. intelligence community.

FATA Federally Administered Tribal Areas, seven Pakistani provinces along the Pakistan-Afghanistan border ruled by tribal chiefs and extremist groups that provide a safe haven for al Qaeda and Taliban extremists.

Haqqani network A prominent Taliban insurgent group, active in southeastern Afghanistan.

IED Improvised explosive device, a makeshift bomb often used by insurgents alongside roads.

ISAF International Security Assistance Force, coalition of forces in Afghanistan from 42 nations, led by the United States.

ISI Inter-Services Intelligence, powerful Pakistani intelligence agency that simultaneously assists the United States in fighting the Taliban extremists while at the same time supporting and funding some Taliban groups.

ISR Intelligence, Surveillance and Reconnaissance.

JCS Joint Chiefs of Staff, the top uniformed military officers in the United States, including the chairman, vice chairman and heads of the Army, Navy, Air Force and Marine Corps.

JSOC Joint Special Operations Command, counterterrorism force responsible for planning, preparing and executing rapid and targeted missions to kill or capture high value targets.

LeT Lashkar-e-Taiba (Army of the Pure), terrorist group affiliated with al Qaeda responsible for the November 26 attacks on Mumbai. It was created and continues to be supported by the Pakistani ISI.

NSC National Security Council, composed of the president and his senior foreign policy team, including the vice president, the secretaries of state and defense, the chairman of the Joint Chiefs of Staff, the director of national intelligence and at times the director of the CIA. The NSC staff is headed by the national security adviser.

PDB President's Daily Brief, TOP SECRET/CODEWORD intelligence briefing presented to the president each morning.

POTUS President of the United States.

Quetta Shura The main Taliban insurgent group, headed by Mullah Omar, based in the Pakistani city of Quetta.

RC Regional Command (e.g., RC South, RC East), areas of Afghanistan under the military responsibility of various nations in the ISAF.

RDI Rendition, Detention and Interrogation, controversial covert counterterrorist programs run by the CIA including the transport of suspected terrorists to the U.S. or other countries, CIA detention of terrorists, and interrogation methods employed by the CIA.

SCIF Sensitive Compartmented Information Facility, secure area or isolated room in a building designed to prevent surveillance during sensitive discussions.

SIP Strategic Implementation Plan, a 40-page classified document sent by the White House to the Pentagon on July 17, 2009, stating that a key element of the U.S. mission in Afghanistan was to "defeat the extremist insurgency."

TTP Tehrik-e-Taliban, Pakistani branch of the Taliban that threatens the Pakistani government and the security of its nuclear arsenal. Intelligence showed that the would-be Times Square bomber, Faisal Shahzad, was trained by the TTP.

PRESIDENT OBAMA'S FINAL ORDERS FOR AFGHANISTAN PAKISTAN STRATEGY, OR TERMS SHEET

SECRET/NOFORN
November 29, 2009

MEMORANDUM FOR THE PRINCIPALS
From: National Security Adviser

AFGHANISTAN PAKISTAN STRATEGY

This memorandum summarizes the Afghan option discussed among the principals and with the president, sending significant additional U.S. troops in early 2010 in order to degrade the Taliban and set the conditions for accelerated transition to Afghan authorities beginning in July 2011.

New implementation guidance for Afghanistan

In support of our core goal, new implementation guidance for Afghanistan follows:

United States goal in Afghanistan is to deny safe haven to al Qaeda and to deny the Taliban the ability to overthrow the Afghan government.

The strategic concept for the United States, along with our international partners and the Afghans, is to degrade the Taliban insurgency while building sufficient Afghan capacity to secure and govern their country, creating conditions for the United States to begin reducing its forces by July 2011.

- The military mission in Afghanistan will focus on six operational objectives and will be limited in scope and scale to only what is necessary to attain the U.S. goal. These objectives are:
  - Reversing the Taliban's momentum.
  - Denying the Taliban access to and control of key population and production centers and lines of communication.
  - Disrupting the Taliban in areas outside the secure area and preventing al Qaeda from gaining sanctuary in Afghanistan.
  - Degrading the Taliban to levels manageable by the Afghan National Security Force (ANSF).
  - Increasing the size of the ANSF and leveraging the potential for local security forces so we can transition responsibility for security to the Afghan government on a timeline that will permit us to begin to decrease our troop presence by July 2011.
  - Selectively building the capacity of the Afghan government with military focused on the ministries of defense and interior.

Civilian assistance
- Our military efforts and civilian assistance will be closely coordinated.
- Given the profound problems of legitimacy and effectiveness with the Karzai government, we must focus on what is realistic. Our plan includes the way forward in dealing with the Karzai government has four elements: Working with Karzai when we can, working around him when we must; enhancing sub-national governance; strengthening corruption reduction efforts; and implementing a post-election compact.
  - Afghan-led reintegration and reconciliation are essential pillars of our strategy.

- Principals will ensure appropriate authorities, programs and resources are in place to support a prioritized comprehensive approach.
- We must improve coordination of international political and economic assistance to build Afghan capacity.

- Afghan-led reintegration. We must improve coordination.

This approach is not fully resourced counterinsurgency or nation building, but a narrower approach tied more tightly to the core goal of disrupting, dismantling and eventually defeating al Qaeda and preventing al Qaeda's return to safe haven in Afghanistan or Pakistan.

Achieving the new implementation guidance for Afghanistan

Based on Defense's Option 2A and our discussions with the president, we describe below an approach to enable General McChrystal and ISAF to carry out our implementation guidance and set the conditions for accelerated transition to Afghan authorities.

The key elements of this option, described in detail below, are:

- An additional 30,000 U.S. troops will be deployed immediately in an extended surge of 18 to 24 months to arrive in Afghanistan in the first half of 2010, along with counterpart civilian personnel and funding.
- The secretary of defense is authorized if necessary to commit a limited number of additional enablers to support emerging needs in the range of 10 percent above the 30,000 U.S. troops.
- December 2010, an NSC-led assessment of the security situation and other conditions, including improvements in Afghan governance, development of ANSF, Pakistani actions and international support.

- July 2011, U.S. forces begin transferring lead security responsibility from our forces deployed to the ANSF and begin reducing U.S. forces. Based on progress on the ground, the president will consider the timing for a shift from combat operations to an advise and assist mission and assess the levels at which our military and civilian support will be sustained.

December 2010 is selected as the next assessment point because it is one year after the additional 33,000 U.S. troops committed in 2009 arrived in Afghanistan, providing sufficient time to assess progress and proof of the operational concept.

Concept

In each area secured by U.S. forces, the agreed concept and goal are to accelerate transition to Afghan authorities in 18 to 24 months from July 2009, then to adjust the mission and thin out U.S. forces in that area.

In July 2011, we will assess progress nationwide and the president will consider the timing of changing the military mission.

By July 2011, the 68,000 U.S. forces deployed by 2009 will have been in place for nearly 24 months at least, and in some cases for years longer.

By then we will expect to begin transferring lead security responsibility from these forces to the ANSF and begin reducing U.S. forces to the levels below the extended surge.

The fundamental distinctions between the approach in Option 2 and 2A are the narrower mission and the express tighter timeline in which to show progress and transfer responsibility.

International and Afghan contributions

In effect, this approach provides General McChrystal more troops earlier than his recommended option.

In 2010, the Afghan army intends to reinforce its units in the capital, south and east region with 44 infantry companies above 4,400.

Assessment criteria

The NSC will monitor progress on a monthly basis.

Afghan governance:

- Has Karzai made progress enacting the compact and fulfilling our specific requests in the private message? Specifically has he made merit-based appointments in the ministries, provinces and districts that are most critical to our mission?

- Have we demonstrated that we can assist the Afghans in promoting effective sub-national governance based on our civil/military campaign plan despite the limits of the national government? Specifically, have we and the Afghans generated sufficient civilian capacity to partner with our military forces in the hold, build, transfer phases? And are these resources beginning to take effect?

- Has the Afghan government begun to implement an effective reintegration/reconciliation program?

Pakistan:

- Are there indicators that we have begun to shift Pakistan's strategic calculus and eventually end their active and passive support for extremists?

- Has Pakistan approved our specific request for assistance against al Qaeda and other extremists, including the Afghan Taliban and the Haqqani network?

ANSF development:

- Are we meeting our program for accelerated ANSF growth while improving quality? Is the 2010 program to reinforce the ANA by 44 companies on track?

- Have we established with the government of Afghanistan a program to transfer security responsibility from ISAF to ANSF province by province?

International support:

- Have international partners demonstrated substantial support for the mission in Afghanistan? Specifically has NATO sustained current commitments and generated for 2010 additional troops and trainers (about 5,000 troops) and funded sufficiently the various trust funds? Have international partners contributed substantial additional civilian resources?

- Do we have in place a civilian counterpart to General McChrystal responsible for coordinating the ISAF assistance effort?

Of these four conditions, the one on which we could objectively expect to show best progress in the next several months is in building international support. To line up immediate support (by the December 3/4 NATO foreign ministerial meeting), principals have been engaging their counterparts. The president has spoken to Berlusconi and is scheduled to speak to key allied leaders including Brown, Sarkozy and Merkel in advance of his speech. Leaders must make decisions to stand with the president at this crucial time and only they can make the call on committing additional troops. At a minimum, we expect a strong political statement in support of the president's decision at the ministerial.

Cost

The total cost for this option in Afghanistan is about $113 billion per year for those years in which we sustain nearly 100,000 troops in Afghanistan. Major annual cost factors include: $100 billion for military operations and maintenance; up to $8 billion for the ANSF, depending on annual targets and allied contributions; $5.2 billion for civilian operations and assistance.

CHAPTER NOTES

CHAPTER ONE

The information in this chapter comes primarily from background interviews with seven firsthand sources.

1 *On Thursday, November 6, 2008: American Morning,* CNN, November 6, 2008, http://transcripts.cnn.com/TRANSCRIPTS.

3 *In September 2006, Pakistan:* "Government, Militants 'Ink' NWA Peace Pact," *The Nation* (Pakistan), September 2, 2006.

4 *Although classified, the program:* Candace Rondeaux, "U.S. Airstrikes Creating Tension, Pakistan Warns," *The Washington Post,* November 4, 2008, p. A10.

5 *Fifty-eight people were killed:* Abdul Waheed Wafa and Alan Cowell, "Bomber Strikes Afghan Capital; At Least 41 Die," *The New York Times,* July 8, 2008, p. A1.

8 *But in that part of the world:* Ron Moreau and Mark Hosenball, "Pakistan's Dangerous Double Game," *Newsweek,* September 22, 2008, p. 44.

8 *McConnell said a second:* Pamela Hess and Matthew Lee, "US officials: Yemen Poses Growing Terror Threat," Associated Press Online, September 17, 2008.

9 *The Chinese had hacked into:* Evan Thomas, "Center Stage; Obama's Aides Worried the Clintons Might Steal the Show," *Newsweek,* November 17, 2008, p. 87.

11 *In an Oval Office interview:* Interview with President Barack H. Obama, July 10, 2010.

CHAPTER TWO

The information in this chapter comes primarily from background interviews with fifteen firsthand sources.

14 *Despite his misgivings:* Anne E. Kornblut and Karen DeYoung, "Emanuel to Be Chief of Staff," *The Washington Post*, November 7, 2008, p. A1.

14 *Only months earlier, candidate Obama:* Interview with President Barack H. Obama, July 10, 2010.

15 *Petraeus had almost redefined:* The *Counterinsurgency Field Manual* put together by Petraeus noted the differences from conventional warfare in a section starting on page 47 called "Paradoxes of Counterinsurgency":

Sometimes, the more you protect your force, the less secure you may be.

Sometimes, the more force is used, the less effective it is.

The more successful the counterinsurgency is, the less force can be used and the more risk must be accepted.

Sometimes doing nothing is the best reaction.

Some of the best weapons for counterinsurgents do not shoot.

The host nation doing something tolerably is normally better than us doing it well.

If a tactic works this week, it might not work next week; if it works in this province, it might not work in the next.

Tactical success guarantees nothing.

Many important decisions are not made by generals.

15 *When his 92-year-old father died:* Lisa DePaulo, "Leader of the Year: Right Man, Right Time," *GQ*, December 2008.

16 *The evening before:* David Ignatius, "20 Months in Baghdad," *The Washington Post*, September 17, 2008, p. A19.

16 *"The darkness has receded":* Robert Gates, "Multi-National Force-Iraq Change of Command (Iraq)," September 16, 2008, http://www.defense.gov/speeches.

16 *Gates again showed up:* Robert Gates, "U.S. Central Command Change-of-Command Ceremony (Tampa, FL)," October 31, 2008, http://www.defense.gov/speeches.

16 *Petraeus was the recipient:* Les Carpenter, "NFL Orders Retreat from War Metaphors," *The Washington Post*, February 1, 2009, p. D1.

17 *A popular war hero:* Steve Coll, "The General's Dilemma," *The New Yorker*, September 8, 2008, http://www.newyorker.com/reporting/2008/09/08/080908fa_fact_coll.

17 *On Monday, November 10, Obama:* Sheryl Gay Stolberg, "As the Handoff Begins, a Visit Both Historic and Perhaps Awkward," *The New York Times*, November 10, 2008, p. A16; Dan Eggen and Michael D. Shear, "Obamas Make Symbolic Visit to Future Home: White House," *The Washington Post*, November 11, 2008, p. A4.

18 *Later on November 10: Anderson Cooper 360°*, CNN, November 10, 2008, http://transcripts.cnn.com/TRANSCRIPTS.

19 *In his 1996 memoir:* Robert M. Gates, *From the Shadows* (New York: Simon & Schuster, 1996), p. 419.

20 *When he had talked about the problem:* Defense Department transcript, Secretary Gates Interview with Tavis Smiley, March 11, 2009, http://www.defense.gov/transcripts; Robert Gates, Remarks at the Army War College, Carlisle, PA, April 16, 2009; Robert Gates, U.S. Military Academy Commencement, May 23, 2009, http://www.defense.gov/speeches.

21 *Gates read one of several:* Peter Eisler, Blake Morrison and Tom Vanden Brook, "Pentagon Balked at Pleas from Officers in Field for Safer Vehicles," *USA Today*, July 16, 2007, p. 1A; Tom Vanden Brook and Peter Eisler, "Letter: Add-on Armor Too Heavy for New Vehicles," *USA Today*, July 17, 2007, p. 5A; Tom Vanden Brook and Peter Eisler, "Military Says Troops in Iraq to Get 3,500 Safer MRAP Vehicles," *USA Today*, July 19, 2007, p. 10A; Peter Eisler, "The Vehicle the Pentagon Wants and a Small S.C. Company's Rush to Make It," *USA Today*, August 2, 2007, p. 1A; Blake Morrison, Tom Vanden Brook and Peter Eisler, "When the Pentagon Failed to Buy Enough Body Armor, Electronic Jammers and Hardened Vehicles to Protect U.S. Troops from Roadside Bombs in Iraq, Congress Stepped In," *USA Today*, September 4, 2007, p. 1A.

22 *As one of his first actions:* Emelie Rutherford, "Defense Secretary Approves 'DX' Rating for MRAP Vehicle Program," *Inside the Pentagon*, June 7, 2007, Vol. 23, No. 23.

22 *Gates ordered crash production:* By July 2009, all 16,000 had been built. MRAPs do protect soldiers, but they do not completely overcome the problem of IEDs.

23 *Obama told me that from his time:* Interview with President Barack H. Obama, July 10, 2010.

23 *Later, Obama recalled for me:* Ibid.

24 *At a later press conference:* Robert Gates, media roundtable from the Pentagon briefing room, Arlington, VA, December 2, 2008, http://www.defense.gov/transcripts.

CHAPTER THREE

The information in this chapter comes primarily from background interviews with eight firsthand sources.

27 *A 1987* Chicago Magazine *profile:* Grant Pick, "Hatchet Man: The Rise of David Axelrod," *Chicago*, December 1987, http://www.chicagomag.com/Chicago-Magazine/December-1987/Hatchet-Man-The-Rise-of-David-Axelrod/.

27 *After a February rally:* Perry Bacon, Jr., and Alec MacGillis, "Clinton Takes Strong Exception to Tactics of Obama Campaign," *The Washington Post*, February 24, 2008, p. A11.

28 *She flew to Chicago:* Abdon M. Pallasch, "Hillary in Mystery Motorcade?" *Chicago Sun Times*, November 14, 2008, p. 3.

29 *It had offended him:* Darryl Fears, "Black America Feels the Sting of Ex-President's Comments," *The Washington Post*, January 25, 2008, p. A8.

29 *The former president went public:* Peter Baker and Helene Cooper, "Bill Clinton Said to Accept Terms of Obama Team," *The New York Times*, November 20, 2008, p. A1.

30 *During the course of this courtship:* John Heilemann and Mark Halperin, *Game Change* (New York: HarperCollins, 2010).

33 *In one of the presidential debates:* CNN transcript of the first presidential debate, September 26, 2008, http://www.cnn.com/ 2008/.POLITICS/09/26/debate.mississippi.transcript/.

33 *Accompanied by a single aide:* Barbara Starr, "Emerging Players in Obama's National Security Team," CNN.com, November 24, 2008, http://www.cnn.com.

34 *Mullen had testified:* Ann Scott Tyson, "Pentagon Critical of NATO Allies," *The Washington Post*, December 12, 2007, p. A1.

35 *Obama later said:* Interview with President Barack H. Obama, July 10, 2010.

CHAPTER FOUR

The information in this chapter comes primarily from background interviews with nine firsthand sources.

36 *Jones had expressed distaste:* Bob Woodward, *State of Denial* (New York: Simon & Schuster, 2006), p. 404.

39 *In retirement, he was heading:* Executive Branch Personnel Public Financial Disclosure Report, James L. Jones, January 17, 2009, http://s3.amazonaws.com/propublica/assets/financial_disclosures/Jones_James_278.pdf.

41 *His favorite military book: The Charlie Rose Show*, "A Conversation with Major General Douglas Lute," January 23, 2006, http://www.charlierose.com/view/interview/573.

43 *"We're not losing, but we're not winning":* Report described to the author by two knowledgeable sources.

45 *The gunmen created a spectacle:* Rama Lakshmi, "Dozens Die in Mumbai Attacks," *The Washington Post,* November 27, 2008, p. A1; Somini Sengupta, "Terror Attacks Kill Scores in India," *The New York Times,* November 27, 2008, p. A1.

45 *In his nationally televised address:* Presidential Documents, September 11, 2001, pp. 1301–1302 (Vol. 37, No. 37), http://www.gpoaccess.gov/wcomp/v37no37.html.

45 *Bush was extremely proud:* Interview with President George W. Bush, December 20, 2001.

47 *The ease of the planning:* Based on notes and background interviews with several knowledgeable sources. See also "Expert: Open Internet Best Terrorist Asset," *New Straits Times* (Malaysia), November 12, 2009, p. 13; Jeremy Kahn, "Terrorists Used Technology in Planning and Execution," *The New York Times,* December 9, 2008, p. A14.

CHAPTER FIVE

The information in this chapter comes primarily from background interviews with nine firsthand sources.

48 *The memorial service:* Jacques Steinberg, "At Funeral, Russert's Son Sounds a Theme of Unity," *The New York Times,* June 19, 2008, p. B7.

50 *That meeting was finally arranged:* Sara A. Carter, "Obama Huddles with CIA Director on Security," *The Washington Times,* December 13, 2008, p. A5.

50 *As Richard Helms, the CIA director:* Bob Woodward, *Veil: The Secret Wars of the CIA, 1981–1987* (New York: Simon & Schuster, 1987), p. 25.

51 *"They just arrested the governor":* Carrie Johnson, "FBI Says Illinois Governor Tried to Sell Senate Seat," *The Washington Post,* December 10, 2008, p. A1.

55 *There had been 13, Hayden said:*
The 13 former interrogation techniques, some of which are still current, are:
1. Dietary manipulation. Reduce food intake to as little as 1,000 kcal/day, limiting detainees to a bottle of the diet drink Ensure.
2. Nudity in rooms at least 68 degrees F. It was permissible to exploit a detainee's fear of being seen naked, including when women interrogators are used.

3. Attention grasp. The grabbing of a shirt collar in a quick and controlled motion to pull the detainee forward.

4. Walling. Ramming a detainee into a flexible, false wall up to 20 or 30 times.

5. Facial hold. The interrogator using both palms to hold the detainee's face.

6. Facial slap or insult slap. A slap to the lower part of face between the chin and earlobe.

7. Abdominal slap. A slap with the back of an open hand, not a fist, to the area between the navel and sternum.

8. Cramped confinement. Usually dark. For no more than eight hours at a time, or 18 hours a day. In very small spaces, no more than two hours. Harmless insects could be placed in the space to frighten the detainee, but this technique had not been used.

9. Wall standing. Have the detainee stand several feet away from the wall, arms out with fingers touching the wall. The detainee is not permitted to move, inducing temporary muscle fatigue.

10. Three stress positions: 1. Sitting on the floor with legs extended straight and arms raised; 2. Kneeling on the floor while at a 45-degree angle; and 3. With wrists handcuffed in the front or back, the detainee is placed three feet from the wall and only able to lean his head against the wall. As with wall standing, these postures induce temporary muscle fatigue.

11. Water dousing. Cold water is poured or sprayed on a detainee. The maximum time a detainee can be soaked in water is two thirds of the time at which hypothermia could set in.

12. Sleep deprivation for more than 48 hours. The detainee is standing, his hands are handcuffed and chained to the ceiling, his feet shackled to the floor. The hands are kept between heart and chin. He can only raise his hands above his head for two hours. The detainee cannot support his weight by hanging from the ceiling, though he can also be shackled to a small stool. The detainee may be naked and wearing a diaper. The diaper is for sanitary purposes and "not used for the purpose of humiliating the detainee." Maximum permissible period is 180 hours, or more than one week. Then eight hours of uninterrupted sleep are required.

13. Waterboarding. The detainee is strapped to a board and his feet elevated. A cloth is placed over the detainee's face, and water is poured over the cloth for no more than 40 seconds. This is not

physically painful, but "it usually does cause fear and panic," creating the sensation of drowning. Waterboarding can only be used if there is credible intelligence that a terrorist attack is imminent and the detainee might possess actionable intelligence that could stop the attack. A detainee could only be subjected to two distinct two-hour waterboarding sessions a day for no more than five days, with a maximum of 12 minutes of waterboarding in a 24-hour period. (Khalid Sheik Mohammed, the mastermind of the 9/11 attacks, was waterboarded 183 times.)

56 *Later as president:* Executive Order 13491—Ensuring Lawful Interrogations, signed January 22, 2009, by President Barack H. Obama, http://www.gpoaccess.gov/presdocs/2009/DCPD200900007.htm.

56 *When I asked the president:* Interview with President Barack H. Obama, July 10, 2010.

56 *The 2004 reform law:* "Intelligence Reform and Terrorism Prevention Act of 2004," December 17, 2004, http://www.nctc.gov/docs/pl108_458.pdf.

58 *"Before the election":* Speech by Dennis Blair at the U.S. Chamber of Commerce, July 22, 2009, BNET, http://findarticles.com/p/articles/mi_8167/is_20090722/ai_n50901376/.

60 *"Number three, I've read some":* Leon E. Panetta, "No Torture. No Exceptions," *The Washington Monthly,* January/February/March 2008, p. 40, http://www.washingtonmonthly.com/features/2008/0801.torture.pdf; Leon E. Panetta, "Americans Reject Fear Tactics," *Monterey County Herald,* March 9, 2008.

60 *The Justice Department had approved:* The text of the Justice Department memos on interrogation techniques may be accessed at: http://documents. nytimes.com/justice-department-memos-on-interrogation-techniques.

CHAPTER SIX

The information in this chapter comes primarily from background interviews with six firsthand sources.

62 *On Friday, January 9:* Pamela Constable, "Bomb Kills 3 U.S. Soldiers in Afghanistan," *The Washington Post,* January 10, 2009, p. A10.

65 *After 9/11, CIA and U.S. Special Forces:* In his 2007 memoir, *At the Center of the Storm,* former CIA Director George Tenet told how Karzai's life was rescued at the end of 2001 when he became the leader of Afghanistan (pp.219–220).

65 *Ahmed Wali had been on:* Dexter Filkins, Mark Mazzetti and James Risen, "Brother of Afghan Leader Said to Be Paid by C.I.A.," *The New York Times*, October 28, 2009, p. A1.

70 *Biden threw down his napkin:* Dexter Filkins, "Afghan Leader Finds Himself Hero No More," *The New York Times*, February 8, 2009, p. A1.

72 *Floated in the media that day:* "Obama to Dems: Give Me the Money," *The Situation Room*, CNN transcript, January 13, 2009; Farah Stockman, "Bill Clinton's Policies May Echo at Hearing," *The Boston Globe*, January 13, 2009, p. A1; "No Stumbling Block Expected at Clinton Hearing," *Morning Edition*, NPR, January 13, 2009.

73 *As Obama, Biden and Graham:* "Remarks by President-Elect Obama and Vice President–Elect Joe Biden," Federal News Service, January 14, 2009.

CHAPTER SEVEN

The information in this chapter comes primarily from background interviews with seven firsthand sources.

74 *"Mr. President, I was on television":* Axelrod appeared on Fox News, NBC's *Today* and CBS's *Early Show*.

74 *Credible intelligence showed:* Peter Baker, "Inside Obama's War on Terrorism," *The New York Times on the Web*, Magazine Preview, January 5, 2010, http://www.nytimes.com.

75 *In his address, Obama devoted:* Daily Compilation of Presidential Documents, January 20, 2009, Inaugural Address, http://www .gpoaccess.gov/presdocs/2009/ DCPD200900001.htm.

77 *The 54-year-old retired Army colonel:* See Bob Woodward, *The War Within* (New York: Simon & Schuster, 2008).

CHAPTER EIGHT

The information in this chapter comes primarily from background interviews with six firsthand sources.

82 *Known as the father:* See Bob Woodward, *The War Within* (New York: Simon & Schuster), 2008.

84 *Holbrooke's first assignment:* See George Packer, "The Last Mission," *The New Yorker*, September 28, 2009, p. 39.

85 *The gaunt runner:* David Martin, "McChrystal's Frank Talk on Afghanistan," *60 Minutes*, CBS, September 27, 2009.

85 *When JSOC had killed:* John F. Burns, "After Long Hunt, U.S. Bombs Kill al Qaeda Leader in Iraq," *The New York Times*, June 9, 2006, p. A1;

Sean D. Naylor, "Inside the Zarqawi Takedown," *Defense News*, June 12, 2006, p. 1; Joshua Partlow and Michael Abramowitz, "Officials Detail Zarqawi's Last Hour," *The Washington Post*, June 13, 2006, p. A1.

86 *While teaching at Boston University:* Husain Haqqani, *Pakistan: Between Mosque and Military*, (Washington, D.C.: Carnegie Endowment for International Peace, 2005).

87 *The Hay-Adams, as advertised:* http://www.hayadams.com.

89 *Four months earlier, he had published:* Bruce Riedel, *The Search for al Qaeda* (Washington D.C.: Brookings Institution Press, 2008), p. 12.

89 *He concluded that there was:* Ibid, p. 140.

89 *He matched the description:* William Colby, *Honorable Men: My Life in the CIA* (New York: Simon & Schuster, 1978).

CHAPTER NINE

The information in this chapter comes primarily from background interviews with seven firsthand sources.

91 *Outgoing Director Hayden was watching:* Federal News Service, Hearing of the Senate Select Committee on Intelligence, Subject: The Nomination of Leon Panetta to Be Director of the Central Intelligence Agency, February 5, 2009.

92 *But it was another "slam dunk":* Before the Iraq invasion, then CIA Director George Tenet told President Bush the case for Iraq possessing weapons of mass destruction was a "slam dunk." No WMD were ever found in Iraq after the 2003 invasion.

92 *The next day, Friday, February 6:* Federal News Service, Hearing of the Senate Select Committee on Intelligence, Subject: The Nomination of Leon Panetta to Be Director of the Central Intelligence Agency (Part Two), February 6, 2009.

94 *Jones went along with the whole draft:* General David Petraeus, Commander's Remarks at 45th Munich Security Conference, February 8, 2009, http://www.centcom.mil/from-the-commander/commanders-remarks-at-45th-munich-security-conference.

97 *Obama later said that the worries:* Interview with President Barack H. Obama, July 10, 2010.

98 *The next day the White House:* White House press release, Statement on United States Troop Levels in Afghanistan, February 17, 2009, http://www.gpoaccess.gov/presdocs/2009/DCPD200900089.htm.

98 *It was left to the Pentagon:* Defense Department press release, DOD Announces Afghanistan Force Deployment, February 17, 2009, http://www.defense.gov.

CHAPTER TEN

The information in this chapter comes primarily from background interviews with seven firsthand sources.

109 *Obama put on his jacket:* Scott Wilson, "Obama, in Calif., Says He Hopes to Return 'Balance' to Economy," *The Washington Post*, March 19, 2009, p. A6.

109 *Taping* The Tonight Show *that afternoon:* Daily Compilation of Presidential Documents, March 19, 2009, Interview with Jay Leno of *The Tonight Show* in Burbank, California, http://www.gpoaccess.gov/ presdocs /2009/DCPD200900173.htm.

109 *Later, the president confirmed:* Interview with President Barack H. Obama, July 10, 2010.

CHAPTER ELEVEN

The information in this chapter comes primarily from background interviews with seventeen firsthand sources.

112 *About her conversation with Petraeus:* Author interview with Helen Thomas, January, 2010.

113 *At 9:40 the next morning:* Daily Compilation of Presidential Documents, March 27, 2009, Remarks on United States Military and Diplomatic Strategies for Afghanistan and Pakistan, http://www.gpoaccess.gov/ presdocs/2009/DCPD-200900196.htm.

113 *A* Washington Post *editorial:* "The Price of Realism," *The Washington Post*, March 29, 2008, p. A12.

113 *A* New York Times *editorial:* "The Remembered War," *The New York Times*, March 28, 2009, p. A20.

114 *Secretary of Defense Gates seemed:* Secretary Robert Gates Interview with Fox News, *FOX News Sunday*, March 29, 2009, http://www.defense .gov/transcripts.

116 *Later Obama told me:* Interview with President Barack H. Obama, July 10, 2010.

119 *In late April, Admiral Mullen:* Fisnik Abrashi, "Top Pentagon Commander in Afghanistan," AP Worldstream, April 22, 2009; Rajiv Chandrasekaran, "Pentagon Worries Led to Command Change," *The Washington Post*, August 17, 2009, p. A1.

119 *McKiernan had given his word:* Author interview with Colonel Julian "Dale" Alford, December 1, 2009.

119 *At a Monday, May 11, Pentagon press conference:* Press Conference with Secretary Gates and Admiral Mullen on Leadership Changes

in Afghanistan, May 11, 2009, http://www.defense.gov/
transcripts.

120   *On the choice of McChrystal:* Interview with President Barack H. Obama,
       July 10, 2010.

121   *The headline on this item read:* Author's dictated notes of a Top Secret
       document dated May 26, 2009.

122   *On September 19, 2009, agents:* Al Baker and Karen Zraick, "F.B.I.
       Searches Colorado Home of Man in Terror Inquiry That Reached
       Queens," *The New York Times*, September 17, 2009; Anne E. Kornblut,
       "Obama Team Says Zazi Case Illustrates Balanced Approach to Terror
       Threat," *The Washington Post*, October 6, 2009, p. A8.

122   *Chicago resident David Coleman Headley:* David Johnston, "2 in Chicago
       Held in Plot to Attack in Denmark," *The New York Times*, October 28,
       2009, p. A18; Ginger Thompson, "A Terror Suspect with Feet in East
       and West," *The New York Times*, November 22, 2009, p. A1.

123   *When I later asked the president:* Interview with President Barack H.
       Obama, July 10, 2010.

123   *In his prepared remarks:* Federal News Service, Hearing of the Senate
       Armed Services Committee, Subject: Nomination of . . . Lieutenant
       General Stanley McChrystal, USA, to be General and Commander,
       International Security Assistance Force, and Commander, U.S. Forces,
       Afghanistan, June 2, 2009.

124   *As President Obama spoke:* Scott Wilson, "History . . . Has Always Been
       Up to Us," *The Washington Post*, June 7, 2009, p. A1.

125   *That next Monday, June 8:* News Briefing with Geoff Morrell, June 8,
       2009, http://www.defense.gov/transcripts.

CHAPTER TWELVE

The information in this chapter comes primarily from background interviews
with nine firsthand sources.

127   *During an hour-long conversation:* Author interview with retired General
       Jim Jones, June 21, 2009.

128   *As I entered the spacious office:* Author interview with President Hamid
       Karzai, June 23, 2009.

129   *Goldstein records how:* Gordon M. Goldstein, *Lessons in Disaster* (New
       York: Times Books, 2008), p. 97.

130   *In the morning, the commander:* Author conversation with Brigadier
       General Lawrence Nicholson, retired General Jim Jones and others.

130   *Corporal Matthew Lembke:* Chris Brummitt, "Stalemate in Afghan Ghost
       Town Shows Task Ahead," Associated Press Worldstream, July 1,

2009; Julie Sullivan, "Family Keeps Faith, as Marine Would Want," *The Oregonian*, July 8, 2009.

131 *Lembke was airlifted:* William Cole, "Marine Dies of Injuries in Afghan Roadside Blast," *The Honolulu Advertiser*, July 11, 2009.

131 *The Oregon governor honored:* Press release from the office of the governor of Oregon, "Governor Orders Flags at Half-Staff in Memory of Oregon Soldier," July 16, 2009.

131 *Lembke was:* Josh Boak phone conversation with Anna Richter Taylor, press secretary for Oregon Governor Ted Kulongoski, July 27, 2010.

131 *Five months later:* Richard A. Oppel, Jr., "Marines Lead Offensive to Secure Southern Afghan Town," *The New York Times*, December 5, 2009, p. A9.

131 *Later that morning, Nicholson:* On-the-record briefing attended by the author. See also: Bob Woodward, "Key in Afghanistan: Economy, Not Military," *The Washington Post*, July 1, 2009, p. A1.

135 *In a meeting, the PRT leaders:* Meeting attended by the author.

136 *As a first step, he called in:* Press conference attended by the author.

136 *Zardari sat between two photographs:* Author interview with President Asif Ali Zardari.

139 *Zinni thought he had been offered:* Barbara Slavin, "Zinni Says Iraq Ambassador Job Offer Was Retracted," *The Washington Times*, February 4, 2009, p. A13; Eric Schmitt and Mark Landler, "General Says Iraq Envoy Job Was Offered, Then Retracted," *The New York Times*, February 6, 2009, P. A8.

140 *A few days after returning:* Bob Woodward, "Key in Afghanistan: Economy, Not Military," *The Washington Post*, July 1, 2009, p. A1.

142 *Mullen then gave an interview:* Ann Scott Tyson, "No Limit in Place for Pending Request on Troops in Afghanistan," *The Washington Post*, July 2, 2009, p. A10.

142 *At his daily briefing:* White House press briefing by Robert Gibbs, July 1, 2009, http://www.whitehouse.gov.

143 *In a column for* The Weekly Standard: William Kristol, "A Whiskey Tango Foxtrot Presidency?" *The Weekly Standard*, September 21, 2009 (Vol. 15, No. 1).

CHAPTER THIRTEEN

The information in this chapter comes primarily from background interviews with 13 firsthand sources.

146   *The classified SIP was signed:* Author's review and dictated notes of the July 17, 2009, Strategic Implementation Plan.

146   *But in public, Holbrooke downplayed:* Richard Holbrooke, Special Briefing on July 2009 Trip to Pakistan, Afghanistan and Brussels, July 29, 2009, http://www.state.gov/p/sca/rls/rmks/2009/126669.htm.

149   *McChrystal's staff had hastily organized:*
      Members of the McChrystal review team:
         General Stanley McChrystal
         Colonel Chris Kolenda, review coordinator
         Colonel Daniel Pick, assistant review coordinator
         Stephen Biddle, Council on Foreign Relations
         Anthony Cordesman, Center for Strategic and International Studies
         Catherine Dale, Congressional Research Service
         Étienne de Durand, Institut Français des Relations Internationales
         Andrew Exum, Center for a New American Security
         Fred Kagan, American Enterprise Institute
         Kimberly Kagan, Institute for the Study of War
         Whitney Kassel, U.S. Office of the Secretary of Defense
         Terry Kelly, The RAND Corporation
         Luis Peral, European Union Institute for Strategic Studies
         Lieutenant Colonel Aaron Prupas, U.S. Air Force, CentCom

153   *McChrystal soon became the chief:* Dexter Filkins, "His Long War," *The New York Times Magazine*, October 18, 2009, p. 36.

154   The Washington Post *called the report:* Ann Scott Tyson, "General: Afghan Situation 'Serious,' " *The Washington Post*, September 1, 2009, p. A1.

154   The New York Times *warned:* Peter Baker and Dexter Filkins, "Obama to Weigh Buildup Option in Afghan War," *The New York Times*, September 1, 2009, p. A1.

154   *McChrystal had signed off:* Ann Scott Tyson, "9 Officers Blamed in Tillman Death, but No Coverup Found," *The Washington Post*, March 27, 2007, p. A2.

154   *The issue resurfaced:* Federal News Service, Hearing of the Senate Armed Services Committee, Subject: Nomination of . . . Lieutenant General Stanley McChrystal, USA, to be General and Commander,

404 CHAPTER NOTES

International Security Assistance Force, and Commander, U.S. Forces, Afghanistan, June 2, 2009.

155 *In August, members of the Senate:* Nahal Toosi, "McCain Calls for More US Troops in Afghanistan," Associated Press, August 18, 2009.

CHAPTER FOURTEEN

The information in this chapter comes primarily from background interviews with nine firsthand sources.

157 *Petraeus read a September 2 column:* David Ignatius, "A Middle Way on Afghanistan?" *The Washington Post*, September 2, 2009, p. A17.

158 *Rebutting Ignatius's critique:* Michael Gerson, "In Afghanistan, No Choice but to Try," *The Washington Post*, September 4, 2009, p. A23.

159 *The vice president had flown:* Michael Finnegan, "Biden Helps Boxer Raise Reelection Funds," *Los Angeles Times*, September 13, 2009, p. A42; Thomas Hines, "Memorial at Dodger Stadium Honors Fallen Firefighters," *San Gabriel Valley Tribune*, September 12, 2009.

160 *Obama later explained to me:* Interview with President Barack H. Obama, July 10, 2010.

161 *Obama had read McChrystal's:* Author's review of the SECRET assessment.

170 *Instead, the CentCom commander:* http://www.nfl.com.

171 *On Monday, September 14, a long op-ed:* Lindsey Graham, Joseph I. Lieberman and John McCain, "Only Decisive Force Can Prevail in Afghanistan," *The Wall Street Journal*, December 14, 2009, p. A15.

CHAPTER FIFTEEN

The information in this chapter comes primarily from background interviews with eight firsthand sources.

172 *Admiral Mullen appeared:* Hearing of the Senate Armed Services Committee, Subject: Nomination of Admiral Michael Mullen for a second term as chairman of the Joint Chiefs of Staff, September 15, 2009.

172 *"The Taliban insurgency grows":* Ibid.

173 *The chairman had a Facebook page:* See http://www.facebook.com/admiralmikemullen; http://twitter.com/THEJOINTSTAFF; http://www.youtube.com/view_play_list?p=EC6B9257769B13D0; and http://www.defense.gov/home/features/2008/0708_mullen1/.

174 *"Mullen: More Troops 'Probably' Needed":* Ann Scott Tyson, "Mullen: More Troops 'Probably' Needed," *The Washington Post*, September 16, 2009, p. A1.

176 *On the second page:* Author's review of the classified Commander International Security Assistance Force Initial Assessment. A searchable copy declassified by the Defense Department on September 20, 2009, is available at http://www.washingtonpost .com/wp-dyn/content/article/2009/09/21/AR2009092100110 .html?sid=ST2009092003140.

177 *Because of "inadequate intelligence":* Ibid. The nonredacted sentence reads, "The insurgents control or contest a significant portion of the country, although it is difficult to assess precisely how much due to a lack of ISAF presence *and inadequate intelligence.*" (Emphasis added.)

179 *The June 30, 1971, Supreme Court:* R. W. Apple, Jr., "Times Topics: Pentagon Papers," *The New York Times*, June 23, 1996, http://topics .nytimes.com/top/reference/timestopics/subjects/p/pentagon_papers/ index.html.

179 *I reached General Jones:* Author phone call with General Jim Jones, September 19, 2009.

180 *Within an hour:* Author conference call with Marcus Brauchli, a *Washington Post* lawyer, Secretary Gates, General Jones, Tom Donilon and General James E. Cartwright, September 19, 2009.

181 *At a press conference two weeks earlier:* Press conference with Secretary Gates and Admiral Mullen, September 3, 2009, http://www.defense .gov/transcripts.

181 *In addition, Obama was appearing on five:* "Highlights," *The Washington Post*, September 19, 2009, p. C8.

181 *On Sunday, Brauchli:* Eleven A.M. meeting at the Pentagon attended by the author, Marcus Brauchli, Rajiv Chandrasekaran, General Cartwright, Geoff Morrell and Michèle Flournoy, September 20, 2009.

182 *Brauchli noted that Gates and others:* Federal News Service, Hearing of the Defense Subcommittee of the Senate Appropriations Committee, Subject: Federal Budget for Fiscal Year 2010, Witnesses: Robert Gates, Secretary of Defense, and Admiral Michael Mullen, Chairman of the Joint Chiefs of Staff, June 9, 2009.

182 *That evening, the Pentagon provided:* Both a PDF version (http://media .washingtonpost.com/wp-srv/politics/documents/Assessment_ Redacted_092109.pdf?sid=ST2009092003140) and a searchable html version (http://www.washingtonpost.com/wp-dyn/content/ article/2009/09/21/AR2009092100110.html?sid=ST2009092003140) of the assessment are available on the *Washington Post*'s Web site.

182 *The headline in the September 21:* Bob Woodward, "McChrystal: More Forces or 'Mission Failure,' " *The Washington Post*, September 21, 2009, p. A1.

182 *Within a few minutes,* The New York Times: Eric Schmitt and Thom Shanker, "General Calls for More Troops to Avoid Afghanistan Failure," *The New York Times,* September 21, 2009, p. A1.

183 *Retired Army Colonel Pat Lang:* Pat Lang, "An Interesting Monday," *Sic Semper Tyrannis* (blog), September 21, 2009, http://turcopolier.typepad .com/sic_semper_tyrannis/2009/09/an-interesting-monday.html.

183 *Peter Feaver, who had been on:* Peter Feaver, "Bob Woodward Strikes Again! (McChrystal assessment edition)," *Shadow Government* (blog), September 21, 2009, http://shadow.foreignpolicy.com/ posts/2009/09/21/bob_woodward_strikes_again_mcchrystal_ assessment_edition.

183 *At the morning press briefing:* Air Force One press gaggle by Robert Gibbs, September 21, 2009, http://www.whitehouse.gov.

183 *In my interview with the president:* Interview with President Barack H. Obama, July 10, 2010.

CHAPTER SIXTEEN

The information in this chapter comes primarily from background interviews with 14 firsthand sources.

186 *It had already appeared:* Brad Knickerbocker, "Obama Faces Critical Decision on How to Proceed in Afghanistan," *Christian Science Monitor,* September 26, 2009, p. 10; Elisabeth Bumiller, "Top Officers Weigh Need to Increase Troop Levels," *New York Times,* September 26, 2009, p. A4.

186 *At 3 P.M. on Wednesday, September 30:* Peter Baker, "Inside the Situation Room: How a War Plan Evolved," *The New York Times,* December 6, 2009, p. A1.

192 *The 11-page document:* Author's review and dictated notes of "Resourcing the ISAF implementation strategy," General McChrystal's SECRET/NOFORM September 24, 2009, troop request.

192 *McChrystal listed three:* Ibid.

193 *Around that time, the CBS show:* David Martin, "McChrystal's Frank Talk on Afghanistan," *60 Minutes,* CBS, September 27, 2009.

193 *The bloggers pounced:* Peter Baker, "From General's Mouth to Obama's Ear," *The New York Times,* September 30, 2009, p. A12.

193 *Obama was flying:* Peter Slevin, "Obama's Personal Bid for the Olympics," *The Washington Post,* September 20, 2009, p. A1.

193 *During McChrystal's October 1 speech:* General Stanley McChrystal, special address on Afghanistan to the International Institute for

Strategic Studies (IISS), October 1, 2009, http://www.iiss.org/recent
-key-addresses/general-stanley-mcchrystal-address/.

193 *After his prepared remarks:* John F. Burns, "Top U.S. Commander
in Afghanistan Rejects Scaling Down Military Objectives," *The
Washington Post*, October 2, 2009, p. A12.

194 *Obama and McChrystal met:* Michael D. Shear, "McChrystal Flown to
Denmark to Discuss War with Obama," *The Washington Post*, October
3, 2009, p. A4; Peter Baker, "Obama Meets Top Afghan Commander
as He Mulls Change in War Strategy," *The New York Times*, October 3,
2009, p. A6.

195 *In his 1995 book,* In Retrospect: Robert S. McNamara, *In Retrospect*
(New York: Vintage, 1996), pp. 187–88.

198 *The criticism had grown so intense:* Karen DeYoung, "In Frenetic White
House, a Low-Key 'Outsider,' " *The Washington Post*, May 7, 2009,
p. A1; Helene Cooper, "National Security Adviser Takes Less Visible
Approach to His Job," *The New York Times*, May 7, 2009, p. A10.

198 *On June 11, Fox News:* "Jones on the Outs with Obama?" Fox News,
June 11, 2009, http://www.foxnews.com/politics/2009/06/11/jones
-outs-obama-gates-defends-national-security-adviser/.

198 *On October 1, the day of the McChrystal speech:* White House press
release, Deputy National Security Adviser, NSC Chief of Staff Mark
Lippert Returning to Active Duty in the US Navy, October 1, 2009,
http://www.whitehouse.gov.

198 *Jones was quoted as saying:* Ibid.

201 *It reimbursed allies:* "Combating Terrorism: Increased Oversight and
Accountability Needed over Pakistan Reimbursement Claims for
Coalition Support Funds," U.S. Government Accountability Office,
http://www.gao.gov/products/GAO-08-806.

CHAPTER SEVENTEEN

The information in this chapter comes primarily from background interviews
with 13 firsthand sources.

204 *Clinton and Gates went off:* Roundtable discussion with Secretary Gates,
Secretary Clinton, Christiane Amanpour and Frank Sesno, October
5, 2009, http://www.gwu.edu/explore/aboutgw/thegwexperience/
secretariesgatesclintondiscussdefenseanddiplomacy.

204 *At 2:30 P.M. on October 6:* See Scott Wilson, "Afghan Strategy Divides
Lawmakers," *The Washington Post*, October 7, 2009, p. A1.

205 *But Graham's comments a few days earlier:* Senator Lindsey Graham
     Interview with Fox News, *Fox News Sunday*, October 6, 2009,
     http://www.foxnews.com/story/0,2933,560000,00.html.

207 *Graham decided to back off:* Meet the Press, NBC, October 11, 2009.

210 *There are tens of thousands:* See "Today Siachen Is Weeping, Tomorrow
     the World Will Cry," *The News* (Pakistan), December 30, 2006,
     http://www.thenews.com.pk/top_story_detail.asp?Id=5021.

CHAPTER EIGHTEEN

The information in this chapter comes primarily from background interviews
with 10 firsthand sources.

213 *Obama awoke that next morning:* Scott Wilson, "Nobel for Obama Brings
     Praise, Ire," *The Washington Post*, October 10, 2008, p. A1.

214 *He had published one short story:* Ben Rhodes, "The Goldfish Smiles, You
     Smile Back," *Beloit Fiction Journal*, vol. 15, Spring 2002.

214 *Obama appeared at a podium:* Daily Compilation of Presidential
     Documents, October 9, 2009, Remarks on Winning the Nobel Peace
     Prize, http://www.gpoaccess.gov/presdocs/2009/DCPD-200900793
     .htm.

CHAPTER NINETEEN

The information in this chapter comes primarily from background interviews
with 10 firsthand sources.

231 *"This is a long war":* See "Vietnam, Not Afghanistan, Still Longest War:
     Holbrooke," *The Two-Way* (blog), NPR, June 7, 2010, http://www.npr
     .org/blogs/thetwo-way/2010/06/vietnam_not_afghanistan_still.html.

CHAPTER TWENTY

The information in this chapter comes primarily from background interviews
with 11 firsthand sources.

234 *The Afghanistan commander responded:* Contents described to the author
     by a knowledgeable source.

237 *Under the law as a member:* See U.S. Code, Title 10, Subtitle A, Part I,
     Chapter 5, 151, Subsection d, http://www.law.cornell.edu/uscode/
     html/uscode10/usc_sec_10_00000151——000-.html.

237 *And the law said that the chairman:* Ibid.

242 *At least one copy never made it back:* Author review and dictated
     notes of Petraeus's October 14, 2009, memo entitled "Lessons on
     Reconciliation."

CHAPTER TWENTY-ONE

The information in this chapter comes primarily from background interviews with 13 firsthand sources.

246 The Washington Post *and ABC News:* ABC News/*Washington Post* Poll: Afghanistan, "Drop for Obama on Afghanistan; Few See a Clear Plan for the War," October 21, 2009, http://abcnews.go.com/images/ PollingUnit/1095a3Afghanistan.pdf.

247 *Former Vice President Dick Cheney:* "Cheney: 'We Cannot Protect This Country by Putting Politics over Security, and Turning the Guns on Our Own Guys,' " former Vice President Dick Cheney, October 21, 2009, http://www.centerforsecuritypolicy.org/p18209.xml.

247 *At the White House press briefing:* White House press briefing by Robert Gibbs, October 22, 2009, http://www.whitehouse.gov.

249 *A survey of the Kandahar population:* "District Assessment: Kandahar-city, Kandahar Province," commissioned by the Canadian Department of Foreign Affairs and International Trade, November 2009, p. 23.

249 *The survey was later heralded:* Major General Michael T. Flynn, USA, Captain Matt Pottinger, USMC, and Paul D. Batchelor, DIA, "Fixing Intel: A Blueprint for Making Intelligence Relevant in Afghanistan," Center for a New American Security, January 2010, p. 25, footnote 10, http://www.cnas.org/files/documents/publications/ AfghanIntel_ Flynn_Jan2010_code507_voices.pdf

255 *Just before midnight:* Michael Fletcher and Ann Gerhart, "In Pre-Dawn Darkness, Obama Salutes Victims of War," *The Washington Post,* October 30, 2009, p. A2; Jeff Zeleny, "Obama Visits Air Base to Honor Returning Dead," *The New York Times,* October 30, 2009, p. A16.

CHAPTER TWENTY-TWO

The information in this chapter comes primarily from background interviews with 12 firsthand sources.

260 *On October 30, Gates sent Obama:* Author's review and dictated notes of Secretary Gates's October 30, 2009, memo.

261 *The U.S. ambassador to Afghanistan had sent:* Eikenberry's cables can be viewed in document form at http://documents.nytimes.com/ eikenberry-s-memos-on-the-strategy-in-afghanistan. See also Elisabeth Bumiller and Mark Landler, "Envoy Expresses Doubt on Forces for Afghanistan," *The New York Times,* November 12, 2009, p. A1; and Eric Schmitt, "Cables Detail Envoy's Worry on Karzai Role," *The New York Times,* January 26, 2010, p. A1.

263 Newsweek *had put him on its cover:* Cover story, Rod Nordland, "Iraq's Repairman," *Newsweek*, July 5, 2004, p. 22.

264 *Only about 42 percent of the Afghan populace:* Central Intelligence Agency, "Afghanistan," *The World Factbook*, 2009, https://www.cia.gov/library/publications/the-world-factbook/geos/af.html.

264 *So for example, they would not have to worry:* Ibid.

CHAPTER TWENTY-THREE

The information in this chapter comes primarily from background interviews with 10 firsthand sources.

266 *About noon on Veterans Day:* Jeff Zeleny, "Obama Salutes Fallen Americans on Veterans Day," *The New York Times on the Web*, November 12, 2009, http://www.nytimes.com/2009/11/12/us/12obama.html; James Gordon Meek, "My Solemn Surprise Meeting with the President at My Friend's Resting Place," *The Daily News*, November 12, 2009, p. 4. See also Daily Compilation of Presidential Documents, November 11, 2009, Remarks at a Veterans Day Ceremony in Arlington, Virginia, http://www.gpoaccess.gov/ presdocs/2009/DCPD-200900902.htm.

266 *They walked around Section 60:* Rick Atkinson, "Where Valor Rests," Washington, D.C.: *National Geographic*, 2009, p. 21.

266 *Around 2 P.M. on Veterans Day: CNN Newsroom*, CNN, November 11, 2009, http://transcripts.cnn.com/TRANSCRIPTS.

268 *The* Journal *story quoted:* Peter Spiegel, "Obama Receives New Afghan Option," *The Wall Street Journal*, November 11, 2009, p. A10.

272 *Eikenberry wrote:* Eikenberry's cables can be viewed in document form at http://documents.nytimes.com/eikenberry-s-memos-on-the-strategy-in-afghanistan. See also Elisabeth Bumiller and Mark Landler, "Envoy Expresses Doubt on Forces for Afghanistan," *The New York Times*, November 12, 2009, p. A1; and Eric Schmitt, "Cables Detail Envoy's Worry on Karzai Role," *The New York Times*, January 26, 2010, p. A1.

275 *In my interview with the president:* Interview with President Barack H. Obama, July 10, 2010.

279 *This was the second lesson:* Gordon M. Goldstein, *Lessons in Disaster* (New York: Times Books, 2008), p. 69.

279 *I later pressed the president twice:* Interview with President Barack H. Obama, July 10, 2010.

279 *"Hooah, Sir!" Dowd said, using the universal:* This loose definition of "hooah" is frequently cited but rarely explained by members of the

military. According to a humorous definition on usmilitary.about.com, definitions of "hooah" can include: "Referring to or meaning anything and everything except 'no,' " "What to say when at a loss for words," "Message received," "Welcome," "I don't know the answer, but I'll check on it," "I haven't the foggiest idea," "Thank you," "Go to the next slide," "I don't know what that means, but I'm too embarrassed to ask for clarification" and "Amen!" See Rod Powers, "Dictionary Definition of Hooah," Military Jokes and Humor, http://usmilitary. about.com/od/militaryhumor/a/hooahdef.htm. See also Martha Brant, "West Wing Story: You're in the Army Now," *Newsweek (Web Exclusive)*, December 19, 2002.

281 *Three days later, Mullen:* Author's review of the graph entitled "Alternative Mission in Afghanistan," November 14, 2009.

282 *In my interview with the president:* Interview with President Barack H. Obama, July 10, 2010.

CHAPTER TWENTY-FOUR

The information in this chapter comes primarily from background interviews with 14 firsthand sources.

284 *"I don't think anybody believes":* Jenna Jordan, a Ph.D. candidate at the University of Chicago, published a study in late 2009 that suggested the targeted killing of terrorist group leaders was mostly ineffective at stopping the group. Her study, "When Heads Roll: Assessing the Effectiveness of Leadership Decapitation," examined 298 incidents between 1945 and 2004. It found that large, decades-old, religious-based groups were largely resilient to targeted killing. Jordan wrote, "Decapitation is not ineffective merely against religious, old, or large groups, it is actually counterproductive for many of the terrorist groups currently being targeted. In many cases, targeting a group's leadership actually lowers its rate of decline. . . . Moreover, going after the leader may strengthen a group's resolve, result in retaliatory attacks, increase public sympathy for the organization, or produce more lethal attacks." See Jenna Jordan, "When Heads Roll: Assessing the Effectiveness of Leadership Decapitation," http://cpost.uchicago .edu/pdf/Jordan.pdf. See also Andrew Exum, "Two Documents of Note: The Ridiculous and the Sublime," *Abu Muqawama* (blog), April 14, 2010, http://www.cnas.org/blogs/abumuqawama/2010/04/ two-documents-note-ridiculous-and-sublime.html.

284 *In the two-page letter:* Author's review of President Obama's letter to President Zardari, November 11, 2009.

287 *Later in November, Zardari answered Obama:* Author's review of President
     Zardari's letter to President Obama, November 25, 2009.

289 *The president told me:* Interview with President Barack H. Obama,
     July 10, 2010.

CHAPTER TWENTY-FIVE

The information in this chapter comes primarily from background interviews
with nine firsthand sources.

307 *Obama had met that week:* Michael D. Shear and Paul Kane, "President
     vs. Party on Troop Increase," *The Washington Post*, November 26, 2009,
     p. A1.

307 *On a conference call with bloggers:* Ibid.

CHAPTER TWENTY-SIX

The information in this chapter comes primarily from background interviews
with eight firsthand sources.

311 *When I asked the president about this advice:* Interview with President
     Barack H. Obama, July 10, 2010.

CHAPTER TWENTY-SEVEN

The information in this chapter comes primarily from background interviews
with three firsthand sources.

CHAPTER TWENTY-EIGHT

The information in this chapter comes primarily from background interviews
with nine firsthand sources.

328 *After the 9/11 attacks, President Bush:* Bob Woodward, *Bush at War*
     (New York: Simon & Schuster, 2002), p. 30.

331 *"The days of providing a blank check are over":* President Obama, Address
     to the Nation on the Way Forward in Afghanistan and Pakistan,
     December 1, 2009, http://www.whitehouse.gov.

331 *I went back and read Eisenhower's:* President Dwight Eisenhower,
     Farewell Address, January 17, 1961, http://millercenter.org/scripps/
     archive/speeches/detail/3361.

CHAPTER TWENTY-NINE

The information in this chapter comes primarily from background interviews with 10 firsthand sources.

334 *Obama, wearing a dark suit:* President Obama, Remarks at the U.S. Military Academy at West Point, New York, December 1, 2009, http://www.gpoaccess.gov/presdocs/2009/DCPD-200900962.htm.

335 *Although most news coverage:* Sheryl Gay Stolberg and Helene Cooper, "Obama Adds Troops, but Maps Exit Plan," *The New York Times*, December 2, 2009, http://www.nytimes.com/2009/12/02/world/asia/02prexy.html.

335 *The day after the West Point speech:* Federal News Service, Hearing of the Senate Armed Services Committee, Subject: Afghanistan, December 2, 2009.

337 *Later, at the White House press briefing:* Chip Reid, "White House: July 2011 Is Locked In for Afghanistan Withdrawal," *Political Hotsheet* (blog), December 2, 2009, http://www.cbsnews.com/8301-503544_162-5868282-503544.html.

337 *Gates went to Afghanistan and declared:* Media availability with Secretary Gates en route to Afghanistan, December 8, 2009, http://www.defense.gov/transcripts.

337 *At a December 13 regional security conference:* Address by General Petraeus, Panel on Regional Security Architecture, IISS Manama Dialogue, IISS Regional Security Summit, December 12, 2009, http://www.iiss.org/conferences/the-iiss-regional-security-summit/manama-dialogue-2009/plenary-sessions-and-speeches-2009/fifth-plenary-session/fifth-plenary-session-general-david-petraeus/.

340 *On Christmas Day 2009:* Dan Eggen, Karen DeYoung and Spencer S. Hsu, "Plane Suspect Was Listed in Terror Database," *The Washington Post*, December 27, 2009, p. A1; Elisabeth Bumiller, "Napolitano Says No Evidence of Wider Terrorist Plot," *The New York Times*, December 28, 2009, http://www.nytimes.com.

340 *On vacation in Hawaii:* Daily Compilation of Presidential Documents, December 29, 2009, Remarks on Improving Homeland Security in Kaneohe, Hawaii, http://www.gpoaccess.gov/presdocs/2009/DCPD-200901019.htm.

342 *The final six-page report:* Memorandum on the Attempted Terrorist Attack on December 25, 2009: Intelligence, Screening, and Watchlisting System Corrective Actions, January 7, 2010, http://www.gpoaccess.gov/presdocs/2010/DCPD-201000009.htm.

342 *After it was released:* Press briefing, January 7, 2010, http://www
     .whitehouse.gov/briefing-room.

343 *"I think of Jim as the glue":* David Ignatius, "Jim Jones's Team," *The
     Washington Post,* June 7, 2009, p. A17.

CHAPTER THIRTY

The information in this chapter comes primarily from background interviews
with eight firsthand sources.

356 *Things were closing in on them:* Mark Mazzetti and Dexter Filkins,
     "Secret Joint Raid Captures Taliban's Top Commander," *The New York
     Times,* February 16, 2010, p. A1.

CHAPTER THIRTY-ONE

The information in this chapter comes primarily from background interviews
with 10 firsthand sources.

358 *The operation into the town of Nawa:* Rajiv Chandrasekaran, "In
     Helmand, a Model for Success?" *The Washington Post,* October 22,
     2009, p. A1.

359 *Even though a blight:* Richard A. Oppel, Jr., "Mysterious Blight Destroys
     Large Portion of Afghan Poppy Harvest," *The New York Times,* May 13,
     2010, A12.

361 *Several days earlier:* Kimberly Dozier, "Petraeus: Times Square Bomber
     Likely Acted Alone," Associated Press, May 7, 2010.

363 *During my Oval Office interview:* Interview with President Barack H.
     Obama, July 10, 2010.

369 *When I interviewed President Obama:* Ibid.

CHAPTER THIRTY-TWO

The information in this chapter comes primarily from background interviews
with six firsthand sources.

370 *The CIA had won and the feud:* Walter Pincus, "Senate Panel Backs DNI
     in Turf Battle with CIA," *The Washington Post,* July 23, 2009, p. A3;
     Washington Post editorial, "Settling an Intelligence Turf War," *The
     Washington Post,* November 17, 2009.

370 *"Covert action programs":*
     DNI Principles for Covert Action:
     1. Covert action should be employed only to support an
        overarching set of clearly defined, well articulated U.S. policy
        objectives.

2. Covert action should not be employed for the purpose of circumventing a lack of U.S. public support for any particular overt policy.

3. The secrecy and flexibility of covert action does not make it a substitute for overt diplomatic efforts, strategic communications, economic sanctions or incentives, or military action. It should be employed only as a complement to robust overt policy objectives and activities.

4. Covert action to influence the short-term policies and actions of other governments should be routinely evaluated to ensure it is not undermining the development of stable, non-corrupt and representative governments that respect the human rights of their citizens, control their territory and borders, and resist aggression from their neighbors.

5. Not every clandestine activity conducted by the U.S. government is or must be an unacknowledged covert action activity. For example, the Department of Defense, the Drug Enforcement Administration, the FBI and other elements can and do conduct activities that will be undertaken in the manner intended to minimize the likelihood of discovery, but those activities are not necessarily covert activities.

6. Covert action programs should continually be considered for transition to non-covert activities, whether classified or unclassified.

371 *Within several minutes:* Jake Tapper, "Exclusive: President Obama to Replace Director of National Intelligence Dennis Blair," *Political Punch* (blog), ABC News, http://blogs.abcnews.com/politicalpunch/2010/05/exclusive-president-obama-to-replace-director-of-national-intelligence-dennis-blair.html.

371 *It contained some disparaging and mocking comments:* Michael Hastings, "The Runaway General," *Rolling Stone*, June 25, 2010, http://www.rollingstone.com/politics/news/17390/119236.

372 *"I believe that General McChrystal":* Defense Secretary Gates Statement on McChrystal Profile, June 22, 2010, http://www.defense.gov/releases/.

373 *"Is removing the general from his position":* White House press briefing by Robert Gibbs, June 22, 2010, http://www.whitehouse.gov.

373 *Obama told me:* Interview with President Barack H. Obama, July 10, 2010.

373 *At 1:43 P.M. on Wednesday, June 23:* President Obama, Remarks on the Resignation of General Stanley A. McChrystal as Commander of the

NATO International Security Assistance Force in Afghanistan, June 23, 2010, http://www.gpoaccess.gov/presdocs/2010/DCPD -201000525.htm.

CHAPTER THIRTY-THREE

The information in this chapter comes primarily from an on-the-record interview with President Obama.

375 *In the interview I had with the president:* Interview with President Barack H. Obama, July 10, 2010.

375 *This was the speech he gave:* State Senator Barack Obama, "Against Going to War in Iraq," October 2, 2002, http://www.asksam.com/ebooks/ releases.asp?file=Obama-Speeches.ask&dn=Against%20Going%20 to%20War%20with%20Iraq.

375 *Isn't this undetermined cost:* Interview with President Barack H. Obama, July 10, 2010.

377 *Near the end of the interview:* Ibid.

378 *"For war was not just a military campaign":* Rick Atkinson, *The Day of Battle: The War in Sicily and Italy, 1943–1944* (New York: Henry Holt, 2007), p. 121.

378 *"I sympathize with this view," he said:* Interview with President Barack H. Obama, July 10, 2010.

378 *"The instruments of war do have a role":* President Obama, Remarks on Accepting the Nobel Peace Prize in Oslo, Norway, December 10, 2010, http://www.gpoaccess.gov/presdocs/2009/DCPD-200900985.htm.

ACKNOWLEDGMENTS

This book is based almost entirely on my own reporting, interviews, a review of documents and meeting notes. I am deeply indebted to the reporters and authors who have covered the war in Afghanistan and the Obama administration. They blazed the trail. Their work and insights provide a significant and essential foundation.

I want to thank all sources, those named and those unnamed. These individuals often agreed to take the time to answer all my questions, provide me with notes and other written material, and give context to the scenes in this book. Without their help, the effort to make this a serious and authoritative history would have been impossible. I am grateful.

Alice Mayhew, my editor at Simon & Schuster for 38 years and 16 books, continues to offer wisdom that is shrewd, fair and always to the point. No one edits with more grace than Alice. Her devotion to revealing history in a clear, compelling way is a gift. She has my admiration and affection.

Jonathan Karp enthusiastically leapt into his new job as publisher at Simon & Schuster. He gave dozens of concrete suggestions and ideas that strengthened this book. Simon & Schuster and its authors are fortunate to have at the helm a publisher who immerses himself in the details of a manuscript. Simon & Schuster CEO Carolyn K. Reidy remains the kind of ally who all writers should have. My deepest appreciation also goes to Roger Labrie, senior editor; Elisa Rivlin, senior vice president and general counsel; Victoria Meyer, executive vice president of publicity; Tracey Guest, director of publicity; Jackie Seow, art director and jacket designer; Irene Kheradi, executive managing editor; Tristan Child, assistant managing editor; Karen Thompson, associate editor; Paul Dippolito, designer; Lisa Healy, senior production editor; Nancy Inglis, director of copyediting; John Wahler, associate director of production.

Josh Boak, Evelyn Duffy and I have profound gratitude for master copy editor Fred Chase, who came from Texas to join our team and work on his sixth book with me. Fred is a man of immense experience and common sense. His company, good humor, eye for detail and typographical saves make his help invaluable.

Many thanks to Barbara DeGennaro for indexing this book in such a short time.

Washington Post executive editor Marcus Brauchli has steered the institution I love with intelligence and courage. He possesses an eye for scoops, a competitive drive and the unflappable presence needed during this tumultuous time in the industry. Many thanks also to publisher Katharine Weymouth, whose pride in the work, mission and future of the newspaper is essential.

Post chairman and CEO Don Graham is a stalwart friend. No media CEO could be more of a champion of journalism and journalists. He knows the importance of ensuring that independent voices are heard.

My friend Steve Luxenberg, associate editor, gave willingly of his ingenuity and judgment to help excerpt this book for *The Washington Post*, and he has my lasting gratitude.

Washington Post reporters and editors whose work on Afghanistan and Pakistan was of tremendous assistance include Karen De-Young, Rajiv Chandrasekaran, David Ignatius, Joby Warrick, Greg Jaffe, Joshua Partlow, Al Kamen, Walter Pincus, Scott Wilson, Anne E. Kornblut, Ann Scott Tyson, Pamela Constable, Griff Witte, Rama Lakshmi, Emily Wax, Karin Brulliard, Cameron Barr, Carlos Lozada and many others. A great deal of significant background and understanding came from others on the *Post*'s foreign and national staffs. Special thanks to Rick Atkinson, Steve Coll and David Maraniss.

My appreciation also goes to Michel du Cille, Wendy Galietta and the rest of the *Post*'s incomparable photo staff who supplied nearly all of the pictures used in this book.

I will always be indebted to my friend and mentor Ben Bradlee, whose exacting standards and enduring principles are a legacy for all who have passed through the *Post*'s newsroom.

And special thanks to Carl Bernstein, a friend, colleague and source of endless ideas and insight.

I was also helped immeasurably by the reporting and analysis in *The New York Times*, *The Wall Street Journal*, the *Chicago Tribune*, the *Los Angeles Times*, *The New Yorker*, *Politico*, *Dawn* (Pakistan), *The Nation* (Pakistan), the Associated Press, and countless other news organizations both foreign and domestic.

The following books were useful points of reference and would make for excellent further reading: *The Accidental Guerrilla* by David Kilcullen; *Counterinsurgency Warfare: Theory and Practice* by David Galula; *Decoding the Taliban: Insights from the Afghan Field* edited by Antonio Giustozzi; *Descent into Chaos* by Ahmed Rashid; *Game Change* by John Heilemann and Mark Halperin; *Koran, Kalashnikov and Laptop: The Neo-Taliban Insurgency in Afghanistan* by Antonio Giustozzi; *Lessons in Disaster* by Gordon M. Goldstein; *My Life with the Taliban* by Abdul Salam Zaeef; *Pakistan: Between Mosque and Military* by Husain Haqqani; *The Promise* by Jonathan Alter; and *The Search for Al Qaeda* by Bruce Riedel.

My assistants and I found the following blogs helpful as well: *Abu Muqawama* (http://www.cnas.org/blogs/abumuqawama); *The AfPak Channel* (http://afpak.foreignpolicy.com/); *At War* (http://atwar.blogs.nytimes.com/); *The Cable* (http://thecable.foreignpolicy.com/); and *Mike Allen's Playbook* (http://www.politico.com/playbook/).

Robert B. Barnett, my agent, attorney and friend, again proved indispensable. His counsel is always welcome and informed. Bob looks out for his authors and their interests with an unmatched zeal. Because he represents President Obama, Secretary of State Clinton and other political figures, he was not consulted on the contents of this book and did not see it until it was printed.

Josh, Evelyn and I are fortunate for the presence of Rosa Criollo and Jackie Crowe in our lives. Long days are shortened and challenges eased by their able assistance.

My elder daughter, Tali, spent a week in Washington reviewing the manuscript. Her smart recommendations helped make sometimes dense subject matter more understandable. Tali has a natural touch and feel for the written word. My younger daughter, Diana, is fast becoming a spirited and caring young woman and a highly readable writer in her own right. Both are joys in my life.

Elsa Walsh, my wife, lived through this book from the first interviews to the final proofs. Her advice has always proven enlightening, and her company an abiding comfort. She devoted an intense week to marking up drafts. This book—and my previous ones—are richer because of her. Elsa is the anchor of our family and the source of the love that matters.

PHOTOGRAPHY CREDITS

INDEX